The Mini Farming Bible

The Mini Farming Bible:

The Complete Guide to Self-Sufficiency on ¼ Acre

Brett L. Markham

Skyhorse Publishing

Skyhorse Publishing books may be purchased in bulk at special discounts for sales promotion, corporate gifts, fund-raising, or educational purposes. Special editions can also be created to specifications. For details, contact the Special Sales Department, Skyhorse Publishing, 307 West 36th Street, 11th Floor, New York, NY 10018 or info@skyhorsepublishing.com.

Skyhorse® and Skyhorse Publishing® are registered trademarks of Skyhorse Publishing, Inc.®, a Delaware corporation.

Visit our website at www.skyhorsepublishing.com.

10 9 8 7 6 5 4

Library of Congress Cataloging-in-Publication Data is available on file.

Print ISBN: 978-1-62914-490-0
Ebook ISBN: 978-1-63220-047-1

Printed in China

For my daughter, Hannah

Contents

Introduction

Welcome to *The Mini Farming Bible!* I am pleased to say that *The Mini Farming Bible* is comprehensive, containing everything you need to know to support yourself and your family on a minimal amount of real estate.

In an effort to reduce my food bills while still providing plentiful and wholesome food for my family, I started work on the Mini Farming concept in 2004. My backyard became a laboratory for trying different methods of growing plants, breeding varieties tailored to my locale, controlling pests, making compost, raising chickens, growing fruits, and so much more. I tried many popular methods, noted their strengths and weaknesses, and made constant incremental improvements until I arrived at the method I call Mini Farming.

Wholesome food is important for good health, and it is unfortunately rare for Americans to eat enough fruits and vegetables. In my research, I discovered there are three primary barriers that prevent people from eating enough fruits and vegetables: cost, taste, and sugar addiction.

On a calories per dollar basis, fresh fruits and vegetables are some of the most expensive foods available outside of fine wines, caviar, and similar luxury items. On a limited budget, a box of instant macaroni and cheese or cereal will get you a lot more calories for your dollar than carrots or apples. You can get up to 350 calories per dollar using a fast-food dollar menu, or 250 calories per dollar when choosing a candy bar. You'd have to spend $10 on tomatoes to get that many calories. In essence, vegetables are not affordable enough to form a major portion of many people's diets. Growing your own vegetables cost effectively solves this problem.

Taste is also a factor. Most vegetables you can buy at the store are not particularly tasty. There are many reasons for this. In commercial agriculture, even organic agriculture, crop varieties are selected on the basis of shipping and keeping qualities so that they arrive at the grocery store looking good. The problem is that the variety of a crop best-suited for mechanical harvesting and shipping 3,000 miles in a truck is unlikely to be the variety that tastes best. Some crops, such as tomatoes, are harvested before they are ripe and then artificially ripened with ethylene gas, so they don't develop the flavor complexity and sweetness of a naturally ripened product.

Taste is also affected by the time between harvest and purchase, which can be as long as a month for some products. The term "fresh" merely means it hasn't been frozen, it doesn't mean it was harvested yesterday. Taste is also affected by the way the product is grown, and the way commercial agriculture operates is not conducive to creating the most flavorful vegetables.

If you think about it, this makes sense. Vegetables are bought and sold on a commodity market where a carrot is a carrot is a carrot. If you are a farmer, you'll get the same price for a carrot grown for the best flavor and nutrition as you will

for a bland carrot. The biggest factor in grading your carrot is its visual aesthetic, its color and lack of visible blemishes. The fact it tastes vaguely of turpentine (thus discouraging a kid from wanting seconds) is irrelevant. So, of course, we have lots of nice-looking vegetables at the supermarket that don't taste good enough to tempt us to eat them in quantities conducive to good health.

Growing your own vegetables also solves this problem. When you grow your own, you can select the varieties that taste best. As you aren't mechanically harvesting or shipping them 3,000 miles on a truck, you can select for flavor and allow foods to ripen naturally. You can supply all the micronutrients they need and provide optimum fertility. My daughter, Hannah, hates celery, but loves the celery that I grow. Until she started eating my salads, she would sing a song about salads: "Icky salad, I want to burn it, so I don't have to eat it...." But once I convinced her to try the salads made from my homegrown vegetables, she looked forward to them as her favorite part of a meal. I even convinced her to eat them for breakfast! Vegetables you grow yourself really are that good. They're so good you'll eat a lot of them. It's not unusual for me to pick and eat a cucumber right off the vine or pick some mustard leaves and shove them into my mouth while I'm out back. Delicious!

The third cause of inadequate vegetable consumption is addiction to both direct and indirect sugar. Concentrated sugars and high carbohydrate diets are relatively new on the human scene, and they can cause both physiological and psychological addiction. Because of this, when a choice is available, the sugar-laden alternative is chosen. Though starting a mini farm won't fix this, I've written a book, *Modern Caveman*, that discusses sugar addiction in-depth and gives solutions.

So Mini Farming solves the problems of cost and taste, encouraging optimum levels of vegetable consumption for a healthy life. But it does more than that.

Mini Farming enhances your health through providing movement that maintains your proprioception, balance, and flexibility. In addition, because the food is more fresh, it can contain as much as 300% more of some nutrients than the food you buy at the store. Even better, using Mini Farming methods will enhance the micronutrient content of your food, and many experts believe that the deficiency of micronutrients in our food supply is indirectly responsible for a host of human ills. Simply on the basis of health alone, Mini Farming is a good idea.

But Mini Farming is about more than physical health, it's about economic health as well. Gardening is a hobby. Farming is an economic pursuit. Mini Farming can certainly be a hobby, but it is fundamentally an economic pursuit designed to produce the greatest amount of the healthiest food for the least amount of investment in terms of real estate, time, and money. The fact that it is enjoyable and gives you healthy exercise is a bonus.

Usually, the goals of food being healthy AND taking less time and money are a zero-sum game. If you go to the grocery store to buy organic food, you'll find it can cost as much as 500% more than conventionally-grown food of the same type. Likewise, many of the small-space gardening techniques in vogue may work well on the scale of a hobby, but when you try to increase them enough to support a family, they are either inordinately time consuming for modern American lifestyles, or they become too expensive.

Over time, I discovered the core elements necessary to meet the economic goals without sacrificing the quality of the product. These elements are: close spacing in raised beds using wooden frames, organic methods of soil management, crop rotation, a three-part pest control strategy, composting for fertility preservation, seed saving, food preservation, and calorically-dense crops.

Mini Farming uses raised beds surrounded by a wooden frame. The beds are usually double-dug, and generous quantities of compost are included along with any needed organic soil amendments. Using raised beds allows the season to last about two weeks longer, eliminates soil compaction so the soil is more productive, and allows amendments to be applied only to areas used for growing food. Though beds can be made by mounding instead of using wooden frames, such beds have to be reconstructed regularly and will have substantial issues with erosion. Close spacing within the beds sometimes allows a single 4" x 8" bed to produce as many vegetables as a 100-row one. It also shades weeds and conserves moisture.

Organic methods of soil management and pest control are crucial for the economic success of a mini farm. Although it is more expensive initially, within five years the fertility and tilth of the beds is so transformed that you can work the soil with your bare hands, without tools, and the health of the plants make problems with pests and diseases rare or nonexistent. Composting to conserve fertility will also reduce the amount of amendments needed over time. By reducing pest problems and the need for fertilizers, the cost of the mini farm is reduced, so you realize greater profitability even if you only grow food for your own use.

Seed saving is also important. I remember when I first started trying to produce as much food as I could. I was easily spending more than

$250/year just on seeds. But now that I exclusively grow open-pollinated plant varieties and save most of my own seed, I spend less than $30/year on seeds, yet grow even more food! When you save seeds, you select seeds from the plants that had the fewest problems with pests and diseases, and were the most productive. After a few years, you will have crops that are well-adapted to your own locale, are very productive, and have few problems.

Food preservation via canning, freezing, and dehydrating is also a key element of self-sufficiency because it allows you to have food when the garden is blanketed with three feet of snow. I can't tell you how many times I've been thankful for the results of preserved foods. This weighty tome also includes very advanced methods of food preservation by teaching you to make wine, vinegar, and other fermented foods.

Controlling your food supply can also bring you peace of mind. Several times a year some food poisoning incident makes the news, and it is often caused by careless farming practices such as fertilizing spinach with raw manure too close to harvest. Likewise, the measurements of multiple pesticides in foods, whose long-term effects are unknown, can be alarming. When you grow your own food, you know how it is handled so you can eat it with confidence. The economic value of providing your own food can also reduce pressure in other areas of your life by reducing how much money you need to earn, or freeing up that money for other purposes. It can also come in really handy when the power goes out for several days during an ice storm and the shelves of the grocery store are cleaned out within hours. It's hard to put a value on that.

The core ideas of *Mini Farming* were developed until the first book in the series was published in 2010. The book became a huge success, and I started getting questions, feedback, and suggestions from people via my website. This input from readers and friends inspired the rest of the books in the series, as well as some fine-tuning of methods and additional techniques to save time and money.

I must credit my two editors, Jenn McCartney at Skyhorse and my wife, Francine, for all their help with the *Mini Farming* series. Though I did pretty well on my own later in the series, my early writing needed a lot of organizational help, and Francine helped make those books as good as they are. Jenn McCartney was a great sounding-board and helped me refine my ideas regarding what should (or shouldn't) be included in my books.

I believe you'll find this book very useful. It represents years of hands-on research and progressive refinement that will help you produce incomparable fruits, vegetables, eggs, meat, and even wine from the modest resources of your own backyard. Your home will become a center of production that pays for itself rather than an expensive hotel. You'll be more healthy, and you'll have greater peace of mind.

—Brett L. Markham

PART I
Basics of Mini Farming

Overview of Intensive Agriculture

1

Intensive agricultural techniques, and their productivity compared to traditional row gardening methods, have been well documented in the past several decades, and certain methods have been used for centuries. They all share a number of common characteristics.

All of the intensive methods use raised beds and grow vegetables much more closely than traditional row methods and therefore require less land—thus requiring less water and labor while reducing the need for weeding. Intensive gardens produce the same amount of food in 20% of the space or even less than that, leading to greatly reduced costs.

Traditional row gardening is one-dimensional—that is, a straight line. A small furrow is dug with a hoe, and seeds are sprinkled in from a packet. After the seeds germinate, the farmer goes back down the row and thins plants to the recommended spacing. Each row takes its own space, plus space for walking paths on either side, and the walking paths become compacted under foot traffic. The enti~ area—rows and paths—is watered and fertilized. Because the r~ are exposed to the drying effects of sun and wind on both

Row gardens adapted from commercial agriculture are wasteful of space and resources on a home scale.

mulching is required to conserve water and prevent weeds. The typical 100-foot row takes up at least 300 square feet of space. As a basis of comparison, the expected yield of carrots for that row is about 100 pounds.

In contrast, intensive mini-farming is three-dimensional. Seeds are planted in the raised bed using within-row spacings in all directions, giving a two-dimensional space, and crops such as pole beans are grown on trellises, adding a third dimension. This vastly increases the quantity of a given crop that can be produced per unit area. In the case of carrots, a garden bed 4 feet wide and 6 feet long (24 square feet) will yield 100 pounds of carrots. That's the theoretical yield, but in practice I've found 32 square feet

are required to get a full 100 pounds. Still, that's an amazing increase in space efficiency! Using trellising and pole beans instead of bush beans and indeterminate (vining) tomatoes instead of determinate (bush) tomatoes will also increase the yield per plant.

Using row gardening, the farmer has to fertilize, mulch, weed, and water 300 square feet of space to get 100 pounds of carrots. But by using raised beds and intensive gardening techniques that use close spacing, the farmer has to fertilize and water only 24 square feet—less than 1/10 the space and thus less than 1/10 the fertilizer and water. The cost savings are immense, and the intensive farmer can also dispense with mulching, because the plants are growing so closely together that they shade each other's stems and the ground, conserving moisture and shading out weeds. The shade provided by growing plants closely is also helpful in protecting beneficial soil microbes from the damaging effects of ultraviolet radiation from the sun. Last season I kept records of how much weeding was required per 100 square feet averaged across crops as diverse as broccoli and tomatoes, and because of the living mulch aspect of intensive gardening, less than 30 minutes *per season* were required per 100 square feet.

There are three schools of thought regarding the spacing of plants in intensively planted beds. The Grow Biointensive method recommends a hexagonal pattern using various sorts of hexagonal and triangular jigs. The Square Foot method recommends using a grid of squares dividing every square foot into a number of subsquares appropriate to the spacing of the crop being grown. My own method is to plant a properly spaced row, go up the distance within a row, and then plant seeds in parallel.

⊗ Carrots planted intensively in a raised bed yielded 100 pounds in just 32 square feet.

A little analysis yields a few facts. The Grow Biointensive method actually fits more vegetables into the same space compared to the other two, but for most vegetables the difference is 10% or less. Offsetting this advantage is the fact that the Grow Biointensive planting method is painstaking and that the average person interested in farming isn't about to envision a hexagon as being composed of a series of equilateral triangles. However, this process *will* increase yields for a farmer handy enough to set up the proper jigs to make the planting process easy. The jigs are plywood triangles composed of three 60-degree angles and with all three sides the same length as the planting distance between each plant of each different crop. A seed is planted at each of the three points.

The Square Foot method is about as simple as can be imagined geometrically: Everything is a square. Spacing can be figured easily based on within-row spacing of a given plant. The only downside is that you are subdividing individual square feet that need to be laid out within the beds. This works great on a small scale, but on a larger scale this can be problematic, especially when adding large-volume soil amendments to beds such as compost. Grids can be made that can be readily removed, but this again is more labor. For a 200-square-foot garden, the work is no big deal, but when the garden is scaled to 6,300 square feet to provide for the needs of a family plus marketable vegetables, the task of making and maintaining grids to set apart individual square feet becomes enormous. Thus the Square Foot method, where each square foot is individually marked off, is more suitable for hobby gardening than a mini-farm.

When I came up with my own way of intensive planting, I wanted something simple enough that my daughter would be able to do it.

First, look at the seed packet to determine the final distance between plants after thinning (circled in the illustration). Second, grab a small ruler and a blunt pencil. Third, use the ruler and pencil to put quarter-inch holes in the ground to mark off a square grid the size of the area you want to plant. The distance between holes is the final distance between plants after thinning. Put a seed in each hole, cover with dirt, and tamp it down—then water daily until the seeds sprout.

Note that all of these methods will eliminate the need to thin plantings. As a result, they conserve seed and thereby conserve money and save labor.

⊗ Use the final thinning distance as your initial planting distance for intensive agriculture.

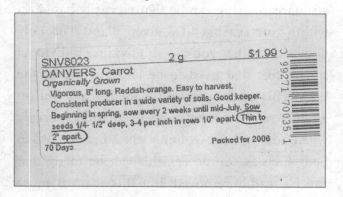

The yield differential for the carrots given in the example isn't atypical. A 100-foot row of lettuce spaced every six inches will fit into a 4-foot × 6-foot intensively planted bed with the same yield. Comparing the 24 square feet to the 300 square feet (including walking paths), and understanding that an acre contains 43,560 square feet, you will quickly see that a 3,500-square-foot intensive garden will produce the same output as an acre farmed conventionally.

Along with close spacing, intensive agriculture emphasizes vertically grown crops such as cucumbers, vining tomatoes, and pole beans. There are two reasons for this. First, using the third dimension of height allows you to get more production per unit area. Second, vining varieties produce more total food yield over the course of the season. Growing crops vertically on a trellis also makes harvesting easier, reduces diseases, and has the aesthetic advantage of growing consistently straight cucumbers.

So that crops grown on a trellis don't shade out other crops, trellises should be constructed on the north side of raised beds. The ultimate height of a trellis depends somewhat on what is being grown but also on your convenience. For most people, a trellis can be six or even seven feet high without causing inconvenience.

I use a variety of trellis structures including A-frames, boards screwed together, and electrical conduit. Anything will work as long as it is mechanically strong enough to handle winds while fully loaded with plants without falling over.

The approach to intensive agriculture called "mini-farming" in this book contains elements from many different systems that have been tested by the author at various times. While not

⊗ Trellises maximize efficiency by allowing plant growth in three dimensions.

every approach can be listed, the most influential systems are described along with some references so that anyone who is interested can learn more about these ideas.

The French Intensive method of agriculture was originally developed to cope with the small yard sizes in France. It emphasizes a technique called "double-digging" to create the beds and depends on a considerable input of horse manure for fertilizer. The most comprehensive book on the topic is *Intensive Culture of Vegetables* by P. Aquatias.

The Biodynamic method was created by Rudolph Steiner in 1924 because of his observations of the detrimental effects of artificial fertilizers. It emphasizes the concept of the farm as a self-contained biological organism. The book *What Is Biodynamics?* includes seven lectures on the topic by Rudolph Steiner and gives a good overview of the method and its fundamentals.

The Grow Biointensive method is a combination of the French Intensive and Biodynamic methods first synthesized by Alan Chadwick and continued by Ecology Action, a nonprofit group focusing on sustainable agriculture. It keeps the

double-dug raised beds of the French Intensive method and adds many aspects of the Biodynamic method. The book *How to Grow More Vegetables* by John Jeavons covers the method comprehensively.

Square Foot gardening was invented by Mel Bartholomew in the 1980s because of his observations of community gardens and his desire to improve the efficiency and enjoyability of gardening. The method emphasizes the use of raised beds using custom-made soil fertilized with organic amendments. The book *All New Square Foot Gardening* by Mel Bartholomew covers his methods in detail.

There are other approaches to intensive agriculture with a variety of names, but all of them are essentially composed of elements already incorporated in one of the four methods already listed. The methods of intensive agriculture advocated in this book are no different—they pull from the experiences of others and add the experience of the author. As a result, the approach that I present differs somewhat from earlier methods. I will explain the reasoning for the differences in the chapters ahead, but for now I think it would be worthwhile to point out the major differences.

My mini-farming technique differs from the Square Foot method in that I do not mark off individual square feet of bed or use the bed shape, special soil mix, or individual-plant hand-watering techniques advocated by that method.

Mini-farming differs from the Grow Biointensive method mainly in its lack of emphasis on growing grains, but it also dispenses with the seed-starting and plant-spacing methods, among others.

Mini-farming differs from the Biodynamic method in that it doesn't use special herbal preparations for preparing compost, plant seeds by moon phases, or consider the farm to be a self-contained entity. There are so many other differences, they can't all be listed.

My approach to mini-farming differs from the French Intensive method in that it doesn't rely on massive inputs of horse manure. In other respects the French method is similar to Grow Biointensive, so those differences apply as well.

Learning and Observation

Intensive agricultural practices are constantly being refined, extended, amended, and developed by well-known practitioners and by individual farmers. Agriculture is, at its heart, a biological rather than industrial process. As a result, it is subject to laws of nature that we humans are only beginning to understand. The path to success with intensive agriculture, as with any other endeavor, is through constantly expanding knowledge.

A constant input of new information is most easily and economically acquired through a library. Land-grant universities have a substantial selection of agricultural books and magazines available, and use of the facility is not limited to students. Likewise, the Internet has a wide array of resources available.

Experience is also an excellent teacher, and hands-on experience will provide insight unavailable in a book. Along with gaining experience, a mini-farmer should keep detailed records of events and observations.

I keep several journals for each year. One journal lists every plant variety to be grown that year, where the seed was acquired, and general information about that plant and its requirements. Following this are journal entries describing where, when, and how the seeds were started; transplantation information; and significant events that affected the crop up through harvest. Any pest problems are noted in the journal, along with the effectiveness of any remedies and especially information that might give a clue as to why some plants of a given crop may have been more or less affected.

Another important journal entry specific to intensive agriculture is plant spacing. A starting value for two-dimensional plant spacing is the within-row thinning distance specified on the seed package. This will give optimal yields in a row-type system and will often give optimal yields in a raised-bed intensive system, but a little experimentation is in order because yields relative to

Plant Journal

Broccoli, Arcadia F1
Start 12 wks before last frost
Plant out 5 wks before last frost
should be ready end of June
Spacing: 12"
Special: use 1/2 tsp borax mixed into fertilizer per 32 sq. ft.
     add some dolomite lime to hole w/ each
     plant when transplanting.
Start 2nd batch on last frost date
Plant out 1 wk. after 1st batch is harvested.

Beans, Blue Lake Pole
Plant seeds in ground on last frost date
Pre-soak seeds 2-4 hrs before planting
Use innoculant
Spacing 2"
Expect harvest Aug 10 - Aug 30

⊗ Journals are an important tool for learning and improvement.

spacing will vary with soil and climate conditions. In the case of lettuce in my own garden, I have discovered that eight-inch spacings work better than six-inch spacings—but those results will be different for a different soil and climate.

All of this information helps to fine-tune the environment that I give the plant from year to year so that my reliance on fertilizers, horse manure, and other external inputs—even if organic—can be reduced from year to year.

A journal of crop-specific information also helps me to decide if I want to grow a particular crop variety the next year or perhaps grow it differently. In 2005, I grew a particular kind of carrot that tasted horrible raw but was fine when cooked. Since I grew it in the summer, I might decide to instead grow it as a winter or fall crop this upcoming year to see how that affects the taste. If my family usually eats carrots when raw, I might want to consider a different variety of carrot altogether. That carrot was also grown in soil that had received some composted horse manure. It would stand to reason that the carrot might taste better raw if grown in a different bed that has been fertilized with only vegetable-based compost. (And this *is* the case! Carrots shouldn't be grown in anything close to fresh manure, and I learned this through my journals!) With all of this information, I can fine-tune my carrots until they are the finest quality carrots available.

Another journal that I keep lists weather events, particularly abnormalities or anything that affects crops. Such a journal allows me to know that, in my area, I need to protect young spinach plants from hail when they are planted before the last frost date. Having this knowledge in hand allows my crops to be more productive and suffer less damage.

I also keep a calendar/planner that lets me lay out across the year when I need to perform various tasks—such as starting and transplanting seedlings or harvesting green manures. Such a calendar allows me to see and work around labor bottlenecks in advance. I note in the planner the date of first harvests for each crop based on published maturity dates for the crops, and I make note of instances where a particular crop matured earlier or later than I expected. Predicted harvest dates also allow me to see in advance when succession planting or starting a crop at a time when I ordinarily wouldn't will serve to reduce peak workloads for food preservation so the work can be spread out better.

My final journal lists practically everything I do related to soil fertility, including digging beds, compost contents, organic amendments added to soils, crop rotations, and so forth. This information is correlated with information about harvests of various crops and pest or disease problems.

The idea of all of this journaling is to put all of my experiences and observations into a context that allows me to use that information effectively to make better decisions each year than I made the year before. Working with biological systems is a process of constant learning, and a mini-farmer will ultimately benefit from keeping detailed notes.

Intensive agriculture, because it grows plants close together in a relatively small land area, is a field with a lot of room for experimentation and it makes the results of that experimentation more easily observable by the farmer. This gives mini-farmers an opportunity to make improvements in technique much more rapidly than those involved in industrial farming.

How Mini-Farming Works for You

2

Many homeowners undertake the task of gardening or small-scale farming as a hobby to get fresh-grown produce and possibly save money over buying food at the supermarket. Unfortunately, the most common gardening methods end up being so expensive that even some enthusiastic garden authors state outright that gardening should be considered, at best, a break-even affair.[1]

Looking at the most common gardening methods, such authors are absolutely correct. Common gardening methods are considerably more expensive than they need to be because they were originally designed to benefit from the economies of scale of corporate agribusiness. When home gardeners try to use these methods on a smaller scale, it's a miracle if they break even over a several-year period, and it is more likely they will lose money.

The cost of tillers, watering equipment, large quantities of water, transplants, seeds, fertilizers and insecticides adds up pretty quickly. Balanced against the fact that most home gardeners grow only

---

[1] Bird, C. O. (2001) *Cubed Foot Gardening*

vegetables, and vegetables make up only less than 10% of the calories an average person consumes,[2] it quickly becomes apparent that even if the cost of a vegetable garden were zero, the amount of actual money saved in the food bill would be negligible. For example, if the total economic value of the vegetables collected from the garden in a single season amounted to about $350,[3] and the vegetables could be produced for free, the economic benefit would amount to only $7 per week when divided over the year.

The solution to this problem is to both cut costs and increase the value of the end product. This can be accomplished by growing your own seedlings from open-pollinated plant varieties so you can save the seeds and avoid the expense of buying both transplants and seeds, using intensive gardening techniques that use less land, conscientiously composting to reduce the need for fertilizers, and growing calorie-dense crops that will supply a higher proportion of the household's caloric intake.

Using this combination, the economic equation will balance in favor of the gardener instead of the garden supply store, and it becomes quite possible to supply all of a family's food except meat from a relatively small garden. According to the USDA, the average annual per capita expenditure on food was $2,964 in 2001, with food costs increasing at a rate of 27.7% over the previous 10 years.[4] Understanding that food is purchased with after-tax dollars, it becomes clear that home agricultural methods that take a significant chunk out of that figure can make the difference, for example, between a parent being able to stay at home with children and he or she having to work, or it could vastly improve the quality of life of a retiree on a fixed income.

The key to making a garden work to your economic benefit is to approach mini-farming as a business. No, it is not a business in the sense of incorporation and taxes unless some of its production is sold, but it *is* a business in that by reducing your food expenditures, it has the same net effect on finances as income from a small business. Like any small business, it could earn money or lose money depending on how it is managed.

Grow Your Own Seedlings

Garden centers are flooded every spring with home gardeners picking out seedlings for lettuce, broccoli, cucumbers, tomatoes, and so on. For those who grow gardens strictly as a hobby, this works out well because it allows them to get off to a quick start with minimal investment of time and planning. But for the mini-farmer who approaches gardening as a small business, it's a bad idea.

⊗ These broccoli plants grown from seed saved a lot of money in the long run.

[2] Jeavons, J. (2002) *How to Grow More Vegetables*
[3] Bartholomew, M. (2005) *Square Foot Gardening*
[4] USDA (2001) *Agriculture Factbook 2001–2002*

In my own garden this year, I plan to grow 48 broccoli plants. Seedlings from the garden center would cost $18 if discounted and possibly over $30. Even the most expensive organic broccoli seeds on the market cost less than a dollar for 48 seeds. If transplants are grown at home, their effective cost drops from $18 to $30 down to $1. Adding the cost of soil and containers, the cost is still only about $2 for 48 broccoli seedlings.

Considering that a mini-farm would likely require transplants for dozens of crops ranging from onion sets to tomatoes and lettuce, it quickly becomes apparent that even if all seed is purchased, growing transplants at home saves hundreds of dollars a year.

Prefer Open-Pollinated Varieties

There are two basic types of seed/plant varieties available: hybrid and open-pollinated. Open-pollinated plant varieties produce seeds that duplicate the plants that produced them. Hybrid plant varieties produce seeds that are at best unreliable and sometimes sterile and therefore often unusable.

Although hybrid plants have the disadvantage of not producing good seed, they often have advantages that make them worthwhile, including aspects of "hybrid vigor." Hybrid vigor refers to a poorly understood phenomenon in plants where a cross between two different varieties of broccoli can yield far more vigorous and productive offspring than either parent. Depending on genetic factors, it also allows the creation of plants that incorporate some of the best qualities of both parents while deemphasizing undesirable traits. Using hybridization, then, seed companies are able to deliver varieties of plants that incorporate disease resistance into a particularly good tasting vegetable variety.

So why not just use hybrid seeds? Because there's no such thing as a free lunch. For plants that normally self-pollinate, such as peppers and tomatoes, there is no measurable increase in the vigor of hybrids. The hybrids are just a proprietary marketing avenue. So buying hybrids in those cases just raises costs, and since the tomato seeds can't be saved, the mini-farmer has to buy seeds again the next year. The cost of seeds for a family-sized mini-farm that produces most of a family's food for the year can easily approach $200, a considerable sum! Beyond that, seed collected and saved at home can not only reduce costs but be resold if properly licensed. (Here in New Hampshire, a license to sell seeds costs only $100 annually.)

Another reason to save seeds from open-pollinated plant varieties is if each year you save seeds from the best performing plants, you will eventually create varieties with genetic characteristics that work best in your particular soil and climate. That's a degree of specialization that money can't buy.

Of course, there are cases where hybrid seeds and plants outperform open-pollinated varieties by the proverbial country mile. Corn is one such example. The solution? Use the hybrid seeds or, if you are so inclined, make your own! Hybridization of corn is quite easy. Carol Deppe's excellent book *Breed Your Own Vegetable Varieties* gives all of the details on how to create your own hybrids.

Hybrid seeds that manifest particular pest- or disease-resistant traits can also be a good choice when those pests or diseases cause ongoing problems. When using hybrid seeds eliminates the need for synthetic pesticides, they are a good choice.

Use Intensive Gardening Techniques

A number of intensive gardening methods have been well documented over the past century. What all of these have in common is growing plants much more closely spaced than traditional row methods. This closer spacing causes a significant decrease in the amount of land required to grow a given quantity of food, which in turn significantly reduces requirements for water, fertilizer, and mechanization. Because plants are grown close enough together to form a sort of "living mulch," the plants shade out weeds and retain moisture better, thus decreasing the amount of work required to raise the same amount of food.

Intensive gardening techniques make a big difference in the amount of space required to provide all of a person's food. Current agribusiness practices require 30,000 square feet per person or 3/4 acre. Intensive gardening practices can reduce the amount of space required for the same nutritional content to 700 square feet,[5] plus another 700 square feet for crops grown specifically for composting. That's only 1,400 square feet per person, so a family of three can be supplied in just 4,200 square feet. That's less than 1/10 of an acre. In many parts of the United States, land is extremely expensive, and lot sizes average a half acre or less. Using traditional farming practices, it isn't even possible to raise food for a single person in a half-acre lot, but using intensive gardening techniques allows only half of that lot—1/4 acre—to provide nearly all the food for a family of four, generate thousands of dollars in income besides, allow raising small

[5] Duhon, D., Gebhard, C. (1984) *One Circle*

livestock plus leave space for home and recreation. Intensive gardening techniques are the key to self-sufficiency on a small lot.

Compost

Because growing so many plants in such little space puts heavy demand on the soil in which they are grown, all intensive agriculture methodologies pay particular attention to maintaining the fertility of the soil.

The law of conservation of matter indicates that if a farmer grows a plant, that plant took nutrients from the soil build itself. If the plant is then removed from the area, the nutrients in that plant are never returned to the soil, and the fertility of the soil is reduced. To make up for the loss of fertility, standard agribusiness practices apply commercial fertilizers from outside the farm.

The fertilizer costs money, of course. While there are other worthwhile reasons for avoiding the use of nonorganic fertilizers, including environmental damage, the biggest reason is a mini-farm with a properly managed soil fertility plan can drastically reduce the need to purchase fertilizer altogether, thereby reducing one of the biggest costs associated with farming and making the mini-farm more economically viable. In practice, a certain amount of fertilizer will always be required, especially at the beginning, but using organic fertilizers and creating compost can ultimately reduce fertilizer requirements to a bare minimum.

The practice of preserving soil fertility consists of growing crops specifically for compost value, growing crops to fix atmospheric nitrogen into the soil, and composting all crop residues possible (along with the specific compost crops) and practically anything else that isn't nailed down. (Chapter 5 covers composting in detail.)

A big part of soil fertility is the diversity of microbial life in the soil, along with the presence of earthworms and other beneficial insects. There are approximately 4,000 pounds of bacteria in an acre of fertile topsoil. These organisms work together with soil nutrients to produce vigorous growth and limit the damage done by disease-causing microorganisms known as "pathogens."

Grow Calorie-Dense Crops

As already noted, vegetables provide about only 10% of the average American's calories. Because of this, a standard vegetable garden may supply excellent produce and rich vitamin content, but the economic value of the vegetables won't significantly reduce your food bill over the course of a year. The solution to this problem is to grow crops that provide a higher proportion of caloric needs such as fruits, dried beans, grains, and root crops such as potatoes and onions.

Raise Meat at Home

Most Americans are accustomed to obtaining at least a portion of their protein from eggs and meat. Agribusiness meats are often produced using practices and substances (such as growth hormones and antibiotics) that worry a lot of people. Certainly, factory-farmed meat is very high in the least healthy fats compared to free-range, grass-fed animals or animals harvested through hunting.

The problem with meat, in an economic sense, is that the feeding for one calorie of meat generally requires anywhere from two to four calories of feed. This sounds, at first blush, like a very inefficient use of resources, but it isn't as bad as it seems. Most livestock, even small livestock like poultry, gets a substantial portion of its diet from foraging around. Poultry will eat all of the ticks, fleas, spiders, beetles, and grasshoppers that can be found plus dispose of the farmer's table scraps. If meat is raised on premises, then the mini-farmer just has to raise enough extra food to make up the difference between the feed needs and what was obtained through scraps and foraging.

Plant Some Fruit

There are a number of fruits that can be grown in most parts of the country: apples, grapes, blackberries, pears, and cherries to name a few. Newer dwarf fruit tree varieties often produce substantial amounts of fruit in only three years, and they take up comparatively little space. Grapes native to North America, such as the Concord grape, are hardy throughout the continental United States, and some varieties, like muscadine grapes, grow prolifically in the South and have recently been discovered to offer unique health benefits. Strawberries are easy to grow and attractive to youngsters. A number of new blackberry and raspberry varieties have been introduced, some without thorns, that are so productive you'll have more berries than you can imagine.

Fruits are nature's candy and can easily be preserved for apple sauce, apple butter, snacks, jellies, pie filling, and shortcake topping. Many fruits can also be stored whole for a few months using root cellaring. Fruits grown with minimal or no pesticide usage are expensive at the store, and growing your own will put even more money in the bank with minimal effort.

Grow Market Crops

Especially if you adopt organic growing methods, you can get top-wholesale-dollar for crops delivered to restaurants, organic food cooperatives, and so forth. If your property allows it, you can also set up a farm stand and sell homegrown produce at top retail dollar.

According to John Jeavon's 1986 research described in *The Complete 21-Bed Biointensive Mini-Farm*, a mini-farmer in the United States could expect to earn $2,079 in income from the space required to feed one person in addition to actually feeding the person. Assuming a family of three and correcting for USDA reported rises in the value of food, that amounts to $10,060 per year, using a six-month growing season.

Mel Bartholomew in his 1985 book *Ca$h from Square Foot Gardening* estimated $5,000 per year income during a six-month growing season from a mere 1,500 square feet of properly managed garden. This equates to $8,064 in today's market.

A mini-farm that sets aside only 2,100 square feet for market crops would gross an average of $11,289 per year.

It is worthwhile to notice that two very different authorities arrived at very closely the same numbers for expected income from general vegetable sales—about $5.00 per square foot.

Extend the Season

A lot of people don't realize that most of Europe, where greenhouses, cold frames, and other season extenders have been used for generations, lies north of most of the United States. Maine, for example, is at the same latitude as southern France. The reason for the difference in climate has to do with ocean currents, not latitude, and latitude is the biggest factor in determining the success of growing protected plants because it determines the amount of sunlight available. In essence, anything that can be done in southern France can be done throughout the continental United States.

The secret to making season extension economically feasible lies in working with nature rather than against it. Any attempt to build a

super insulated and heated tropical environment suitable for growing bananas in Minnesota in January is going to be prohibitively expensive. A simple unheated hoop house covered with plastic is fairly inexpensive and will work extremely well with crops selected for the climate.

Extending the season brings two big advantages. First, it lets you harvest fresh greens and seasonal fare throughout the year including held-over potatoes, carrots, and onions, thus keeping the family's food costs low. Second, it allows for earlier starts and later endings to the main growing season, netting more total food for the family and more food for market. It also provides a happy diversion from dreary winters when the mini-farmer can walk out to a hoop house for fresh salad greens in the middle of a snowstorm.

Understand Your Market

As a mini-farmer you may produce food for two markets: the family and the community. The family is the easiest market to understand because the preferences of the family can be easily discovered by looking in the fridge and cabinets. The community is a tougher nut to crack, and if you decide to market your excess crops, you will need to assess your community's needs.

Food is a commodity, meaning that the overwhelming majority of food is produced and sold in gargantuan quantities at tiny profit margins that are outside the reach of a mini-farmer. The proportion of crops that are grown for market cannot hope to compare with the wholesale costs of large commercial enterprises. Therefore the only way the mini-farmer can actually derive a profit is to sell at retail direct to the community or high-markup organics at wholesale.

Direct agricultural products can work, as can value-added products such as pickles, salsas, and gourmet vinegars.

Your products can appeal to the community in a number of ways, but the exact approaches that will work in a given case depend on the farmer's analysis of the needs of that community. You should keep careful records to make sure that the right crops are being grown.

The Economic Equation

According to the Federal Bureau of Labor Statistics, as of October 2005, the average nonfarm wage earner in the United States earns $557.54 per week or $28,990 per year for working 40.7 hours every week, or 2,116 hours a year. According to the Tax Foundation, the average employee works 84 out of 260 days a year just to pay taxes deducted from the paycheck, leaving the average employee $19,620.

According to the 2001 Kenosha County Commuter Study, conducted in Wisconsin before our most recent increases in fuel costs, the average employee spent $30 per week on gas just getting back and forth to work, or $1,500 per year, and spent $45 per week on lunches and coffee on the way to work, or $2,340 per year. Nationwide, the cost of child care for children under age 5 was estimated at $297 per month for children under age 5 and $224 per month for children aged 5 to 12. This estimate is from an Urban League study in 1997, so the expense has undoubtedly increased in the meantime. Assuming a school-age child though, the expenses of all this add up so that the average worker has only $13,092 remaining that can be used to pay the mortgage or rent, the electric bill, and so forth.

Though there can be other justifications for adopting mini-farming, including quality-of-life issues such as the ability to homeschool children, it makes economic sense for one spouse in a working couple to become a mini-farmer if the net economic impact of the mini-farm can replace the income from the job. Obviously, for doctors, lawyers, media moguls, and those in other highly paid careers, mini-farming may not be a good economic decision. But mini-farming can have a sufficient net economic impact that most occupations can be replaced if the other spouse works in a standard occupation. Mini-farming is also sufficiently time efficient that it could be used to remove the need for a second job. It could also be done part-time in the evenings as a substitute for TV time.

The economics of mini-farming look like this. According to Census Bureau statistics from 2003, the average household size in the United States is 2.61 people. Let's round that up to 3 for ease of multiplication. According to statistics given earlier, accounting for the rise in food prices, the cost of feeding a family of 3 now amounts to $3,210 per person, or $9,630 per year. A mini-farm that supplied 85% of those needs would produce a yearly economic benefit of $8,185 per year—the same as a pretax income of $12,200, except it can't be taxed.

That would require 2,100 square feet of space, and 10 hours a week from April through September—a total of 240 hours. This works out to the equivalent of nearly $51 per hour.

If the farm also dedicated 2,100 square feet to market crops, you could also earn $10,060 during a standard growing season, plus spend an additional five hours a week from April through September. This works out to nearly $84 per hour.

When the cash income is added to the economic benefit of drastically slashing food bills, the minimum net economic benefit of $14,920 exceeds the net economic benefit of the average job by nearly $2,000 per year.

This assumes a lot of worst-case conditions. It assumes that the mini-farmer doesn't employ any sort of season extension, which would increase the value generated, and it assumes that the mini-farmer deducts none of the expenses from the income to reduce tax liability. In addition, once automatic irrigation is set up, the mini-farmer needs to work only three to four hours a day from April through November. Instead of working 2,116 hours per year to net $13,092 after taxes and commuting like the average wage earner, the mini-farmer has worked only 360 to 440 hours per year to net $14,920. At the end of the workday, the mini-farmer doesn't have to commute home—because home is where the farm is, and the workday has ended pretty early.

In this manner, the mini-farmer gains back more than 1,500 hours a year that can be used to improve quality of life in many ways, gains a much healthier diet, gets regular exercise, and gains a measure of independence from the normal employment system. It's impossible to attach a dollar value to that.

For families who want to have a parent stay at home with a child or who want to homeschool their children, mini-farming may make it possible—and make money in the process, by having whichever parent who earns the least money from regular employment go into mini-farming. For healthy people on a fixed income, it's a no-brainer.

3

Raised Beds

Raised beds and properly constituted soil make mini-farming practical. Modern people in the industrialized world have a lot less spare time and a lot less available land than their ancestors.

Raised beds offer so many advantages over row gardening that it is hard to imagine why everyone except big agribusiness cartels isn't using them. Especially in northern climates, raised beds can help gardeners lengthen their growing season because they can raise soil temperature by 8 to 13 degrees compared to ground soil temperatures.

By raising the level of the soil, farmers and gardeners can start their crops earlier because excess moisture drains easily so the cold spring rains won't overwhelm new crops. Raised beds are also easily fitted with attachments, such as cold frames.

A raised bed is essentially a bottomless and topless box laid on the ground and filled with soil. The boxes can be built from wood, plastic boards, cement, and other materials. Raised beds can be made from mounded earth, but surrounding them with a box structure limits erosion of the carefully prepared soil of the bed.

⊗ Raised beds extend the season and reduce problems related to excess water.

Material Choices

The frames of raised beds are in constant contact with damp earth and can be subject to rotting. Ordinary lumber will last two or three years before replacement is needed. This can be delayed by carefully painting all exposed surfaces of the frames with a water-based exterior latex paint and allowing them to dry thoroughly before putting them to use. Do not use oil-based paints or paints containing antimildew ingredients or else you'll poison the soil in your beds. Because of the weight of the soil, boards used should be at least 1.5 inches thick to avoid bowing, and opposite sides of long runs should be tied together every eight feet or so. The biggest benefits of lumber lie in its easy availability and easy workability.

Ordinary concrete blocks are inexpensive and easy to use. They are readily available, durable, and heavy enough to hold the soil in a raised bed without need for mortar. They can be picked up and moved around to relocate or expand beds, and they can be reused almost indefinitely. The only downside is their weight—45 pounds for

each. That means that in spite of their compact size, only 22 at a time can be hauled in a pickup truck rated to haul a half ton. Since each block is eighteen inches long, a pickup-sized load gives only 33 linear feet.

Boards made from recycled plastic used for decks and other outdoor structures have become more available in recent years and combine the assets of the easy handling of traditional lumber with the durability of concrete block. Several raised-bed kits are on the market that use plastic boards, and these may be a good idea if you plan on doing a small amount of gardening, but because of the expense of the kits, they don't make sense on the scale needed to feed a family. For a mini-farm, save expense by buying the plastic boards at the lumber store and cutting them to the right size yourself.

It is true that more modern pressure-treated lumber uses less toxic components than it used

⊗ Raised beds can be made from a variety of materials. This one is made with cinder blocks and landscape timbers.

to, but the components are still toxic, and they can leach into the soil of the growing bed, so they are best avoided.

Many other materials can be used, ranging from landscaping timbers to poured concrete forms. Just let imagination, cost, durability, and the potential toxicity of anything you might use guide the decision. Keep in mind that using materials that leach poisons into the growing beds completely defeats the purpose of the home garden or mini-farm because consuming the products grown in those beds can be extremely hazardous. (The arsenic in pressure-treated wood, for example, is both directly toxic and highly carcinogenic.)

Shape and Orientation of Raised Beds

The most common and useful shape for raised beds is rectangular. Certain planters for flowers are circular, and this works fine as long as the diameter is not so great that the gardener has to step into the bed. Another common shape is a 4-foot square. This works well for casual vegetable-only gardening on a small scale, but at the scale of providing all the needs of a family, it becomes wasteful of space and material.

I recommend a rectangular shape because it makes maximum use of space and minimal material while making it easy to add standardized structures like hoop houses.

Any rectangular bed is going to be longer than it is wide. To give maximum sun to crops and avoid shading, ensure that the long sides face north and south. Any trellising for vining crops should be established along the north edge to get the advantage of sunshine without shading other crops.

Size of Raised Beds: Width

Everyone has an opinion on the proper size of raised beds. The Grow Biointensive method favors a width of 5 feet and a length of 20 feet to establish a "microclimate" for intensive agriculture. Square Foot enthusiasts advocate a maximum width of 4 feet, because it is easy to reach into a bed that is 4 feet wide from either side and get to whatever is in the middle. Many experienced organic farmers use even narrower raised beds.

The five-foot width advocated by Ecology Action requires, for many people, stepping into the bed onto a board intended to more widely distribute the weight and minimize damage to the soil structure. But stepping into the garden bed at all, even using a board, defeats the purpose of careful management of the soil structure by compacting the soil. The board would need to be set up so it can be laid across the sides of the bed structure and be rigid enough that it won't bend when someone is standing on it. (This would be impossible using the complete Grow Biointensive method since, in that method, the raised beds are only mounded soil without structural sides. My method uses structural sides instead.)

The 4-foot width is narrow enough that most people can reach into the garden from both sides since only a 2-foot reach is needed. This will not work, however, when trellised crops that grow food on both sides of the trellis are grown against one of the long sides of the bed. In that case, picking pole beans, for example, requires a 4-foot reach, which most people don't have. My wife and I did this with a 4-foot-wide bed one year, and watching my wife balance on one of the frame boards while reaching for the beans with one hand and holding on to me with the other was a sure sign that I would need to make some changes the following year!

For reasons of experience and convenience, then, I recommend that beds should be four feet wide if they aren't going to be used for tall vines like pole beans. They should be three to three and a half feet wide otherwise.

Size of Raised Beds: Length

We already know that beds need to be rectangular for economic reasons and three to four feet wide for convenience—but how long can they be? Technically, they can be as long as the farmer wants, but there are some aspects of length worth considering.

One of the biggest causes of insect and disease problems is growing the same plants in the same space year after year. Bacterial, fungal, and viral diseases often have preferred host plants—and sometimes won't even grow in plants of an unrelated genus. Since these pathogens are competing against more beneficial microbes in compost-enriched soil, they can survive for only a limited period of time—usually three years or less—in soil that doesn't provide a suitable host.

Insect pests (some of which spread diseases) are quite similar. They have a particular appetite—a particular niche—such as cabbage. Such pests not only eat cabbage and infect it with diseases but also lay their eggs in the soil around the cabbage so that their offspring will emerge right next to their favorite food. One important way of foiling such pests is to make sure that when their offspring awaken in spring, they find plants that aren't appetizing.

Limiting the length of raised beds so that you have more room to create several of them makes it easy to practice crop rotation because the soil in one bed is isolated from the soil in the others. Making sure the same crop isn't grown in the same bed for three years solves a lot of problems in advance. In my own mini-farm, beds range in length from 8 to 24 feet.

Start at the Right Time and Grow Slowly

The time between when the soil can first be worked in the spring and when the early spring crops need to be planted is about three weeks. This is simply not enough time to create enough raised beds.

Ultimately, for total food self-sufficiency, you will need about 700 square feet per person. If you plan to raise market crops, you'll need even more. That will require a lot of beds. The number will depend on the length you choose.

Assuming the creation of beds that are 4-feet × 25-feet, that means you'll need at least seven beds per person or 21 beds for a family of three. Using 4-feet × 8-feet beds, that would be 22 beds per person or 66 for a family of three. In practice, depending on dietary preferences, chosen crop varieties, climate, and other factors, a larger or smaller number of beds could actually be used.

Initial creation of raised beds takes a considerable amount of time and is very labor intensive, but once they've been created, they require very little work to maintain. Raised beds can be created in a number of ways, but even the most time-efficient methods will take a few hours per bed. If you have limited time, getting all the beds made in spring will be physically impossible.

Therefore the best time to embark upon mini-farming is *the summer or fall before* the first growing season. This way the beds can be prepared in a more leisurely fashion and then sowed with cover crops for overwintering. In the spring, you only have to cut the cover crops and put them into the compost pile, cultivate existing beds, and start planting. (Cover crops are explained in the next chapter.)

It may be best to start mini-farming slowly—say, by initially creating enough beds for just a single individual's food—and then keep adding beds as time and materials allow until the required number has been established. This is because of the trade-off between time and money. If the prospective farmer has the time to establish all of the required beds initially, that's great. But if time is lacking, the only way to shortcut the system is to pay for heavy equipment and truckloads of compost.

I don't want the fact that fall is the best time to get started to discourage you from starting in either the spring or summer if that is when you want to start. It is always better to start than to delay because even just a couple of raised beds can produce a lot of food. If you get started in the spring or summer, just keep in mind that you'll want to add new beds in the fall as well.

Creating the Beds

For reasons of economy and productivity, I recommend creating the beds initially by double-digging. Lay out the area to be dug using stakes and string, then once it is dug, surround that area with the material you have chosen to create the box for the bed. Because the process of double-digging will loosen the soil, the level of the dug area will be between four and six inches higher than the surrounding soil.

Double-digging has been a standard agricultural practice for soil improvement in various places around the world for untold generations, and it is what I recommend because it is the most effective for the money required. The idea behind double-digging is that plants send their roots deeply into the soil, and making sure there are nutrients and aerated soil two feet deep provides ideal growing conditions. Up where I live in New Hampshire, any attempt at digging, no matter how modest, can be difficult because of the large number of rocks encountered. Did you ever wonder where all those picturesque rock walls in New England came from? Yep—they came from farmers getting rocks out of their fields.

My grandfather never double-dug anything but his asparagus beds. But, then again, he had 96 acres of land, horse teams, plows, tractors, four sons, and three daughters, so he wasn't trying to squeeze every ounce of productivity out of every square foot like a modern mini-farmer either. Nevertheless, the asparagus grown in a double-dug bed was far superior to any other.

Although many plants, especially grasses, can send roots several feet deep, the majority of a plant's root system exists in the top six inches of the soil. That's why Mel Bartholomew's Square Foot gardening system, which uses only six inches of soil, works. But in spite of the fact that six inches of perfectly prepared soil can be adequate, there can be no doubt that two *feet* of soil will necessarily hold a greater reservoir of nutrients and water.

As my father would say, with my apologies to our beloved cat, Patrick, in advance, "there's more than one way to skin a cat." Meaning, of course, that double-digging is not the only suitable way to prepare soil for mini-farming. There are actually three ways of digging the beds.

Digging Methods

The old-timers where I grew up never used the term *double-digging*. In the United States and Great Britain, that practice has been historically known as "bastard trenching" to differentiate it from full or "true" trenching. Most modern texts don't mention it, but there are actually three sorts of trenching that are useful under different circumstances. All three types of trenching are brutally hard work, particularly in areas with a lot of large rocks or with soils composed mainly of clay, but they offer benefits worth the effort. These three types of trenching are *plain digging*, *bastard trenching*, and *trenching*.

Plain digging relies on using a garden spade to dig into and turn over the soil to the depth of a single spade. The area to be dug is laid out using string or other marking, and a garden spade is used to remove the soil one-spade wide and a single-spade deep across the width of the bed, and that soil is placed into a wheelbarrow. Then a couple of inches of compost is added to the bottom of the first trench, and the soil from the next parallel trench is added on top of the compost in the first trench. This process continues until the last trench is dug and compost added to the bottom, and then the soil saved from the first trench is added to the hole left by the last trench.

The only difference between plain digging and double-digging (a.k.a. bastard trenching) is that in the latter, after a trench is dug a single-spade deep and before the compost is added, a digging fork is worked into the soil at the bottom of the trench to lift and break up the soil. Finally, more compost is added on top and mixed with the top six inches of soil. I perform this last step after I've built the form around the dug area.

Both plain digging and double-digging can be useful for newly created beds and can be especially useful for an area that is covered with grass as the spits of dirt (the dirt that makes up

⊗ The garden fork and digging spade are indispensable tools for double-digging.

a spade-full is known as a "spit") can be turned grass-side down in the adjacent trench as they are dug. It is extremely useful in either case, where the land to be used for farming was previously weeds or lawn, to sift through the soil to remove wireworms and grubs as you go along. When I use either of these trenching methods, I not only put compost in the bottom of the trenches but add some across the top of the finished bed and mix it in as well.

True or full trenching is serious work, but it is appropriate for regenerating soil in beds that have been previously double-dug or where the soil can be worked deeply without using a backhoe. A properly maintained bed should never need regeneration, but true trenching can be useful when dealing with land that was previously overfarmed using conventional methods since it exchanges the subsoil with the top soil. In true trenching, the first trench is dug a single-spade deep and the soil from that set aside, and then the same trench is dug another spade deep and that soil is set aside as well, separately from the soil from the top of the trench. Then a digging fork is used to break up the soil in the bottom as deep as the tines will go, and compost is added.

When the second adjacent trench is dug, the spits from the top are added to the bottom of the first trench, then the spits from the bottom are added to the top of that. In this way, the topsoil is buried, and the subsoil is brought to the top. Continue in this way until the last trench is dug, at which time the top spits from the first trench are put into the bottom of the last trench, and then those spits are topped with those that remain.

Because true trenching exchanges the topsoil with the subsoil, and subsoil tends to have far less organic matter, generous amounts of aged compost should be added to the top layer, worked in thoroughly, and allowed to sit for a couple of weeks before putting the new bed to use.

In any of the three trenching methods, you will be using hand tools to move, literally, thousands of pounds of soil for each bed. This can be grueling work, and you should always use spades and digging forks that have been either bought or modified to accommodate your height. The correct height of a spade or fork (plus handle) can be judged by standing the tool vertically next to you, then seeing how high it reaches on your body. The top of the handle should fall somewhere between your elbow and the middle of your breastbone.

Digging forks and spades can be purchased with either straight or "D" handles. You should get the "D"-handled versions, as they will lessen the amount of required back twisting. When using the tools, keep your back straight, and avoid both twisting and jerky movements. Work at a comfortable pace, and take breaks when needed. This way you get an excellent and safe aerobic workout that improves your strength and flexibility while improving the soil.

What about "No-Dig" Beds?

In my experience, I have found nothing that competes, in terms of sheer productivity, with properly double-dug raised beds. However, this can be a lot of work, and folks without a lot of time or with physical disabilities might not want to undertake the effort. You can still get very good results, though, using a no-dig method that I've tested.

Illustrated Double-Dig

Every year I expand my mini-farm a little by adding a few raised beds. The beds in my farm vary in size depending on the materials I had available at the time of construction, but most of them are 3-1/2 feet wide and 8 feet long. In the spring of 2006, I added a few beds and had my wife take pictures of the process so I could include them for your reference.

1   Mark off the area to be dug. In my case, I just laid out the boards where I would be digging. Notice a completed bed in the foreground and boards marking where the new bed will be in the background.

2   Dig the first row across the width of the bed one-spade deep, and put the dirt from that row in a wheelbarrow.

3   Loosen the soil in the bottom of the trench with a digging fork.

4   Add compost to the bottom of the trench.

5   Dig the second trench parallel and adjacent to the first one.

6   Because, in this instance, I am digging an area that was covered with grass, I turn the

⊗ Boards are used to mark off the new bed. You could just as easily use string or chalk.

⊗ Loosening the soil.

⊗ First row dug.

⊗ Adding compost.

⊗ Digging the second trench. Beware the author's stylish footwear!

⊗ Putting spits in the trench upside down.

spits from the second trench upside down in the first trench.

7   Work some additional compost into the top few inches of the finished bed.

As you can see from the photo tutorial, preparing raised beds by double-digging is a pretty straightforward and very physical process. It is great exercise and loosens the soil to a depth of two feet, placing organic material throughout the entire depth. The yields from beds that I work like this are phenomenal!

⊗ Working compost into the top few inches of the new bed.

Save up old newspapers—just the black-and-white portions, not the glossy parts. In the fall, build your frame out of 2 × 4 lumber right on the ground. Lay down the newspaper several layers thick, and then fill the bed completely with finished compost. Don't skip the newspapers because their purpose is to smother the grass underneath. If the grass isn't smothered, and if you are using only 2 × 4 lumber, you'll end up with a lot of grass growing in the bed.

When spring rolls around and the ground thaws, just use the digging fork to fluff it up a little; then plant, and you are done.

For no-dig beds it is particularly important to keep them planted with cover crops when fallow during the off-season because you are depending on the action of plant roots to mix the soil and keep it loose.

Because seeds don't always germinate well in compost, I'd recommend using the bed for transplanted crops for the first year, and then a good soil builder like beans the next year. In all other respects, you can treat this just like a regular raised bed. If fresh compost is added yearly, after three years the productivity will be the same as for a double-dug bed.

Trellising for Raised Beds: Flexible Trellising System

Trellises are necessary for certain crops and can be a valuable adjunct for others. Because raised beds don't provide much room for sprawling plants such as cucumbers or pole beans, adding a trellis makes growing these crops more practical and space efficient.

Many crops are more productive in vining versions than bush versions. This includes beans, peas, cucumbers, tomatoes, and more. Pole beans, for example, can yield almost twice as much product per square foot as bush beans. This means that a row of pole beans grown on a trellis along the north side of an 8-foot bed using only 8 square feet of space can produce nearly as many beans as 16 square feet of bush beans. This same calculation applies to other vegetables.

⊗ Electrical conduit makes a sturdy and versatile trellis.

As mentioned earlier in the chapter, beds will ideally be located with the long sides facing north and south. Trellises should be established on the north side. If, for some reason, this orientation isn't convenient, the second-best choice is to have the long side upon which trellises will be established on the north west or, in the worst case, west side. Don't establish trellises on the south or east sides of a bed or they will shade crops during the times of day that are most sunny.

There are as many ways to erect trellises as there are farmers, and I've used many different methods over the years. In the past few years, my preferred method of trellising uses rebar, electrical conduit, and conduit fittings. Electrical conduit comes in lengths 10 feet long. By cutting it to strategic lengths and using appropriate fittings, you can vary its height and length. By fitting it over rebar driven into the ground, you can lift it off the rebar easily in the fall for storage, and moving it to a different bed is a snap.

Because lumber used to create the beds is eight feet long, the longest you need the conduit to be is eight feet. This is for the horizontal piece on top. Meanwhile, trellis heights can range all the way from two feet for peas to four feet for tomatoes to even six feet for pole beans. A trellis height of more than six feet isn't a good idea, as reaching the top would be tiring or—even worse if a stool is required—dangerous.

The easy way to get a flexible system is to buy 10-foot lengths of conduit six pieces at a time. Three are cut into an 8-foot and a 2-foot piece, two are cut into a 6-foot and a 4-foot piece, and the final length of conduit is cut into two 4-foot pieces and one 2-foot piece. When done, you have three 8-foot horizontals, two 6-foot verticals, four 4-foot verticals, and four 2-foot verticals. In addition to these, for every six pieces of conduit, you will need six 90-degree elbows, four screw couplings, and six pieces of 2-foot rebar. (You can find rebar already cut to length and bundled at Home Depot and similar stores.)

Once the rebar is hammered into the ground on either end of the beds, you can completely assemble or disassemble a trellis of any height from 2-foot to 8-foot in two-foot increments using only a screwdriver.

⊗ Driving the rebar into the ground.

⊗ Placing an upright over the rebar.

Complete Trellis Creation, Step-by-Step

1 Hammer 2-foot pieces of rebar into the ground at either end of the raised bed, leaving 6 inches protruding above the ground.

⊗ Attaching the horizontal to the bend.

⊗ Deck screws drilled into the edge and protruding 3/8 inch.

Deck Screws

4   Put deck screws into the side of the raised bed along the trellis every 6 to 12 inches. Leave them protruding about a quarter of an inch.

5   Run string between the horizontal bar on top and the deck screws in the side of the raised bed.

6   Now you have a completed trellis!

« Run string between the horizontal and the deck screws.

2   Slip your vertical piece of conduit over the rebar. Repeat for the other side.

3   Attach a 90-degree elbow to each vertical piece of conduit, and then secure the horizontal conduit to the elbows.

Completed trellis. »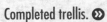

Soil Composition and Maintenance

4

The productivity and fertility of the farm and plant resistance to pests and disease depend on the quality of the soil. Soil quality can be enhanced and outside inputs reduced through proper tillage, compost, cover cropping, and crop rotation. These are crucial to maintaining the high level of fertility required for the close plant spacing in a mini-farm without spending a lot of money on fertilizer.

When French Intensive gardening was developed, horses were the standard mode of transportation, and horse manure was plentiful and essentially free. This explains the reliance on horse manure as a source of soil fertility. According to the Colorado State University Cooperative Extension Service, the average 1,000-pound horse generates 9 tons—18,000 pounds—of manure occupying nearly 730 cubic feet per year.[6] The sheer volume, smell, and mess of such quantities of manure often mean that places that board horses will give it away for the asking to anyone willing to haul it away.

---

[6] Davis, J. G., Swinker, A. M. (2004) *Horse Manure Management* Retrieved Jan 29, 2006, from http://www.ext.colostate.edu/pubs/livestk/01219.html

⊗ Horse manure should be composted and not added directly to the bed.

Horse manure is good food for crops as well. According to the same source, horse manure contains 19 pounds of nitrogen per ton, 14 pounds of phosphate, and 36 pounds of potassium. This works out to about 1% nitrogen, 0.7% phosphate, and 1.8% potassium.

There's no such thing as a free lunch, and horse manure is no exception. Raw horse manure can spread a parasitic protozoan called giardia and E.coli as well as contaminate water sources and streams with coliform bacteria. Raw manure can also contain worm eggs that are easily transmitted to humans, including pinworms and various species of ascarid worms. Horse manure is high in salts, and if used excessively, it can cause plants grown in it to suffer water stress, even if well watered. The highest permissible rate of application of horse manure assuming the least measurable salinity is between two and three pounds of manure per square foot per year.[7] In addition to the above objections, horse manure doesn't have a balanced level of phosphorus,

meaning that it should be supplemented with a source of phosphorus when used.

Straight horse manure is also in the process of composting. That is, the process has not yet finished. Unfinished compost often contains phytotoxic chemicals that inhibit plant growth. For horse manure to be directly usable as a planting medium, it must first be well rotted, meaning it either should be composted in a pile mixed with other compost materials such as plant debris or should at least sit by itself rotting for a year before use. The former method is preferable since that will conserve more of the manure's valuable nitrogen content. The potential problems posed by horse manure are eliminated through composting the manure with other materials first and then liberally applying the resulting compost to beds. The composting process will kill any parasites, dilute the salinity, and break down phytotoxins.

Making perfect soil from scratch, on a small scale, works quite well. The Square Foot gardening method gives a formula of 1/3 coarse vermiculite, 1/3 peat moss, and 1/3 compost by volume plus a mix of organic fertilizers to create a "perfect soil mix."[8] My own testing on a 120-square-foot raised bed confirms that the method works beautifully. For small beds, the price of the components is reasonable. A six-inch-deep 4-foot 6-foot bed would require only four cubic feet of each of the components. Coarse vermiculite and peat moss currently sell for about $18 for a four-cubic-foot bale. Assuming free compost, the cost of making perfect soil mix comes to $1.50 per square foot of growing area. This works quite well on a small scale, but when even 700 square

[7] Ibid

[8] Bartholomew, M. (2000) *Ca$h from Square Foot Gardening*

feet are put into agricultural production, the cost can become prohibitive.

Double-digging was covered in the previous chapter, and it is what I recommend for mini-farming. Although it is more difficult in the beginning, it affords the best opportunity to prepare the best possible soil for the money invested. No-dig beds, also described in the previous chapter, are a second option.

Water-Holding Capacity and pH

Few soils start out ideal for intensive agriculture or even any sort of agriculture. Some are too sandy, and some are too rich in clay. Some are too acidic, and others are too alkaline. Many lack one or more primary nutrients and any number of trace minerals.

Soil for agricultural use needs to hold water without becoming waterlogged. Sandy soils are seldom waterlogged, but they dry out so quickly that constant watering is required. They make root growth easy but don't hold on to nutrients very well and are low in organic content or humus. (There is some dispute among experts on the exact definition of *humus*. For our purposes, it can be defined as organic matter in the soil that has reached a point of being sufficiently stable that it won't easily decompose further. Thus, finished compost and humus are identical for our purposes.) Clay soils will be waterlogged in the winter and will remain waterlogged as long as water comes to them. As soon as the water stops, they bake and crack, putting stress on root systems. Clay soil is clingy, sticky, and nearly impenetrable to roots. Loam soil is closest to the ideal, as it consists of a mix of sand and clay with a good amount of humus that helps it retain water and nutrients in proportions suitable for agriculture.

Both sandy and clay soils can be improved with vermiculite. Vermiculite is manufactured by heating mica rock in an oven until it pops like popcorn. The result is a durable substance that holds and releases water like a sponge and improves the water-holding characteristics of practically any kind of soil. Because it is an insoluble mineral, it will last for decades and possibly forever. If the soil in your bed isn't loamy to start with, adding coarse or medium vermiculite at the rate of four to eight cubic feet per 100 square feet of raised bed will be very beneficial. (Vermiculite costs $4 per cubic foot in four-cubic-foot bags at the time of this writing.)

If you can't find vermiculite, look instead for bails of peat moss. Peat moss is an organic material made from compressed prehistoric plants at the bottom of bogs and swamps, and it has the same characteristic as vermiculite in terms of

⊗ Vermiculite enhances the water-holding capacity of the soil.

acting as a water reservoir. It costs about the same and can also be found in large bales. It should be added at the same rate as vermiculite—anywhere from four to eight cubic feet per 100 square feet of raised bed. Keep in mind that peat moss raises the soil's pH slightly over time and decomposes, so it must be renewed.

The term *pH* refers to how acidic or alkaline the soil is and is referenced on a scale from 0 to 14, with 0 corresponding to highly acidic battery acid, 14 to highly alkaline drain cleaner, and 7 to neutral distilled water. As you might imagine, most plants grown in a garden will perform well with a pH between 6 and 7. (There are a few exceptions, such as blueberries, that prefer a highly acidic soil.) pH affects a lot of things indirectly, including whether nutrients already in the soil are available for plants to use and the prevalence of certain plant disease organisms such as "club foot" in cabbage.

On the basis of a pH test, you can amend your soil to near neutral or just slightly acid, a pH of 6.5 or so, with commonly available lime and sulfur products. To adjust the pH up 1 point, add dolomitic limestone at the rate of 5 pounds per 100 square feet of raised bed and work it into the top two inches of soil. To adjust the pH down 1 point, add iron sulfate at the rate of 1.5 pounds per 100 square feet of raised bed and work it into the soil. To adjust the pH by half a point, say from 6 to 6.5, cut the amount per 100 square feet in half.

pH amendments don't work quickly. Wait 40 to 60 days after adding the amendments, and then retest the soil before adding any more. If amendments are added too quickly, they can build up in the soil and make it inhospitable for growing things.

Fertilizers

The fertility of soil is measured by its content of nitrogen, phosphorus, and potassium, and fertilizers are rated the same way, using a series of numbers called "NPK." The N in NPK stands for nitrogen, the P for phosphate, and the K for potassium. A bag of fertilizer will be marked with the NPK in a format that lists the percentage content of each nutrient, separated by dashes. So, for example, a bag of fertilizer labeled "5-10-5" is 5% nitrogen, 10% phosphate, and 5% potassium.

A completely depleted garden soil with no detectable levels of NPK requires only 4.6 ounces of N, 5 ounces of P, and 5.4 ounces of K per 100 square feet to yield a "sufficient" soil. In the case of root crops, less than 3 ounces of N are needed.

Inexpensive soil tests are available to test the pH, nitrogen, phosphorus, and potassium content of soil. A couple of weeks after the soil in the bed has been prepared and compost and/or manure have been worked in, you should test the soil's nutrient content and amend it properly. The most important factor in the long-range viability of your soil is organic matter provided by compost and manures, so always make sure that there is plenty of organic matter first, and then test to see what kind of fertilization is needed.

You can buy a soil test kit at most garden centers, and most give results for each nutrient as being depleted, deficient, adequate, or sufficient. The latter two descriptions can be confusing because in ordinary English, they have identical meaning. For the purposes of interpreting soil tests, consider "adequate" to mean that there is enough of the measured nutrient for plants to survive but not necessarily thrive. If the soil test indicates the amount to be "sufficient," then there is enough of the nutrient to support optimal growth.

The Rapitest soil test kit is commonly available, costs less than $20, and comes with enough components to make 10 tests. The LaMotte soil test kit is one of the most accurate available and can currently be purchased via mail order for less than $55. When preparing a bed, I recommend adding enough organic fertilizers to make all three major nutrients "sufficient."

Organic fertilizers are a better choice than synthetic ones for several reasons. Organic fertilizers break down more slowly so they stay in the soil longer and help build the organic content of your soil as they break down. Synthetics can certainly get the job done in the short term, but they also carry the potential to harm important microbial diversity in the soil that helps to prevent plant diseases, and they also hurt earthworms and other beneficial soil inhabitants. For these reasons, I strongly discourage the use of synthetic fertilizers.

Organic fertilizers, like synthetics, are rated by NPK, but because they are made from plant, animal, and mineral substances, they contain a wide array of trace minerals that plants also need. Probably the biggest argument in favor of using organic fertilizers is taste. The hydroponic hothouse tomatoes at the grocery store are grown using exclusively synthetics mixed with water. Compare the taste of a hydroponic hothouse tomato with the taste of an organic garden tomato, and the answer will be clear.

There is one thing to keep in mind with organic fertilizers: Many of them are quite appetizing to rodents! One spring, I discovered that the fertilizer in my garage had been torn open by red squirrels and eaten almost entirely! Ever

⊗ The LaMotte soil test kit is very accurate.

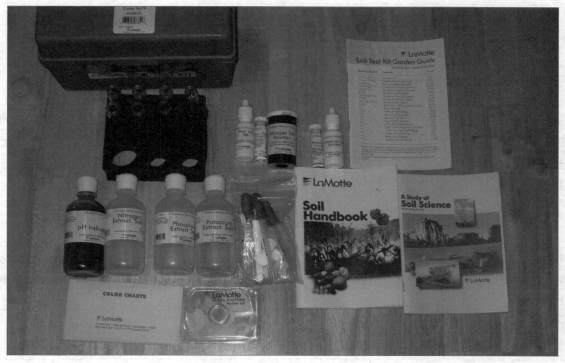

since, I store organic fertilizers in five-gallon buckets with lids.

There are a number of available sources for organic fertilizers. Some come premixed, or you can make them yourself from individual components.

Making your own premixed fertilizer is easy. For N, you can use alfalfa meal, soybean meal, or blood meal. For P, bone meal and rock phosphate work well. For K, wood ashes, greensand, and seaweed will work. The foregoing list is far from exhaustive, but the materials are readily available from most garden or agricultural stores.

Table 1 contains two numbers notated as either "leaf" or "root" because root crops don't need as much nitrogen as leafy vegetable crops. In fact, too much nitrogen can hurt the productivity of root crops. There's also no reason to formulate a fertilizer for depleted soil since that shouldn't happen after the first year, and maybe not even then if adequate compost has been added. If it does, just add triple or quadruple the amount used for adequate soil. Looking at these tables, it should be pretty easy to formulate a couple of ready-made fertilizers.

A "high nitrogen" fertilizer for vegetative crops like spinach could consist of a mix of 10 ounces of blood meal, 6 ounces of bone meal, and 21 ounces of wood ashes.

As long as you keep the proportions the same, you can mix up as much of it as you like to keep handy, and you know that 37 ounces of

Table 1: Nitrogen Sources

Nitrogen Source	%N	Ounces per 100 sq. ft. for depleted soil	Ounces per 100 sq. ft. for adequate soil
Alfalfa meal	2.50	184 leaf/120 root	52 leaf/34 root
Soybean meal	6.00	76 leaf/50 root	21 leaf/14 leaf
Blood meal	12.00	38 leaf/25 root	10 leaf/7 r oot

Table 2: Phosphorus Sources

Phosphorus Source	%P	Ounces per 100 sq. ft. for depleted soil	Ounces per 100 sq. ft. for adequate soil
Bone meal	21.00	23	6
Rock phosphate	39.00	13	4

Table 3: Potassium Sources

Potassium Source	%K	Ounces per 100 sq. ft. for depleted soil	Ounces per 100 sq. ft. for adequate soil
Wood ashes	7.00	77	21
Greensand	5.00	108	30
Seaweed	5.00	108	30

the mixture are required for each 100 square feet. Just a tad over two pounds.

A "low nitrogen" fertilizer for root crops like parsnips could consist of a mix of 34 ounces of alfalfa meal, 4 ounces of rock phosphate, and 30 ounces of greensand.

Just as with the first formulation, as long as you keep the proportions the same, you can mix up as much as you'd like, and you know that 68 ounces are required for each 100 square feet—a hair over four pounds.

Your actual choice of fertilizers and blends will depend on availability and price of materials, but using a variety of components guarantees that at some point practically every known nutrient— and every unknown nutrient—finds its way into your garden beds. Wood ashes should be used no more often than once every three years because of the salts they can put into the soil and because they can raise the soil pH.

Fertilizers should be added to the soil a couple of weeks before planting and worked into the garden bed; any additional fertilizer should then be added on top of the ground as a side dressing, perhaps diluted 50/50 with some dried compost.

The reason for dilution is that some organic fertilizers, such as blood meal, are pretty powerful— as powerful as synthetics—and if they touch crop foliage directly, they can damage plants.

Liquid fertilizers are worth mentioning, particularly those intended for application directly to leaves. These tend to be extremely dilute so that they won't hurt the plants, and they are a good choice for reducing transplant shock.

In some cases, liquid fertilizers can be a lifesaver. One year, I planted out cabbage well before last frost in a newly prepared bed. Having added one-third of the bed's volume in compost of every

⊗ Popular organic liquid fertilizers.

sort imaginable, I made the mistake of assuming the bed had adequate nutrients. What I had forgotten is that plants can't use nitrogen when the soil is too cold. A couple of days after the cabbage plants were planted, they turned yellow, starting from the oldest leaves first, which is a classic symptom of severe nitrogen deficiency.

As an experiment, I added a heavy sidedressing of mixed blood meal, bone meal, and wood ashes and watered it in on all the cabbage plants, but for half of them, I also watered the leaves with a watering can containing liquid fertilizer mixed according to package directions. The result was that all of the plants watered with the liquid fertilizer survived and eventually thrived, while a full half of the plants that received only a side-dressing died.

Now, I use liquid fertilizer—specifically Neptune's Harvest—whenever I transplant, especially in early spring.

Soil Maintenance

Believe it or not, soil is a delicate substance. More than merely delicate, it is quite literally alive. It is the life of the soil, not its sand and clay, that makes it fertile and productive. A single teaspoon of good garden soil contains millions of microbes, almost every one of which contributes something positive to the garden. The organic matter serves as a pH buffer, detoxifies pollutants, holds moisture, and serves to hold nutrients in a fixed form to keep them from leaching out of the soil. Some microbes, like actinomycetes, send out delicate microscopic webs that stretch for miles, giving soil its structure.

The structure of soil for intensive agriculture is maintained through

- cover crops (explained later in this chapter) to maintain fertility and prevent erosion;
- regularly adding organic matter in the form of left over roots, compost, and manures;
- crop rotation; and
- protecting the soil from erosion, compaction, and loosening.

Once the soil in a bed has been prepared initially, as long as it hasn't been compacted, it shouldn't need more than a fluffing with a broad fork or digging fork yearly and stirring of the top few inches with a three-tined cultivator. Digging subsequent to bed establishment is much easier and faster than the initial double-dig.

It was noted earlier that you shouldn't walk on the garden beds. An occasional unavoidable footprint won't end life on earth, but an effort should be made to avoid it because that footprint compacts the soil, makes that area of soil less able to hold water, decreases the oxygen that can be held in the soil in that area, and damages the structure of the soil, including the structure established by old roots and delicate microbial webs. Almost all species of actinomycetes are aerobic—meaning that they require oxygen. Compacting the soil can deprive them of needed oxygen.

The microbial webs in soil are extremely important in that they work in symbiosis with root systems to extend their reach and ability to assimilate nutrients.[9] Damaging these microbial webs—which can stretch for several feet in each direction from a plant—reduces the plant's ability to obtain nutrients from the soil.

My wife thought I was overreaching on this point and insisted on occasionally walking in the beds to harvest early beans, so I did an experiment. I planted bunching onions from the same packet of seeds in places where she had walked in the beds and in places where she hadn't. The results? Total yield per square foot, measured in pounds, was 20% lower in the places where my wife had walked. She only weighs 115 pounds! The lesson is plain: Maximum productivity from a raised bed requires avoiding soil compression.

Some gardeners favor heavy duty tilling of agricultural land at least yearly and often at both the beginning and end of a season. The problem with such practices lies in the fact that the very same aspects of soil life and structure that are disrupted by compaction are also disrupted by tilling, particularly deep tilling.

[9] Howard, D. (2003) Building fertile soil *Mother Earth News*, Issue 198, June/July 2003

Soil amendments, such as compost and organic fertilizers, should be mixed with the soil—no doubt. But this doesn't require a rototiller. A simple three-tined cultivator (looks like a claw), operated by hand, is sufficient to incorporate amendments into the top couple of inches of soil. Earthworms and other soil inhabitants will do the job of spreading the compost into deep soil layers.

The Amazing Power of Biochar

Most of us are used to thinking of charcoal as an indispensable aid to grilling, and that it certainly is! But less well-known is its equally beneficial effect when added to ordinary garden soil. The standard charcoal you buy at the grocery store may be impregnated with everything from saltpeter to volatile organic compounds intended to aid burning, so it may not be a good choice. There are some "all natural" or even organic charcoals out there that can be used, such as Cowboy Brand Charcoal, though. In addition, some companies make charcoal specifically intended for agricultural use, such as Troposphere Energy.

Of course, if you have access to hardwood, making your own charcoal isn't terribly difficult. In fact, for agricultural use, you don't even need hardwood—just any old vegetable matter—and you can make the charcoal that is trendy nowadays to call "biochar."

The benefits of biochar mixed in the soil are many and were first discovered by the peoples inhabiting the Amazon basin in pre-Columbian times. They discovered that turning their vegetable matter into charcoal, pulverizing it, and adding it to the soil enhanced the soil's productivity. Soil scientists have now discovered that charcoal, previously thought to be inert in soil, lowers the soil's acidity; creates a haven for the beneficial bacteria that live in symbiosis with the root hairs of crops; helps to keep fertilizers in the soil instead of letting them be washed out, thus decreasing the need for fertilizer; and helps to loosen tight soils. In addition, it helps to sequester carbon from the atmosphere, thereby reducing global warming. More benefits are being discovered all the time.

⊗ The three-tined cultivator is a workhorse for raised beds.

The easiest way to add this incredible fertilizer to your garden beds is to make it right where you want it used: in your beds. Use a hoe to make a couple of one-foot-wide and six- to nine-inch-deep trenches running the length of the bed. Place dried branches, leaves, and other vegetable matter neatly, but not too tightly packed, in the trenches. Then, light them on fire in several places. (Avoid using chemicals such as charcoal lighter or gasoline as these could seriously poison the soil.) Once the material is burning well and the smoke has turned gray, cover with the mounded-up soil on the sides of the trenches to deprive it of oxygen, and let it smolder until the pieces are no larger than a deck of cards. Then, douse the embers with plentiful quantities of water. If you do this every fall with garden refuse and other vegetable matter, you will soon have soil that, taken together with the other practices here, will have astonishing levels of productivity.

Cover Crops and Beneficial Microbes

Today we know a lot more than our great-grandparents did about the relationship between plants and microorganisms in the soil. It turns out that the microorganisms in soil are not merely useful for suppressing diseases but actually an integral part of a plant's root system.[10] Up to 40% of the carbohydrates that plants produce through photosynthesis are actually transported to the root system and out into the soil to feed microorganisms around the root system. In turn, these microorganisms extend the plant's root system and make necessary nutrients available.

Friendly microorganisms grow into the roots themselves, setting up a mutually beneficial cooperation (symbiosis) and respond with natural production of antibiotics when needed to protect their host. Planting cover crops will serve to keep these critters fed through the winter months and protected from environmental hazards such as sun and erosion. This way they are healthy and well fed for the next planting season.

For these reasons, harvesting should be considered a two-part process in which the task of harvesting is followed as soon as possible with the sowing of cover crops, which can also be known as green manures.

Green manures are plants grown specifically for the role they play in sustaining soil fertility, but they also reduce erosion and feed beneficial microbes outside the growing season. The benefits of green manures on crop yield are far from merely theoretical. In one study, for example, the use of hairy vetch (a common legume) as a green manure and mulch increased tomato yields by more than 100%.[11] Green manures are generally either grains or legumes; grains because of their ability to pull nutrients up into the topsoil from a depth of several feet,[12] and legumes because of their ability to take nitrogen out of the air and fix it in nodules in their roots, thereby fertilizing the soil. They are either tilled directly into the ground once grown or added to compost piles. Legumes use up their stored nitrogen to make seed, so when they are used as green manures, they need to be cut just before or during their flowering. During the summer growing season, green manures should be grown in

---

[10] Ibid.

[11] Abdul-Baki, A., Teasdale, J. (1993) A no tillage tomato production system using hairy vetch and subterranean clover mulches *Horticultural Science* 28(2) pp. 106–108

[12] Jeavons, J. (2002) *How to Grow More Vegetables*

Table 4: **Cover Crops/Green Manures and Nitrogen Yields**

Name	Sow	Harvest	N Yield	Notes
Hairy vetch	Spring or fall	Fall or spring	160 lbs/acre	Sow in August–September, can become a weed if followed by grains, don't follow with lettuce
Red clover	Spring or fall	Fall or spring	105 lbs/acre	Sow in August for winter cover, good choice under fruit trees, shade tolerant
Field peas	Spring	Summer	100 lbs/acre	Won't overwinter north of Maryland, good for interplanting with brassicas
Cereal rye	Fall	Spring	None	Sow in early fall, wait four weeks after cutting in spring before sowing subsequent crops because rye suppresses germination of other plants
Alfalfa	Spring	Summer	130 lbs/acre	Prefers well-drained soils, highest N fixation
Barley	Spring	Summer	None	Doesn't work in acid soils
Oats	Spring	Summer	None	Established quickly
Winter wheat	Fall	Spring	None	High in protein

beds that will be followed by heavy-feeding plants, such as cabbage, as part of a crop rotation plan.

An important aspect of making a mini-farm economically viable is the use of green manures to provide and enhance soil fertility and reduce dependence on purchased fertilizers. To that end, cover crops should be grown over the winter to start the spring compost pile and should also be planted in any bed not in use to prevent leaching of nutrients and promote higher fertility. The careful use of green manures as cover crops and as specific compost ingredients can entirely eliminate the need for outside nitrogen inputs. For example, alfalfa makes an excellent green manure during the growing season in that it leaves 42

percent of its nitrogen in the ground when cut plus provides biologically fixed nitrogen to the compost pile. I recommend that 25 to 35 percent of a mini-farm's growing area should be sown in green manures during the growing season, and all of it should be sown in green manures and/or cover crops during the winter.

Green manures interplanted with crops during the growing season can form a living mulch. Examples include sowing hairy vetch between corn stalks at the last cultivation before harvest or planting vegetables without tilling into a bed already growing subterranean clover.[13] On

[13] Sullivan, P. (2003) *Overview of Cover Crops and Green Manures*

⊗ Hairy vetch is an excellent cover crop.

my own mini-farm, I grow white clover between tomato plants.

Cover crops aren't a cure-all, and they can cause problems if used indiscriminately. For example, using a vetch cover crop before growing lettuce can cause problems with a lettuce disease called sclerotina.[14] Because the increased organic matter from a cover crop can cause a short-term increase in populations of certain pests such as cutworms, it is important to cut or till the cover crop three or four weeks before planting your crops.[15] Legume green manures, such as peas, beans, vetch, and clovers, also need to be covered with the correct type of bacterial inoculant (available through seed suppliers) before they are sown to ensure their health and productivity.

Given these complications, how does a farmer pick a cover crop? Cover crops need to be picked based on the climate, the crop that will be planted afterward, and specific factors about the cover crop—such as its tendency to turn into an invasive weed. Legumes and grains are often, though not always, sown together as a cover crop. Some cover crops, like oats and wheat, can also serve as

---

[14] Thomas, F. et al. (2002) *Cover Cropping in Row and Field Systems*
[15] Ibid

food. If this is anticipated, it might be worthwhile to investigate easily harvested grains like hull-less oats. However, keep in mind that the choice of green manures will be at least partially dictated by climate. Many crops that grow fine over the winter in South Carolina won't work in Vermont.

Crop Rotation

Crop rotation is one of the oldest and most important agricultural practices in existence and is still one of the most effective for controlling pest populations, assisting soil fertility, and controlling diseases.

The primary key to successful crop rotation lies in understanding that crops belong to a number of different botanical families and that members of each related family have common requirements and pest problems that differ from those of members of other botanical families. Cabbage and brussels sprouts, for example, are members of the same botanical family, so they can be expected to have similar soil requirements and be susceptible to the same pest and disease problems. Peas and beans are likewise part of the same botanical family; corn belongs to yet another family unrelated to the other two. A listing of the botanical names of most cultivated plant families with edible members follows:

Amaryllidaceae—leek, common onion, multiplier onion, bunching onion, shallot, garlic, chives

Brassicaceae—horseradish, mustards, turnip, rutabaga, kale, radish, broccoli, cauliflower, cabbage, collards, cress

Chenopodiaceae—beet, mangel, Swiss chard, lamb's quarters, quinoa, spinach

Compositae—endive, escarole, chicory, globe artichoke, jerusalem artichoke, lettuce, sunflower

Cucurbitaceae—cucumber, gherkin, melons, gourds, squashes

Leguminosae—peanut, pea, bean, lentil, cowpea

Solanaceae—pepper, tomato, tomatillo, ground cherry, potato, eggplant

Umbelliferae—celery, dill, carrot, fennel, parsnip, parsley

Gramineae—wheat, rye, oats, sorghum, corn

Amaranthaceae—grain and vegetable amaranth

Convolvulaceae—water spinach, sweet potato

Some plants will do better or worse depending on what was grown before them. Such effects can be partially canceled by the use of intervening cover crops between main crops. Thankfully, a large amount of research has been done on the matter, and while nobody is sure of all the factors involved, a few general rules have emerged from the research.

- Never follow a crop with another crop from the same botanical family (e.g., don't follow potatoes with tomatoes or squash with cucumbers).
- Alternate deep-rooted crops (like carrots) with shallow-rooted crops (such as lettuce).
- Alternate plants that inhibit germination (like rye and sunflowers) with vegetables that don't compete well against weeds (like peas and strawberries).
- Alternate crops that add organic matter (e.g., wheat) with crops that add little organic matter (e.g., soybeans).
- Alternate nitrogen fixers (such as alfalfa or vetch) with nitrogen consumers (such as grains or vegetables).

The most important rule with crop rotations is to experiment and keep careful records. Some families of plants have a detrimental effect on some families that may follow them in rotation but not on others. These effects will vary depending on cover cropping, manuring, and composting practices, so no hard and fast rules apply, but it is absolutely certain that an observant farmer will see a difference between cabbage that follows carrots as opposed to cabbage that follows potatoes. Keeping careful records and making small variations from year to year while observing the results will allow the farmer to fine-tune practices to optimize quality and yields.

A three-bed rotation applicable to where I live in New Hampshire might give you an idea of how crop rotation with cover cropping works. We'll start with the fall.

Table 5: **Example Three-Bed Rotation with Cover Cropping**

	Bed 1	**Bed 2**	**Bed 3**
Fall Year 1	Rye	Hairy vetch/rye	Hairy vetch/oats
Spring Year 2	Peas	Tomatoes	Corn
Midsummer Year 2	Broccoli/cabbage	White clover is sown between plants	Pole beans are sown between stalks
Fall Year 2	Hairy vetch/rye	Hairy vetch/oats	Rye
Spring Year 3	Tomatoes	Corn	Peas
Midsummer Year 3	White clover is sown between plants	Pole beans are sown between stalks	Broccoli/cabbage

Compost

5

Anytime you pass by a forest or a long-abandoned field, you see tons of vegetation even though it is pretty obvious nobody is fertilizing the wilderness. Forests and fields don't need fertilizer, because they exist within the framework of a sustainable nutrient cycle that returns nutrients to the soil via natural composting.

A tree takes elements from the earth and turns them into leaves that turn brown and fall to earth in the autumn, forming a layer on top of last year's leaves. Progressing down the layers, within just a few inches, the leaves have turned into a sweet-smelling, living compost. This gets mixed into the existing soil through the action of earthworms and other organisms. The same mechanism is at work when a squirrel eats an acorn and drops the shell to the forest floor and then relieves himself. It all combines in the forest floor so that everything goes back whence it came and becomes available for reuse.

This same is true even in death. The squirrel eaten by a hawk has all of its parts, in some form or another, returned to the earth; likewise, a huge tree hit by lightning decomposes into the earth for reuse.

Nature is already equipped to sustain itself, as it has for billions of years. Taking energy only from the sun, nature follows the Law of Conservation of Matter to recycle all of the elements that it takes from the earth. This cycle does not work within a given area of land when elements are removed from that area more quickly than they can be replaced without taking elements from somewhere else.

This is where conventional farming cartels find themselves. They export all of their fertility from their farms in the form of crops and then replenish that fertility with artificial chemicals or with manures brought in from several states away. Such a system can endure for a long time, but it is pretty expensive and geared best to large-scale operations. Smaller-scale home-sized operations work least expensively when every effort is made to maintain as much soil fertility as possible from sources within the operation. Conscientious attention to the nutrient cycles of the mini-farm can make a huge difference in crop yield and the amount of outside amendments and fertilizers that must be brought in—which in practical terms means reduced costs.

The nutrient cycles of the mini-farm encompass the life-death-rebirth of plants and animals as well as the grow-eat-excrete-grow of the plants and animals on the farm. The mini-farmer uses composting and fertilizer crops to accelerate the natural process of these cycles to maintain a high level of fertility in the soil.

The importance of compost in a mini-farm or even a small garden can't be overstated. Broadly, compost is the rotted remains of plant and animal products and by-products that have been aerobically decomposed so that the individual constituents cannot be distinguished. This is exactly what happens in nature, and the mini-farmer simply helps the process along. Once this has occurred, the resulting product becomes agriculturally indispensable.

Compost not only serves as a reservoir of fertility because of the individual elements and nutrients that it contains but also serves to destroy plant and animal diseases and toxins while improving the texture and moisture handling of the soil to which it is added. One commercial California vegetable grower was able to reduce pesticide use by 80% in just three years through applications of compost.[16]

The Composting Process

The core process of composting is simply this: The farmer stacks up a bunch of organic matter that, given time, air, and moisture, decomposes. Organic matter includes leftovers from the table, crop debris, grass clippings, leaves raked in the fall, and animal manure. In essence, anything that was either once alive or produced by something that was alive.

A combination of elements are responsible for organic decomposition but most notably microorganisms such as bacteria and fungi that are already present in soil, on plants, and even in the intestines of animals. When an environment hospitable to their growth and multiplication is created, the microorganisms digest the organic material. Along with this, a number of larger organisms such as earthworms get into the act of digesting the organic matter, thus creating an

[17] Hoitink, H. A. J., Fahy, P. C. (1986). Basis for the control of plant pathogens with compost *Annual Review of Phytopathology* 24 pp. 93–114

entirely different substance than what existed in the first place.

Microorganisms, like people, have different dietary and climate preferences. Some prefer to eat leaves, some prefer to eat straw, and others prefer to eat apples. As a result, the best level of decomposition and fertility occurs from adding a variety of organic substances to the pile.

Microorganisms are likewise competitive. Every species (and even variant of a given species) wants to make room for itself and its offspring. Because of this, many microorganisms have developed a variety of weapons that can be used against other microbes in the compost pile. The most widely understood is the production of antibiotics by a variety of organisms intended to inhibit the growth of other organisms. Heat-loving bacteria in a compost pile endeavor to heat up the pile to a high-enough temperature that other bacteria can't tolerate the heat and die off. But once they've finished their job, mesophilic bacteria move back into the pile and take over again, along with fungi and finally earthworms.

Composting to Destroy Pathogens

The microorganisms that create compost can be broadly classified as being either thermophilic—meaning "heat loving"—or mesophilic—meaning "intermediate loving"—both terms referring to the temperatures preferred and created by such microorganisms. A compost pile is called either thermophilic or mesophilic depending on the temperatures it achieves.

The most important aspect of the relative heat of a compost pile is pathogen death. Thermophilic composting will kill all known human pathogens—including parasitic worm eggs, bacteria, viruses, and protozoa—along with plant disease organisms and weed seeds. Using thermophilic composting, it is both possible and practical to recycle not just ordinary plant material such as leaves and grass clippings but also leftover fried chicken. In other words, thermophilic composting makes a much broader array of compost ingredients both practical and safe.

There are two factors affecting the death of plant or animal pathogens and weed seeds in compost. The temperature achieved by the compost, as mentioned, is a big factor. Another important factor is the time that the compost is held before being used. Microbial pathogens require particular hosts to complete their life cycles, and their spores can remain inert—and thus viable—only in a warm, moist compost pile for so long. Even if a compost pile isn't thermophilic, adequate holding time will still render the compost both safe and beneficial. Weed seeds can be killed by the high heat of a thermophilic compost pile, but they can also be killed by virtue of the fact that the warmth of even a mesophilic pile can induce premature germination, thus interrupting the life cycle of the weeds.

The holding time for mesophilic compost is two years if it contains, or is likely to contain, pathogens from infected crops, dead animals, or other ingredients. Thermophilic compost that contains any or all of these things need only be held for a year. Compost made from solely nondisease-infected vegetation can be used after six months, no matter the temperature of the pile.

Many books and articles on home composting contain long lists of things not to compost, and that list contains diseased crops, meat scraps, peanut butter, cooking oils, carnivore or omnivore feces, and so forth. Such a list of banned items makes perfect sense when dealing with mesophilic compost (or meeting organic certification standards), especially if it won't be held for a couple of years to ensure pathogen death—and most home composting is mesophilic. But by using thermophilic composting, the list of banned items can go into the compost pile,[17] and you can recycle all of your uneaten leftovers.

It is possible to compost human manure safely; however, the procedure isn't covered in this book. The proper procedures for recycling human manure are thoroughly covered with extensive documentation by Joseph Jenkins in *The Humanure Handbook*. (Mr. Jenkins has kindly made an electronic version of the book available on the Internet at no cost. Just look for it in a search engine.)

Thermophilic Composting

Four things are required to achieve thermophilic composting: adequate bulk, adequate aeration, adequate moisture, and a proper ratio of carbon to nitrogen, known as C/N ratio.

Composting methods are usually described as either batch methods or continuous methods. Batch methods add all of the ingredients at once, while continuous methods add to the pile progressively. Most mini-farmers and home gardeners are continuous composters by default. As a result the initial stages of a compost pile may not have enough bulk to retain the heat of thermophilic composting. This problem can be solved

[17] Jenkins, J. (2005) *The Humanure Handbook*

through timing: Start new compost piles in the spring, so that by the time cool weather arrives, the pile already has plenty of bulk to retain heat through the winter.

In the spring, you not only add the leaves that fell on the yard during the fall but also harvest green manures that were planted in the fall for a spring harvest and add those to the pile as well. You can also add livestock manure (if available) and any grass clippings or remaining crop debris. This gets the pile off to a good start with plenty of bulk. If leaves aren't available, straw or hay will work just as well. The various ingredients are added to the pile in alternating layers no more than two inches thick so that grass clippings or leaves don't get matted down to form a layer impermeable to air. If you wind up with a layer a little too thick, don't worry because the next time you turn the compost pile, the layers will all get mixed up.

Aeration is important because thermophilic composting is aerobic, requiring oxygen. There are two sorts of microorganisms involved in decomposing organic materials—aerobic microorganisms that work in the presence of oxygen, and anaerobic microorganisms that work in the absence of oxygen. Aerobic composting reduces or eliminates odors and allows for thermophilic microbes, whereas anaerobic composting smells like a septic tank and seldom develops much heat. Therefore, aeration is important to make good compost and maintain peace in the neighborhood. Aeration is achieved by regularly turning over and mixing compost piles. Practically every book or article written about composting advocates frequent turning of the pile to ensure adequate aeration. The idea of turning compost is so entrenched that a number of companies even

⊗ Drilled PVC pipe used for compost aeration.

make fairly expensive gadgets for helping people turn and tumble their compost.

Too much turning of compost is unnecessary and can actually be counterproductive by causing a loss of both valuable nitrogen and organic matter.[18] Turning a compost pile will also serve to dissipate any heat. The solution to the problem is to build the compost pile in such a way that it is self-aerating.[19] This is accomplished by layering in straw as you go along—just keep a couple of

bales handy next to the compost pile. By adding a layer of straw and making sure that no layer in the pile of any given ingredient is more than a couple of inches thick without being broken up by either straw or another ingredient, a self-aerating pile is ensured. Or, you can try my method, in which large-diameter PVC pipes with holes drilled in them are buried vertically in the pile.

Not all piles can be constructed in a fashion that guarantees self-aeration, of course; in such cases turning the pile up to five times per year is absolutely necessary. In fact, if a pile is not self-aerating, it should be turned regularly. After prolonged heavy rains that can soak into the pile

[18] Brinton, W. F. Jr. (1997) Sustainability of modern composting–Intensification versus cost and quality *Biodynamics*, Summer 1997
[19] Jenkins, J. (2005) *The Humanure Handbook*, p. 50

⊗ Watering the pile as it is turned is important.

and force out the oxygen, turning is a good idea. In addition, the composting process uses a great deal of water, so when compost is turned, water should be added as needed.

Adequate moisture is another important factor in composting. Too much moisture in compost forces out the air, leading to anaerobic decomposition, which is not thermophilic and almost always smells bad. Too little moisture in compost causes the microorganisms to go dormant or work less effectively. Thankfully, the ideal range for compost is actually pretty tolerant and can be anywhere in the range of 40% to 60%,[20]

---

[20] Campbell, S. (1990) *Let It Rot* p. 95

and all that is required is for any dry layers added to the pile (such as leaves or sawdust) be dampened with a hose if rain isn't in the forecast. Any additional moisture needed will be supplied by rain in most of North America. Extremely rainy climates might require that the pile be covered with a tarp on occasion, and drought conditions will require that the pile be checked and water added if its moisture content isn't about that of a wrung-out sponge. Remember, again, that when turning compost, check to see if water is needed, and add it if necessary.

Just like humans require nutrients in given amounts to be most productive, microorganisms responsible for making compost have dietary needs. The most relevant dietary requirement of microbes in the manufacture of thermophilic compost is the ratio of carbon to nitrogen in the pile. Microbes need nitrogen to build proteins, and they need carbon for practically everything. A ratio of carbon to nitrogen of 30:1 will result in thermophilic compost.[21] This ratio need not be followed slavishly. Microbes are picky but not *that* picky. Anywhere from 35:1 to 25:1 will work fine.

The proper carbon/nitrogen ratio can be achieved by mixing ingredients with higher and lower C/N ratios in approximate proportions. For example, cow manure with a C/N ratio of 20:1 can be mixed with oak leaves with a C/N ratio of 50:1 to get the desired ratio of 30:1. Even more easily, green vegetable wastes mixed half and half with dry vegetable wastes will achieve the same result. A table listing the C/N ratios of common materials is below to use as a guide.

Table 6: Carbon to Nitrogen Ratios of Commonly Composted Materials

Material	Ratio
Vegetable wastes	12–20:1
Alfalfa hay	13:1
Cow manure	20:1
Leaves	40–80:1
Corn stalks	60:1
Oat straw	74:1
Wheat straw	80:1
Sawdust	100–500:1
Grass clippings	12–25:1
Coffee grounds	20:1
Poultry manure	10:1
Horse manure	25:1

If a compost pile is constructed, and it just won't seem to heat up, check the moisture and add water or drain as needed, then poke holes deep in it with a pole for aeration. If neither of these works, nitrogen needs to be added. Ideally, this would be done by mixing in green vegetation, but blood meal mixed with water and dumped into the aeration holes will work too. Blood meal is common and can be bought at garden stores and possibly the local Walmart. If my piles aren't heating up the way they should because of inadequate nitrogen, what I do is add a standard organic fertilizer containing nitrogen and a bit of compost activator every so often as I turn them.

A soil and/or compost thermometer can be purchased inexpensively so you can judge the performance of your pile. (I use a long laboratory thermometer because I have several already.) You want the pile to reach from 130 to 160 degrees for no less than 15 days total. In practice, your compost is unlikely to stay at such a temperature for 15 days in a row. By using a thermometer, you can see when the temperature is starting to drop. Mix the pile thoroughly every time you see the temperature drop, and within a couple of days, the pile will heat back up again if the moisture level is right. This way, you can be pretty certain of at least 15 days of thermophilic temperatures in your compost.

At thermophilic compost temperatures of 140 degrees, roundworm and other eggs are killed in two hours or less, and most other protozoans, bacteria, and viruses are killed within minutes. The most tenacious dangerous germ is salmonella, and it is killed in about 20 hours.[22] By

---

[21] Jeavons, J. (2002) *How to Grow More Vegetables* p. 39

[22] Feachem et al. (1980) *Appropriate Technology for Water Supply and Sanitation: Health Aspects of Excreta and Sullage Management*

providing 15 days at temperatures exceeding 130 degrees, you are creating compost that is absolutely safe to apply to crops that touch the soil, practically without regard to its ingredients.

Compost Aging

As noted earlier, both temperatures and retention time have an impact on pathogen destruction, along with the biochemistry of the compost pile. For a pile made from nondiseased plants and manures, an extensive retention time is not required to ensure that the compost is hygienic, but a minimum retention time is definitely required to make sure that the compost is *mature*. Immature compost can contain phytotoxins that retard germination and can use up the nutrients from any beds it is added to. The standards of the Canadian Council of Ministers of the Environment specify that six months is adequate retention time for compost,[23] and that works whether the composting has been mesophilic or thermophilic as long as diseased materials weren't used. If disease organisms were likely present (because debris from infected crops or meat products were added), then compost should be retained a year if thermophilically composted, and two years otherwise.

Proper aging of compost can be tested without a fancy laboratory using radish seeds, because radishes are extremely sensitive to the phytotoxins in immature compost.

Purchase some commercial seed-starter mix, dampen it, and put it in a seed-starting container. Put the compost to be tested in another container

---

[23] Composting Council of Canada (1999) *The Composting Process: Compost Maturity*

in the same environment as the first, then plant 20 radish seeds in each flat. Water both regularly, and keep at 70 degrees F.

Observe the germination. If the germination rate of the seeds in the compost is less than 80% of that in the commercial seed-starter mix, the compost needs to age some more.

Compost Activators

Almost every gardening magazine carries advertisements in the back for so-called compost activators. These products typically contain a mix of bacteria and fungi that help the composting process. While these products certainly won't hurt your compost, they aren't usually necessary either, because compost activators are all around you and free.

The two most useful compost activators are the prior year's compost and good garden soil. These contain a wealth of suitable bacterial and fungal spores that will seed your pile. Only a shovel or two of these mixed into the pile periodically is sufficient.

I have tried a couple of commercial compost activator products and found no difference between piles in which they had been used and piles in which they had not—except for cases where a pile has refused to heat up adequately because of lack of moisture. In these cases, adding the activator layered in with the additional water increases the rate at which the pile heats up.

The Grow Biointensive method of making compost—a mesophilic method—specifies that fully 1/3 of the final weight of your compost should be from garden soil. The reasoning for this is that it keeps the compost pile "cool" so that it will compost slowly. This has the benefit of preserving more organic matter and more nitrogen because a thermophilic phase is never reached.

I cannot deny this benefit, but I don't advocate this technique because the benefits of thermophilic composting—removing disease organisms and allowing a wider range of compost ingredients—outweigh the slightly greater loss of organic matter. So use a shovelful of garden soil or last year's compost as an activator, but don't get carried away or you'll end up with compost that won't reach high enough temperatures to kill disease organisms.

The Big Picture

Plant cover crops in the fall that are harvested in the spring and used to start a thermophilic compost pile when combined with leaves, straw, and other high-carbon materials. Add household organic wastes like food leftovers liberally to the pile, along with any animal manures available. Use straw or sawdust as a cover material when adding anything that would attract dogs or rodents or just bury it deeply in the pile. Add crop debris in the fall and then a good cover of hay or straw on top for the winter. In the spring, start a second pile, and let the first one sit for a year to cure, since uncured compost can hurt the soil's fertility; allowing a year to cure also ensures hygienic compost. The following spring, the first pile is available for use.

If potentially pathogenic material has been composted or the compost never reached a thermophilic phase, it is best to hold the compost for a couple of years to be absolutely sure it is safe.

I have a three-bin system made out of chicken wire with a large bin in the center and bins half

⊗ The author's three-bin composting system.

the size of the center one on either side. The larger center bin is used for current compost. By midsummer, the center pile has shrunk, and I shovel it into one of the two side bins. The next batch of compost from the center bin goes into the other side. By then, the compost in the first side is fully cured.

6

Plant Nutrients In-depth

In the past couple of chapters we have discussed the major macronutrients, soil structure, cover cropping, crop rotation, and other soil-building practices in a fair amount of detail. But this level of information is not sufficient in and of itself. It's a lot like saying that a human needs carbohydrates, fats, proteins, air, and exercise—but forgetting to mention vitamins.

Plants make their own vitamins, which is one reason why they are so nutritious. But to make them, or sometimes even survive at all, they need a wide array of both macronutrients and micronutrients. Most of the micronutrients take care of themselves between using various compost ingredients, specifically adding kelp or seaweed to compost once in awhile if available, and using commercial liquid kelp fertilizers such as Neptune's Harvest or Root Boost in the beds. In spite of this, deficiencies sometimes develop. In my garden, because I grow a lot of cabbage-family plants, boron can especially be an issue because with inadequate boron, broccoli grows with hollow stems. So I specifically add a teaspoon of borax (mixed with a cup of blood meal for easy dispersal) to every garden bed at the beginning of each gardening season.

⊗ These hollow stalks are the result of boron deficiency.

Macronutrients

Calcium: Calcium stimulates rhizobia bacteria, is critical for healthy cell walls, assists with movement of carbohydrates within plants, aids in the absorption of trace elements, and aids the activity of enzymes. Adequate calcium (or its even uptake) is necessary to prevent potato scab, blossom end rot, black lesions on carrots, and other diseases. Adding lime (which contains calcium) to the hole when transplanting brassicas can help prevent a fungal disease called "club foot." Bioavailable calcium is necessary for proper utilization of nitrogen.

Plants use large amounts of calcium, so it is important to ensure sufficient levels in the soil. Most often, this is done through adding lime of various sorts. Calcium can be added in the form of regular garden lime; dolomitic limestone, which also contains magnesium; and pulverized oyster shells. All of these take time to work and become bioavailable, so I generally recommend adding them to beds in the fall so they have time to work before the garden season starts in spring. In general, you should add eight pounds of lime yearly to every 100 square feet of garden beds. I generally recommend using dolomitic lime as magnesium and calcium work in concert in a way that benefits the plants.

Nitrogen: Nitrogen is an essential element for life as, combined with carbon and hydrogen, it is a building block for amino acids, which combine to make proteins and even the basic data of life: RNA and DNA. Nitrogen is critical for every metabolic process in a plant and for the formation of important compounds such as chlorophyll. Predictably, plants need a lot of it. We covered nitrogen sources and quantities in a previous chapter.

Phosphorus: Phosphorus is an ingredient in the protoplasm within cells and is important for all cell division and growth. It is the single most important element for the germination and growth of plants, followed shortly by nitrogen. Almost all soils are deficient and need supplementation as described in a previous chapter. The most obvious place where phosphorus deficiency will become evident is in seedlings, because starting media is usually nutrient deficient. In these cases, the leaves will develop a purplish color on the underside. For seedlings, a complete liquid fertilizer containing phosphorus such as Neptune's Harvest (if growing organically) or Miracle Gro otherwise will head this off at the pass. Apply fertilizer to seedlings after the first set of leaves appear and every two weeks thereafter if using a nutrient-free growing medium. For crops in the ground, use the information from chapter 4.

Potassium: Plants require a large and continuous supply of potassium to help in the metabolism and movement of carbohydrates, protein synthesis, growth, and cell division.

Adequate potassium supplies ensure better shape, color, and flavor of vegetables and fruits. The chief sign of deficiency can be seen in leaf edges that appear "scorched." Root crops, especially, require adequate potassium and perhaps even increased levels for best production. Chapter 4 contains information on the proper levels of potassium to maintain in your beds.

Micronutrients

Boron: Though classified as a micronutrient because of the small amount required, it is absolutely crucial to practically all life processes of plants including hormone activity, ion exchange, nutrient movement, and water metabolism. Every plant shows boron deficiency a bit differently, depending on the severity. In beans, the beans are deformed. In broccoli, the stems are hollow. Because deficiency symptoms can be easily confused with deficiencies in other elements, the best bet, short of a professional soil test, is to ensure adequate supply routinely. Because excess boron can be toxic to plants, and plants will absorb it in excess if too much is available, you have to be careful to only add what is needed. You can add three teaspoons of borax per 100 square feet of bed space once a year, and this will generally work out fine. You should mix it thoroughly with something like powdered lime or bone meal before broadcasting to ensure even distribution, and then work it into the top couple of inches of soil.

Copper: Copper plays an important role in root metabolism, photosynthesis, and enzyme activation, as well as protecting plants from adverse effects of excessive nitrogen. Copper, like boron, is required in only small amounts and is toxic in excess. It is available in the form of copper sulfate crystals and should be added to the beds yearly at the rate of 1-1/2 ounces (four tablespoons) per 100 square feet of bed. Because it is hard to distribute such a small quantity evenly over such a large space, it should be thoroughly mixed with something being added to beds in a larger quantity, such as lime, bone meal, or other fertilizer.

Iron: Though required in only small amounts, iron is essential for the chlorophyll cycle in plants. Without it, plants start to appear "bleached out" (called chlorosis) and suffer from stunted growth. Toxicity isn't a big issue with iron, as plants tend to self-regulate how much they take from the soil. Nevertheless, because it is required in only small amounts, excess shouldn't be supplied. Iron can be added incidentally through the use of blood meal as a nitrogen source. Because I use blood meal in my garden, iron deficiency has never been an issue. However, some may prefer not to use blood meal, in which case preventively adding six ounces of iron (or ferric) sulfate per 100 square feet of garden bed every year should do the trick. Another more organic alternative is to deliberately include nettle plants, which are very high in iron, in the compost pile.

Magnesium: Magnesium is an important element throughout the garden. It speeds up composting, makes nitrogen more readily available, stimulates rhizobia bacteria, assists in root development, and is necessary for carbohydrate motility within plants. It interacts in balance with calcium in a variety of ways and reduces the effects that could arise (however unlikely) from excess quantities of aluminum, manganese, or iron in the soil. Magnesium coexists with calcium in dolomitic lime, and you will have no problems from magnesium deficiency as long as you use dolomitic limestone as a source of calcium in your beds. Barring this, magnesium sulfate—also known as Epsom salt—is available at grocery stores or pharmacies and can be used at the rate of 24 ounces yearly per 100 square feet of garden bed.

Manganese: Though manganese is required only sparingly, its presence in adequate quantities can have an enormous positive effect on crop yields, especially for root crops. Deficiency is seen as a uniform yellowing in new leaves. This makes sense, because manganese is essential for the production of chlorophyll. Most soils have adequate naturally available manganese, but if the pH of the soil is higher than 6.5, supplementation may be needed. As well, overfarmed soils may be deficient. If you suspect deficiency, you can add 12 ounces of manganese sulfate per 100 square feet to your beds once every three years.

Molybdenum: Molybdenum is an essential catalyst for the formation of enzymes and synthesis of amino acids and proteins. Although it is essential, in excess it is extremely toxic to plants. If you accidentally add too much molybdenum to your beds, treat them with copper sulfate, which will reduce the bioavailability of the molybdenum so it will be less toxic. Most soils today, especially those in agricultural usage, are deficient in molybdenum. If you supplement with manganese when molybdenum is already deficient, that makes matters worse—so I recommend always using molybdenum and manganese together. Supplementation can be in the form of molybdic acid, ammonium molybdate, or sodium molybdate at the rate of 1-1/2 ounces per 100 square feet of garden bed mixed with something else to facilitate even application.

Molybdenum disulfide, used as a lubricant, isn't suitable because it is so stable that it has no effective biological availability.

Sulfur: Sulfur is an important ingredient of essential amino acids required for building plant proteins. In essence, without sulfur, plants cease to exist. On the other hand, sulfur exists in many different forms, and some are more useful to plants than others while yet others are absolutely toxic. In general, the sulfate forms of sulfur are healthful to plants whereas the sulfide forms of sulfur are deleterious. Because sulfur compounds tend to acidify the soil a bit, you should keep an eye on the soil pH and add lime if needed to offset the effects of the sulfur in terms of pH. Sulfur is usually applied in the form of plain elemental sulfur, known as "flowers of sulfur." Evenly distribute over the beds at the rate of 24 ounces per 100 square feet once yearly.

Zinc: Zinc is crucial for seed production, metabolism, and regulation of the water and carbon dioxide equilibrium in plants. Zinc deficiency is not particularly common, but when it shows up, it can be identified in the form of chlorotic bands within the leaves of a plant. Zinc is much more available in acidic (pH less than 7) than in alkaline (pH greater than 7) soils. Thus, the 12 ounces of zinc sulfate per 100 square feet of bed that are needed to correct or prevent deficiency would need to be multiplied by five for a total of 60 ounces if the soil in the beds is alkaline.

Making a Micronutrient Mix

Once your mini-farm has been up and running for three years or so, this will probably be unnecessary for established beds because the soil fertility practices will conserve a lot of plant nutrients. But, when just getting started, it may be needed. For enough for 300 square feet, combine the following ingredients in a bucket, and dry mix thoroughly:

> Borax: 1-1/2 ounces
> Copper sulfate: 4-1/2 ounces
> Ferric sulfate: 18 ounces
> Magnesium sulfate: 72 ounces
> Manganese sulfate: 12 ounces
> Sodium molybdate: 4-1/2 ounces
> Sulfur: 36 ounces
> Zinc sulfate: 36 ounces

Nutrient Conservation

Other than boron, I've never had to supplement with a micronutrient on my farm. The primary reason is because the biochar in the soil holds nutrients so they don't leach, the use of cover crops keeps the nutrients from becoming mobile, and conscientious composting of all plant matter from the garden preserves the nutrients that have entered the plants from the soil so they can be returned to the soil.

The other reason is variety of inputs. When I use organic fertilizers, I use a variety. One time, I might use alfalfa meal for nitrogen, but another time I might use blood meal. For potassium I might use greensand at the beginning of a season but wood ashes at the end. And all throughout, the compost bin collects a wide array of materials ranging from crop debris and lawn clippings to stale eggs and the entrails of slaughtered animals. As a result, because the animals largely receive feed from off the farm, the compost contains more nutrients than were taken out of the soil in the first place, making it an incredible fertilizer.

This is important. Everything that you can't make yourself or conserve on your mini-farm becomes something that will eventually cost you money. Keeping costs down is the secret that makes mini-farming an economic activity that is more beneficial than simple gardening.

Time and Yield

7

Most of the United States, even the northern plains, has a growing season long enough to allow for multiple plantings of many crops. Moreover, well-orchestrated timing allows harvests to be timed either to allow a little at a time to be harvested for daily use or marketing—which is useful for crops like lettuce—or to allow multiple large harvests for the purpose of preservation and storage. Many crops are frost hardy, and second plantings will allow harvests to continue for as long as a month after the first fall frost, without using anything to extend the season. For example, two crops of broccoli or spinach can be raised in the same area as one crop, doubling production per unit area.

Succession Planting

This is a technique for maximizing productivity of garden space by having a new crop ready to plant as soon as an earlier crop is harvested. An example is planting a second crop of broccoli in the same space where a first crop of broccoli was harvested at midsummer. Another example is sowing spinach early and then planting beans where the spinach used to be as soon as the spinach is harvested.

Crops that work well for the early planting in a succession are anything from the cabbage family, spinach, peas, radishes, turnips, beets, and onions from sets. ("Sets" are the miniature onions for planting that you can buy in a mesh bag at the garden center. They aren't the same as supermarket onions.) The foregoing crops are usually harvested no later than the middle of July. Crops that can be planted in mid-July for a late summer or fall harvest include bush beans, lettuce, spinach, carrots, turnips, beets, parsnips, and anything in the cabbage family.

Timed Planting

Timed planting means spreading out harvests by staggering the planting dates for a particular crop across a few weeks rather than planting it all at once. The result is a steady supply of a particular crop for market or a continual harvest that can be frozen, eaten, or canned in small sessions.

The easiest way to do this is to take the total number of plants intended for a given crop and divide it by three. Sow the first third on the first sowing date for that crop, the second third a week later, and the final third two weeks later. This will give the same total harvest as planting the whole crop at once but will spread out the harvest over a two-week period.

The next aspect of timed planting is replanting. Take carrots, for example; if carrots were planted in four sessions, each two weeks apart, when the first planting is harvested, that area can be replanted with more carrots so the space never sits idle. By the time the final crop

of carrots is ready for harvest, you are only two weeks away from yet another first harvest.

Succession planting and timed planting both provide a little insurance so if serious weather hits early or late, there's still a harvest. All that you need to know to successfully use succession and/or timed planting is the days to maturity for the crop under consideration and its frost hardiness.

Interplanting

Interplanting is used in two ways. It is used to give green manures a head start on the winter and to maximize the amount of food that can be harvested from a given area. Carefully chosen, interplanted crops can save on fertilizer as well, as when a nitrogen producer such as beans or clover is interplanted with a nitrogen consumer such as tomatoes or corn.

There are some practical considerations to interplanting, and chief among them are overcrowding and shade. Plants that require a lot of space or sunlight, such as tomatoes, could have difficulty if planted in an established stand of

⊙ Interplanting crops creates synergies.

corn. If planted before the corn has germinated, the tomatoes would shade the seedlings. On the other hand, white clover works well with most plants, as do beans.

Perhaps the most famous example of successful interplanting is the so-called Three Sisters of the Native Americans—corn, beans, and squash, which they grew together. In this case, the pole beans and squash vines used the corn stalks for support.

Fall Gardening

Frost hardy crops and biennials kept alive over the winter for seed production (called "overwintering") can be planted first in the spring, harvested in the summer, and then replanted for a second fall or early winter harvest. Late harvests can be achieved for many crops without going to the trouble of using season extension structures. Overwintering crops, so they can be used either as needed or for seed production, is more problematic. In the South or Pacific Northwest, it can be done outdoors. In the upper Midwest or Northeast, such plants have to be brought indoors for the winter or else protected with, at minimum, an unheated greenhouse or cold frame.

For purposes of fall gardening, crops can be divided into three categories: tender, semihardy, and hardy. Tender crops are damaged by a light frost. Semihardy crops will tolerate a light frost, and hardy crops will tolerate hard frosts.

The best bets for fall gardening are semihardy and hardy crops. Some hardy crops, like broccoli and spinach, often taste better when grown in the fall rather than in the spring. Semihardy crops should be timed for harvests within 28 days after the first frost, and hardy crops should be timed

within 56 days after the first frost. For this, the time to harvest needs to be known. Each variety of a given crop has slightly different dates of maturity, and those dates are indicated in seed catalogs and on seed packets. Because growth is slower in the fall, 10 days should be added to the maturity date, so plant 10 days earlier for fall harvests.

Table 7: **Crop Hardiness**

Tender	*Semihardy*	*Hardy*
Beans	Beets	Broccoli
Corn	Carrot	Brussels sprouts
Cucumber	Cauliflower	Cabbage
Eggplant	Celery	Kale
Melon	Chard	Onion
Okra	Lettuce	Parsley
Pepper	Parsnip	Peas
Squash	Potato	Spinach
Sweet potato		Turnip
Tomato		

Using Seedlings for a Head Start

Some crops, such as cucumbers, can be directly seeded in the garden or transplanted. Transplanting seedlings gives the plants a head start and can allow maximum production from the number of growing days in the season.

Winter squash, requiring 80 or more days to harvest, is a good candidate for transplanting seedlings, particularly in the northern half of the United States where there are often fewer than 90 frost-free days in a row in the growing season. Since squash shouldn't be direct seeded until 14 days after the last frost, leaving fewer than 80 remaining growing days, growing transplants instead will increase the amount of squash harvested without requiring the farmer to use season extension devices.

The same applies for crops in the fall garden. In the late season, broccoli can be direct seeded, but giving it a four-week head start by growing seedlings inside and then transplanting them will accelerate the harvest.

One place where I have used this technique to good effect is with a crop that most authors will tell you not to transplant: corn. Grown on the agribusiness scale, seed for sweet corn is usually coated with a fungicide to keep it from rotting in the ground. Seed corn is prone not just to rot but to being eaten by wireworms. In addition, it doesn't all germinate at the same time. On a very large scale, this all evens out. But on a small

scale—say growing 48 plants in a 4-foot × 8-foot raised bed—it can be a problem. Transplanting seedlings is an ideal solution.

What I do is start 64 seedlings indoors about two weeks before the first frost-free date. It's important to not try any longer than two weeks because corn grows a taproot, and after that, transplant shock can be too great. After two weeks, some may not have germinated, and some will be taller than others. What I do is pick the 48 most uniform plants and transplant them into the bed. I keep the others handy for a week just in case cut worms or some similar pest strikes.

You can use this technique for most crops outside of root crops. By starting from seed indoors, you gain an advantage of anywhere from two to six weeks.

Example Timeline

The following table is part of the calendar for my own mini-farm in New Hampshire, so the exact dates may not work for you. Nevertheless, the examples given should be helpful.

Table 8: **Example Activity Schedule**

Date	Activity	Date	Activity
02/11/06	Start onion and leek seeds inside	05/06/06	Start cucumber, melon, and squash inside
02/18/06	Start broccoli, cabbage, and kale inside	05/07/06	Sow radish and salsify seeds outside
02/25/06	Start cauliflower inside	05/13/06	Sow 1/2 of carrots, beets, parsnips, and turnips; cut cover crops and add to compost pile
03/01/06	Start lettuce inside	05/27/06	Plant tomato and pepper transplants outside
04/01/06	Start tomatoes and peppers inside	05/28/06	Sow corn seed and second 1/2 of carrots, beets, parsnips, and turnips

Date	Activity	Date	Activity
04/15/06	Start marigold, nasturtium, pyrethrum, and dill seeds inside	06/03/06	Harvest radishes and plant cucumber, melon, and squash transplants where the radishes were
04/22/06	Transplant broccoli, cabbage, and kale outside	06/23/06	Harvest broccoli and kale and replant with new transplants for a second crop
04/23/06	Plant potatoes and peas outside, covered with hoop house	07/07/06	Harvest cauliflower and replant with new transplants for a second crop
04/29/06	Start new broccoli seedlings inside for second planting	07/20/06	Harvest potatoes and carrots, prepare potato area, and sow with carrots and spinach
05/06/06	Plant cauliflower transplants outside	07/24/06	Pull up pea plants and add to compost pile, sow area with lettuce

Watering and Irrigation

Making sure that crops have the proper amount of water without overwatering them is important. Properly watered crops are more resistant to pests, absorb nutrients more consistently, and are generally stronger and more productive.

While it is possible to water crops a little bit daily, such an approach presents problems. For one thing, if enough water isn't used to soak down deep into the soil, the roots of the plants will stay close to the surface, making it impossible for the farmer to skip watering for a couple of days.

A better approach is to water extremely thoroughly but less frequently. A "thorough" watering is the equivalent of one inch of rain, which equates to about five pints of water per square foot of garden bed. Under normal conditions, this much water will soak deeply into the soil so that plant roots will become better established, and watering will be required only once a week, or twice a week during extremely hot weather. (Later in this chapter I describe how to determine how much watering is required if it has rained.)

Garden soil, when dry, initially repels water. If water is simply dumped on top, the water will flow to the lowest spot it can find and pool there until it is absorbed. Get the soil a little damp first, and it will soak up water like a sponge.

There are as many approaches to watering gardens as there are gardeners. The Square Foot method waters each square foot of a raised bed individually using a ladle. The reasoning for this is not just water conservation but the fact that keeping foliage from being damp helps to prevent disease problems. This is true, but the problem lies in the fact that such a method of watering becomes burdensomely time-consuming when done on the scale of even a few hundred square feet.

The Grow Biointensive method imitates natural rainfall by using special watering attachments that make small droplets and let the water fall with only the force of gravity. By watering thoroughly each time, the frequency of watering is kept to about once a week. This is a lot less time-consuming than watering each square foot individually, and because it waters thoroughly rather than frequently, it is better than daily watering regimens in terms of disease, though not as good as the Square Foot method in that regard. Agriculture, like anything else, requires compromises! All things being equal, using a watering wand is the best technique for a mini-farmer in the first couple of years.

Use of a Watering Wand

A watering wand can be used to duplicate natural rainfall. This is worthwhile, as typical watering attachments can allow the water to

» A watering wand allows delivery of water at the proper rate.

be too forceful, causing erosion and disrupting seeds and seedlings.

Most watering wands, but not all, have a movable head that allows the use of different settings for water flow. If you get one like this, make sure to select the "shower" setting. Unfortunately, when watering by hand, it is difficult to know how much water is being delivered. Luckily, it is easy to figure out.

Take a garden hose with the shower watering attachment installed, place it in a five-gallon bucket, and turn it on. (The shower watering attachment is also known as a "watering wand." Use *nothing but* a watering wand if watering by hand or you'll damage your plants.) Use the sweep second hand on a watch to see how long it takes to fill up the bucket. If it takes two minutes to fill up the bucket, then you know that the flow rate of the hose and attachment is 2.5 gallons per minute. A 100-square-foot garden bed requires 62 gallons

of water once a week. By dividing 62 by 2.5, you will discover that by watering the bed evenly for 25 minutes, you will add sufficient water. If your farm is anything like mine, most of the beds are roughly 4-foot × 8-foot, or 32 square feet. That's roughly 1/3 of 100 square feet, so if you divide the 62 gallons of water for a 100-square-foot bed by three, you get 20 to 21 gallons of water for a 32-square-foot bed. If your attachment waters at 4 gallons per minute, then that means watering the bed for five minutes.

This is obviously time-consuming. A three-person self-sufficient mini-farm will have more than a few beds, so hand watering would require a lot of time and be pretty boring. One way of avoiding monotony is to divide up the beds so that 1/5 of the beds are watered on each day of the week. Once you have expanded to a big enough mini-farm that watering chores are eating a lot of your time, you should arrange some sort of irrigation system (if possible) to optimize time usage.

Drip Irrigation

Probably the best approach in terms of time, efficiency, and disease prevention is drip irrigation in which tubes carry water to discrete areas of the garden at a predetermined rate of flow. It can be pretty expensive to install initially, but in the long run it pays for itself by freeing your time. One of the best aspects of drip irrigation systems is that they are modular and use standardized fittings, meaning that a farmer can start small and expand the system gradually as time and finances allow. Drip irrigation gives the benefits of watering each plant individually and keeping the foliage dry and thus discouraging diseases while saving considerable time.

⊗ Use the "shower" setting to avoid damaging plants.

Drip irrigation systems are rated in gallons per hour, either per foot or per emitter. (An emitter is a small device that delivers water from the system to the plants.) In the case of intensive agriculture, emitters should be spaced every 6 or 12 inches because the plants grow so closely together. Drip tape is ideal for intensive applications and should be run according to manufacturer's directions in such a way that there is at least one emitter per square foot of raised bed. An automatic timer can be installed so that if the flow rate of the emitters is known, the time can be set to allow precisely the right amount of water. Keep a rain gauge in the garden, and you will know that the garden needs to be watered only when the amount of rain in a week is less than one inch. When the amount of rain that fell is *less than one inch*, the amount of water (in gallons) needed per square foot can be calculated using the following formula: $0.62 \times (1 - z)$ where z is the number of inches of rain that fell that week.

Soaker Hoses

Not every mini-farmer will choose to install a drip irrigation or gray water recycling system. A good alternative is the use of soaker hoses. Soaker hoses can be laid lengthwise on top of the garden bed and snaked back and forth so that successive runs are no more than one foot apart.

⊗ Two popular styles of soaker hose.

Alternatively, they can be buried in the garden beds no more than four inches deep. I tried burying a soaker hose about eight inches deep in a bed, and since most of a plant's roots are in the top six inches of soil, it didn't work out so well. Soaker hoses need to be on top of the soil or buried no more than four inches deep.

The watering rates of soaker hoses will vary by manufacturer. One brand, made by Fiskars, waters at the rate of one gallon per hour per 10 linear feet of hose if connected to a 10-psi pressure regulator. Up to six lengths of soaker hose of up to 100 feet length each can be run from the same spigot/pressure regulator. Adding an automatic timer to the system makes watering effortless.

Calculating how long to leave the soaker turned on is straightforward. One inch of rain on a 100-square-foot garden bed is 62 gallons of water, and that is what is needed weekly for optimal plant health. If laid out properly, a 4-foot × 25-foot garden bed will use 100 feet of soaker hose. Since the hose waters at the rate of one gallon per hour per 10 linear feet, then 100 linear feet will put out 10 gallons of water an hour. So in six hours or so, 62 gallons will be delivered. When the automatic timer is set to water for six hours once a week, you are then free from watering chores except in the case of young seedlings that need to be watered by hand.

Gray Water Recycling

Gray water recycling is seldom considered as a means of watering crops. Household waste water is designated as either black water, meaning that it contains human waste, or gray water, which is everything else. If a home is equipped to handle gray water separately, then water that would otherwise go to waste can be used to water raised beds. The microbes in the raised beds and the plants themselves purify the gray water and derive nutrients from it. Such a system would contain a gray water holding tank and a pump, and the beds would contain embedded pipes with small holes drilled in them. (The Johnny Appleseed rest area in Massachusetts uses this technique.) Gray water can also be recycled using artificial wetlands that can double as a home for ducks or aquaculture of farm-raised fish. It stands to reason that toxic substances should never be dumped into a gray water system, so homes anticipating such a use need to "go green" in terms of the cleaning products they use.

9

Crop Proportions and Sizing

How much of each crop to grow depends on a number of factors but most importantly on your needs and the requirements of market outlets if you choose to grow enough to sell. Averages come in handy for general planning, but nobody is really average. What this means is nobody can make a chart telling you exactly what to grow.

Folks in the United States eat notoriously unhealthy diets. According to the USDA Center for Nutrition Policy and Promotion, only 10% of Americans have a healthy diet.[24] So before we get into crop proportions and sizing, let's take a brief look at nutritional requirements.

As of 2006, the USDA food pyramid specifies the servings per day of different food groups (see Table 9).

By examining what constitutes a "serving" in each case and doing a little multiplication, we can create target production suitable for a healthy diet, which can later be modified if necessary to match the family's food preferences and activity levels.

---

[25] Basiotis, P. et al. (2002) *Healthy Eating Index 1999–2000* published by U.S. Department of Agriculture Center for Nutrition Policy and Promotion

Table 9: 2006 USDA Food Pyramid

Person	Grains	Vegetables	Fruits	Milk	Meat
Male, age 25–50	11	5	4	2	2.8
Female, age 25–50	9	4	3	2	2.4
Teenage male	11	5	4	3	2.8
Teenage female	9	4	3	3	2.4

For grains, a serving is a single slice of bread; 1/2 cup of rice, pasta, or cooked breakfast cereal; or one ounce of ready-to-eat breakfast cereal. Serving equivalents are computed on the basis of 1/2 ounce of flour per serving.

For vegetables, a serving is one cup of green leafy vegetables or a half cup of any other sort of vegetables, whether raw or cooked. Three-quarters of a cup of vegetable juice also constitutes a serving. Potatoes count as a vegetable, with half of a cup constituting a serving. Botany defines tomatoes as a fruit, but U.S. law defines tomatoes as a vegetable. For the purposes of the food pyramid, tomatoes are a vegetable.

With fruits, an average-sized whole fruit or 1/2 cup of fresh berries or canned/cooked fruit constitutes a serving. Three-quarters of a cup of fruit juice is also a serving of fruit.

All forms of meat but also dry beans, eggs, and nuts fall into the meat category. For red meat, poultry, and seafood, 2.5 ounces is a serving. One egg, half of a cup of tofu, half of a cup of cooked dried beans, and 1/4 of a cup of dried seeds each constitute a serving. One cup of milk or yogurt or 1.5 to 2 ounces of cheese constitutes a serving of milk.

Using food pyramid guidelines and serving sizes, we can determine the target production numbers for one person, as shown in Table 10.

Table 10: Per-Person Yearly Food Requirements

Crop	Per-Person Yearly Requirement
Vegetables	456 lbs
Fruit	365 lbs
Wheat, corn, oats, and rice	250 lbs
Total lean meats and eggs	159 lbs

What those numbers indicate is that the yearly diet for a family of two adults and one teenager requires 1,368 pounds of vegetables, 1,095 pounds of fruits, 750 pounds of grains, and 477 pounds of meat and eggs. This is, of course, subject to food preferences and allergies, so at the individual crop level, nobody can tell you what to grow. But at the level of gross nutrients, the USDA food pyramid can give you a good starting spot from which to customize.

Different crops give different yields per unit of space, and a mini farmer has to be aware of the expected yields to plan space allocation. Table 11 (page 86) gives approximate yield information for planning purposes based on a number of assumptions. Nonhybrid plant varieties in ordinary soil with sufficient water are assumed. Actual yield will depend on the variety of a given crop grown and individual growing conditions.

And, it is quite possible (even likely) that a farmer with richly composted soil will exceed these yields.

Our hypothetical family of three (two adults and one teenager) requires 1,368 pounds of vegetables for the year. Averaging the yield of various vegetables, you get 220 pounds per 100 square feet of bed space, meaning that all of a family's vegetable needs can be provided easily in 700 square feet of bed space, assuming a variety of vegetables.

The same hypothetical family needs 1,095 pounds of fruit for the year. Muskmelons, cantaloupes, and watermelons all count as fruits. Unfortunately, in most cases, these don't keep very long past the growing season. Fruit trees and vines are best to produce fruit in significant quantities. These aren't grown in raised beds and are instead grown in the ground.

A dwarf apple tree can yield up to 160 pounds of fruit annually. Apples store pretty well in a root cellar and are easily made into applesauce, and dehydrated apples make a tasty addition to oatmeal. Another good source of fruit is sweet and sour cherries, which will yield 300 and 150 pounds of fruit per tree, respectively. Blackberry canes are easy and trouble free to grow and will yield up to 50 pounds of blackberries per 100 square feet. Strawberries will yield around 100 pounds per 100 square feet.

Any number of combinations of fruit could work, but one example that would yield the 1,095 pounds of fruit is as follows:

- 100 square feet of strawberries (100 lbs)
- 100 square feet of melons (200 lbs)
- 200 square feet of blackberries and raspberries (100 lbs)
- 2 sour cherry trees (300 lbs)
- 5 dwarf apple trees (800 lbs)

Knowing that the hypothetical family of three requires 750 pounds of grains, it is easy to calculate the space that would be needed for grain crops from the information in Table 11. Oats produce only 10 pounds per 100 square feet, but wheat can produce as much as 20 pounds in the same space. Even at that, dividing 750 by 20 and multiplying by 100 gives 3,750 square feet, which is an awful lot of space for a relatively small amount of food carbohydrates. On top of that, this small scale of growing grains isn't enough to justify buying a thresher, so the grain would have to be threshed by hand—an incredibly time-consuming chore. There is also the process of turning it into meal and/or flour by hand. I've done a lot of that over the years, and it is serious work.

Raising grains can become more practical if a suitable thresher is available at modest cost, and a number of public domain designs are available for folks who are mechanically proficient. Two of the most promising designs were cocreated by Allen Dong and Roger Edberg; these were donated into the public domain by the creators as a gift to humanity. These designs are included on pages 177–178 and 179–180.

In spite of the fact that the USDA counts potatoes as a vegetable, they can be substituted for a portion of the grains in the diet, and doing so may have positive effects on overall health, energy, and mood.[25] Three hundred and fifty pounds of potatoes can easily be grown in 200 square feet. Substituting that for a portion of the grain crops would leave only 360 pounds of grains still being needed.

The growing of grains for food purposes (as opposed to cover cropping) in a mini-farm needs

---

[25] Desmaisons, K. (1998) *Potatoes Not Prozak*

to be carefully considered from an economic perspective. In 2006, the most expensive organic wheat sells for less than $15 for a 50-pound bag. Fifty pounds of the finest organic bread flour on the market currently costs $28. It would take 300 square feet of beds to grow that much wheat, and that same amount of space could grow over $1,400 worth of marketable crops instead. In addition, hand threshing wheat is time-consuming and must then be followed by grinding. Overall, within the United States, it really doesn't make sense for a mini-farmer to grow grains for their food value. This is why my approach to mini-farming, unlike the Grow Biointensive approach, doesn't emphasize growing grains at home.

⊗ If you grow grains at home, you'll need a grain grinder.

Unless you can make a thresher economical and don't mind digging 3,800 square feet for growing grain, a much better approach is to learn how to use a bread machine. Purchasing bulk flour and whole grains, using a bread machine, and learning how to make grain-based products at home from scratch will ultimately be more economically beneficial and less time-consuming than growing grains for food unless you live in a remote region where such an otherwise economically unwise approach is necessary. Bread machines are the greatest thing since . . . sliced bread. Organic bread at the health food store routinely costs $4 per loaf as of this writing. By using a bread machine and buying the ingredients in bulk, you end up with chemical-free bread costing about $0.50 per loaf.

Table 11: Average Crop Yields Planted Intensively

Crop	Yield in Pounds per 100 Square Feet
Green beans (as a vegetable)	100
Green beans (dried, as a protein)	20
Beets (just the roots)	200
Beets (just the greens)	200
Broccoli	75
Cabbage	300
Cauliflower	200
Carrots	350
Chard	550
Corn (on the cob)	55
Corn (dried for corn meal)	18
Cucumber	360
Eggplant	100

Crop	Yield in Pounds per 100 Square Feet
Kale	120
Leeks	500
Leaf lettuce	320
Head lettuce	180
Muskmelons	100
Onions	300
Peppers	120
Peas	100
Parsnips	290
Pumpkins	120
Spinach	130
Sunflower (shelled seeds)	6
Summer squash	250
Winter squash	200
Tomatoes	250
Watermelons	180
Barley	20
Oats	10
Rye	20
Wheat	20

Of all the dietary requirements, protein is the hardest to meet. Depending on your preferences, meat may need to be purchased, although it is feasible to produce meat and eggs at home by raising poultry. Larger livestock such as sheep and cattle are too big to be raised cost-effectively on smaller lots. The details of raising small livestock will be covered in a later chapter, so you may wish to consider space for a chicken coop in your farm plan.

But meat is not the only source of protein! Dried beans such as pinto, kidney, black turtle, soy, and others are rich in protein and easy to raise. I sow my dried beans in between my corn stalks, so they effectively require zero space. As noted earlier in this chapter, a mere half cup of cooked dried beans constitutes a serving of meat according to the USDA. That's only 1/4 cup of beans in their dried state. Vegetable proteins are seldom complete, meaning that they lack one or more amino acids, but this deficiency can be addressed by supplementing the beans with protein from grains such as wheat and corn. This way the entire mix of essential amino acids is available. I'm not jumping on the vegetarianism soapbox here. What I am saying instead is that if you can eat cooked dried beans and whole grain breads a couple of times per week, your health won't suffer, and you'll save a lot of money on meats.

In summary, assuming that whole grains and flours are purchased rather than raised at home, the core food needs of the family (other than meat) can be met by growing 700 square feet of vegetables and 200 square feet of potatoes or other tubers, purchasing flour in bulk, and growing a variety of fruit trees and vines. Protein can be acquired through purchasing meats, raising meat, and using beans and grains.

Pest and Disease Control

10

Pest and disease problems are an unavoidable fact of life for the mini-farmer. Sometimes, they are barely noticeable and cause no significant problems. But at other times they can cause major crop losses.

There are, unfortunately, hundreds of pests and diseases that affect vegetable crops. Going into the detail of identifying these is beyond the scope of this book, so instead I'll refer you to *The Organic Gardener's Handbook of Natural Insect and Disease Control,* published by Rodale and edited by Barbara Ellis and Fern Bradley. This 500-page book is loaded with color pictures and extensive explanation for every disease or pest you are likely to encounter, including specific details of organic methods for dealing with problems. What follows in this chapter is an overview that concentrates more on principles than details, along with my own unique passive-active-reactive pest management strategy developed specifically for the needs of mini-farms.

Since the old adage that "an ounce of prevention is worth a pound of cure" is true, mini-farming focuses automatically on passive prevention by giving plants what they need. Active prevention is used when experience or reliable data indicate that a particular pest or disease is likely to be a problem. Active reaction is employed when the value of likely crop damage will exceed the costs of active reaction methods.

Passive prevention is the application of good farming practices: well-composted and appropriately amended healthy soil, adequate sunshine, proper watering, crop rotation, and sufficient airflow. In essence, this simply means to give plants growing conditions that are as close to optimal as possible. This will make them healthier and thus less susceptible to diseases and less attractive to pests.

Active prevention uses active measures to prevent diseases or repel insect pests. Examples include applying repellent garlic or hot pepper sprays on plants to deter pests, installing physical barriers, putting out traps, or spraying the plants periodically with a fungus preventative. Sometimes, for certain types of pests, poisons that are usually used as a reactive measure may be required as active prevention.

Active reaction occurs when preventative measures fail and a problem already exists. Active reaction will often employ the same methods as active prevention, only with greater intensity, but it will also include, in most cases, the application of natural botanical or synthetic poisons or fungicides.

Pest management needs to be viewed holistically, as part of a bigger picture, to minimize crop damage while simultaneously protecting the long-range viability of the mini-farm. As part of this view, it is good to establish a threshold for what constitutes an acceptable level of damage before reactive, as opposed to preventative, measures need to be taken. This threshold is established economically, considering that the time, costs, and risks associated with active pest control measures will diminish the net grocery savings. So the threshold of acceptable damage for a given crop, in terms of percentage crop loss, is

⊗ Potato beetles are a common garden pest.

the level at which the value of the lost crop portion exceeds the cost of active control measures.

Passive Prevention

Passive prevention gives the biggest bang for both your time and money because the focus lies mainly in performing ordinary farming chores. Soil, water, sunshine, and crop rotations are the foundation of pest and disease control; all of these create an environment inhospitable to the persistence of pests and disease.

A healthy, living soil with plenty of nutrients allows for vigorous growth so that crops can outgrow problems. In addition, healthier plants are less attractive to pests and less susceptible to disease in most cases. Healthy soil plays host to various portions of the life cycles of many beneficial insect populations, along with beneficial microbes that compete with nasty pathogens for nutrients and generate antibiotics to eliminate them. It is no mistake that forests thrive independent of human intervention, and the more closely a farmer's garden approximates naturally optimal conditions for a crop, the less susceptible it will be to pest and disease problems.

An important aspect of healthy soil, particularly with intensive agriculture, is compost. As discussed in chapter 5, merely using compost in your soil can significantly reduce pest and disease problems.

Proper watering is another important aspect of disease control. Plant diseases spread most easily when plant tissues are wet; both excessive watering and overhead watering can increase the likelihood of disease problems. However, adequate moisture is also important because drought-stressed plants become more attractive to pests.

Crop rotation is impossible to over empha-size. Just like there are viruses and bacteria that affect some mammals but not others—such as feline leukemia—there are numerous plant dis-eases that affect one family of vegetables but not others. Since these microbes need a host hos-pitable to their reproduction to complete their life cycles, depriving them of the host they need through crop rotation is extremely effective at controlling many diseases. The same applies to insect pests, so the same crop should not be grown in the same bed two years in a row. Ide-ally, crop rotation will prevent crops of the same family from growing in the same bed any more often than once every three years.

Specific plant variety selection is another important preventative. Notwithstanding the

⊗ Dill is a common attractant of beneficial insects.

economic benefits of using open-pollinated seeds (described in the next chapter), some hybrids carry disease- and pest-resistance genes that can make them a better choice if certain diseases or pests become a repetitive problem. On my farm, for example, I now grow hybrid cucumbers that are resistant to bacterial wilt disease.

Finally, never discount the power of the sun. The same UV rays that make excessive sunshine a risk factor for skin cancer also scramble the genetic code in bacteria and viruses, rendering them incapable of infection. Sunshine sanitizes.

Attracting beneficial insects is also useful. Most beneficial insects feed on or invade pest species at some point in their life cycle, but they also require certain plants for their well-being. Providing these plants in the garden will give beneficial insects a base of operations they can use to keep pest species controlled.

A small planting of early, intermediate season, and late-blooming beneficial insect attractors in each garden bed will help stack the deck in the farmer's favor. Ladybugs love to eat aphids; dandelion, marigold, and hairy vetch will attract them. Tachanid flies help keep cabbage worms and stink bugs in check; a planting of parsley or pennyroyal will give them a home. Ben-eficial insect attractors that bloom early include sweet alyssum, columbine, and creeping thyme. Intermediate bloomers include common yarrow, cilantro, edging lobelia, and mints. Late bloomers include dill, wild bergamot, and European gold-enrod. An easy plan is to plant a few marigolds throughout the bed, a columbine plant, a bit of cilantro, and some dill.

You should familiarize yourself with the properties of beneficial plant attractors before planting them in your beds. Don't just run out

Table 12: **Preventative Plantings**

Beneficial Insect	Controlled Pests	Plants to Provide
Parasitic wasps	Moth, beetle, and fly larvae and eggs, including caterpillars	Dill, yarrow, tansy, Queen Anne's lace, parsley
Hoverflies (syrphid flies)	Mealybugs, aphids	As above, plus marigold
Lacewings	Aphids, mealybugs, other small insects	Dandelion, angelica, dill, yarrow
Ladybugs	Aphids	Dandelion, hairy vetch, buckwheat, marigold
Tachanid flies	Caterpillars, cabbage loopers, stink bugs, cabbage bugs, beetles	Parsley, tansy, pennyroyal, buckwheat

and plant mint in the garden bed directly, for example, because it will take over the entire bed. Instead, plant mint in a pot and then bury the pot in the garden soil so that the upper edge sticks out of the soil 1/2 inch or so.

You may also want to choose some plants that you will already use in some other way—such as mint for tea, dill for pickling, and cilantro for salsa. That way you are making maximum use of limited space. There is nothing wrong with growing goldenrods just because they are pretty!

Another valuable addition to the garden and yard, once the seeds have sprouted and the plants are growing well, would be chickens or guineas. Both types of birds, but guineas particularly, wreak havoc on bugs, especially bugs like ticks that nobody wants around anyway. Such livestock can effectively keep many sorts of garden pests from reaching the critical mass of population necessary to be threatening to crops.

Active Prevention

Active prevention is often necessary when a particular pest or disease problem is a practical certainty. In such cases, the active prevention is tailored to the expected problem and can often encompass methods used for both passive prevention and intervention. For example, you may notice your garden is regularly infested with earwigs. Once the bugs are noticed inside a cauliflower plant, they've already done a lot of damage. A weekly spraying with pyrethrin (a natural insecticide) or hot pepper wax (a repellent) will increase the usable harvest significantly.

The materials and techniques most often used for active prevention include traps, immune boosters, compost extracts, imported beneficial insects, and application of repellents, fungicides, and pesticides. (The latter is particularly important with certain fruit trees.)

Lures and Traps

Many insect pests can be caught in traps. In commercial operations, traps are usually used to monitor pest populations to determine the optimal timing for the application of pesticides. In a mini-farm, because of the smaller land area involved, it is often practical to employ enough traps to completely eradicate a particular pest (or one of the sexes of that pest) in the garden without resorting to poisons. Examples of pests easily trapped are codling moths, Japanese beetles, and apple maggots. Traps can also be employed for cucumber beetles, white flies, and a number of other pests, but they tend to be less effective. The time when various insects emerge varies from area to area. Because the lures used in traps often have limited lifespan, the timing of their deployment can be important. This is something you'll learn from keeping notes, and within a couple of years you'll have no trouble with the timing of traps.

Immunity Boosters and Growth Enhancers

One immune booster for plants on the market at the moment is marketed by Eden Bioscience in the form of harpin protein. Harpin protein, which is produced naturally by the bacterium that causes fire blight in apples and pears, elicits a broad immune response from vegetables that makes them more resistant to a wide array of pests and diseases while enhancing their growth. Eden Bioscience uses this discovery in a product called Messenger that is nontoxic and relatively inexpensive at my local agricultural supply store.

A company called Vitamin Institute sells a product called Superthrive that is advertised to improve the growth rate of plants and whose primary ingredient is thiamine. I have done some side-by-side testing, and the results have been ambiguous.

On the other hand, I have found a growth enhancer called Root Boost to live up to its advertising. It is not a fertilizer but rather an enhancer that is primarily based on kelp extract with the addition of humic acids. This product, when used as directed, really does enhance the soil and the plants that depend on it.

Compost Extract and Compost Tea

Compost extract is the most well-known and most widely studied homemade disease preventative. It is exactly what it sounds like: a shovel of properly aged compost in a water-permeable sack immersed in a bucket of water and steeped for 7 to 14 days.

As the chapter on composting pointed out, compost extract contains a cocktail of microbes and the chemicals that they produce. Compost extract contains a mix of beneficial bacteria and fungi that, when sprayed onto plants, eats the food substances that would otherwise be eaten by disease-causing organisms. As a result, the disease-causing organisms get starved out. A biweekly spray of compost extract is a good idea, and numerous studies attribute properties to the substance that are nothing short of miraculous. It can help prevent diseases such as black spot and powdery mildew. Best of all, it's free.

The next step up from compost extract is compost tea. Compost tea differs from an extract in that it is the result of an active attempt to increase the amount of fungi and bacteria in the solution through aeration. Still water (as used in compost extract) doesn't have much dissolved oxygen in it, and the beneficial microbes in compost require oxygen. So, actively aerating the water in which the compost is steeped will serve to boost populations of beneficial microbes from the compost. This can be done inexpensively by putting a fish tank aerator and air pump in the bottom of a container containing the water and compost. Some reasonably priced and favorably reviewed commercial options are also available through Keep It Simple, Inc. (www.simplici-tea .com) or Alaska Giant (www.alaskagiant.com).

Importing Beneficial Insects and Nematodes

Imported beneficial insects have their greatest applicability in greenhouses because, being quite mobile, when applied outdoors they are prone to fly away. Even outside they can be useful though, particularly when applied to crops infested with their favorite pest species and also provided with their favorite plants. Table 12 (earlier in this chapter) lists which beneficial insects to use for what problem and what sorts of plants should be established in advance of their arrival so they will stay in the garden.

Beneficial nematodes are extremely small worms that wait underground for a chance to work their way into pest insects and kill them. Beneficial nematodes are harmless to plants and pollinators and shouldn't be confused with pest nematodes such as root knot nematodes. Once inside the host, the nematodes release their gut bacteria, *Xenorhabdus luminescens*, into the insect's interior, where the bacteria multiply and the nematodes feed on them. The pest species eventually dies from infection. There are two commonly used species of nematodes, listed in Table 13. Beneficial nematode products often contain both species to be as broadly useful as possible.

Beneficial nematodes require extreme care in their handling and are usually shipped by overnight courier in a refrigerated package. They are stored in the refrigerator until they are used. It is

Table 13: **Beneficial Nematodes**

Species	Pests Controlled	Notes
Steinernema spp	Webworms, cutworms, vine borers	Not effective against grubs
Heterorhabditis spp	White grubs, vine weevils, root weevils	

best to wait until ground temperatures are above 50 degrees, the ground is damp, and a light rain is falling. Then put the nematodes in a pump-style sprayer and apply them to the ground where you want them. The reason for this is that beneficial nematodes are very prone to dehydration, and the falling rain helps them get into the soil. If you live north of Maryland, you'll need to apply them yearly because they can't survive the winter. If you live in a more southerly clime, the nematodes will probably survive, so a second application may not be needed.

Pest Repellents

Organic repellent mixtures are not 100% effective, but they serve as a valuable part of an integrated strategy for pest management. One repellent mixture is simple hot pepper. Capsaicin, the active ingredient in hot peppers, repels onion, carrot, and cabbage maggots. Simply finely chop up a cup of hot peppers, and steep it for a day in a gallon of water to which a single drop of dish soap has been added. Another repellent mixture is garlic, manufactured the same way. One thing that I do, with great success, is make hot pepper and garlic mixtures in a coffee maker that has been set aside for agricultural use only. There are some commercial repellent preparations worth noting as well, including CropGuard and Hot Pepper Wax™.

There is *some* evidence that certain plants can repel pest insects. According to numerous sources, for example, nasturtiums and radishes repel cucumber beetles. I have experimented extensively with this practice and found no difference in cucumber beetle populations between cucumber plants surrounded by radishes and intertwined with nasturtiums and cucumber plants grown on their own. On the other hand, I have found that onion family crops repel wireworms, so I interplant leeks with my parsnips. A number of sites on the Internet list repellent plants, so I encourage you to experiment with the reputed properties of repellent plants and keep notes to see what works best for your garden.

Active Reaction

Even the most conscientious farming practices and most vigilant preventive measures will often fail to prevent pest and disease problems. Once these problems become apparent, reactive measures are in order.

Reactive measures will often include some of the same materials and methods as passive and active prevention. For example, many fungal infections can be eradicated by the timely application of compost tea, neem oil, or garlic oil. (Neem oil is an oil extracted from a tree in India.) Most often, though, reactive measures will involve the use of fungicides and/or natural or synthetic pesticides. Because these reactive measures use substances with greater potential

to harm people or the environment, I don't recommend their application unless the farmer is certain that a likelihood exists that failure to apply them will result in an unacceptable level of crop loss.

Another tip to make active measures most effective is to take a cue from doctors treating HIV and tuberculosis: Never treat an insect or disease problem with only one active agent at a time. Using only one active agent increases the odds of survivors living to convey immunity to that agent in the next generation. When you mix two or more active agents, you increase the odds of success while decreasing the odds of creating resistant organisms.

When Disease Prevention Fails

Plant diseases fall into four broad categories: bacterial, viral, protozoan, and fungal. Usually, these are impossible to distinguish by the naked eye except through experience with their symptoms. (See also the Rodale book recommended earlier in this chapter.) All such diseases present the problem that once a plant is infected, it becomes a storehouse of infective particles that can be spread to other plants via insects, wind, or handling. The longer an affected plant remains in the garden, the greater the odds that it will infect other plants. Diseases caused by viruses, bacteria, and protozoans are seldom treatable, but sometimes you can save a plant by pruning out the affected portions. Many fungal diseases, though, *are* treatable through a combination of pruning and spraying.

When a plant infection of any sort is first noticed, you may be able to save the plant by applying compost tea and/or Messenger. These products can stimulate an immune response that helps the plant overcome the infection. Their usefulness in that regard varies depending on the plants and diseases involved, so try it and keep notes of the results. A number of spray fungicides can also be used. Common fungicides include copper sulfate, Bordeaux mix (a mixture of copper sulfate and lime), baking soda, garlic oil, and neem oil. Baking soda is mixed two tablespoons per gallon of water with one ounce of light horticultural oil added, and the others are mixed according to label directions.

Some less well-known antifungal agents can have surprising results. I had a problem with powdery mildew on my lawn last spring (we had an especially wet spring), and I eliminated the infection by spraying with a mix of neem oil and fixed copper.

If saving the plant is either unsuccessful or inadvisable, then the plant should be removed from the garden immediately. Removing an infectious plant can be problematic since it can be covered with microscopic spores that will spread all over the place if the plant is disturbed. The solution is to spray the plant with something that will hold any spores in place and inactivate as many as possible before attempting removal. A good spray for this is made of two tablespoons of castile soap, one tablespoon of copper sulfate, one tablespoon of lime, and one tablespoon of light horticultural oil all mixed together in a gallon of water. The soap and oil will make the plant sticky so that spores can't escape, while the copper sulfate and lime serve to actually kill many infectious organisms. Spray the plant thoroughly with this (though not until it is dripping), and then cut it out and remove it, being as careful as possible to avoid letting it touch any other plants.

When dealing with plant diseases, you should consider your hands and tools to be a mode of disease transmission. When handling known diseased plants, it makes sense to handle *only* the diseased plants before hand washing and also to immediately sterilize any tools used on the diseased plants with bleach. A suitable sanitizing solution is one tablespoon of bleach per quart of water.

Diseased plant materials can be thermophilically composted with minimal or no risk as long as proper retention times are observed. If the farmer uses mesophilic composting instead, then diseased plant debris should be burned or placed in the curbside trash. It is also very important not to grow the same family of plant in the same area the next year. If a variety of the plant that resists that disease can be found, it would be a good idea to switch to that variety for at least a year or two, if not permanently.

When Pest Prevention Fails

The best soil management and prevention mechanisms will not be 100% effective against insect pests. For example, naturally attracted beneficial insects exist in balance with pest insects. If the beneficial insects were to eat all of the pest species, then the beneficial insects would starve or move somewhere else, and the pest species would experience a resurgence in the absence of its natural enemies.

Reactive control measures include anything used in the preventive stages, along with importing beneficial insect populations, applying microbial insecticides, and using substances that actually kill insects directly, such as soaps, oils, and natural or synthetic insecticides. Synthetic insecticides should be reserved as a last resort since they would reduce the healthfulness of the crop (as described later in this chapter) and would make it impossible for you to sell your produce as organic for several years if you wish to do so.

Both natural and artificial insecticides can also harm beneficial helpers, such as necessary pollinators and earthworms, and disrupt the life of the soil and thus harm fertility in the long run, so they are best employed only when absolutely necessary. Because natural insecticides don't last as long in the garden, they have less potential to do unintended damage.

Microbial Insecticides

Microbial insecticides are microbes (or toxins produced by microbes) that are deadly to pest insects but harmless to beneficial insects and humans. They have the advantage of being relatively benign but the disadvantage of being fairly species specific. For example, *Bacillus popilliae* is deadly to Japanese beetle larvae but harmless to other white grubs that infest lawns. They aren't contact poisons, and they must be eaten by the insect to be effective. Microbial insecticides have become increasingly popular, even among conventional farmers, and are readily available at agricultural stores.

Soaps and Oils

Plain old soap (not detergent, but soap) kills a number of insects by dissolving a waxy coating that they need to breathe and preserve moisture. Specialized insecticidal soaps can be used, or else a pure castile soap (such as Dr. Bronner's), mixed two tablespoons per gallon of water. Insecticidal

Table 14: **Common Microbial Insecticides**

Microbe	Pests Controlled	Notes
Bacillus thuringiensis var. *kurstaki*	The caterpillar stage of a wide variety of moths	Will not control codling moths
Bacillus thuringiensis var. *israelensis*	Mosquito, black fly, fungus gnat	
Bacillus thuringiensis var. *san diego*	Colorado potato beetle	
Nosema locustae	Grasshoppers	Because of grasshopper mobility, may not work for small yards

soap will effectively control aphids, white flies, scale, spider mites, and thrips. It needs to be reapplied fairly frequently—about weekly—to interrupt the life cycle of the target pest.

Light horticultural oils are highly refined mineral oils that control the same insects as insecticidal soap by covering and smothering the pest and its eggs. Mix and apply according to label directions.

Both oils and soaps should be tested on a single plant first, then wait a day, because they can be toxic to certain plants. (Their degree of toxicity to plants varies with heat, sunshine, humidity, general plant health, and other factors. Most often, they won't cause a problem, but it never hurts to test first.)

Natural Insecticides

The fact that something is natural doesn't mean that it is harmless. Ebola, smallpox, and strychnine are all 100% natural, for example. Natural insecticides fall under the same category and thus require care in their use. Natural insecticides can be purchased, or they can be grown and made at home. From a cost standpoint, the latter approach is preferable, though certain natural insecticides aren't practical for home manufacture.

Pyrethrin is a contact insecticide that controls most aphids, cabbage loopers, stinkbugs, codling moths, and whiteflies among other pests. It does not affect flea beetles, imported cabbage worms, or tarnished plant bugs.

To make your own pyrethrin, grow pyrethrum daisies (*Tanacetum cinerarifolium*) somewhere in the garden. Cut the flowers when they are in full bloom for the highest concentration of poison, and hang them upside down in a cool, dry, dark place to dry. Once they are dried, take a quart jar of the dried flowers and grind them up using an old food processor or blender that you pick up at a yard sale and that *you will never use for food again*. Mix it with one gallon of water and two drops of dish liquid, and allow it to steep for three days, stirring every once in a while. When done, filter it through cheese cloth that you will throw away afterward, store in a tightly capped bottle in a cool dark place, and label it appropriately as a poison so nobody drinks it accidentally. You dilute this for use by mixing one quart of the poison with three quarts of water, shaking, and applying via a sprayer. (I cannot stress strongly enough that all bottles containing poisons of any sort be labeled appropriately. Not far from where I live, a child died tragically a couple of years ago because of an unlabeled container of insecticide.)

Other natural insecticides are widely available. They can be purchased at most garden centers or via mail order and should be used with as much care and caution as synthetics, because they can be toxic to humans.

Synthetic Pesticides

While this book focuses on organic methods, synthetic pesticides available to home gardeners bear mentioning. Ideally, because of a combination of growing conditions, attraction of natural predators, and other factors, pests won't be a problem so no pesticides will be needed—synthetic or otherwise. But that's the ideal. Reality can be far different, especially when first beginning a mini-farm. Even the most careful planning won't completely eliminate pest problems.

As a mini-farmer, you are trying to put a lot of food on the table, and you are trying to put *safe* food on the table. Perhaps, like me, you are an organic purist. But what happens when the theory of being an organic purist runs into the reality of a pest problem that threatens an entire crop? In my case, since I sell my produce as organic at 200% higher rates than conventional produce, it is actually better for me to lose a crop entirely than use synthetic pesticides. But what if my operation were strictly oriented toward putting food on the table? In that case, *maybe* I would use them, albeit cautiously and as a last resort, because some research shows that the synthetic pesticides available at the hardware store can be just as safe as botanical insecticides—and more effective—when used properly.

Please note that I said "maybe," "cautiously," and "as a last resort" for a reason. First off, in a mini-farm established using the methods in this book, economically threatening insect problems should be rare, and insect problems that won't respond to natural remedies even more rare. In fact, I have had only *one* pest problem where synthetics would have possibly been the better short-term solution.

Second, the government agencies charged with ensuring the safety of foodstuffs, drugs, and insecticides have a poor track record. For example, an article in *USA Today* disclosed that in 55% of FDA meetings regarding drug approvals, over half of the participants had financial conflicts of interest serious enough to note.[26] According to the same article, committees approving such things are actually *required by law* to include officials representing the industry in question. This is not exactly a recipe that would inspire confidence in most objective observers and perhaps explains the dozens of chemicals (including various insecticides and drugs) approved by government agencies and subsequently recalled after people have been harmed or killed.

Finally, studies indicate that synthetic pesticides make food less healthful by reducing the ability of plants to create antioxidants.[27] This explains my caution regarding synthetic pesticides. If you are nice enough to buy my book, should I repay your kindness by giving you advice that could hurt you without totally disclosing the facts as I know them? Government agencies have a poor track record, and research in universities is often funded by self-interested parties. The extent to which this affects the results and conclusions of research is impossible to tell. So I am going to give you information on two synthetic insecticides, understanding that the research I have available says they are safe but that it could be discovered later that you shouldn't touch them with the proverbial 10-foot pole.

The use of natural insecticides like pyrethrin is perfectly acceptable under the National Organic Program, but in practical terms these substances are every bit as toxic as commonly available synthetics while being less effective in many instances. The main difference is that the natural insecticides break down into nontoxic compounds very quickly under the influence of heat, sunshine, wind, and rain so they won't make it into your food supply if used properly, whereas the synthetics are specifically formulated to be more persistent.

Let's take pyrethrin as an example. Pyrethrin is a natural neurotoxin that insects quickly absorb through the skin. Once it is absorbed, the race is on between the insect's enzymes that detoxify the pyrethrin and the pyrethrin's toxic effects. Many insects, if they receive a sublethal dose, will pick themselves up and dust themselves off less than an hour after apparently being killed! Synthetic pyrethrins approach this problem by mixing the product with a substance like piperonyl butoxide that delays the insect's ability to make the enzymes to detoxify the pyrethrin, thus lowering the threshold considerably for what would constitute a lethal dose. Moreover, semisynthetic pyrethrins, such as allethrin, are often more toxic to insects while being less

[26] Couchon, D. (2000) Number of drug experts available is limited *USA Today*, Sept 25, 2000
[27] Asami, D., Hong, Y., Barrett, D., Mitchell, A. (2003) Comparison of total phenolic and ascorbic acid content of freeze-dried and air-dried marionberry, strawberry and corn grown using conventional, organic and sustainable agricultural practices. *Journal of Agricultural Food Chemistry,* Feb 26, 2003

toxic to mammals (such as humans) than their natural counterparts.

So a semisynthetic pyrethrin spray combined with piperonyl butoxide would require less poison to be used and be more effective, and the type of pyrethrin being used would be less toxic to humans.[28]

According to a metabolic study, neither natural nor synthetic pyrethrins accumulate in the body or show up in breast milk because they are quickly detoxified in the human body.[29] Any allethrin consumed by a human is rapidly transformed into something less toxic and eliminated.[30] In addition, allethrin is broken down into nontoxic compounds through the action of air and sunlight within a few days,[31] though not as quickly as natural pyrethrin.

The piperonyl butoxide used to increase the effectiveness of pyrethrins is a semisynthetic derivative of safrole—an oil found in the bark of sassafras trees. It works by inhibiting enzymes that detoxify the pyrethrins in the insect's body. Safrole is a known carcinogen, but the status of piperonyl butoxide as a carcinogen is disputed. Unlike allethrin, piperonyl butoxide is stable in the environment and doesn't break down easily.[32]

Given current information, the allethrin doesn't worry me much, but I am sufficiently uneasy about the persistence of piperonyl butoxide in the environment that I wouldn't personally use it. Either way, synthetic pyrethrins and those containing piperonyl butoxide should be used according to label directions and never be used on crops within a week of harvest; even then harvested crops should be well washed.

Carbaryl (also known as "Sevin") is another common synthetic insecticide used in home gardens. There is no clear evidence that carbaryl is carcinogenic or causes birth defects, and 85% of carbaryl is excreted by humans within 24 hours.[33] Carbaryl has a half-life of 7 to 14 days in sandy loam soil, and the manufacturer (GardenTech) states that it is not absorbed by the plant.[34] Therefore, if used according to label directions, and produce is carefully washed, it should be safe. According to numerous studies, "Carbaryl breaks down readily and experience shows it readily decomposes on plants, in soil and water to less toxic byproducts. Accumulation in animal tissues and biomagnification of residues in food chains with carbaryl and its metabolites does not occur."[35]

Certainly, the preponderance of science says that carbaryl is perfectly safe when used according to label directions. It definitely takes care of cucumber beetles much more effectively than my organic approaches. Nevertheless, common sense and the fact that it is a neurotoxin that takes a lot longer than most botanical insecticides to break down would dictate that it be used only as a last resort. All in all, if I were to use a synthetic insecticide, I would use carbaryl in preference to

[28] Extoxnet (1994) *Pyrethrins* from http://pmep.cce.cornell.edu/profiles/extoxnet/pyrethrins-ziram/pyrethrins-ext.html. Retrieved May 20, 2006,

[29] Elliot, M. et al. (1972) Metabolic fate of pyrethrin I, pyrethrin II and allethrin administered orally to rats *Journal of Agricultural Food Chemistry 20*

[30] Kidd, H., James, D. (eds) (1991) *The Agrochemicals Handbook, Third Edition*

[31] Napa County Mosquito Abatement District (2006) Retrieved June 12, 2006, from www.napamosquito.org/Pesticide/pesticide.htm

[32] New York State Health Department (2000) Retrieved March 13, 2006, from http://www.health.state.ny.us/nysdoh/westnile/final/c3/c3summry.htm

[33] Extoxnet (1996) (Extoxnet is a government-funded database of toxic substances located at http://extoxnet.orst.edu)

[34] GardenTech (2006) Retrieved July 5, 2006, from http://www.gardentech.com/sevin.asp

[35] Hock, W. *Sevin (Carbaryl): A Controversial Insecticide*

the others available. And, in fact, that is what I used before switching to organic gardening.

Animal Pests

So far, in this chapter, when discussing pests we've largely been talking about insects. But one ignores larger pests, such as raccoons, rabbits, and deer, at his or her farm's peril. For many years, my farm ran along just fine with only minor damage from moles who ate strawberries and ripe tomatoes, and raccoons who occasionally stole an ear of corn. But one year, my entire crop of beans, sweet potatoes, and Brussels sprouts was wiped out in just one night by a herd of hungry deer. And they kept coming back to nibble at the sad remains. Clearly, action was needed.

Moles can be a bit of a nuisance in my garden. They are there, primarily, to eat grubs. If you get rid of the grubs by applying milky spore or beneficial nematodes, you will dramatically reduce the mole population. For faster relief, there are a number of castor oil products on the market that put castor oil into the dirt. When the moles dig, they get the castor oil on their fur, and they lick it off. This gives them diarrhea, and they move on within a couple of weeks. I've found this quite effective. A number of companies sell a battery-powered spike that generates noise that is supposed to deter moles. These may work for you, but I've found them ineffective.

Rabbits are only an occasional problem and don't usually do much damage on the farm. What I do is mix a milky spore product with anything else I happen to be spraying and use it to wet the leaves. This serves as sufficient deterrent.

⊗ Products for deterring furry pests.

Deer are another matter entirely. I tried all the standard tricks. Bars of soap, hair clippings, urinating around the property line, and similar homespun remedies did nothing. Spraying the plants with hot pepper wax was inadequate and only marginally effective. I have found only three things that really work. The first is quite expensive: an impenetrable physical barrier in the form of a fence eight-feet tall. The second is a product called Deer Scram, which is a deterrent scent that is sprinkled around the area to be protected. The third is the use of a baited electric fence.

A baited electric fence is a regular electric fence that has been baited with peanut butter wrapped in aluminum foil. Deer adore peanut butter, so they put their mouth right on the aluminum foil and get zapped. This works incredibly well and requires only a single strand of fencing about four feet off the ground where pets are safe. This same trick works for raccoons if you add another strand about 18 inches off the ground.

11

Seed Starting

It is a good idea to learn to start seedlings for three reasons. The first reason is economic: Starting seedlings at home saves money. The second reason is variety: Starting seedlings at home vastly increases the range of crop choices because certain varieties may not be available at your local garden center. Finally, since seedlings grown at home were never in a commercial greenhouse, you'll have a known-good product that is unlikely to be harboring pests.

Starting seeds is simple: Place seeds in a fertile starting medium in a suitable container; provide water, heat, and light; and that's it. Many seeds—such as grains and beets—are sowed directly in a garden bed, but others such as tomatoes, broccoli, and peppers, must be either started in advance or purchased as small plants ("seedlings") and then transplanted.

Timing

Seedlings need to be started indoors anywhere from 2 to 12 weeks before transplant time, depending on the particular crop. Transplant

Table 15: **Spring and Fall Planting Guide**

Crop	Start Spring and Summer Seedlings Relative to Last Spring Frost	Transplant Spring and Summer Seedlings Relative to Last Spring Frost	Start Fall Seedlings Relative to First Fall Frost	Transplant Fall Seedlings Relative to First Fall Frost
Broccoli	–12 weeks	–6 weeks	Transplant date –42 days	Frost date +32 days –days to maturity
Brussels sprouts	–12 weeks	–4 weeks		
Cabbage	–13 weeks	–5 weeks	Transplant date –56 days	Frost date +25 days –days to maturity
Cantaloupe	–2 weeks	+2 weeks	N/A	N/A
Cauliflower	–12 weeks	–4 weeks	Transplant date –56 days	Frost date +18 days –days to maturity
Celery	–13 weeks	–3 weeks	Transplant date –70 days	Frost date +11 days –days to maturity
Collards	–12 weeks	–4 weeks	Transplant date –56 days	Frost date +18 days –days to maturity
Cucumber	–3 weeks	+1 week	N/A	N/A
Eggplant	–8 weeks	+2 weeks	N/A	N/A
Kale	–13 weeks	–5 weeks	Transplant date –56 days	Frost date +25 days –days to maturity
Lettuce	–8 weeks	–2 weeks	Transplant date –42 days	Frost date +4 days –days to maturity
Okra	–4 weeks	+2 weeks	N/A	N/A
Onions	–12 weeks	–6 weeks	Transplant date –42 days	Frost date +32 days –days to maturity
Peppers	–6 weeks	+2 weeks	N/A	N/A
Pumpkins	–2 weeks	+2 weeks	N/A	N/A
Squash (summer)	–2 weeks	+2 weeks	N/A	N/A
Squash (winter)	–2 weeks	+2 weeks	N/A	N/A
Tomatoes	–7 weeks	+0 weeks	N/A	N/A
Watermelon	–2 weeks	+2 weeks	N/A	N/A

time is reckoned in weeks before or after the last predicted frost of the year for spring and summer crops and in weeks before the first predicted frost for fall and winter crops. The timing of transplanting is dictated by the hardiness of the particular crop. Broccoli is pretty hardy, so it is often planted 6 weeks before the last predicted frost, whereas cucumber is very tender, so it is planted 1 or 2 weeks after.

So the most important information that you will need for starting seeds is the date of the last frost for your geographic region. This can be found from the Cooperative Extension Service or from an Internet search in most cases. The National Climatic Data Center maintains comprehensive tables on the Internet that give the statistical likelihoods of frost on a given date along with the probabilities of the number of frost-free days, broken down by state and city. Weather.com also provides data relevant to gardening.

Once you've determined the average date of your last spring frost, determine the date for starting seeds and transplanting seedlings into the garden by adding or subtracting a certain number of weeks from the date of the last frost, depending on the crop (see Table 15).

If my average last spring frost is June 1st, then I would start my tomato plants seven weeks before June 1st and set them out on that date. Cabbage would be started 13 weeks before June 1st and set out in the garden 5 weeks before June 1st. Eggplant would be started 8 weeks before June 1st and set out 2 weeks after June 1st.

Anything that can be planted in the garden before the last spring frost can also be grown as a fall crop. For fall cabbage, if my average date of the first fall frost is on September 6th, and my cabbage requires 65 days to mature according to the seed package, then I would transplant my cabbage seedlings on July 28th. This is computed by adding 25 days (from the table) to September 6th then subtracting 65 days for the days to maturity (from the seed package). I can tell when to start my cabbage from seed by subtracting 56 days (from the table) from the transplant date. So I should start my cabbage seedlings for fall on June 2nd.

Starting Medium

Gardening experts have many varied opinions on the best starting medium. To confuse matters, seed catalogs try to sell all kinds of starting mediums for that purpose, and the number of choices can be confusing.

Whatever is used as a seed-starting medium should be light and easy for delicate roots to penetrate, and it should hold water well and not be infected with diseases. It should have some nutrients but not too heavy a concentration of them. Commercial seed-starting mixes are sold for this purpose and work fine, as do peat pellets of various shapes and sizes. At the time of writing, commercial seed-starting mixes cost about $3 for enough to start 150 plants, and peat pellets cost about $5 per 100.

Compared to the cost of buying transplants from a garden center, the price of seed-starting mixes or peat pellets is negligible. But for a farmer growing hundreds or even thousands of transplants, it may be economical to make seed-starting mixes at home. Most seed-starting mixes consist mainly of finely milled peat moss and vermiculite. The Territorial Seed Company recommends a simple 50/50 mix of vermiculite and peat moss,[36] but some authorities recommend adding compost to the mix because it can suppress diseases.[37] Some farmers also add a little clean sand. If these latter two ingredients are added, they shouldn't constitute more than 1/3 of the soil volume in aggregate. Don't use garden soil, and don't use potting soil. It is extremely important that any compost used to make seed-starting mix be well finished so that it contains no disease organisms or weed seeds. (Garden soil can be used as an ingredient if it is first sifted through a 1/4-inch mesh screen and then sterilized. Instructions for sterilizing are given later in this chapter. Potting soil can be used under the same conditions—if it is sifted then sterilized.)

A little compost or worm castings mixed into seed-starting mixes is fine and can be helpful in warding off diseases. But even organic fertilizer in too great a concentration will create an environment ideal for the growth of various fungi that will invade and harm the seedlings. An indoor seed-starting environment is not like the great outdoors. Wind movement, sunshine, and other elements that keep fungi at bay are greatly reduced in an indoor environment. As a result, the teaspoon of solid fertilizer that does so much good outdoors can be harmful to seedlings.

Another reason for keeping the nutrient content of seed-starting medium low is the lower nutrient concentrations cause more aggressive root growth. Improved root growth leads to a transplant that will suffer less shock when it is planted outdoors.

Here is my own recipe:

- Finely milled sphagnum peat moss, 4 quarts
- Medium vermiculite, 1 pint
- Well-finished compost passed through a 1/4-inch screen made from hardware cloth, 1 pint
- Worm castings (available at any agricultural store), 1 pint

Again, the simple 50/50 mix of peat moss and vermiculite recommended by the Territorial Seed Company and most commercial seed-starting mixes work perfectly fine. Feel free to experiment!

Because the starting medium used for seeds is deliberately nutritionally poor and provided in insufficient quantity to meet a seedling's nutritional needs, it will become necessary to fertilize seedlings periodically once their first "true" leaves appear. The first two leaves that appear, called the cotyledons, contain a storehouse of nutrients that will keep the plant well supplied until the first true leaves emerge. (Plants can be divided into two categories—those with two cotyledons, called "dicots," and those with one cotyledon, called "monocots." The first true leaves look like the leaves that are distinctive for that plant.) Adding solid fertilizer to the cells of a seedling tray would be both harmful and impractical, so liquid fertilizer will need to be used.

Seedlings are delicate, and full-strength fertilizer is both unneeded and potentially harmful. A good organic kelp, fish, or start-up fertilizer diluted to half strength and applied every two weeks after the first true leaves appear should work fine.

Containers

Mini-farming is not a small hobby operation. The average mini-farmer will grow hundreds

---

[36] http://www.territorial-seed.com/stores/1/March_2001_W133C449.cfm retrieved on 2/27/2006
[37] Coleman, E. (1999) *Four Season Harvest*

or perhaps thousands of seedlings. The best methods for starting seeds on this scale include cellular containers like those used by nurseries, peat pellets, and compressed soil blocks.

The use of undivided flats is advocated in the Grow Biointensive method. In this method, a rectangular wooden box of convenient size and about 2 inches deep is filled with starting medium, and seeds are planted at close intervals. The seeds are kept moist and warm, and once the cotyledons have appeared, the seedlings are carefully picked out and transplanted into a new flat with a greater distance between seedlings. This process is repeated again when the growth of the plant makes it necessary, and the final time the plant is transplanted, complete with a block of soil, it goes straight into the garden. The most obvious benefit of this method is that it is inexpensive. The largest detriment is that it is extremely time-consuming. Grow Biointensive publications also state that this method produces a beneficial microclimate and stronger transplants, but my own experiments have shown no appreciable difference between seedlings grown this way and seedlings grown exclusively in soil blocks or peat pellets. Certainly, this technique works well, and in a situation where the farmer is rich in time but poor in cash, it is a very good option.

The commercial growers who make the small six-packs of transplants for the garden center use plastic multicelled containers. These containers cost money, of course, but also save on labor costs and are easily transplanted. These units have a hole in the bottom of every cell, fit into rectangular plastic boxes that provide for bottom watering, and can be picked up at most agricultural stores for around $2 or $3 for a tray and eight 6-pack containers. The price of these works out to about

Broccoli seedlings destined for market.

$6 per 100 plants, which isn't expensive considering that the containers can be reused year to year as long as they are well washed between uses so they don't spread diseases. If you sell seedlings, as I do, you will want to take the cost of these containers (and labels) into account in setting your price. In practice, once acquired, the economics of using these is sound since the per-plant cost drops dramatically after the first year, and they save a lot of time compared to using undivided flats.

The disadvantage of multicelled containers is that each cell contains only two or three cubic inches of soil. This means that the soil can't hold enough nutrients to see the seedling through to transplanting time, so bottom watering with liquid fertilizer is required. Also, because of the small amount of space, roots grow to the sides of the cell and then wind around and around, contributing to transplant shock. Finally, because of the small soil volume, multicelled containers can't be left unattended for more than a couple of days because their water supply is depleted rapidly. Even with these disadvantages, they are the method of choice for producing seedlings for sale because of their convenience.

Peat pellets have a significant advantage over multicelled containers when it comes to transplant shock. Taking a transplant from a multicelled pack and putting it directly into garden soil can set the plant back for a few days as it acclimates to the new soil conditions. Peat pellets get around this problem because transplants are put into the garden without being disturbed, and roots can grow right through them into the soil. This allows for gradual acclimatization and virtually eliminates transplant shock.

Peat pellets cost about $5 per 100 and can be purchased at agricultural supply stores and occasionally at places like Walmart. They come as compressed dry wafers and are expanded by placing them in warm water. Once the pellets expand, the seeds are placed in the center and lightly covered, then the pellet is bottom watered as needed until time to plant in the garden. In the case of peat pellets, the seed-starting mix of a peat pellet is essentially devoid of nutrients altogether, making liquid fertilizer a must. If you use peat pellets, be sure to carefully slit and remove the webbing at transplanting time so it doesn't bind the roots.

Peat pots suffer from the same disadvantages that affect multicelled containers because

⊗ Peat pots often fail to break down quickly.

of their small soil volume, plus they don't break down well, and they constrain root growth in many cases, so I don't recommend them. When I worked some compost into my beds last spring, I dug up perfectly intact peat pots that had been planted a year earlier.

Compressed soil blocks, while not aesthetically acceptable for commercial sale, are the best available choice for the farmer's own seedlings. That's because a compressed soil block contains 400% more soil volume than a peat pellet or multicelled container, meaning it will contain more nutrients and moisture. Seedlings raised in compressed soil blocks using a properly constituted soil mix may require no liquid fertilizer at all. Because roots grow right up to the edge of the block instead of twisting around, and the block is made of soil so decomposition isn't an issue, transplant shock all but disappears. They are also the least expensive option when used in volume.

Compressed soil blocks are made with a device called a "soil blocker" into which a soil mix is poured, and the mix is then compressed.

A standard mix for the soil used in the blocker contains 30% fine peat moss, 30% good finished compost, 30% sterilized garden soil and 10% fine sand.[38] A balanced organic fertilizer such as Cockadoodle DOO is added to the mix at the rate of 1/2 cup per four gallons of soil mix, and the pH is adjusted with lime if necessary to fall between 6.2 and 7.0. My own mix is 50% peat moss, 40% worm castings, and 10% coarse vermiculite with a bit of balanced fertilizer. (Garden soil can be sterilized by spreading

[38] Patry, S. (1993) *Soil Blocks Increase Space Utilization and Plant Survival* Retrieved March 7, 2006, from http://www.eap.mcgill.ca/MagRack/COG/COG_H_93_02.htm

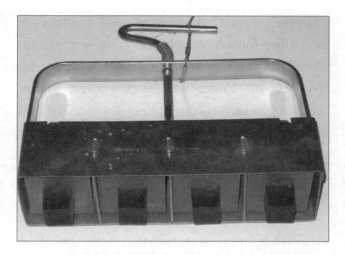

A standard 2-inch soil blocker with rectangular inserts.

so large twigs don't interfere with the operation of the soil blocker.

Even though the devices for making soil blocks cost about $30 each, they are made of steel and will last many years, so they will save many times their cost compared to multicelled containers. I bought mine from Peaceful Valley Farm Supply over the Internet.

One particular technique for using soil blockers merits attention. An insert can be purchased for the 2-inch soil blocker that makes a 3/4-inch cubic indentation in the block to accept 3/4-inch soil blocks. This is a great idea because it allows germination to be accomplished in smaller soil blocks that are then transplanted into the larger ones. That way you aren't taking up a large soil block with seed that won't germinate.

it no more than 1-inch thick on a baking pan and baking in the oven at 200 degrees for 20 minutes. Don't use a good pan!) It is important that the ingredients used in a soil mix be sifted

Use 1/4-inch hardware cloth to screen out debris.

⊗ Soil blocks with sprouted lettuce seedlings.

Light

Plants evolved with needs for light intensity that match the output of the sun, which provides light that is so intense that merely looking at it can permanently damage the eye. Naturally, seedlings grown inside also need an intense light source that can provide enough light without also making so much heat that plants get burned.

With the exception of certain flowers, most plants do not need light to germinate. In fact some plants, like those in the brassica family, may have their germination inhibited by light. But once the first plant parts emerge above the ground, all plants need light to grow. In most of North America and Europe, there is not enough sunshine coming through even a south-facing window to adequately start seedlings during the winter months when most seed starting takes place, so a source of artificial light is required. Selecting an artificial light source should be based on an understanding of the plants' requirements.

Plants require light of various wavelengths or colors for various purposes. Red wavelengths, for example, regulate dormancy, seed production, and tuber formation, whereas blue wavelengths stimulate chlorophyll production and vegetative growth. Violet wavelengths affect plants' tendency to turn toward a light source. The best light sources for starting seedlings, then, should generate a wide spectrum of light wavelengths that encompass both the blue and the red ends of the spectrum.

There is a growing number of options for artificial lighting; unfortunately, most of these are quite expensive. Following is my particular approach that inexpensively meets the light needs for seedlings.

⊗ A homemade rack for seedlings works great and costs little.

All sorts of special carts costing anywhere from $200 to $1,000 are sold for this purpose, but with a little ingenuity you can create a suitable contrivance, made like the one illustrated, at very low cost.

This device is made from a simple wire rack sold in the hardware department of Walmart for $50. Three racks hold up to four large seed trays each, and two 48-inch shop light fluorescent light fixtures are hung over each rack using simple adjustable chains from the hardware store. This way, the lights can be independently raised and lowered to keep them the right distance above the plants as they grow. The six lights (or fewer if you don't need them all) are plugged into an electric outlet strip that is plugged into a timer. Each light holds two 40-watt 48-inch fluorescent tubes.

The fluorescent tubes need to be selected with the needs of plants in mind. Cool white fluorescents put out more blue light, and warm white fluorescents put out more red light. Combining the two in the same fixture gives a perfectly acceptable mix of wavelengths. It's what I use, and a good many farmers use it successfully.[39] There are also special tubes for fluorescent light fixtures that are specifically designed for growing plants or duplicating the sun's wavelengths— and these work well too but at a cost roughly six times higher than regular tubes and at a reduced light output. The thing to watch for with fluorescent lighting generally is light output, because plants need a lot of it. Go with the highest light output tubes that will fit in a 48-inch shop light fixture. Because the lights are used approximately five months out of the year, the tubes need to be

replaced only every other year. Replace them even if they look and work fine, because after being used for two years, their measurable light output will have declined.

The intensity of light decreases in inverse proportion to the square of the distance from the source. In other words, the further away the lights are, the less light the plants will get. Fluorescent tubes need to be set up so that they are only an inch or two above the seedlings for them to get enough light. Because plants grow, either the height of the lights or the bottom of the plants needs to be adjustable.

Plants need a combination of both light and darkness to complete their metabolic processes, so too much of either can be a bad thing. Because even closely spaced florescent lights are an imperfect substitute for true sunshine, the lights should be put on an inexpensive timer so seedlings get 16 hours of light and 8 hours of darkness every day.

Don't forget: Once seeds sprout, shine the light on them!

Temperature

Many publications provide various tables with all sorts of data about the optimum temperatures for germination of different garden seeds. For starting seeds in the house, almost all seeds normally used to start garden seedlings will germinate just fine at ordinary room temperatures. The only time temperature could become an issue is if the area used for seed starting regularly falls below 60 degrees or goes above 80.

If seed-starting operations get banished to the basement or garage where temperatures are routinely below 60 degrees, germination

[39] Murphy, W. (1978) *Gardening under Lights*

A heating mat is especially useful for peppers and tomatoes.

could definitely become a problem. The easiest solution for this situation is to use a heat mat (available at any agricultural supply store) underneath your flats that will raise the soil temperature about 20 degrees higher than the surrounding air.

Water

Seedlings should be bottom watered by placing their containers (which contain holes in the bottom or absorb water directly) in water and allowing the starting medium to evenly water itself by pulling up whatever water is needed. Seedlings are delicate and their roots are shallow, so top watering can disrupt and uncover the vulnerable roots.

It is important that the starting medium be kept moist, but not soaking, for the entire germination period. Once the germination process has begun and before the seedling emerges, allowing the seed to dry out will kill it. Most containers used for seedlings are too small to retain an appreciable amount of water; for this reason seedlings should stay uniformly damp (though not soggy) until transplanted.

Unfortunately, dampness can cause problems with mold growth. Often, such mold is harmless, but sometimes it isn't, and telling the difference before damage is done is difficult. If gray fuzz or similar molds appear on top of the seedling container, cut back the water a bit, and place the container in direct sunlight in a south-facing window for a few hours a day for two or three days. This should take care of such a problem.

Another cause of mold is the use of domes over top of seedling flats. These domes are advertised to create an environment "just like a greenhouse." In reality, they create an environment extremely conducive to mold, even in moderately cool temperatures. No matter how clean and sterile the starting medium, anytime I have ever used a dome on top of a seed flat, mold has developed within two or three days. I recommend that you do not use domes.

Fertilizer

As mentioned earlier, once seedlings have their first set of true leaves, they should be bottom watered with a half-strength solution of organic liquid fertilizer once every two weeks in addition to regular watering. Since starting medium is nutritionally poor, some fertilizer will be a benefit to the seedlings, but anything too concentrated can hurt the delicate developing root system and cause problems with mold. The only exception to this is soil blocks, which can contain enough nutrients that liquid fertilizer isn't needed because of their greater soil volume.

Hardening Off

A week or two before the intended transplant date, you may wish to start the process of "hardening off" the transplants; that is, the process of gradually acclimating the plants to the outdoor environment.

This generally means bringing the seedlings outside and exposing them to sun and wind for an hour the first day, progressing to all day on the last day of the hardening-off period, which lasts about a week before transplanting. The process of hardening off serves to make the transplants more hardy.

In my experience, hardening off makes little difference with plants that are transplanted after the last frost, but it does have an effect on the hardiness of plants that are transplanted before the last frost. It should be done with all transplants anyway, because there is no way to know with absolute certainty if an unusual weather event will occur. I've seen no case in which hardening off transplants has been harmful and numerous cases in which it has helped so it is a good general policy for a mini-farm in which maximum yields are important.

12

Selecting
and Saving Seed

The selection of seeds can seem like an overwhelming task, especially
if you are looking at a half dozen seed catalogs on a cold winter's day in
January. When I look at seed catalogs, my eyes get bigger than my belly,
and my mouth starts watering at each description of a different variety
of each plant. Pretty soon, I have checked off enough different kinds of
seeds that if I were to actually grow all of them, I would need a 600-acre
farm and an impressive staff of workers.

Seeds are a very compact form of material wealth. A single packet
of 30 tomato seeds that costs $2 can easily produce bushels and bushels
of tomatoes—enough to make salsa and spaghetti sauce for the family
for a year with leftovers to sell or give away. In addition, seeds, when
properly selected and saved, are an insurance policy against hard
times.

Anyone with limited space should be picky about seed selections in
terms of climate preferences, productivity per unit area, disease resistance, and taste preferences. And if you save seed from plants grown
the prior year, you will dramatically reduce the need to purchase seed.

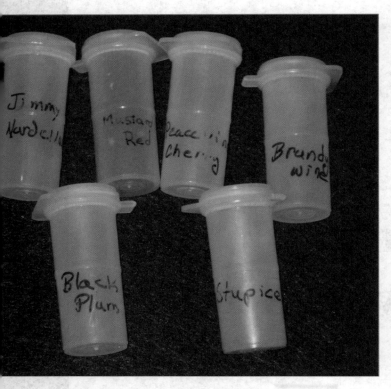

⊗ Home-saved seeds in airtight vials.

Explanation of Plant Varieties

There are two terms that will be used interchangeably in the remainder of this chapter and are used periodically throughout this book that need to be understood: *variety* and *cultivar*. In the sense in which I use the terms, they have the same meaning, but to explain what I mean, I have to get into a bit of biology.

Living things are categorized by biologists according to broad categories first and then into ever-finer categories. The broadest categories would be, for example, "plants" and "animals." The order of classification by plant scientists is kingdom, division, class, order, family, tribe, genus, and species. A variety is a subset of a species, and a cultivar is a cultivated variety.

The actual meaning of the word *species* is disputed even among scientists, but the generally accepted definition is that a species is made up of a population capable of interbreeding. Typically, two plants are considered to be members of the same species if they can interbreed and produce seeds that will grow plants that will also produce seeds. Thus cabbage, cauliflower, and broccoli are all members of the same species because they can interbreed with each other. However, there are certainly significant differences between these plants! The fact that two plants are members of the same species doesn't make them identical.

If you look through a seed catalog under "broccoli," you will find anywhere from 3 to 20 different types of broccoli. The sixth edition of the *Garden Seed Inventory* lists 32 different open-pollinated types of broccoli. These various types of broccoli have differences in taste, color, disease resistance, vitamin content,

Also, raised-bed practices don't sow seeds in a row too closely together and then go back and thin out half the plants—thus wasting the seeds—as the directions on the seed packet instruct. In intensive agriculture, each seed is planted individually at the optimal spacing the first time around—so not a single seed is wasted.

Thus, the seed orders placed by a mini-farmer after the second year of farming will likely be a small number of hybrid vegetables selected for a particular reason, a few plants for which saving seed was either too difficult or unsuccessful, and a handful of new crop varieties that the farmer wants to try out. The full order for a mini-farm that will feed a family of three plus generate optional replacement income will probably amount to only $100 worth of seeds plus shipping after the second year if the farmer saves seeds from annual vegetables.

how long they take to produce a broccoli stalk, and a host of other important characteristics. Each of the different types of broccoli is its own *variety*. Some food crops, like broccoli, have a very small number of varieties in existence, but others, like tomato, have over a thousand different varieties.

You might select a particular variety of a given crop for any number of reasons—taste, pest resistance, short season, and so on. This is what I am referring to when I talk about a plant variety. In open-pollinated varieties, the traits that distinguish one variety from another are reliably inherited from one generation to the next.

Existing plant varieties are the culmination of untold thousands of years of careful selection for various traits; new varieties are created in the same fashion all the time. Since plant characteristics are heritable, as a mini-farmer, you will have the ability to select the best-growing plants of a given variety as parents for new seeds, and over time you can end up creating your own specifically adapted plant varieties.

Selecting Plant Varieties

A mini-farmer needs four types of information to select plant varieties: local climate, available varieties, personal tastes, and plant spacing/yields. To this basic information you will eventually add your own experiences.

Local climate information can be found from the local agricultural extension service or from the Web site of the National Climatic Weather Center. The Web site Weather.com also has a section specifically for gardens. The idea is to find out the length of the local growing season, so that plant varieties can be selected that have enough

time to fully mature. A farmer in Virginia will have a much wider selection of appropriate corn and watermelon to choose from than a farmer in Vermont.

Because open-pollinated varieties of crops produce seeds that can be used to grow the same crop again the next year, they are a much better choice for mini-farmers. Seed can be saved from the most productive or hardy plants so that, over time, the open-pollinated variety that the farmer started with has been specifically adapted to that farm's climate and growing conditions. None of this is possible with interbred hybrids, which don't produce reusable seed, making open-pollinated seeds the better default choice of the farmer.

The matter of hybrids has been oversimplified a bit. Given a few years of careful selection and adequate space, it is possible with many (though not all) hybrids to convert them into a new true-to-type open-pollinated variety that preserves the desired traits of the hybrid but allows for saving seeds. For details on how to do this, see Carol Deppe's excellent book *How to Breed Your Own Vegetable Varieties*.

There are also some cases in which hybrids provide a significant advantage over otherwise equivalent open-pollinated varieties; corn is probably the best example. The difference in productivity between hybrid and open-pollinated corn can be huge, with the hybrid producing considerably more, and when a farmer is raising food in a very small area, differences in productivity make a difference. There are also instances in which hybrid plants incorporate traits such as disease resistance, and using a hybrid variety can save the farmer from needing to use fungicides on the crops. Outside of such cases, the overwhelming preponderance of a farmer's crops should be open-pollinated.

The good news about open-pollinated seeds is that they have become increasingly popular and are available from a number of companies at good prices. The Seed Saver's Exchange publishes a book called *Garden Seed Inventory* that describes and lists all of the open-pollinated varieties available for every garden plant along with commercial sources for every plant listed. The Seed Saver's Exchange is also a membership organization ($35/year) in which members make thousands of varieties of homegrown seeds available to each other at modest cost via two annually published compendiums provided to members.

A list of seed companies with whom I have had good experiences is provided at the end of this book, but use it as a starting place rather than a limitation. The open-pollinated seed business is very competitive, and excellent service is the rule rather than the exception. Most seed companies provide free written catalogs and Web sites containing a wealth of valuable information.

An important aspect of selecting seeds is the need for experimentation. There are hundreds of varieties of peas, beans, carrots, and other crops available, and each variety will perform differently because of climatic and soil differences as well as genetic variations that affect flavor. It is good to set aside a small area just for experimenting with new crop varieties and keep careful notes of the results.

Selecting Parents

Since many important characteristics of a plant variety are hereditary, it makes sense to save seeds from plants that do best in your own environment and to avoid saving seeds from plants that do poorly. This is most reliable when dealing with self-pollinating, plants, as both the mother and the father of the seed are known. For insect- or wind-pollinated plants, though, only the mother is known. Even so, it is better to know that at least one of the parent plants was superior.

The problem of unknown parentage can be dealt with by culling inferior-performing plants before they are mature enough to pollinate or by using hand pollination to ensure that both parents are known. Either way, by selecting parentage, the farmer constantly increases the seed pool in quality and productivity.

Saving Seeds

As previously noted, one of the advantages of open-pollinated seeds is that they can be saved so that the need to purchase seeds each year is reduced. Like anything else, there are costs and benefits that the farmer has to consider, and in all likelihood you will end up saving seeds from some crops but not others. A mini-farm exists as a way to produce food rather than an exercise in seed saving. Some seeds, like tomato and pepper, can be saved with minimal effort or inconvenience while others such as cauliflower will require significant efforts and land.

If the production and sale of seeds is something you are interested in, then extraordinary efforts to save seed are worthwhile. Outside of that, if buying a packet of seed for $1.50 saves hours of effort and tying up land that would otherwise be productive, it makes sense to buy the seeds. You will need to make that determination on the basis of your own circumstances and interests.

Saving seeds is a broad enough topic that entire books have been written on this subject alone. The gist, though, is straightforward: Nature mandates that plants reproduce themselves, and plants procreate by producing seeds. If these seeds are saved and replanted, they will re-create the original plant.

There are three major sets of plant attributes that affect seed saving. The first is whether the plant is annual, biennial, or perennial. Annual plants produce seed every year and are planted newly each year. Biennial plants require two years in the ground to produce seed. Perennial plants will continue to grow from year to year but often produce seed annually. Second is whether the plant is predominantly self-pollinating or predominantly cross-pollinating. Cross-pollinators require pollen from another plant to make seed, while strongly self-pollinating plants may fertilize their own flowers before the flowers even open! This attribute exists on a continuum with beans, for example, being almost exclusively self-pollinated and corn being exclusively cross-pollinated. Finally, the actual seeds will require either dry processing or wet processing, depending on the nature of the fruit. Spinach seeds are dry like grains and will be processed differently from tomato seeds immersed in fluid.

These attributes ultimately determine how much effort and land the farmer has to invest to produce seed. Biennials require overwintering and, especially north of Maryland, special attention so that they live through the winter. Plants that are predominantly cross-pollinating require a fairly large population, sometimes as many as 400 plants, to avoid a phenomenon known as "inbreeding depression" in which seed produced from an insufficient quantity of parent plants exhibits progressively decreased vigor and productivity. Seed processing generally, whether wet or dry, can require a fair amount of time. Table 16 lists the seed-saving characteristics of a number of common crops.

Saving seed from biennial plants presents difficulties for the mini-farmer whose every square foot of garden bed is important, and also because plants that are wintered-over in the garden complicate crop rotation schedules and the use of cover crops. Luckily, most biennial plants flower and set seed early in spring so they are out of the way in time for summer planting.

A good compromise for farmers who wish to raise their own biennial seeds is to set aside one or two beds for the specific purpose of producing seed. Such beds can be protected over the winter with a hoop tunnel such as the one described in chapter 13.

Inbreeding Depression and Genetic Diversity

In Table 16 is a column labeled "Min #." This signifies, for outbreeding/crossing plants, the minimum number of plants of that variety that must be grown together to avoid inbreeding depression.

For those plants that are self-pollinating, the number in that column (followed by an asterisk) represents the minimum number of plants from which seed should be saved to preserve a good cross-section of the gene pool for that particular variety. These numbers represent the plant populations used in commercial seed production. If the seed is being produced for home use, there is generally little harm in reducing the population by 25% or even 50%.

Isolation Distance

For seed production, it is important to observe the minimum isolation distances given in Table 16. These distances are for producing seed for home use. For commercial distribution, the distances would be greater in many cases. These isolation distances specify the minimum distance that a plant has to be from another plant of the same species but a different variety to keep the two from interbreeding and producing seeds that won't duplicate either plant. At first glance, this looks easier than it actually is for the following reason.

On a farm that occupies less than a quarter acre, all of the plants are within 100 feet of each other, meaning that for purposes of seed saving, there won't be enough isolation distance available to grow more than one variety of a given species without using isolation cages or other special seed-saving techniques to prevent interbreeding. This isn't a problem with self-pollinators like peas, beans, and tomatoes but can pose a real challenge with squash, spinach, or corn.

Isolation by Time

Some brassica family plants, like broccoli, are annual while others, like cauliflower, are biennial. This means that isolation between the two can be based on timing as broccoli will have long since made its seed before cauliflower flowers the following spring. The same technique can be used if the time of flowering is different for two varieties of the same species because of differences in maturation rates. Orchestrating this sort of isolation would be somewhat delicate but certainly possible.

Another method for the farmer dedicated to saving seeds is to make use of the fact that many seeds retain their viability (ability to sprout and grow a healthy plant) for a number of years and therefore don't need to be grown for seed each year. Cucumber seeds, for example, will remain viable for at least five years if stored properly. You could grow a different variety of cucumber each year for three years and save the seed from each variety. Then, on the fourth year, grow the same variety that you grew the first year. That way you are maintaining the seeds for three different varieties of cucumbers without having to do anything exotic to keep the varieties from interbreeding.

Barrier Isolation

Barrier isolation is the practice of using a physical barrier to keep flowers from one plant from pollinating another. The two methods most practiced are alternate-day caging and hand pollination.

Alternate-day caging is done by building cages out of fine window screen or floating row cover that will fit over the plants—two varieties of carrots, for example. On the first day, one variety is covered with a cage, and on the second day, the other variety is covered. This allows insects to pollinate both without cross-pollinating them.

Hand pollination is easiest on plants with large flowers—like cucumbers and squash—but can be done on many other plants given a sufficiently steady hand. Hand pollination is made easy with members of the squash and cucumber family because of the fact that they grow large male and female flowers separately. A bag is used to protect the female flower from undesirable pollen until it is hand pollinated using a male flower of the farmer's choosing. The female flower is protected with a bag again until it is no longer receptive to pollen, and that fruit is marked for seed usage. If female flowers are caught before they first open, hand pollination can be very successful at maintaining purity even in instances where multiple varieties of the same species are grown.

Dry Processing

Seeds that are naturally dry—such as those of spinach and wheat—are processed to separate the seeds from other plant materials by screening and winnowing. Screening is done with a screen selected for a mesh size that allows the seeds through but nothing larger. (Southern Exposure Seed Exchange sells screens that are presized for particular types of seeds.) This eliminates the larger debris. Debris smaller than the seeds is removed by winnowing. Winnowing can be accomplished by pouring the seeds from one container to another in front of a stiff breeze or a fan. Lighter materials get blown away, and seeds get preserved. (Getting good at this takes practice!)

Some dry seeds require threshing to be saved in appreciable quantities. Threshing is a technique that uses physical force to break away the pods surrounding the seeds and can be accomplished in a number of creative ways. Traditionally, farmers used a flail resembling a set of nunchakus for this task. The plants requiring threshing would be placed in a sturdy sack, and then the sack would be beaten with the flail and all the seeds would end up in the bottom of the bag. Another common technique is to place the plants to be threshed on a tarp, put another tarp on top so the plants are sandwiched in between, and then walk around on them.

Melons, winter squash, and green peppers are wet fruit, but their seeds can be saved like dry seeds by washing them in water to remove any traces of pulp and then drying before storage.

Wet Processing

For plants whose seeds are embedded in damp flesh, studies have shown that the viability of the seeds is highest if the fruit is allowed to become a bit more than fully ripe before harvesting.

Such wet seeds will also benefit from fermentation processing. In fermentation processing, the seeds and pulp are scraped into a glass container—a clean pint jar for example—and about half that volume of tap water is added to the jar. Swirl and mix, then cover the container and put it in a warm place. Three days later, the contents of the container have grown a rather disgusting mold, and the good seeds have sunk to the bottom. The seeds that have sunk to the bottom are removed, washed, and dried.

Fermentation is not strictly necessary, but studies indicate that this sort of processing mimics natural processes and has been demonstrated to reduce the incidence of diseases in the seeds.

Storing Seeds

The length of time that seeds are viable depends on how you store them, and this applies to both purchased seeds and homegrown seeds. The two most important factors affecting the longevity of seeds are heat and moisture.

Studies have demonstrated that between the temperatures of 32 degrees F and 112 degrees F, the time that a seed is viable *doubles* for every

Table 16: **Seed Characteristics**

Plant	Annual/ Biennial	Wet or Dry	Pollinator	Min #	Years Viable	Isolation Distance
Asparagus	Perennial	Dry	Insects	10		1,200'
Beans	Annual	Dry	Self	20*	2–3	150'
Beets	Biennial	Dry	Wind/cross	25	3–5	1,200'
Broccoli	Annual	Dry	Insects/cross	50	3–5	300'
Brussels sprouts	Biennial	Dry	Insects/cross	50	3–5	300'
Cabbage	Biennial	Dry	Insects/cross	50	3–5	300'
Carrots	Biennial	Dry	Insects/cross	75	2–3	1,200'
Cauliflower	Biennial	Dry	Insects/cross	100	3–5	300'
Celery	Biennial	Dry	Insects/cross	25	2–3	1,200'
Chives	Perennial	Dry	Insects/cross	20	1	1,200'
Corn	Annual	Dry	Wind/cross	200	2–3	500'
Cucumber	Annual	Wet	Insects/cross	25	5–10	500'
Eggplant	Annual	Wet	Self	20*	2–3	10'
Kale	Biennial	Dry	Insects/cross	50	3–5	300'
Leek	Biennial	Dry	Insects/cross	20	2	1,200'
Lettuce	Annual	Dry	Self	12	2–3	20'
Melons	Annual	Dry	Insects/cross	25	5–10	500'
Onion	Biennial	Dry	Insects/cross	30	1	1,200'
Parsley	Biennial	Dry	Insects/cross	25	2–3	1,200'
Parsnip	Biennial	Dry	Insects/cross	75	2–3	1,200'
Pea	Annual	Dry	Self	20*	2–3	20'
Peppers	Annual	Dry	Self/cross	10*	2–3	20'
Pumpkin	Annual	Dry	Insects/cross	25	2–5	500'
Radish	Annual	Dry	Insects/cross	75	3–5	500'
Soybean	Annual	Dry	Self	20*	2–3	200'
Spinach	Annual	Dry	Wind	75	2–3	1,200'
Squash	Annual	Wet	Insects/cross	25	2–5	500'
Tomato	Annual	Wet	Self	20*	5–10	10'
Turnip	Annual	Dry	Insects/cross	25	3–5	1,200'

9 degrees F that the temperature is lowered.[40] The moisture content of the seeds is also important, as similar studies have shown that an increase in seed moisture of as little as 5% to 10% can reduce seed viability more rapidly than increasing the temperature from 68 degrees F to 104 degrees F.[41] (Seed banks store seeds in chest freezers at below-freezing temperatures. For home seed

---

[40] Bubel, N. (1988) *The New Seed Starter's Handbook* p. 204

[41] Ibid p. 205

⊗ Tools for properly drying seeds for storage.

savers, storing seeds at temperatures below freezing is unusual because the moisture level of the seed must be carefully controlled to keep such cold temperatures from damaging the seed.)

Therefore, keep seeds cool and dry. This is easy to accomplish using moisture-indicating silica gel, small muslin bags like those used for spices, and mason jars with sealing tops. Moisture-indicating silica gel and the small muslin bags can be purchased from the Southern Exposure Seed Exchange. When dry, moisture-indicating silica gel is blue, and when damp it is pink. Once it becomes pink, put it on some aluminum foil on a pan in the oven on the lowest setting and gently heat it until it turns uniformly blue again. It can be reused indefinitely, so it's a good investment.

Place the seeds to be stored in a mason jar either within paper seed packets or not, because the seed packets pass moisture readily. (You might do this with commercial seed packets you received in the mail, just to make sure they are properly dehydrated before storage.) Put two or three tablespoons of moisture-indicating silica gel in a drawstring muslin bag and put it in the jar with the seeds and seal. A week later, remove the bag containing silica gel from the jar, reseal, and place the jar in a cool basement or a refrigerator. If you use this method, your seeds should remain viable for a long time, and your investment in either purchased seeds or the personal effort of saving seeds is protected.

13

Season Extension

While season extension isn't an absolute necessity for the mini-farmer, it has some advantages. The most obvious is that season extension will allow you to grow warm season crops like sweet potatoes that require more growing days than available in your area, but there are other less obvious advantages.

A simple, unheated hoop house, constructed with two layers of plastic, will allow many crops, such as parsnips and carrots, to be stored in the ground rather than harvested in fall. It will also allow many biennial plants, such as cabbage, to successfully overwinter for purposes of seed production. Finally, it will allow you to grow many cold-hardy crops for sale or consumption, such as spinach and other salad greens. Along with these more practical benefits comes the psychological value (for us northeastern farmers) that such a structure will have in midwinter when the inviting growing foliage can be seen inside against a backdrop of dismal snow.

There are a lot of approaches to season extension ranging from simple cold frames to fancy heated greenhouses with specialized glass and framing. The approach to this, as with everything else in mini-farming, is economic.

Cold frames are simple, four-sided rectangles that are open on the bottom and sloped on the top and oriented so that the downward end of the slope faces the sun. Usually, they are covered with old windows, so they can be made cheaply. The only heat provided is that of the sun, so they can be placed just about anywhere. A cold frame will provide a temperature about 20 degrees warmer than the outside air during the day but will drop to within 5 degrees of outside temperature overnight unless it is well insulated or has provisions for heat retention. If raised beds are used, cold frames can easily be made to fit.

Hotbeds are cold frames that have a mechanism for heating built in. A couple of hundred years ago, hotbeds were made by digging a pit three feet deep, filling it to within six inches of the top with fresh horse manure that would provide heat as it composted and then covering that with six inches of regular garden soil in which crops were planted. More modern hotbeds use either buried heating cables underneath where the plants grow or pipes carrying warm water. Obviously, hotbeds keep crops warmer than cold frames, but the amount of warmth they provide varies with design.

⊗ A cold frame can extend the season by several weeks.

The unheated hoop house is a simple skeleton framework of hoops covered with the kind of plastic that folks in the northern parts of the United States use to cover their windows during the winter. Because it holds a far greater volume of air, it will tend to provide more warmth than a cold frame. There are a number of hoop house kits available from companies such as Hoop House Greenhouse Kits (www.hoophouse.com), and the most expensive of these cost less than $1,000. For farmers who are handy, there are also a number of free plans available on the Internet, including an easily built and inexpensive structure designed by Travis Saling viewable at westsidegardener.com. The pvcplans.com Web site has a number of free plans available describing how to make greenhouses from PVC pipe.

The idea of an unheated environment that gets all of its heat from the sun can be taken further to create a solar greenhouse. Unlike a hoop house, which is translucent on all sides, a solar greenhouse is translucent only on the side facing the sun, and the other sides are insulated to retain heat while drums of water painted black sit against the back wall creating a solar mass. Portions of the back wall are often reflective to put more light onto the plants. A solar greenhouse is certainly more expensive to construct than a hoop house, but it has the advantage of having smaller ongoing operational costs than a traditional greenhouse because it doesn't use supplemental heating.

Either a hoop house or a solar greenhouse can be made into a heated greenhouse by adding supplemental heat. Supplemental heat can be provided by a heating appliance of practically any type compatible with your budget.

What to Grow

The decision on what to grow decides the design of the season extension adopted, rather than the other way around. Miner's lettuce grows only a couple of inches tall, so it will work fine in a cold frame, but kale is so tall that a hoop house would be required. Winter-hardy crops like spinach and kale don't require supplemental heat, lettuce would require only a little, and tender crops like tomatoes would require a considerable amount. Especially with increasing fuel costs, it is important to consider whether growing frost-tender crops like tomatoes in the winter makes economic sense, and most often it does not.

I recommend growing hardy crops using no supplemental heat or semihardy crops using just enough supplemental heat to prevent freezing. Under such conditions, growth of crops is slow, and it is best to establish them late in the summer or early in the fall so that by the time winter hits, the season extender is serving mainly to extend the harvest rather than actively grow crops.

So what crops are suitable for this purpose? Carrots, parsnips, and parsley will do well in a hoop house or cold frame. Both parsnips and carrots started at midsummer will taste sweet come January. Salsify planted just at the first fall frost can be harvested a bit past Yule. Many leaf lettuces will grow, though their outer leaves may sustain some damage. (Try the Winter Density variety.) Beets will hold in the ground in a cold frame, and chard may grow if you are south of Pennsylvania. Kale will hold well and even grow, as will Brussels sprouts and green onions or leeks. (The American Flag variety of leek will work well.) Both Brunswick and January King cabbage can be harvested around New Year's if planted midsummer.

There are a few particularly cold-hardy crops ideal for season extension, including miner's lettuce, corn salad (a.k.a. "mache"), italian dandelion, wintercress, and purslane. While these are unusual, they are a real taste-treat that adds character to winter salads.

Besides winter crops, an unheated hoop house can also help the farmer get a head start on spring season crops and even extend the season long enough to grow crops or varieties that would otherwise be impossible, such as the aforementioned sweet potatoes in the Northeast. A hoop house also expands the possibilities for cover crops and green manures because of the change in environment.

Special Considerations

A hoop house, cold frame, or hotbed is inherently protected from precipitation. The good news is water is completely in the farmer's control. The bad news is the lack of rainfall will tend to concentrate salts in the soil in the protected area, which will hurt plant growth. It takes three or four years for this to happen, but it is still a problem. Another problem with a more permanent structure is that the space within it can accumulate pests and diseases. Especially since pests have nowhere to go, the enclosed area can cancel some of the benefits of crop rotation within that space.

The most space-efficient way to handle this is to make the structure easily erected and dismantled, and dismantle it late every spring. For more permanent greenhouse designs, the plastic can be removed during the late spring through early fall, which would have the same effect. For large structures, such as 90-foot-long greenhouses, it is obviously too time-consuming, but for structures of the size usually employed in a mini-farm, it is will be feasible if they are designed with easy maintenance in mind.

Larger farms in Europe and the United States have movable greenhouses on rails that are rolled from one location to another with each season to accommodate growing needs and diminish the problems of a permanent standing structure. This may be a bit beyond the needs of a mini-farmer, but it can be accomplished with a little ingenuity and moderate expense by a farmer who is so inclined.

Improving Greenhouse Efficiency

An unheated hoop house can do a great deal to extend the growing season, but a few simple modifications at very low cost can dramatically improve the light and heat utilization of such a structure.

In the winter when the sun is low in the sky, a good proportion of the light that hits a hoop house will enter the south side and exit the north side without ever touching a plant.

If a reflective sheet is installed along the entire north wall up to the ridge pole, light that would otherwise escape will get reflected back onto the plants, thus increasing the light available to the plants and raising the temperature. A good material for this purpose is reflective insulation, available inexpensively from most home improvement stores. Not only will the aluminum surface of the insulation reflect light, but it will also reflect 97% of radiant heat that would have escaped through the plastic back into the hoop house.

The next modification is to add a method of heat retention. A simple hoop house will lose temperature quickly after sunset, and one way to slow down the temperature drop is to line up a number of black-painted barrels against the north wall of the hoop house—though not actually touching the reflective insulation—and fill them with water. The drums of water will absorb the heat from the sunlight during the day and then radiate that heat back into the hoop house at night. The value of this approach is enhanced by the addition of the reflective insulation because the radiant heat gets reflected back into the enclosed space from all directions. Barrels can be emptied and moved anytime the greenhouse is moved, or they can be used for raising fish, with exchanged water being used as nitrogen-rich liquid fertilizer. (Yes, fish *can* be raised in a barrel using the technology of *aquaculture*, but aquaculture isn't covered in this book.)

So, what happens if there is no sun for a week and the water drums freeze? South of Connecticut, this is unlikely to be a problem, but it is a possibility further north. You may need to abandon using barrels or abandon the simple hoop house design altogether and build a solar greenhouse. There are a number of solar greenhouse designs available on the Internet. What they all have in common is significant insulation (R-30) everywhere but in the windows that face south and reflective coating on all interior walls.

Portable Hoops for Raised Beds

Raised beds lend themselves to easily constructed and inexpensive attachments for season extension, particularly if constructed with a width of four feet. The easiest attachments are cold frames mentioned earlier and portable hoops.

⊗ Loops on the frame of a raised bed.

Raised beds can be equipped to accept portable hoops by attaching 1-inch rings to the outside of the beds at the ends and every two feet.

The portable hoops are made from 10-foot-long pieces of 1/2-inch PVC pipe that have been cut in half for ease of storage. To build the hoops, the two 5-foot pieces of PVC are connected via a straight coupling, and then each end is inserted into one of the 1-inch rings on each side of the bed. The hoops are covered with translucent plastic sheeting 10 feet wide available at any hardware store. The plastic can be secured at the long edges by sandwiching it between 1-inch × 2-inch boards so it can be easily rolled up and deployed, or it can by secured with homemade snap clips made by slicing pieces of garden hose lengthwise. Which technique will work best depends on the strength of prevailing winds in your area.

⊗ Insert the PVC pipes into the loops.

⊗ Completed hoop house.

14

Fruit Trees and Vines

Fruit trees and vines can provide an enormous amount of food compared to the effort invested. Many fruit and nut trees produce, literally, bushels of fruits or nuts, and some blackberry variants produce gallons of berries per vine. Unfortunately, even though berries may even produce in their first or second season, full-sized fruit and nut trees take several years to come into production and may produce nothing at all for the first few years. Dwarf trees will normally produce fruit within three years, but the volume of fruit they produce is lower.

To offset this problem, diversify! If possible, in the year preceding the start of your mini-farm, plant a small section with berry and perhaps some grape vines for the next year's harvest. Along with these, plant dwarf fruit trees and some full-sized nut trees. In this way, the harvest starts modestly with berries the first year and expands to include dwarf cherries the next year, dwarf apples the year after that, and so on. Within seven years, the farmer is producing enough fruit and nuts for the family plus some surplus.

Fruits are full of idiosyncrasies in terms of disease and pest problems, pruning requirements, suitable climate, and so on. This is particularly true of vinifera grapes, apples, peaches, and other popular fruits. I recommend reading as widely as possible about the fruits you plan to grow and selecting hardy varieties specific to your area, using a reputable nursery, and trying to purchase varieties that are resistant to expected diseases.

I recommend St. Lawrence Nurseries in Potsdam, New York, but there are other reputable nurseries as well. An invaluable Internet resource at the time of this writing is Garden Watchdog, at www.davesgarden.com. Garden Watchdog has a listing for almost every company in the gardening business and a list of feedback from customers along with ratings. Check out any mail-order nurseries with Garden Watchdog before ordering.

In addition to ordering high-quality trees that are likely to be less susceptible to problems, you should work proactively to keep pest problems minimal by making sure plants that attract beneficial insects are already established where the trees will be planted. Most notably, this means clover. Clover attracts insects that feast on the most tenacious pests of apple-family trees and fruits such as codling moths, apple maggots, and plum curculios. The exact type of clover to be planted will vary with the condition of the soil, expected temperatures, and expected precipitation. A good resource for selecting the right variety of clover is a comprehensive organic gardening catalog like that from Peaceful Valley Farm Supply.

Plant trees in the spring, and spray them for the first time in the fall with dormant oil that smothers and controls overwintering insects. The following spring spray the trees with a lighter horticultural oil in spring when the buds have swelled but not yet blossomed. Also spray them with either a lime sulfur or organic copper-based fungicide according to label directions every spring after their first year. Traps for common problem insects such as codling moths or apple maggots should be set out and maintained at a high enough density to trap out all of the males of the species.

Fruits and nuts often have specific pollination requirements that make it necessary to plant more than one tree. Sometimes the trees have to be of slightly different variants because trees of the same variety were propagated by grafting and are therefore genetically identical and self-sterile. A few nurseries sell trees propagated from seed rather than grafting, and these trees will pollinate each other without issue even if the same variety. Be sure to pay attention to catalog information and ask questions of the nursery staff to avoid later disappointment!

Pruning will be necessary to maximize the productive potential of the trees. There are many schools of thought on the subject of pruning, and numerous weighty tomes have been written, but the basics are easily described.

Blackberries and Raspberries

Cane fruits, like raspberries and blackberries, grow long and heavy enough that the tips of the canes touch the ground—where they then set a new root and grow more new canes. This isn't necessarily desirable, as it leads to an ever-expanding impenetrable thorny mess, so it is best to trellis the canes to prevent this. The easiest trellising for cane fruits is a four-foot-tall "T" at each end of the row of canes with galvanized wire run from each end of the T along the

⊗ Raspberries are nutritious and easy to grow.

should be *topped* during their first year of growth, meaning they should have their tops cut off just about 4 inches above the trellis. This will cause them to send out lateral shoots so that when they bear fruit the next year, they will bear more abundantly.[42] The lateral shoots should be trimmed to 12 inches to 18 inches.

The same general technique applies to raspberries, with some minor changes. Yellow and red raspberries shouldn't be topped, and the laterals that form on purple and black raspberries should be trimmed to just 10 inches. Ever-bearing raspberry varieties fruit in the late summer of the primocane stage and then again in the early summer of the floricane stage. After the early summer fruiting, the floricanes should be removed. The easiest way to distinguish floricanes in ever-bearing raspberries is that the first-year fruit is on the top of the cane and the second-year fruit is at the bottom.[43]

Grapes

Grapes can be divided into three general varieties: European, American, and muscadine. European grape varieties (*Vitis vinifera*) are vulnerable to a nasty pest called phylloxera, which is a tiny louselike insect that causes all sorts of problems, especially in the eastern United States. Muscadine grapes, native to the southern United States, can be successfully grown only south of Maryland because of their climate requirements. Other American grape varieties are naturally resistant to phylloxera and can be grown

length of the row. The wire holds up the canes so they don't touch the ground, and new canes are trained to stay behind the wire. This makes the berries easy to pick as well.

Blackberries are pruned by distinguishing between *primocanes* and *floricanes*. Primocanes are canes in their first year that bear leaves but no flowers or fruit. Floricanes are those same canes in their second year, when they bear flowers and fruit. After a cane has fruited, it slowly dies, so fruiting canes should be cut out and removed once their fruiting season has passed. Primocanes

⊗ This sort of T-trellis is easily made and works well

3-1/2'

4'

---

[42] Strik, B. (1993) *Growing Blackberries in Your Home Garden* Oregon State University

[43] Lockwood, D. (1999) *Pruning Raspberries and Blackberries in Home Gardens*

practically anywhere in the continental United States. For varietal wine production, scion wood of European grape varieties is often grafted onto American variety root stocks to reduce their vulnerability to phylloxera.

Since grape vines are expensive and can last for decades, it is important to pick a grape variety appropriate for your local climate. Check a reputable vendor for recommendations. All grape varieties can be used to produce jams, jellies, raisins, and wines for home use. Grapes do best in *moderately* fertile soil because soil as

⊗ Properly pruned grape vines yield good crops.

fertile as that in a vegetable garden will cause the leaves to grow so quickly and in such volume that the fruit will be shaded by the leaves, which will keep them damp and increase the likelihood of disease.

It is possible to start a grape vine in the fall, but odds of success are far greater if it is started in the spring because that gives the transplant more time to get established and store energy in its root system for overwintering.

When you first bring home a grape vine, it will likely have numerous shoots coming out of the root system. Cut off all of the shoots but the strongest one, then cut that one back to only three or four buds. Plant the vine in well-drained soil in a locale with plenty of sun, and water thoroughly. Pretty soon new shoots will emerge at the buds, plus some more from the roots. Cut off the ones that emerge from the roots, and once the new shoots from the buds have grown to about 12 inches, select the best and strongest of these and cut off the others. The best shoot will be pretty much upright. Drive a strong stake into the ground close to the plant, and throughout the summer keep the shoot tied nice and straight to that stake.

Meanwhile, set up your training and trellising system. There are many types, but about the easiest is the Kniffin system using two horizontal galvanized steel wires at three feet and six feet from the ground tied to two strong posts secured in the ground.

The first spring a year after planting, take the chosen shoot (which should have grown to a length somewhat taller than the bottom wire), and select the two strongest lateral shoots and tie those to the bottom wire while continuing to tie the growing trunk vertically to the stake.

Later in the season, once the growing trunk has grown to slightly below or slightly above the top wire, cut it off there and select the two strongest lateral shoots to tie to the top horizontal wires.

Occasionally, the chosen shoot that will serve as the trunk won't put out lateral shoots the first year. If that occurs—it's no big deal. Grape vines are vigorous and forgiving, so if a mistake is made in one year, it can always be corrected the next year. Just take the main shoot that serves as the trunk once it is slightly above the first wire, and tie it to one side of the wire and trim it back to three or four buds. These will form shoots. Select the two strongest of these—one of which will be run horizontally in the opposite direction on the wire, and the other of which will be run vertically up the stake and handled as detailed previously.

Ongoing pruning will be important to maintain fruit production because grapes produce on the shoots that come from one-year-old wood. So any shoots that arise from wood that is more than one year old won't bear fruit. That means that the horizontal shoots selected the first year should be removed for the second year and new shoots from the trunk trained along the wires.

⊘ The Kniffin system is one of the easiest for training grapes.

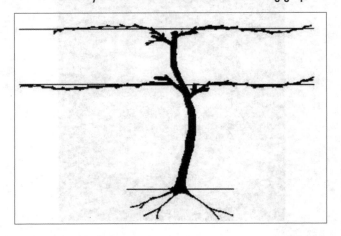

The foregoing is not the final word on grape pruning and training, as many other systems are available to those desiring more information—but this should be enough to get you started.

Grapes are prone to black rot and botrytis fungus, as well as birds and deer. Because of the rot and fungal problems, it is important to avoid sprinkler irrigation of grapes and practice good sanitation by consistently removing old fruit and leaves at the end of each season. A copper-based fungicide applied at bloom time is most effective against rot and fungus.[44]

On a small scale, birds and deer can be foiled with netting; on a larger scale, some creativity (such as noisemakers and fencing) will be required. I grow my grapes far away from everything else, and the birds and deer haven't found them so far!

Strawberries

Very few fruits are as prolific and easy to grow in limited space as strawberries. Moreover, because of their delicate nature, they are expensive to ship long distances, so they sell well in season if you decide to market them. Beds are easy to establish and require minimal maintenance on the scale of a mini-farm.

Strawberries come in three basic types: spring-bearing, ever-bearing, and day-neutral. The spring-bearing variety produces a single crop; the ever-bearing variety produces crops in spring, summer, and fall; and the day-neutral strawberry produces fruit throughout the season. Spring-bearing varieties can be early season, middle season, or late season, meaning that through

44 Baugher, T. et al. (1990) *Growing Grapes in West Virginia*

⊗ Strawberries do extremely well in raised beds.

careful selection of more than one spring-bearing variety, it is possible to extend the length of harvest substantially. Consider the intended use of the strawberries—preservation or fresh eating—in selecting varieties for either a continuous small crop or one or more larger harvests.

Strawberry plants can be spread either through seeds or through plants and runners. The best bet in most cases is to buy strawberry plants of known characteristics and then let them spread by runners. Runners are a long stem that emerges from the crown of the strawberry plant and establishes a new crown and root system wherever it contacts suitable earth. Simply place the runners where they will fill in the gaps in your planting—no more than four strawberry plants per square foot.

Strawberries should be well fertilized with compost and any needed organic amendments and be mulched with straw or fallen leaves after the last frost. They occasionally fall prey to botrytis blight, a gray mold that can grow on the berries. To keep this controlled, keep the beds clear of debris, make sure strawberries are harvested when ripe or slightly underripe, and spray with an organic fixed-copper fungicide as needed.

Apples and Pears

Apples and pears are the quintessential home fruit trees and can be grown in almost any part of the United States. A wide selection of modern and heirloom varieties are available that are suitable for fresh eating, preservation, and pies.

Apples and pears offered in nurseries are usually produced by grafting the scion wood of the desired variety onto a more hardy compatible rootstock, such as that of flowering crab. The original rootstock can produce shoots below the graft (known as "suckers"), and these should be trimmed as soon as they are spotted.

Apples and pears should be pruned and trained when they are quite young or else they will become difficult to manage and produce inferior fruit. The objective of training the tree is to provide optimal air circulation and sunlight

⊗ Pears are a bit easier than apples to keep pest free.

while keeping the fruit low enough to the ground so that it can be picked without a crane.

It is easiest for a mini-farmer is to select dwarf or semidwarf trees from the beginning. This will reduce pruning requirements and make maintenance easier and safer. Ideally, the tree will be pruned so that the shape is similar to a Christmas tree, which will allow maximum penetration of sunlight and easiest spraying while keeping the greatest bulk of the fruit closest to the ground.

A large number of articles on the specifics of pruning and training pomme fruits are available, but it isn't hard to master if a few rules are followed. (Apples, pears, and quinces are collectively referred to as *pomme fruits*. The word *pomme* comes from the French word for *apple*.)

When the young tree is first planted, tie it to a straight, eight-foot-long stake driven at least three feet into the soil for strength, cut off any limbs that are larger than 50% of the diameter of the trunk, and trim the trunk back to a height of three feet. Branches are strongest when they leave the trunk at an angle between 60 and 75 degrees, so when the branches are young, it is easy to bring them back to that angle by tying them with string or inserting small pieces of wood between the branch and the trunk. The branches on trees will tend to grow toward the sun, so that tendency will have to be countered the same way because you want the tree to grow straight and well balanced.

Subsequent pruning is best done in late winter or very early spring. The first spring after planting, remove any limbs closer to the ground than two feet and any limbs that are larger than 50% of the diameter of the trunk. If the tree has developed more than seven limbs, select the seven best distributed around the tree to be saved, and prune the rest. It is important when a limb is pruned that it be pruned back all the way to the trunk, otherwise it will sprout a bunch of vertically growing wood and create troubles. Once the pruning is done, limbs that need it should be tied or fitted with spacers to get the right angle to the trunk.

Beware of cutting off just the tips of the remaining limbs, because this can delay fruiting. Once the tree has been fruiting for a couple of years, such cuts can be used sparingly for shaping, but it is better to solve shading problems by removing entire limbs.

For all following years use the same rules by aiming for a well-balanced upright tree without excessive shading.

Stone Fruits

Stone fruits include cherries, apricots, peaches, plums, and nectarines. Because most stone fruits are native to warm climates and are thus susceptible to problems from winter injury or frost killing the flowers in the spring, it is important to carefully select varieties suitable for your area by consulting with a knowledgeable seller with a good reputation. No matter what cultivar is selected, it should be planted in an area protected from wind and with good sunshine and drainage. It is best to select a one-year-old tree five or six feet tall with good root growth.

Like apples and pears, stone fruits can be grafted onto dwarfing rootstocks. Unfortunately, none of the dwarf varieties grow well north of Pennsylvania.[45] The good news is that a number of hardy stone fruit varieties native to North America are available. The bush cherry (*Prunus*

---

[45] Pennsylvania State University (2001) *Small Scale Fruit Production: A Comprehensive Guide* http://ssfruit.cas.psu.edu/chapter5/chapter5h.htm

⊗ Nectarines are easy to grow and easy to can or freeze.

besseyi), American wild plum (*Prunus americana*), and American beach plum (*Prunus maritima*) can be grown throughout the continental United States, and Indian blood peach (Prunus persica) can be grown south of Massachusetts. All of these are available in seed form from Bountiful Gardens (www.bountifulgardens.org) and are also available from a number of nurseries.

Almost all nursery stock is grafted rather than grown from seed for a number of reasons, but the effect of this is that if two trees of the same type and variety are selected, they may be genetically the same exact plant and thus incapable of pollinating each other, causing low fruit yields. More than one of any stone fruit should be selected to aid in pollination, and it is important to consult with knowledgeable nursery personnel about exactly what varieties need to be grown to ensure proper pollination. Space nectarines, peaches, plums, and apricots anywhere from 15 to 20 feet apart, and space cherries anywhere from 20 to 30 feet apart for best pollination and fruit yields.

Stone fruits should be planted in early spring by digging a hole big enough to accommodate the entire root system without bunching it up or looping it around and deep enough that the graft union is about two inches above the ground. Once the soil is filled back into the hole, the area should be watered thoroughly to help the soil settle around the roots. Stone fruits should be fertilized in early spring only (using a balanced organic fertilizer) and never later in the summer. Fertilizing in late summer will cause vigorous growth that the root system hasn't grown enough to support so the tree could be harmed and have difficulty overwintering. By fertilizing in the early spring, the tree has a chance to grow in a balanced way across the entire growing season so it will overwinter properly.

A good fertilizer can be made by mixing together 1 pound of bone meal, 1/2 pound of dried blood, and 3 pounds of dried kelp or greensand. Apply 1/2 pound to the soil surface around the drip line of the tree (the "drip line" is the area on the ground just under the widest branches) by using a crowbar to make four to eight holes six inches deep in a circle around the plant and sprinkling some of the fertilizer in each hole. Use 1/2 pound the first year, then an additional half pound every year thereafter until, in the ninth and subsequent years, 5 pounds are being used each spring. Stone fruits prefer a pH of 6.0 to 6.5, and if a soil test shows amendment to be needed, that can be done in the spring as well. Keep in mind, however, that lime can take several months to work, so don't overlime and raise the pH above 6.5.

The following pruning directions are equally applicable to both dwarf and full-size trees. Because all stone fruits are susceptible to brown rot, they should be trained to an open center rather than a central leader (a single main trunk that reaches all the way to the top of the tree) like an apple tree. This will allow maximum light and air penetration to keep brown rot problems under control.

When the tree is first planted, cut off any branches closer than 18 inches to the ground, and cut the central leader at 30 inches above the ground. This will force branches to grow out at 18 to 30 inches above the ground, which will yield branches at the right height when the tree is mature. Select three or four good branches that are growing evenly spaced around the trunk, and prune back the others all the way to the trunk, then prune back the central leader to just above the topmost selected branch. These selected branches will be the main *scaffolds* of the tree, referring to their structural importance. Stone fruit branches are strongest when they leave the trunk at an angle between 60 and 90 degrees, so now is the time to establish those angles and the direction of growth using a combination of ropes and wooden spacers inserted between the branch and the trunk.

Stone fruits should not be pruned in winter because of susceptibility to winter injury and because of a disease called cytospora canker. Rather, they should be pruned between the time they bloom and the first week after the flower petals have fallen.

The first pruning after planting should occur just after blooming in the early spring of the next year. At that time, any branches that are broken and diseased should be removed, and the main scaffolds should be cut back half their length to an outward facing bud. Any vertically growing shoots should likewise be removed, and spacers or ties for maintaining branch angles should be checked and adjusted as necessary.

The second pruning after planting will occur at the same time the next year. By this time, the main scaffold branches will be developing new branches on them. Select three or four sublimbs on each main scaffold to be preserved. These should be on opposite sides of the scaffolds, not growing straight up or bending down, and be at least 18 inches away from the main trunk. The main scaffold branches should then be cut back by 1/3 to an outward-facing bud, and all limbs but the selected sublimbs should be cut back to the branch or to the trunk as appropriate.

Subsequent pruning simply needs to maintain the open center by removing vertical limbs and limbs that grow inward toward the center. Limbs and sublimbs should be headed back to an outward-facing bud each year to make sure new fruiting wood is growing each year, and limbs should be pruned as needed to maintain the desired shape and size of tree and to avoid broken limbs.

Nut Trees

Compared to fruit trees, nut trees are easier to prune and care for. The only downside is that, except for filberts, they grow to be quite large and thus require as much as 50 feet between trees. Walnuts and, to a lesser extent, pecans and hickories produce a chemical called juglone in their root systems that inhibits the germination of other plants, so they shouldn't be planted close to a garden. A number of trees are unaffected by juglone, including cherries, oaks, pears, and most cone-bearing trees, among others. The only vegetables unaffected by juglone are onions, beans, carrots, corn, melons, and squash.

Most nut trees aren't self-fruitful and therefore must be planted in pairs. The same caveat applies to nuts as to fruits in that many nut trees are made by grafting and thus are genetic clones. For this reason, two different varieties of

⊗ Chestnuts, walnuts, and other nuts are highly nutritious.

the same nut will need to be planted unless those trees were grown from seed, in which case two trees of the same variety will work fine.

Nut trees can be grown from seed as long as the requisite period of cold stratification is met to break dormancy. (Cold stratification means exposing the seed to a period of subfreezing temperature for a period of time. Many seeds for trees require this or they will never sprout.) If you plant the seed in the fall and protect it from rodents, it will sprout in the spring. Plant it about two feet deep and mulch with hay over the winter, then remove the mulch in early spring.

The tree should be transplanted into a hole big enough to handle the entire root system. About 2/3 of the soil should be carefully shoveled around the roots and then well watered and the remaining soil shoveled in and tamped down. The area around the tree should then be mulched to reduce competition with weeds and the trunk protected with a circular hardware cloth protector to keep deer and other critters from eating

the bark. (Hardware cloth is available at any hardware store at minimal cost.)

Because nut trees have a long taproot that grows slowly, they need to have about half of their top growth pruned back during transplanting, leaving several buds. This balances the upper and lower portion of the tree to enhance survivability. New vertical-growing shoots should emerge from the buds left behind, and when they are 8 to 12 inches long, the most vigorous should be selected as the tree's new central leader, and the remainder cut off even with the trunk.

From that point forward, you are mainly aiming for a balanced tree, so prune to keep the tree balanced. Conduct all pruning in late winter or very early spring, and remove all dead or damaged branches. At the same time, progressively shorten the lowest limbs a little each year until the tree is about 20 feet high, at which point all limbs lower than 6 feet should be removed flush with the trunk. This preserves the food-making ability of the lower limbs until it is no longer needed.

Growing distance/productivity for such large trees can be troublesome on a small lot, but there are ways to get around the problem. Table 17 gives the ultimate distance that the trees should be from each other when fully grown.

Table 17: **Nut Tree Planting Distance**

Type of Nut Tree	Distance between Trees
Black walnut, hickory, pecan, and hican	50 feet in all directions
English and Persian walnut	35 feet in all directions

Type of Nut Tree	Distance between Trees
Chestnut (Chinese, most American chestnuts succumbed to the chestnut blight)	40 feet in all directions
Filberts	15 feet in all directions

Keep in mind that nut trees produce nuts long before reaching full size and that nut wood is some of the most expensive, so selling it could net a nice bundle. If you wish to do so, plant the nut trees about 10 feet apart and then selectively harvest them for wood as their branches come close to touching. In the end, you have properly spaced highly productive nut trees and hopefully a wad of cash.

Diseases and Pests

There's no such thing as a free lunch—or even free fruit! Fruit and nut trees are prone to numerous pest and disease problems. Thus, they require a regular schedule of sanitation and spraying to keep them healthy and productive, and they can pose a challenge to mini-farmers, particularly if they are committed to raising fruit without synthetic pesticides. This is more of a problem with fruits than with nuts, but it can be made manageable through advanced planning and a thorough understanding of the requirements. Pomme fruits such as apples and pears share common pests and diseases, as do stone fruits such as cherries, plums, and peaches. No matter what fruits you grow or what diseases are prevalent, meticulous cleanup of debris around the trees and vigilant pruning

of diseased tissues will provide the proverbial "ounce of prevention."

The difficulties of raising apples and pears explain the high concentrations of toxic contaminants in nonorganic varieties. Therefore you should carefully consider if some other fruit might be more suitable given the amount of time you will need to spend if you wish to produce organic apples and pears. According to the Agricultural Sciences department at Pennsylvania State University, as many as 6 to 10 pesticide applications might be required yearly to produce reasonably appealing apples, though as few as 2 or 3 applications are feasible with scab-resistant varieties. Spraying is simplified, and pomme fruits are more practical if dwarf varieties are selected.

Scab is a fungal disease of apples and pears. The spores mature over a four- to six-week period of wet weather in the spring that corresponds with the wet weather required for the release of the spores. The spores take up residence on the leaves of the tree where they grow and produce more spores, starting a cycle of reinfection that infects the fruit as well, causing ugly, misshapen fruit. If all debris (apples/pears and leaves) is removed before the spores can be released, and a good antifungal agent (such as fixed copper or Bordeaux mix) is applied every 10 to 14 days starting in early spring and extending through early summer, scab infection can be controlled. A better solution, because antifungal agents can injure the tree, is to plant apple varieties that are naturally resistant to scab, such as Liberty. Carefully research the varieties you plan to grow.

There are a number of other apple or pear diseases, such as fire blight, that require comprehensive management programs to produce good fruit. Antibiotics are combined with pruning of diseased tissue for treatment of fire blight once it becomes established.

The most prevalent pest of pomme fruits is the apple maggot, a little white worm. Luckily, the apple maggot is one of the few insects that can discern—and are attracted to—the color red. They can be effectively controlled by hanging red-painted balls coated with a sticky coating (such as Tangletrap). The balls should be hung just after flowering and remain through harvest, being renewed periodically to keep them sticky. Several are required for each tree.

The codling moth is another serious pest. This nondescript gray and brown moth lays eggs on the fruit. The first eggs hatch when the fruit is slightly less than one inch in diameter, and the small worm burrows into the fruit where it eats until it reaches full size then burrows back out, becomes a moth, and starts the cycle again. Codling moths are conventionally controlled by spraying carbaryl or permethrin at least once every 14 days following petal fall. These poisons can be avoided by aggressive organic measures including "trapping out" the male moths by using up to four pheromone traps per full-sized tree, encircling the tree trunks with flexible cardboard covered with a sticky coating to trap the larvae, and spraying frequently with the botanical insecticide ryania.

Stone fruits, like pomme fruits, require constant spraying to deal with a number of diseases and pests. Chief diseases include powdery mildew, leaf spot, peach leaf curl, crown gall, cytospora canker, black knot, and brown spot. Japanese beetles, fruit moths, aphids, borers, and spider mites round out the threats.

A regular spraying schedule is required for stone fruits. If raising the fruit organically, this includes fungicides such as Bordeaux mix, lime sulfur, and fixed copper and insect controls such as neem oil, horticultural oil, and organic insecticides used according to label directions. The spraying should start when buds swell in the spring and continue with the frequency specified on the product label until the fruit has been harvested. All dropped fruit and leaves should be raked up and removed from the area in the fall.

Black knot of the plum can't be controlled this way and instead requires that any sections of wood evidencing this distinctive infection be completely removed from the tree and destroyed by incineration.

Most nut trees never show signs of disease, and the regular spraying required for fruit trees is not needed in most cases. Major nut tree diseases include chestnut blight, pecan scab, walnut anthracnose, and walnut blight.

Chestnut blight was introduced into the United States before 1900 through the importation of various Asian chestnut species that carry the causative fungus but are resistant to it themselves. The American chestnut, native to Eastern North America, has no resistance to this fungus; within a generation this majestic tree, soaring up to 100 feet and measuring up to 10 feet across, was reduced to little more than a shrub that struggles a few years before succumbing to the threat. To put the impact of chestnut blight into perspective, it is estimated that in 1900, 25% of all the trees in the Appalachians were American chestnuts.

There are four ways of dealing with chestnut blight: prompt removal of infected branches, treatment of cankers in existing trees for five years with injections of a hypovirulent strain of the fungus, planting resistant Asian chestnut varieties, and planting American varieties that have incorporated disease-resistant genes through repetitive backcrossing and selection to maximize native DNA content while retaining resistance genes.[46]

Mini-farmers interested in growing and preserving American chestnuts should seek guidance (and seeds!) from the American Chestnut Cooperators' Foundation (www.accf-online.org). Farmers interested in resistant Asian stocks can find suitable varieties at local nurseries.

Pecan scab, evidenced by sunken black spots on leaves, twigs, and nuts, is more of a problem in the southern than northern states. At the scale of a mini-farm, it is most easily controlled through meticulous sanitation—the raking and disposal of leaves and detritus through burning. Severe infestations require multiple fungicide sprays yearly.[47]

Walnut anthracnose, a disease characterized by small dark spots on the leaves that can grow to merge together and defoliate entire trees in severe cases, affects black walnuts but not Persian varieties. Meticulous sanitation is normally all that is required on the scale of a mini-farm, but springtime fungicide spraying may be needed in severe cases.

Walnut blight is just the opposite in that it affects the Persian walnut varieties but not American black walnuts. Walnut blight looks like small, water-filled sunken spots on leaves, shoots, and/or nuts. The disease doesn't travel back into old wood, so the tree and crop can be saved by spraying fixed copper during flowering and fruit set.

Pest insects in nut trees can be controlled through keeping the area mowed and free of tall grasses that would harbor stinkbugs, meticulous sanitation to control shuckworms, and regular insecticide spraying to control hunkflies, weevils, and casebearers. For a handful of nut trees (unless the mini-farm is in close proximity to a large number of similar nut species), pests are unlikely to become a major problem, and it is likely that spraying will never be necessary.

---

[46] Anagnostakis, S. (2000) *Revitalization of the Majestic Chestnut: Chestnut Blight Disease*

[47] Doll, C., McDaniel, J., Meador, D., Randall, R., Shurtleff, M. (1986) *Nut Growing in Illinois, Circular 1102*

15

Raising Chickens for Eggs

I wrote this book for the purpose of learning about self-sufficiency through mini-farming, and self-sufficiency, in my opinion, has no political agendas attached to it. If, for personal, health, or religious reasons you are opposed to consuming animal food products, then skip this chapter and the next one. If you are a meat eater but are understandably squeamish about eating homegrown eggs or turning animals into meat, I nevertheless encourage you to continue reading simply for your own knowledge.

Nothing says "farm" like the sound of a rooster crowing in the morning, and nothing is more aggravating to neighbors than a rooster that seems to crow all day, every day. Still, small livestock have a place on the mini-farm because of the high-quality protein that they provide. If you currently purchase meat and eggs, know that homegrown meat and eggs can be raised at a very low cost that will save you money.

For the purposes of a mini-farm occupying half an acre or less, cows, goats, and similar livestock will place too high a demand on the natural resources of such a small space and will end up costing more than the value of the food they provide. In such small spaces,

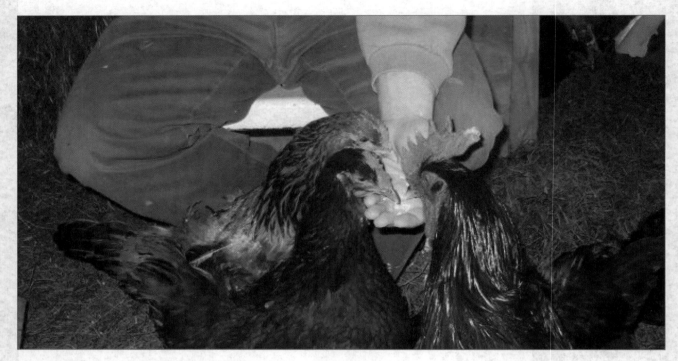

⊗ These chickens are so friendly they eat out of your hand.

the greatest practical benefit can be derived from chickens, guineas, some species of ducks, and aquaculture. Rabbits are also a possibility, but remember that children (and adults!) can get attached to them easily. But chickens, overall, are the most cost-effective choice on a small lot.

Overview

Chickens are foragers that will eat grass, weeds, insects, acorns, and many other things they happen to run across. They will virtually eliminate grasshoppers, slugs, and other pests in the yard, thus keeping them away from the garden. Many cover crops like alfalfa, vetch, and soybeans are delicacies for birds and since cover crops are recommended to be grown anyway, a small flock of 10 or 20 birds can be raised with minimal feed expenditures over the growing season.

Don't expect to get rich in the chicken and egg business because you would be competing at the wholesale level in a commodity market, so it's unlikely to be a direct money maker. But it *is* feasible to produce meat and eggs for yourself at costs that significantly undercut those of the supermarket while selling the odd dozen to friends and coworkers. On our own farm, the eggs we sell completely liquidate the cost of feed so that our own eggs are free, plus we get to keep the chickens valuable nitrogen-rich manure for our compost pile.

Chickens

A flock of 12 laying chickens costs about $6.00 per week to feed during the winter months when they can't be fed by foraging. They will earn their keep by producing about two to four dozen eggs weekly (more during the summer, fewer during the winter). Obviously, the family can't eat that many eggs, so a little negotiation with friends or coworkers who appreciate farm-fresh eggs will net you $2 to $3 per dozen. (Egg cartons cost about $0.20 each from a number of manufacturers. For more information, just type "egg cartons" into an Internet search engine. We get ours at a local get-together known as a "chicken swap.") To put the cost of chicken feed into perspective, a flock of 12 chickens costs less to feed than a house cat.

At the supermarket, a chicken is just a chicken, but eggs run the gamut from cheap generic eggs costing less than a dollar a dozen to organic eggs costing more than five dollars a carton. From the standpoint of raising chickens, there are numerous breeds available, each of which has its strengths and weaknesses. Many chickens are bred specifically for meat yield, and others are bred mainly for laying eggs. There are also dual-purpose varieties that split the difference.

For a mini-farm, I would recommend a hardy egg-laying variety such as the Rhode Island Red, which has the benefit of being good at hatching its own eggs over the more cultured Leghorn (pronounced "legern") varieties. Another good choice would be a dual-purpose breed like the New Hampshire or Orpington. In my experience, the laying productivity of hens diminishes over time, so these birds can be transitioned into the freezer and replaced with younger hens. (Old layers transitioned into the freezer are tough and best used for soups, stews, and chicken pot pies, so label them accordingly.) If you choose to hatch eggs from your chickens to supplement your flock, new roosters of the chosen breed should be brought in every couple of years to reduce inbreeding.

You'll find that hens and roosters are fun to watch and provide endless amusement. When the farmer steps outside, plate in hand, to deliver meal leftovers to the chickens, they'll come running! Then, the chicken that managed to retrieve an especially attractive piece of food will be chased all over the place by other members of the flock. The roosters will be vigilant and defend the rest of the flock against attack but otherwise just strut around looking proud and important. Chickens definitely establish a "pecking order" amongst themselves, so new chickens should be separated from the rest of the flock until they are large enough to defend themselves.

You need only one rooster for every 20 or fewer hens. In fact, you need *no* roosters at all unless you are planning for the hens to raise babies. Too many roosters is a bad idea since they are equipped with spurs on their legs and will fight each other unless the flock is large enough to accommodate the number of roosters. Roosters are not usually dangerous to humans, but there have been cases of attacks against small children, so it's good to keep an eye on kids who are playing in the same yard with roosters. In

With too few hens, roosters leave some bald spots.

addition, if your flock has fewer than 20 birds, the rooster will likely mount the chickens so often that they may develop bald spots.

I recommend the following breeds of general purpose chickens for a mini-farm: Rhode Island Red, New Hampshire, Wyandotte, Sussex, and Orpington. These breeds make good meat and eggs, will get broody and hatch their own eggs, and make good mothers. Especially important around kids or in suburbia, they have gentle dispositions. But don't be complacent, especially about roosters. If they feel that one of the hens is being endangered, they *will* attack, and once they do, breaking them of the habit is difficult.

Caring for Baby Chicks

All birds have requirements in common with any other livestock. They need special care during infancy, food, water, shelter, and protection from predators.

Chickens can be started as eggs in a commercial or home-built incubator. Most often, they are purchased as day-old chicks. They can be obtained at the local feed and seed store in the spring or ordered from a reputable firm such as McMurray Hatchery (www.mcmurrayhatchery.com), Fairview Hatchery (www.fairviewhatchery.com), or Stromberg's (www.strombergschickens.com). After hatching or arrival, baby birds should be provided with a brooder, food, and water. For a mini-farm-scaled operation, a brooder need be nothing more than an area enclosed on the sides free of drafts, an adjustable-height heat lamp, and a thermometer. (These products are available at agricultural supply stores.) The floor of the brooder should be smooth (like flat cardboard or newspapers) for the first few days until the chicks figure out

how to eat from the feeder, and then you can add some wood shavings. Make sure to clean all the droppings and replace the litter daily. Feeding and watering devices for baby birds are readily available.

When the baby chicks are first introduced to the brooder, duck their beaks briefly in the water so they recognize it as a water source. Just before hatching, chicks suck up the last of the yolk so they are all set for up to 24 hours without food after hatching, but you want them to have food and water as soon as possible.

Incubators and brooding areas must be thoroughly cleaned and disinfected before populating them in order to keep a disease called coccidiosis controlled. Coccidiosis is caused by a parasite that is spread through bird droppings and is more dangerous to baby birds than to adults. It is easy to tell if a baby bird has contracted the parasite because blood will appear in the droppings. Feed for baby birds is often formulated with an additive for conferring immunity to the parasite; some small-scale poultry farmers report that the disease can be controlled by adding one tablespoon of cider vinegar per quart to the

◆ Baby chicks in a brooder made from plywood.

birds' drinking water for three days. Either way, the importance of cleanliness and disinfection in areas to be inhabited by baby birds can't be overemphasized.

Disinfection requires a thorough ordinary cleaning with soap and water to remove all organic matter followed by applying a suitable disinfectant for a sufficient period of time. A number of disinfectants are available including alcohols, phenolic compounds, quaternary ammonia disinfectants, and a large number of commercial products sold for that purpose. The most accessible suitable disinfectant is chlorine bleach diluted by adding 3/4 cup of bleach to one gallon of water. This requires a contact time of five minutes before being removed from the surface, then the area has to be well ventilated so it doesn't irritate the birds.

Baby chicks should be started on a type of feed called "starter crumbles" and kept on it for six to eight weeks or until fully feathered. Once fully feathered, they can go on layer rations and be put in the hen house. They don't usually start laying eggs until they are a little over 16 weeks old.

Vaccinations

You should check with the agricultural extension agent in your local area for vaccination recommendations. Poultry are prone to certain diseases, such as Newcastle disease, that are easily protected against by vaccination but are incurable once contracted and can easily wipe out a flock.

I order vaccination supplies from an online veterinary supply company—Jeffers Livestock—and administer the vaccinations myself. Most vaccines come in a size suitable for vaccinating 1,000 birds, which is not particularly suitable for a backyard flock. I vaccinate my laying chickens for Newcastle disease and infectious bronchitis (IB).

Newcastle disease is a highly contagious viral illness of birds that has been recognized since the 1920s. It manifests in various forms, some of which cause as much as 90% mortality in a flock. Newcastle disease infects and is spread by all manner of birds, and it is endemic throughout Western Europe and North America. Most birds don't experience the levels of mortality and debility that manifest in domestic chickens, though. It is primarily spread by droppings. In plain English, this means that all that is needed for your flock to be wiped out is for a sparrow to poop into your chicken yard while flying over. (As a side note, the virus causes a mild conjunctivitis in humans and is particularly toxic to cancer cells in humans while leaving normal cells practically unharmed. Research into this is ongoing.)

So vaccinating your flock is a good idea. Meanwhile, while the Newcastle vaccine is available on its own, it can also be purchased as a combined vaccine for IB.

IB is caused by a highly contagious coronavirus that mutates rapidly. While the immediate mortality rate from IB tends to be low, it can permanently damage the kidneys and reproductive tracts of chickens, hurts shell pigmentation, and makes the eggs unappetizing. Thus, especially if you visit the backyard flocks of other poultry owners, vaccinating your flock for IB makes sense.

So, now that you've decided to vaccinate your flock, how do you go about doing it? First you have to get the vaccine — which I order from Jeffers Livestock. Trouble is, the teeny-weeny 7 ml (less than two teaspoons) vial contains enough dosage for 1,000 chickens. For those of us with a smaller flock of 20 birds or so, it isn't practical to use the watering directions. So how do you administer the vaccine?

The vaccine comes with directions. If you can't find them, you can get them from the company Web site.

Two methods are of interest. The first is to use an included plastic dropper and administer one (very small) drop of vaccine into either the nostril or the eye of each bird. My birds are pretty tame. They jump up onto my shoulders to keep me company and have no real issue with me picking them up or handling them. So in my case, this method works just fine. I set up a chair in the chicken yard and bring a couple of pieces of bread with me, and as each chicken takes a turn jumping up onto my lap, I gently hold its head still and beak closed and put a drop on one nostril. I then briefly close the other nostril with a finger until the drop gets sucked in, give the chicken a piece of bread, and send it on its way.

But not all chickens are so friendly and cooperative. When I was a kid, we had some chickens who thought they were kamikazes or something, and securing their cooperation in such an endeavor was unlikely. So we vaccinated them through their drinking water.

The question is how do you translate dosage instructions intended for 1,000 birds so they work for a small flock of 10–30 birds? Here's how I do it.

I rehydrate the vaccine in the vial using high-quality bottled water. I shake it thoroughly and then dump it into a 100 ml graduated cylinder. I add water to bring the total volume to 100 ml. Now I know that each milliliter has enough vaccine for 10 birds. I set that aside.

Then I turn my attention to the waterer. I take it apart and clean it thoroughly with hot soapy water, rinse it thoroughly, and then dry it with paper towels. My water at home isn't chlorinated. If you have chlorinated water, do the final rinse with bottled water.

Then, I put 1 gallon of bottled water, 1 teaspoon of powdered milk, and 1 ml of vaccine for every 10 birds into the waterer and stir it up. Then I make sure that for the next 24 hours it is the *only* source of water available for the birds. The next day, I clean out the waterer thoroughly and then fill it up with my normal watering solution plus a vitamin supplement. The vaccines are *live virus* vaccines, and they put some stress on the birds, so I give them the vitamins to help them deal with that.

Speaking of live viruses—I should mention that if you aren't careful while playing with this vaccine, you'll get a mild case of conjunctivitis—also known as "pink eye"—or maybe some cold-like symptoms. Nothing serious though.

While I use this method for the Newcastle vaccine, it will also work for other vaccines that are dosed for larger flocks.

Antibiotics

Sometimes vaccinating chickens makes them sick, and they need medicine. Other times, they will get sick from germs you have brought home on your shoes from visiting someone else who has chickens or even from buying a couple of adult birds and introducing them to the flock—even if you keep them in a separated space for 10 days beforehand, which you should always do.

This is a tough situation. If you are raising birds organically and they need antibiotics and you use

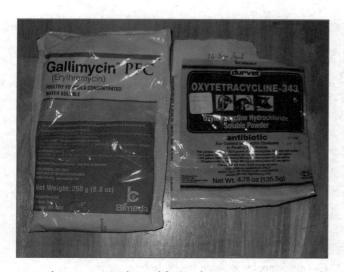

⊗ Antibiotics commonly used for poultry.

other hand, while the meat is safe to eat one day following discontinuance of erythromycin, I have no data indicating that the eggs are ever safe to eat again. So laying chickens treated with erythromycin to cure illness should be transitioned into being meat birds and replaced with new layers.

As with vaccines, antibiotics are usually packaged in sizes suitable for much larger flocks, but a bit of math will let you know how much to use. One thing you will definitely need, though, is an accurate scale weighing in grams. Digital scales used to be quite expensive but can now be found for less than $30.

Food

During the active growing season, birds will provide about half of their own food by foraging if the farmer keeps the size of the flock suitable for the area being foraged, but during the winter and for the first weeks after hatching, they will need to be given commercial feed. (The amount of pasture required per bird depends on the type of vegetation being grown in the area. Start with 300 square feet per bird, and adjust from there.) You can also feed grain and vegetable leftovers—such as bread and pasta—to your chickens. Technically, you can feed them meat as well, but I would avoid the practice because too many diseases are being spread these days by feeding meat to livestock—things like mad cow disease that can spread to humans and is incurable. A small flock of birds will be much less expensive to feed than a house cat, and the feed is readily available at agricultural stores. A number of bird feeders are available commercially, or they can be built by the farmer. Make sure that whatever you use for a feeder, it can be raised or lowered so that

them, the chickens are no longer organic—so you may be stuck destroying the birds.

The most likely reason you would resort to antibiotics with chickens is respiratory illness. These sorts of illnesses aren't all bacterial—some are viral and unaffected by antibiotics. Nevertheless, I have found that most often the respiratory illnesses characterized by wheezing and nasal discharge or sneezing have all responded.

Antibiotics will find their way into the eggs of laying birds, so the eggs should be broken and added to the compost pile during treatment and for a week afterward. The two most common antibiotics used for chickens are variants of tetracycline and erythromycin, both of which are available mail order or right in the feed store without a prescription. A study of tetracycline residues in eggs found that on the second day after finishing treatment, any residues in the eggs were undetectably low.[48] So disposing of the eggs for seven days following treatment is fine. On the

---

[48] Donahue, D., Hairston, H. (1999) Oxytetracycline transfer into egg yolks and albumen, *Poultry Science* 78 pp. 343–345

its lip is even with the backs of the birds. Building the feeder this way, and never filling it more than half full of feed will significantly reduce the amount of feed, that ends up on the floor since chickens have to raise their heads to swallow.

If birds are used for pest control, a fencing system should be created that allows the birds to forage in and around beds that are sown with cover crops but not in beds growing food crops A small flock of birds will devastate a garden in short order because they like to eat most things that humans eat. They make excellent manure that should be added to the compost pile if gathered. Otherwise, just leave it in the beds containing cover crops to naturally degrade and provide free fertilizer for the next growing season.

Commercial feed comes in many varieties. Both medicated and nonmedicated versions of mash, crumbles, and pellets are available. If you specify it is for laying hens, the clerk at the store will know exactly what you need. The medicated versions aren't typically necessary. You can also buy a mix of cracked corn and rye called "scratch feed." Scratch is about half the price of regular feed but is not, in and of itself, a complete ration—although chickens tend to prefer it over regular feed. All feeds are very attractive to rodents, easily rotted by water, and a lure for grain moths, so they should be kept in metal storage containers with tight-fitting lids.

One winter, I kept a feeder with both scratch and regular feed available in the coop for the birds that were confined while the snow was deep. I also kept bales of alfalfa hay in the coop, covered with a tarp. Because the birds preferred the scratch to the complete ration, they became nutritionally deficient and sought to make up the difference by eating the hay. One of the hens

⊗ Containers for keeping feed safe from pests.

developed an obstruction of her crop this way and had to be euthanized. So I have learned not to provide scratch while the chickens are confined, especially if an edible litter—like hay—is used.

What we do instead, when the chickens must be confined because of bad weather, is provide a daily bunch of greens such as lettuce or kale to supplement their feed. This helps give the yolks a nice color and keeps the chickens from getting bored.

Housing

All birds have similar housing requirements though their habits are a bit different. A coop should be built for the birds with about three square feet of floor space per bird. Technically, as few as two square feet can be adequate for chickens, and ducks require only three square feet each, but the coop should be sized to account for temporary increases in flock size during the spring and summer. For a flock of 20 birds, which is the largest practical flock for a small lot, that means a 100-square-foot coop—a size that can be accommodated in a number of configurations such as

8 × 12, 10 × 10, and so forth. Enough floor space helps to reduce stress on the birds and prevents behavior problems. The most prevalent behavior problem resulting from inadequate living space is chickens pecking each other, which can lead to infections and other problems.

The subject of construction techniques required to build a chicken coop is beyond the scope of a book on farming. McMurray Hatchery (www.mcmurrayhatchery.com) has two suitable chicken house plans including a complete bill of materials for less than $15 each as of this writing. Judy Pangman has also written *Chicken Coops,* a comprehensive book containing 45 illustrated plans for chicken coops to suit every circumstance and budget.

For our chicken coop, I used a product called Star Plates available from Stromberg's Chickens. It allows for building a floor in the shape of a

⊗ Nearly completed chicken coop.

⊗ Some hen houses are an exercise in geometry, but they don't need to be.

pentagon and an extremely strong and secure shelter. It also, per square foot, works out to be less expensive than many other approaches plus allows for a natural draft when used with a small cupola.

No matter which way you'd like to build a coop, I'd like to convey a few aspects of coops that I believe to be important.

First, a coop needs to have a smooth floor, made out of plywood, for example, that is well coated with polyurethane or a similar substance that is impervious to moisture and easily cleaned or disinfected. The floor should be strewn with wood shavings, peat moss, or a similar clean absorbent material that is replaced anytime it becomes excessively damp or dirty in order to prevent infections. Some experts recommend against using hay, but that is precisely what we use without any difficulties as long as we don't store the hay bails in the coop.

Second, any windows should be made out of Plexiglas rather than real glass and preferably located high enough on a wall that the chickens can't get to it easily. That way they won't be tempted to fly into it and break their necks.

Third, even the smallest omnivores, like mice and rats, can cause serious problems in a bird coop, so it is important to construct the coop in a fashion that will exclude even the smallest predators. I learned this lesson the hard way back when I was 12 years old and a rat got into our chicken coop and managed to kill three adolescent birds. The easiest way to achieve this is to build the coop on pilings.

Finally, nests should be provided. These are most easily built onto the walls in such a way that the birds can get into them easily via the roosts and they are up away from the floor. Ducks, being more secretive, prefer a covered nesting box on the floor. Nests should be filled with straw, wood shavings, or peat and kept clean. The farmer should provide half as many nests as there are birds.

Because of the way the noses of birds are designed, birds cannot create suction with their

⊗ Adequate and comfortable nesting boxes are important.

beaks. As a result, they have to raise their heads to swallow. What this means in practical terms is that birds sling water all over the place and make the litter on the floor of the coop wet if the lip of a watering device is too low. If the lip of the watering device is even with the level of the backs of the birds, the mess created will be substantially reduced. It is more important with some birds than others, and particularly important with turkeys, to make sure plenty of water is available anytime they are given feed in order to avoid choking. Water provided should be clean and free of debris, and the container should be designed to keep birds from standing in it or roosting on it. If birds stand in or roost over the water source, they will certainly contaminate it with droppings.

Many books on poultry cover the lighting arrangements needed to maximize growth or egg laying. Light affects the hormonal balance in birds and therefore affects when a bird will molt (lose and replace its feathers), lay eggs, desire mating, and so forth. When birds molt, they temporarily stop laying eggs, which is a big deal on a commercial scale. Likewise, egg production naturally decreases as the amount of available light decreases. All of this can be affected by controlling the amount of light that birds receive and, to a lesser degree, the food supply.

This brings up a fundamental difference in the mind-set of a mini-farmer who is raising birds as compared to a large commercial enterprise. In a large commercial enterprise, the life span of a laying chicken is about 16 months because it has been pushed to its physical limits by that time and has outlived its usefulness in terms of the cost of food and water that it consumes compared to the wholesale value of eggs in a commodity market. Likewise, because it has laid eggs

daily without respite since reaching adulthood, the minerals in its body have become depleted and the quality of the egg shells has declined. So by the time a chicken is 16 months old, it is consigned to the compost heap because it isn't even good for eating.

A mini-farmer can have a different outlook because the birds are multipurpose. The birds serve to consume pests and reduce the costs of gardening, consume leftovers, produce fertilizer, provide amusement with their antics, and lay eggs or provide meat for the table. The economic equation for the mini-farmer is strikingly different, so the treatment of the birds will likewise be different. If birds are allowed to molt when the seasons trigger molting and come in and out of egg production naturally because of seasonal light changes, they are subjected to considerably less stress, and their bodies are able to use dormant periods to recover lost minerals and nutrients. In this way, it is not at all unusual for

A radiant heater behind the roosts keeps chickens warm in cold winter climates.

nonspecialized bird breeds to live several years with moderate productivity.

One other thing to consider if you live further north is the need for heat in the coop. Where we live, temperatures below zero are not uncommon, and there can be days in a row with temperatures never budging out of the teens. In these conditions, their water can freeze, and they can suffer frostbite. The water is easily dealt with via a simple water fount heater available at agricultural supply stores. For general heating of the coop, mine is insulated using thermal reflective insulation, and I've installed a simple 400W flat-panel radiant heater behind the roosts so the chickens can stay warm at night.

Collecting and Cleaning Eggs

Chickens usually lay midmorning, but there's no predicting it completely. They're chickens, after all, and lay when they are good and ready. Ideally, you should collect the eggs immediately, but this is seldom practical—especially if, like me, you work a regular job. I've never had a problem with freshness simply collecting the eggs when I get home from work and putting them in the refrigerator immediately.

There are a couple of phenomena pertaining to eggs that may become an inconvenience: dirty and broken eggs. Every once in a while, chickens will lay an egg that has a thin shell and breaks while in the nest. Sometimes, they may lay an egg with no shell at all. When these break, they coat any other eggs in the nest with a slime that makes them unmarketable. Obviously, the proverbial ounce of prevention applies in that having enough nesting boxes will reduce the number

of eggs coated with slime in any given box. However, chickens tend to "follow the leader" to an extent and have a decided tendency to lay eggs in a nesting box where another egg is already present. So even if you put up one nesting box for each bird, this problem wouldn't be solved completely.

Then, of course, there is the problem presented by the fact that eggs leave the body of a hen through the exact same orifice used for excrement. Meaning that sometimes eggs will have a bit of chicken manure on them. Not usually, but sometimes. In addition, chickens who have been running around outside in the mud on a rainy day will track mud back into the nest and make the eggs dirty.

For minor dirt and manure, just scraping it off with a thumbnail or using a sanding sponge is fine. But for slime and major dirt that won't come off easily, water washing is required.

Water washing can be extremely problematic and yield unsafe eggs if done improperly. When the egg comes out of the hen, it has a special

⊗ Farm-fresh eggs are easy to sell as they are qualitatively superior to even the best store-bought eggs.

coating that, as long as it is kept dry, protects the interior of the egg from being contaminated by anything on the shell. But once the shell becomes wet, the semipermeable membrane of the shell can be compromised, and a temperature differential can cause a partial vacuum inside the egg that sucks all of the bacteria on the shell inside—thus creating an egg that is unsafe.

Nevertheless, the techniques and technology for properly water washing an egg are very mature and well understood. Special egg-washing machines exist, but on the scale of a mini-farm, they are so expensive (about $6,000) they don't make sense economically. One alternative that I haven't tried yet is a product called "The Incredible Egg Washer" that sells for less than $120. But let me tell you about the safe and low-cost technique that I use for our small-scale operation.

First, clean your sink and work area thoroughly, and get a roll of paper towels so they are handy. Next, make a sanitizing solution from the hottest tap water by mixing two tablespoons of bleach with one gallon of water. You can multiply this by adding four tablespoons of bleach to two gallons of water, and so on. Put the sanitizer in a cleaned watering can and the eggs in a wire basket. Pour the sanitizing solution over the eggs very generously, making certain to wet all surfaces thoroughly. Wait a couple of minutes, and then use a paper towel that has been dipped in sanitizer to clean the egg. Use a fresh paper towel for each egg. Then, rinse them very thoroughly with sanitizing solution and then set them aside to dry on a wire rack. It's important to let them dry before putting them in egg cartons, because wet eggs tend to stick to egg carton materials.

The Broody Hen

Sooner or later, you are going to run into a hen who is very interested in hatching some eggs. If that is part of your plan—great! She'll sit on any egg, so take some others from adjacent nests that were laid that day, and slide those under her too. If, as in my coop, the standard laying nests are up in the air, make her a new nest that is closer to the ground—6 to 12 inches. That way, once the chicks are hatched, they won't hurt themselves if they fall out of the nest.

Usually, though, when a hen goes broody, you don't want it to happen. The hen will sit on the eggs, keeping them at a high temperature, so that when you collect them a few hours later, they have runny whites and just aren't fresh anymore. Just collecting the eggs out from under her for a while won't work—she'll just keep setting forever. The solution to this problem is a "broody cage."

A broody cage is any cage fashioned with a wire bottom and containing no litter. I've used a small portable rabbit cage for the purpose. If you keep a broody hen in this for 36 to 48 hours, it will break her of the desire to sit on the eggs. It is extremely important that you provide adequate food and water in the cage or you will force her to go into molt.

16

Raising Chickens for Meat

A lot of people are squeamish about killing animals of any sort for food. Still others have moral or religious objections to the practice. If you have moral or religious objections, please skip to the next chapter as there is plenty of other information elsewhere in this book to help you raise a healthy diet without meat. If you are merely squeamish, though, this chapter may put you at ease. Be forewarned, though, that this chapter contains graphic pictures of chicken slaughter.

Selecting Chickens

For sheer efficiency, the easiest choice is to order day-old Cornish cross chicks from your local agricultural supply store. These are also known as "broilers." These are bred to grow quickly with lower feed requirements and to pluck easily. These are a sort of hybrid franken-chicken and are simply voracious eating machines. In fact, they eat so much and gain so much weight so fast that they may start dropping dead or breaking their legs from sheer weight anytime after 12 weeks of age.

⊗ Broilers gathered around a waterer.

Another way to obtain chickens for meat is to let a couple of hens stay broody in the spring and raise a handful of chicks to broiler size by fall. Come fall, pick all the new roosters to be meat birds, plus any of the older hens that aren't laying, leaving yourself with a flock around the same size you started with in the spring—about 10 to 20. The meat birds get processed in the fall, vacuum sealed, and frozen. You should take newly hatched chicks and raise them in the brooder, and thenceforth keep them separate from your regular laying birds. Otherwise, your hens will figure out that you've killed them and get spooked, and your rooster will get aggressive.

Housing for Meat Birds

Unlike chicks of other breeds, broilers can usually be removed from the brooder at about four weeks old because they are pretty well feathered, and it's during a warm time of the year. This is good, because otherwise they'd outgrow the brooder. Regular laying birds raised for meat should be kept in the brooder for six weeks before going outside.

Meat birds are around for only three months of the year, at most, so permanent housing doesn't make as much sense for them as it does with laying hens. What a lot of small farmers use, and we use one too, is a device called a "chicken tractor." A chicken tractor is a portable enclosure that lets the chickens get fresh air and fresh grass. It is moved every day so the chickens don't end up lying around in their own excrement.

There are about a million ways to make a chicken tractor. Just search on the Internet, and you'll find hundreds of designs, many for free. Your choice of design should allow for about four square feet per bird. Many designs are completely enclosed to exclude predators and keep birds from escaping. So far, I've had no real predator problems, and the Cornish crosses that we grow are too heavy to fly, so our chicken tractor is on wheels and has sides made of only three feet of chicken wire.

Feeding Meat Birds

Meat birds should receive a starter/grower from the day they arrive until the week before they are processed. The week before, they should be put on a leaner ration. For this you can use either a finishing feed or ordinary layer crumbles like you give your laying hens. As broilers, particularly, seem to have a nearly insatiable appetite, you should feed them by weight according to the directions on the bag.

⊗ The easiest housing for meat birds is a chicken tractor.

Some breeds of meat birds will forage while in the chicken tractor, but the broiler crosses will mostly just lay around and eat feed. So you shouldn't count on forage providing a lot of their food.

Slaughtering Birds

As a kid, my family raised chickens, and sometimes I got stuck with plucking them, which seemed to take forever and was less than pleasant. But then I got older and wiser and learned of better ways!

Food should be withdrawn from birds destined for slaughter 12 hours before the appointed

⊗ A killing cone. They don't need to be this elaborate.

time, though continuation of water is advisable. This precaution will make sure no food is in the upper digestive tract and thus reduce the possibility of contaminating the meat with digestive contents.

Usually, you should not carry a bird by its feet due to the potential for spinal damage, but for purposes of slaughter it is acceptable if done gently. Catch the bird by its feet and immediately hold it upside down. Swing it a little on its way to the killing cone, and it should settle down. Provide support for its back while carrying if needed. Then insert it head down in the killing cone.

The proper way to slaughter a bird, except for farmers whose religions specify another method, is to cut off the bird's head while the bird is either hanging from its feet or inserted upside down in a funnel-type device called a "killing cone." Use a good, sharp, strong knife for this. Put a leather glove on your weak hand, and grab the bird's head, holding its beak closed. Then, take the knife and cut off the head in one smooth motion. Once the head has been removed, any squawks or twitches observed thereafter are a result of pattern-generating neurons in the spinal cord and *not* conscious volition. I checked with my local veterinarian on this, and he assured me that cutting off the chicken's head is entirely humane. When the head is cut off, the neck will flex all over the place, splattering blood everywhere. I put a piece of Plexiglass in front of the killing cone to avoid getting blood on me. The bird should bleed out in 65 seconds or less, but it doesn't hurt to leave it for a couple of minutes because you don't want to scald a bird if it still has a breathing reflex because it could inhale water while being scalded.

Hanging the bird upside down or using a killing cone is important for two reasons. First,

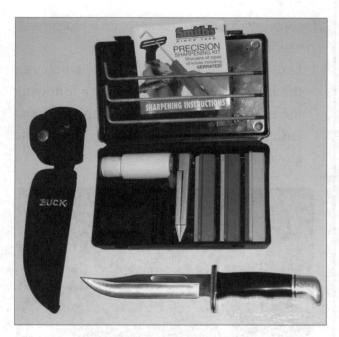

A proper knife makes slaughtering easier.

it helps remove the greatest possible amount of blood from the bird's tissues, which presents a more appetizing appearance. Second, it helps keep the bird from struggling and hurting itself.[49] Blood collected from the bird can be added to the compost pile. If a killing cone isn't used, a noose can be used to hang the bird upside down by the feet.

A killing cone, mentioned previously, is a funnel-shaped device with a large hole on the top into which the bird is inserted headfirst. The hole in the bottom is large enough that the bird's head and neck stick out, but nothing else. The entire device is usually about a foot long. Killing cones can be purchased via a number of poultry suppliers, just be sure to order the correct size for the birds being killed. They are simple enough that anyone can make one from sheet metal and rivets, and many people have improvised by cutting the top off of a small traffic cone.

Once the bird has been killed, it needs to be scalded and then plucked. In scalding, the bird is dipped and then moved around in hot water for 60 to 90 seconds to break down the proteins that hold the feathers in place. Commercial processors use rather elaborate multistage arrangements for this process, but a mini-farmer simply needs to have a bucket of water of the correct temperature ready. Most on-farm slaughtering processes for chickens and guineas use what is called a *hard scald* that loosens the feathers and removes the outer layer of skin. For this, the water temperature should be between 138 and 148 degrees.[50] This temperature range is sufficiently important that it should be measured with a thermometer.

For a small operation, the easiest way to get the right temperature is to fill a five-gallon bucket half full of water and insert a thermometer. Slowly add boiling water from a large pot on the stove until the temperature of the water in the bucket is on the high side of the recommended range. Then, once the bird has been killed, grab it by the feet and hold it under the water for 60 to 90 seconds, sloshing it up and down slightly. The timing on this has some room for flexibility, so you can just count. If more than one bird is being processed, keep an eye on the temperature and add boiling water whenever the thermometer drops close to the low side of the recommended temperature range. The water should be replaced every dozen chickens, any time it has been allowed to sit unused for a half hour or more, or any time the water has obviously been contaminated with feces. In the case of broilers, this is usually for every chicken.

[49] Mercia, L. (2000) *Storey's Guide to Raising Poultry*

[50] Fanatico, A. (2003) *Small Scale Poultry Processing*

The first incarnation of the Markham Farm chicken plucker.

Once the bird has been scalded, the feathers are removed in a process known as plucking. It is easiest to hang the bird by its feet and use both hands to grab the feathers and pull them out. If the bird was killed and scalded correctly, this shouldn't take long, although it *is* messy. The feathers can be added to a compost pile and are an excellent source of nitrogen. A few small "pin feathers" will remain on the bird, and these can be removed by gently pressing with the back side of a butter knife. A few hairs will also remain, and these can be singed off by going very quickly over the carcass with a propane torch. If you process a lot of chickens, you might consider an automated plucker that is easily made at home. The most impressive homemade plucker is the Whizbang Chicken Plucker, designed by Herrick Kimball, and the plans are in his book titled *Anyone Can Build a Tub-Style Chicken Plucker*. I have designed a less expensive table-style chicken plucker and have included complete plans, parts list, and photos in the next chapter.

The bird's entrails should now be removed in a process called evisceration.

1 Loosen the bird's crop, which is between the breast meat and the skin, by following the esophagus down to the crop and loosening it. As you'll note, I wear disposable gloves for processing.

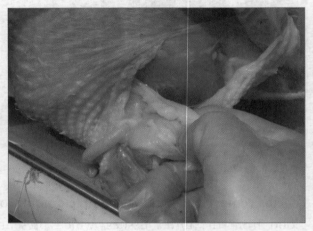

In this photo, the trachea is on the left and the esophagus is on the right.

2 A sharp knife is used to carefully (so as not to puncture any intestines and contaminate the meat) make an incision from the vent in the skin of the abdomen up to the breast bone. There will likely be a layer of fat there, which you can carefully pull apart by hand.

Opening the abdominal cavity.

3   The viscera are carefully removed by hand. With the breast facing up, just reach your hand into the body cavity as far as you can.

⊗ Reach your hand deeply into the cavity.

4   Gently grab a handful of viscera, and pull it completely out of the body cavity. Then scrape the lungs off the backbone. (They are bright pink.) Some people save the heart, liver, and gizzard. If you do, separate them from the rest of the viscera and refrigerate them immediately.

⊗ You may need to remove a couple of handfuls of entrails.

5   Cut out the vent, being careful not to contaminate the bird with the contents. Use a garden hose to wash out the body cavity afterward.

⊗ Carefully cut out the vent.

6   Turn the bird on its back and cut off the neck. A lot of folks use the neck for making chicken stock, so if you do, it should be refrigerated immediately.

⊗ Put the bird on its back and cut off the neck.

7 Turn the bird right-side up and cut off the oil gland.

⊗ Don't forget to remove the oil gland.

8 Now, give the chicken a thorough inside and out rinse with the garden hose and put the completed whole chicken in a tub of ice water. Make sure to keep an eye on the ice and keep it cold! I add a tablespoon of bleach (to kill germs) and a cup of salt (to pull residual blood out of the meat) to the water, but neither is strictly necessary. If you can keep the water ice cold for four hours before freezing the bird, it will be more tender than it would be if frozen immediately.

⊗ Monitor the ice water to make sure it remains icy.

Bird blood, feathers, entrails, and other parts can be composted just like anything else, although many books on composting say to avoid it. Many authors counsel to avoid animal tissues in compost because they can be attractive to stray carnivores and rodents and because in a casual compost pile, sufficiently high temperatures to kill human pathogens may not be achieved. But if you make thermophilic compost, the only precautions needed are to make sure that any big parts of the bird are cut up and that the parts are buried in the middle of the pile with plenty of vegetable matter. In this way, the compost itself acts as a biofilter to stop any odors, and the high-carbon vegetable matter, combined with the high-nitrogen bird parts, will form seriously thermophilic compost in short order. Consequently, the nutrients that the birds took from the land are returned to the land in a safe and efficient manner.

17

The Markham Farm Chicken Plucker

If you are processing only 1 or 2 chickens for meat, just plucking by hand is fine. But we usually process 10 to 15 chickens at a time, and under those conditions plucking becomes too time-consuming for efficiency. I had tried the cheap drill attachments with no luck, and building my own tub-style chicken plucker seemed awfully expensive—hundreds of dollars—to make economic sense. We needed something that could be built much less expensively and still do a good job; thus arose our own chicken plucker design that I'll be sharing with you.

Construction

1   Use the two 7-1/2-inch pieces and two 12-inch pieces of 2 × 4 lumber to construct the drum holder as illustrated, using two deck screws for each union. The center of the second cross-piece is 3-1/4 inch from the connected end. Drill 3/16-inch holes at 1-1/8 inches and 4-3/8 inches from the free ends of the 12-inch pieces. When done, paint the piece and let it dry.

Parts List

1	12" long 1/2" diameter steel shaft	Grainger Part # 5JW35
2	½" Pillow block bearings	Grainger Part # 2X897
2	4" sheaves for 1/2" diameter shaft	Grainger Part # 3X909
1	10" spoked sheave for 1/2" diameter shaft	Grainger Part # 3X934
1	4L V-belt, 1/2" × 54"	
1	2" sheave to fit whatever motor you are using	
1	1/4–1/2 hp motor; 1600–1800 RPM	
1	Piece of 4" diameter PVC pipe, cut 6.5" long	
25	Chicken Plucker fingers	Stromberg's Item # FIN
2	7-1/2" pieces of 2 × 4 lumber	
2	12" pieces of 2 × 4 lumber	
1	24" pieces of 2 × 6 lumber	
1	12" × 20" piece of flat wood 1-1/2" thick	
4	1/4" × 2" lag bolts with 1/2" drive heads	
4	1/4" flat washers	
1	4-1/4" T-hinge with screws	
2	4-1/2" lag bolts	
12	2-1/2" deck screws	
1	12" × 10" piece of 1/4" plywood	
Paint		

Additional hardware as needed to mount the motor to the piece of 2 × 6 board.

⌄ **Unpainted drum holder.**

2   Cut off a piece of 4-inch PVC pipe that is 6-1/2 inches long, and then use a flexible ruler (like the kind you get in the sewing section) to put four longitudinal lines evenly spaced every 3-1/2 inches around the circumference.

3   Mark two of the lines opposite each other at 1-1/4 inch, 2-9/16 inch, 3-7/8 inch, and 5-1/4 inch from one end. Mark the other pair of opposite lines at 1-15/16 inches, 3-1/4 inches and 4-9/16 inches from the same end. Then use a 3/4-inch spade bit to bore holes centered on each mark. After, pull plucker fingers until

⊗ Plucker drum marked longitudinally.

⊗ Plucker drum with fingers installed.

they sit in each hole. This will require some muscle!

4 Complete the drum by inserting the sheaves (with tightening screw facing outboard) into either end of the drum, running the shaft through both sheaves, aligning the outside edge of each sheave with the outside edge of the drum, and then tightening the sheaves to the shaft. Then, secure the sheaves to the drum with epoxy. For this sort of work, I prefer the putty type. Set aside while the epoxy cures.

5 Paint the large board and allow it to dry. Then, insert the steel loop. On the large board, the loop should be 1-1/2 inches from the rear edge and 4-3/4 inches from the right edge. Use pilot holes to keep the steel loops from splitting the boards. Use screws to secure the rectangular end of the T-hinge on the big board with the hinge facing up, the back 8-1/4 inches from the back edge of the board, and the right 1-7/8 inches from the right edge of the board.

6 Paint the 2 × 6 board and allow it to dry. Insert the steel loop centered and

⊗ Completed plucker drum.

⊗ The large board with hinge and hook installed.

1-1/2-inch from the top edge and install mounting hardware for the motor as necessary to position the shaft 13-3/4 inches from the bottom and facing left.

7 Connect the 2 × 6 board to the large board using the T-hinge such that the right edge of the 2 × 6 board is 1-1/4 inches from the right edge of the large board, and then mount the motor to the 2 × 6 board.

8 Attach the drum holder you made in Step 1, holes facing up, to the front of the large board with the left side of the drum holder aligned with the left side of the large board and the rear edge of the drum holder 4-1/2-inch back from the front edge of the large board. Use deck screws drilled in from the bottom of the large board into the long boards of the drum holder.

9 Slide the shafts on either end of the drum into the pillow block bearings, mount the bearings to the drum holder using the 1/4-inch lag bolts and washers, and then loosen the Allen screws in the sheaves so that the shaft is even with the end of the left-hand bearing and projecting a few inches out of the right-hand bearing. Make sure the Allen screws on both bearings are facing left and that the drum is centered and moves freely; then tighten down

⊗ Recycled 2 × 6 board with hook and hardware.

The 2 × 6 board and the large board connected with the T-hinge.

until both are in the same plane. Then attach a bungee cord between the two steel loops to keep tension on the belt. Depending on your arrangement, you may need to use an alternative such as steel wire and a turnbuckle for tensioning.

11 Cut a slot suitable for allowing the shaft to pass through the 1/4-inch plywood, and then paint it and allow it to dry. Finally, attach it to the long right arm of the drum holder with

the Allen screws on the bearings and sheaves. Finally, attach the large spoked sheave to the right side of the shaft with the Allen screw facing to the right.

10 Place the entire machine on a stable flat surface with the drum portion hanging off the edge. Run a V-belt between the sheave on the motor and the sheave that rotates the drum. Adjust the sheaves on their respective shafts

The plucker drum and bearings mounted on the drum holder.

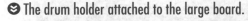

The drum holder attached to the large board.

⊗ Plucker with belt and tensioner installed.

⊗ Safety shield installed. Keep hands away from the belt and pulleys!

short wood screws so that it prevents chicken parts from being caught in the spoked sheave.

About the Motor and Electrical Safety

My first plucker with this design was made using a motor I had picked up at a yard sale for $2, but the design illustrated here features a 1/4 horsepower farm-duty motor I purchased for $110. The motor should be wired according to the directions that came with it, paying close attention to make sure that it is turning clockwise (when viewed from the rear) and properly grounded. The clockwise turning means the chicken feathers will go down toward the ground rather than up into your face during operation.

Because chickens are wet from the scald while being plucked, there is a hazard with water being around electricity. Therefore, it is extremely important that you plug this device into a terminal strip that contains an integral ground-fault circuit interrupter (GFCI). These are not cheap, but they could save your life from an unexpected electrical shock. Don't skip this.

18

Public Domain Thresher Designs

The two main components of the I-Tech rice huller are a hand mill/flour mill or grain grinder and a rubber-faced disk made from

- a rubber disk,
- a steel washer for mounting the rubber disk on the hand mill, and
- cyanoacrylate glue ("super glue" or "krazy glue") to attach the rubber disk onto the steel washer.

The stationary disk (A) is removed and replaced by a rubber-faced disk (B). Turning the auger handle (C) presses rice grains between the rubber-faced disk (B) and rotating disk (D), and then they are rolled out. The soft rubber disk allows the hulls to be removed with minimal damage to the rice kernels. Natural (gum) rubber is used for the rubber disk because it has better abrasion resistance than synthetic rubber. (The "Corona" hand mill is available from R&R Mill Co., 45 West First North Street, Smithfield, UT 84335, USA.)

Short-grain rice can be hulled at a rate of 200 g/min. The percentage of rice hulled varies from 75% to 99% depending on the rice cultivars, the spacing between the stationary rubber disk and the rotating abrasive

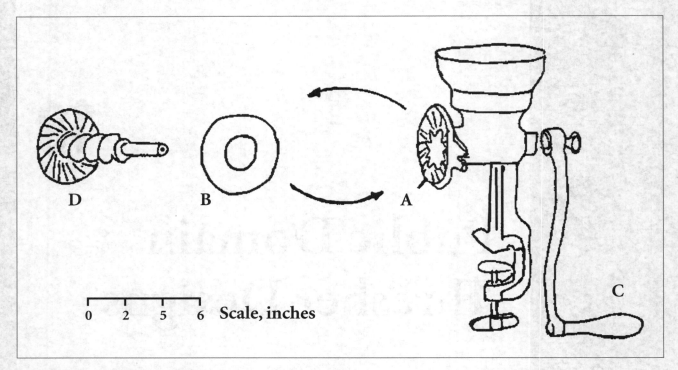

Scale, inches

0   2   5   6

⊗ Standard grain grinder modified to husk rice and spelt.

disk, and the uniformity of spacing between the disks. A tin-plated steel burr disk may produce a black gum residue when hulling rice, until the tin is worn off. No black residue was found when using a cast iron disk or stone disk.

The grain huller also hulls millet (*Panicum miliaceum*), sesame (*Sesamum indicum*), and spelt wheat (*Triticum spelta*) as well as removes saponins from quinoa (*Chenopodium quinoa*). To "wet" hull sesame, soak the seeds in 1% (w: v) lye (sodium hydroxide) solution for 10 seconds to 5 minutes, then rinse with water and 1% solution of acetic acid (Shamanthaka Sastry et al., *J. Am. Oil Chem. Soc.* 46:592A, 1969; Moharram et al., *Lebensmit. Wissen. Tech.* 14:137, 1981). A steel burr disk is preferred for wet hulling sesame, while a stone disk is preferred for hulling spelt wheat.

A hand-operated rice huller has a (A) stationary disk, (B) rubber disk, (C) handle, and (D) rotating disk with auger. Remove the stationary disk and replace with the rubber-faced disk.

In the United States, the C.S. Bell model 60 (cost: $325) and the Corona hand mill (cost: $40) represent two ends of the spectrum of hand mill quality. For serious hulling, the C.S. Bell is the better choice. This mill weighs 54 pounds, its auger shaft is supported by two bronze bearings with oilers, the grinding disks self-aligns and the mill can be motorized. The bronze bearing with oilers allow the shaft to rotate at 300 rpm without heating up (C.S. Bell, PO Box 291 Tiffin, OH 44883, phone 419-448-0791).

The Corona hand mill weighs 14 pounds, it has no bearings, the grinding disks do not self-align, and the mill cannot be motorized (R&R Mill Co., 45 West First North, Smithfield, UT 84335, phone 801-563-3333).

Conversion of a Leaf Shredder/Wood Chipper into a Grain Thresher

This invention was declared public domain August 1994, a gift to humanity.

A portable, engine-driven thresher can be made by modifying a leaf shredder/wood chipper or a hammer mill. Small shredders/chippers use five to eight horsepower gas engines that rotate at 2,800 or 3,600 revolutions per minute (rpm). The modification requires

- converting the free-swinging hammers into rasp bars,
- reducing the rotational speed of the hammers (250 to 1,000 rpm on a 12-inch diameter hammer arms), and
- altering the discharge port to allow smaller, threshed material to pass through a 3/8 to 3/4 inch screen while retaining larger materials.
- (Optional) If electricity is accessible, the gas engine can be replaced with a 1/2- to 3/4-horsepower capacitor start electric motor (1,725 rpm).

Materials: A five horsepower, 2,800 rpm "Roto-Hoe model 500" leaf shredder/wood chipper is used (see picture following the text). Additional parts include

4 2-inch C clamps (A),

6 5/8 × 3-inch bolts (B),

6 1/8 × 1-inch cotter pins (C),

1 5/8-inch inside diameter × 18-inch drip irrigation tubing or garden hose (D) as spacers between hammers, and

1 8 × 10-inch sheet metal or cardboard (E) to block the slotted portion of the leaf shredder/wood chipper exit port.

Modification: The Roto-Hoe shredder has six sets of three free-swinging hammers (F). Convert the six sets of hammers into six rasp bars as follows: Cut the 5/8-inch tubing (D) in segments to fit between the free-swinging hammers (F). Tie the free-swinging hammers (F) together by inserting the 5/8-inch bolt (B) into the hole of the first hammer, followed by a segment of tubing (D) as a spacer, then another hammer, followed by a second segment of tubing, followed by the third hammer. Drill a 5/32-inch hole on the threaded portion of the bolt that protrudes from the third hammer. Reassemble the bolt, hammers, and spacers together and lock the bolt in place with the cotter pin (C) installed in the 5/32-inch hole. This assembly constitutes a rasp bar. Repeat the above procedure and tie together the remaining five sets of free-swinging hammers. Manually rotate the rasp bars and check for clearance between the rasp bars and the walls of the threshing chamber. If there is insufficient clearance, adjust the bolt position, grind the bolt head, or cut the bolt length to obtain the necessary clearance between the rasp bars and the walls.

The Roto-Hoe shredder exit port consists of a slotted section and a 3/4-inch diameter punched-hole screen. Use the sheet metal or cardboard (E) and C clamps (A) to block the slotted portion of the exit port (G). The threshed grain exits through the 3/4-inch holes.

Start the engine and spin the rasp bars. Again, check for clearance between the rasp bars and the walls of the threshing chamber. If there is a knocking sound, grind the bolt down to obtain the necessary clearance.

Operation: Start the engine and spin the rasp bars. Dried plant materials with vines, stems, and leaves are fed in batches through the hopper. After

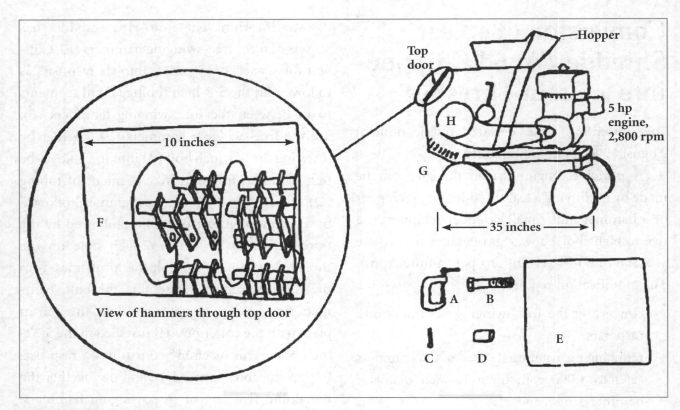

Labels within figure: Top door, Hopper, 5 hp engine, 2,800 rpm, H, G, 10 inches, F, View of hammers through top door, 35 inches, A, B, C, D, E

☣ Leaf shredder converted into a grain thresher.

threshing for one to three seconds, open the top door to eject the longer vines, stems, and leaves that have not been chopped up. Seeds and small bits of plant material exit through the punched holes at the bottom. The mixture of seeds and plant material must be separated after threshing.

The 3/4-inch diameter holes in the exit port are suitable for larger seeds (e.g., beans) and seeds with loosely attached husks (e.g., wheat, bok choy, and amaranth). Small seeds and seeds with tight husk or pods (e.g., barley, clover, and radish) require smaller diameter exit holes to retain the larger unthreshed materials while passing the smaller threshed grains. This can be achieved by attaching a screen with smaller openings under the 3/4 inch diameter punched holes.

Larger seeds crack easier than smaller seeds. Reduce the rasp bar speed to decrease the percentage of cracked seeds. Use a larger pulley (H) and/or reduce the engine speed to achieve the desire rasp bar speed:

250–400 rpm for beans and large seeds

400–800 rpm coriander, radish, sunflower

600–1400 rpm wheat, oats, barley, rice, and small seeds

Typical threshing rates (pounds of seeds per hour):

Amaranth 66

Bok choy 22 to 30

Oats 94

Pinto bean 117

Soy bean 81 to 127

19

Preserving the Harvest

Since the purpose of a mini-farm is to meet a substantial portion of your food needs, you should store your food so that it is available over the course of the year. The four methods of food preservation that I use and will be explaining in this chapter are canning, freezing, dehydrating, and root cellaring. These methods have all been practiced for decades in the United States and can be undertaken with confidence. Each method has its strengths and weaknesses, which is why they are all covered. Advanced techniques that I won't be explaining in this chapter include cheese making, wine making, and meat curing.

Canning

Perhaps the most intimidating form of food preservation for the uninitiated is canning. Stories are everywhere about people dying from botulism because of improperly canned foods, so some people conclude that canning is an art like making fugu (the poisonous Japanese blowfish) in that the slightest mishap will render canned foods unfit. Fortunately, these impressions are not accurate. Modern canning methods are the result of decades of research and can be followed by anybody with a sixth-grade education. (Yes, I knew somebody personally with a sixth-grade education who canned safely.) Those few cases of poorly canned goods resulting in botulism poisoning in the modern era stem from people who do not follow the most basic directions on how to can.

Current standards for home canning come from research by the USDA that is continually updated. Most of the standards haven't changed for decades, because the research methods are quite thorough. The USDA researchers deliberately introduce viable heat-resistant bacteria spores into foods in home canning jars and then use temperature sensors inside the jars as they are canned. After canning, the cans are kept at the precise temperature necessary for best bacterial growth for several months and then opened in a sterile environment and tested for presence of the bacteria or any other spoilage.

The USDA standards published around World War I allowed for up to 2% spoilage, but the standards published since that time require 0% spoilage. This means that foods canned at home using current USDA guidelines are completely safe. Actually, the times and temperatures provided by the USDA also contain a safety factor. This means that if experimenters achieved 0% spoilage at 237 degrees for 11 minutes, the standards specify 240 degrees for 15 minutes. Times and temperatures are always rounded *up*, never down.

There are two methods of canning: boiling water bath and steam pressure. The choice of method depends on the level of acidity of the food being canned. This is because the length of time that spoilage organisms will survive at a given temperature is longer in foods that are *less* acidic. So less acidic foods get canned using the steam pressure method that produces a temperature of 240 degrees; more acidic foods get canned in a boiling water bath that produces temperatures of 212 degrees. The length of time specified for canning is based on how long it takes the heat to fully penetrate a particular food in a particular-sized jar. The standards are written for half-pint, pint, and quart jars. If a mixture (such as stew) is being canned, then the canning time and temperature for the entire mixture is based on that of the ingredient that requires the most time. By using the correct method, container, and processing time, you can be assured of the safety of your canned food.

Home Canning Jars

Jars for home canning are available at Walmart and many hardware and grocery stores, although their availability is seasonal. These jars are heavy walled and specifically designed to withstand the rigors of temperature, pressure, and vacuum created by home canning. Forget the old-style (though attractive) jars with rubber gaskets and wire closures since they are no longer recommended by the USDA. Today's standards specify two-piece caps that include a reusable metal ring called a "band" and a flat nonreusable lid that has a sealing compound around its outer edge. The bands can be used until they have warped or rusted, but the lids must be thrown away once they have been used and bought new.

Home canning jars are expensive—about $7/dozen at the time of writing. So figure a bit over $0.50 apiece. However, their durability easily justifies their cost—home canning jars will last decades. By the time a jar has seen use for 20 seasons, its cost has dropped to $0.02. Once the jars and bands are purchased (new jars usually come with bands), you just need to buy new lids for each use—which are usually less than $0.10 each. There are a handful of brands of home canning jars available, and on the basis of my own experience, I recommend Ball and Kerr, which are both manufactured in the United States by Jarden Corporation. I especially recommend Ball lids, because their underside is coated with a compound that keeps the food from coming into contact with the metal of the lid. This helps food stay fresher longer, and they cost the same as noncoated lids.

My stepmother often used glass jars from spaghetti sauce, mayonnaise, and similar products as long as the bands and lids fit and the rims were free from nicks or imperfections that would prevent a good seal. The good news is that she saved money. The bad news is that sometimes these jars would break and create a mess and lose the food. Most authorities counsel against using these one-trip glass jars because they aren't properly tempered, and their higher risk of breakage could cause injury and loss of valuable food. For these reasons, I recommend using jars specifically designed for home canning. If economy is a big consideration, then it is worthwhile to visit yard sales and flea markets where you can buy inexpensive, properly designed jars for home canning.

Foods and Canning Methods

As I mentioned earlier, the type of canning method required depends on how acidic the food is. Acidic foods (with a pH of less than 4.6) need only a water bath canning method while less acidic foods (with a pH greater than 4.6) require steam pressure canning. Unfortunately, the combination of time and temperature in a pressure canner can render some foods less nutritious and other foods unappetizing. Broccoli is a good example in that it requires such an extensive period of pressure canning to be safe that the results aren't worth eating. Broccoli is much better preserved through either freezing or pickling. The goal, then, is to use the method that preserves the maximum nutrition and palatability while maintaining a good margin of safety. So if I don't list a canning method for a vegetable (Table 19, page 202), it is because I have determined that it is better preserved using some other method.

An age-old method for canning foods that cannot be safely canned otherwise is to raise the acidity of the food by either fermenting it or adding vinegar. Sauerkraut is a great example because cabbage is not suitable for either canning or freezing in its fresh state, but if acidified through lactic acid fermentation (and thereby becoming sauerkraut), it can be canned in a boiling water bath while retaining its most important health benefits. (Technically, with great care, you can freeze grated cabbage, but your results may vary.) Pickles are made either by fermenting vegetables in a brine (which raises their acidity through the production of lactic acid) and/or by adding vinegar. These methods create a sufficiently acidic product so that only a brief period in a water bath canner is required.

Boiling water bath canning is suitable for all fruits, jams, jellies, preserves, and pickles. Tomatoes are right at the margin of pH 4.6, so they can be safely canned in a boiling water bath if a known amount of citric acid (or commercial bottled lemon juice) is added. The correct amount is one tablespoon of lemon juice or 1/4 teaspoon of citric acid per pint. Vinegar can be used instead, at the rate of two tablespoons per pint, but it can cause off-flavors. The only time I would recommend vinegar is in salsa. The acidity (or, rather, the *taste* of the acidity) can be offset by adding two tablespoons of sugar for every tablespoon of lemon juice, which won't interfere with the canning process. While few people choose to can figs (usually they are dehydrated instead), it is worth noting that they are right on the border line of acidity as well and should have lemon juice added in the same proportion as tomatoes if they are being canned. Everything else—vegetables, meats, seafood, and poultry—*must* be canned in a steam pressure canner.

Boiling water canners are pretty much maintenance free. Just wash them like any other pot, and you are done. Pressure canners, on the other hand, require some minimal maintenance. The the accuracy of the dial gage on top of the canner should be checked annually by your Cooperative Extension Service. If it is inaccurate, send it to the manufacturer for recalibration. When the canner is not in use, store it with the lid turned upside down on top of the body. Never immerse the lid or dial gage in water! Instead, clean them with a damp cloth and mild detergent if needed. Clean any vent holes with a pipe cleaner. The rubber seal should be removed and cleaned with a damp cloth after each use. Some manufacturers recommend that the gasket be given a light coat of vegetable oil, and some don't—so be certain to follow the manufacturer's directions. If you follow manufacturer's directions in using your pressure canner, it won't explode, as was sometimes the case years ago. Modern canners have a number of built-in safety features that our grandmothers' models lacked, and aside from deliberately defeating those safety mechanisms, an explosion is practically impossible.

Foods to be canned are packed into hot glass jars using either the fresh-pack or the hot-pack method. The methods are pretty much self-explanatory from their names: Fresh-packed foods are put into the jars fresh and then hot liquid, brine, or syrup is added, and hot-packed foods are put into jars after having been heated to boiling. In some cases, either method can be used. Once packed, the jar is filled with liquid (brine, broth, syrup, pickling juice, etc. depending on the recipe) up to within 1/4 to 1 inch from the top of the jar. This space is called headspace and is needed to accommodate the expansion of the food in the jar as it is heated and allow for a good vacuum seal.

Using a Boiling Water Canner

Boiling water canners come with a wire rack that holds the jars so that they won't be sitting on the bottom of the canner or bumping into each other and breaking. Using a rack ensures that water of the same temperature surrounds the jars on all sides so that heating is even and therefore the best results are obtained.

Jars need to be sterilized for canning. My method is a little different from that in most books, but it works quite well, and I've never had a jar spoil.

1. Fill the canner halfway with the hottest water from the tap.
2. Put the jars you plan to use in the rack, without any lids.
3. Submerge the rack and jars in the canner, adding enough tap water to completely fill all

the jars and stand 1-1/2 inches above the tops of the jars.

4. Put on the lid and bring water to a vigorous boil, then adjust the heat to obtain a steady rolling boil.

5. Meanwhile, put a smaller pot on the stove without water, uncovered, but apply no heat. Put the lids (but not the bands) in this pot, making sure that the sealing compound is facing up.

6. Remove the jars from the canner one at a time using a jar lifter, and empty the boiling water in them into the smaller pot until it is nearly full and set them aside on a dish towel. (Once the smaller pot is full, empty the water in the remaining jars into the sink.) Keep the lids in the standing boiling water at this point—additional heating of the lids is not required.

7. Lift up the rack in the canner so that it is supported by the sides of the canner.

8. Put the product into the jars (a special canning funnel is helpful for this), allowing for proper headspace, get the lids out of the hot water in the smaller pot one at a time using tongs, and place them on the jars, then secure with a screw band tightened only finger-tight. (If you tighten it any more than that, the jar will break when you heat it in the canner.)

9. Put the filled jars in the wire rack, and submerge them in the water in the canner.

10. Turn up the heat on the burner a bit if needed to maintain a steady rolling boil. Start the timer once that boil has been achieved and put the lid on the canner.

11. Once the appropriate time has elapsed, remove the jars and place them on a dish towel at least 2 inches from each other on all sides and allow to sit undisturbed for at least 12 hours.

12. If additional product (more than one canner load) is being processed, pour the water back into the canner from the smaller pot, put clean jars in, and add any needed water to completely fill and submerge with 1-1/2 inches of water on top of the jars, then repeat the process starting at Step 4.

Using a Pressure Canner

Each pressure canner is a little different, so read the manufacturer's directions and employ those in preference to mine if there is a contradiction. Pressure canners don't rely on completely submerging the jars. Instead, they rely on surrounding the jars with superheated steam at 240 degrees. They also come with a rack, but instead of being made of wire to hold jars securely in place like with a boiling water canner, it is a simple aluminum plate with holes in it. Put it in the canner so that the holes are facing up. When using a pressure canner, I don't sterilize the jars before use. Instead, I just make sure they are extremely clean, and I keep them in a large pot of near-boiling water at a simmer. You can also wash them in a dishwasher and keep them hot with the dishwasher's heating element.

1. Put the rack in the canner and put three inches of very hot tap water into the bottom.

2. Put already-filled and lidded jars on the rack using a jar lifter, leaving some space between the jars.

3. Put the lid on the canner, but leave off the weighted gage, turn up the heat until steam starts coming out of the port where you would put the weighted gage, and let the steam exhaust for 10 minutes.

4. Put the weighted gage on the port and keep the heat adjusted for a steady rocking motion

of the gage. Start timing from when the steady rocking motion starts.

5. Once the time is up, turn off the heat and let the canner sit until the dial gage reads zero or when no steam escapes when the weighted gage is nudged. Wait an additional 2 minutes just to be sure.

6. Remove the cover and then remove the jars with a jar lifter and put them on a towel, leaving 2 inches between them on all sides.

7. Leave the jars undisturbed for 24 hours.

Fruits

Practically any fruit can be canned, and all except figs are sufficiently acidic that they can be canned without additives. (Figs require the addition of one teaspoon of lemon juice per pint.) Fruit should be in peak condition, free from obvious blemishes or rot, and well washed. To be sufficiently heated during the canning process, fruits that are larger than one inch should be cut up so that no single piece is larger than a one inch cube. Pits and stones of large-seeded fruit should be removed, and the fruit should be treated in an antioxidant solution, particularly once it has been cut to prevent discoloration. Antioxidant solutions can be bought commercially, or you can make your own by mixing 3/4 cup of bottled lemon juice with a gallon of water.

Fruits are usually canned in sugar syrups because the sugar helps the fruit keep its color, shape, and flavor, although the sugar isn't strictly necessary to prevent bacterial spoilage. If you prefer, can the fruits by using plain water rather than a syrup. I don't recommend the use of artificial sweeteners in syrup because saccharine turns bitter from canning and aspartame loses its sweetness. (If you have ever bought a diet soda and thought that it tasted a bit like dirt, that means that the product was stored in an area of high temperature and the artificial sweetener was damaged.) A "very light" syrup uses two tablespoons of sugar per cup of water, a "light" syrup uses four tablespoons per cup of water and a "medium" syrup uses seven tablespoons per cup of water.

To fresh-pack fruits, add them to the jars and then pour simmering syrup (or water) into the jar until it is filled up to within 1/4 inch of the rim. Put the lids and screw bands on the jars finger-tight, and completely submerge in a boiling water canner for the specified time for that particular fruit. Then remove the jars from the canner and leave them to cool for at least 12 hours. Hot-packed fruits are handled pretty much the same except that the fruit is mixed with the syrup and brought to a light boil, and then fruit and syrup are added to the jar together.

Applesauce

Home-canned applesauce was a favorite of mine as a kid—I'd open up a couple of home-made biscuits on my plate, heap a generous quantity of applesauce on top, and dig in. Applesauce canned at home is simple, delicious, rich, and flavorful—nothing like the homogenized products available at the grocery store. Naturally, the same process used for applesauce can also be used for pears, quinces, and other fruits. Feel free to experiment! Here is my recipe and procedure for semichunky applesauce. Yield: 22–26 pints

Semichunky Applesauce
- 1 bushel of at least two types of apples, one type being rather sweet

- a bag of white and/or brown sugar (the actual amount added depends on your taste and the apples selected)
- cinnamon to taste
- allspice to taste
- nutmeg to taste
- lemon if desired

Procedure

- Wash 3/4 of the apples and remove stems, cut up into 1-inch chunks, including the core and peels, and put into a very large pot with about 1-inch of water in the bottom. (You can buy a simple contraption for a few bucks that cores and cuts apples into segments in just one motion—I recommend it highly!) Dip in an antioxidant solution once cut.
- Cook until all of the chunks are soft throughout. Start off on high heat and then lower to medium-high.
- Run the cooked apples through a strainer to remove the skins and seeds and put them back in the pot. (You can do this hot if you are careful.) I use a Villaware V200 food strainer because I could get it for less than $50 and it came with the right screen for my two favorite foods—applesauce and spaghetti sauce. There are a number of strainers on the market—including the classic Squeezo strainer—that will also work fine.
- Peel and core the remaining apples, cut up into small chunks, and add them to the pot as well. (I have a "Back to Basics" Peel-Away apple peeler that peels, cores, and slices quickly in a single operation. It costs less than $20 at a cooking store.)
- Continue cooking on medium-high until the newly added chunks are soft.

- Add sugar, lemon, and spices to taste. You will probably need less than 1/4 cup of sugar per pint if you used some sweet apples.
- Reduce heat to a simmer to keep the sauce hot while canning.
- Pour the sauce into freshly washed pint or quart canning jars, leaving 1/2 inch of headspace.
- Put on the lids and bands finger-tight.
- Completely submerge jars in boiling water in a boiling water canner for 15 minutes for pints or 20 minutes for quarts.
- Allow the jars to cool in a draft-free place for at least 12 hours before removing the bands, labeling, and storing in a cool dry place for up to two years.
- Enjoy!

Jellies

Jellies are made from fruit juice and sugar, and use heat and sugar for their preservation. The distinctive consistency of jelly comes from an interaction between the acids in the fruit, the pectin it contains, the sugar, and heat. Many fruits contain enough natural acid and pectin to make jelly without having to add anything but sugar. These include sour apples, crab apples, sour cane fruits, cranberries, gooseberries, grapes, and currants. Some fruits are slightly deficient in acid, pectin, or both and will require a small amount of added lemon juice, pectin, or both. These include ripe apples, ripe blackberries, wine grapes, cherries, and elderberries. Finally, some fruits simply won't make jelly without adding a significant quantity of lemon juice and/or pectin. These include strawberries, apricots, plums, pears, blueberries, and raspberries.

Because sugar plays an important role in the preservation of jellies, the amount called for in a recipe shouldn't be reduced. It also plays an important role in making the product gel, so using too little sugar can result in a syrup instead of a jelly.

The juice used to make jelly can be extracted in a number of ways. If you use a juice machine, use it only for fruits that would require added pectin anyway, such as berries, plums, and pears. This is because a juice machine won't properly extract the pectin from high-pectin fruits. The traditional way of extracting the juice is to clean and cut up the whole fruit (it is important to leave the peels on because pectin is concentrated near the peel) and put it in a flat-bottom pot on the stove with added water. For soft fruits, use just enough water to prevent scorching, but with hard fruits like pears you might need as much as a cup of water per pound of fruit. The fruit is cooked over medium heat until soft and then poured through a jelly bag. If you want a crystal-clear product (which I don't personally care about but many folks find aesthetically important), it is important not to squeeze the jelly bag but instead let the juice come through naturally and slowly. You should get about one cup of juice per pound of fruit. Jelly bags in various sizes can be purchased from cooking stores and over the Internet. If you use a juice machine, you should still strain the resulting juice through a jelly bag. If you can't find jelly bags, you can use a double-layer of cheesecloth lining a colander instead.

Once the juice has been extracted, it is combined with sugar and other ingredients (e.g., lemon juice and/or pectin depending on the recipe) and boiled on the stove until it reaches a temperature of 220 degrees as measured with a candy thermometer. The boiling point of pure water is 212 degrees, but that boiling point is raised when other substances such as sugar are added to the water. As water evaporates and the proportion of sugar in the water increases, the boiling point will slowly increase. If you live in the mountains, subtract 2 degrees for every 1,000 feet you live above sea level. So if you live at 3,000 feet, subtract 6 degrees—so boil the mixture only until it reaches 214 degrees. This is because the higher you are above sea level, the more easily water will evaporate because of lower air pressure.

Once the required temperature has been reached, fill sterilized jars with the hot mixture up to 1/4 inch from the top, put the two-piece caps on the jars finger-tight, and process in a boiling water canner for five minutes for half-pint or pint size. There are all sorts of jelly recipes on the Internet, but here are two of my favorites.

Strawberry Rhubarb Jelly
- 3 pints of strawberries
- 1-1/2 lbs of rhubarb stalks
- 6 cups of sugar
- 3/4 cup of liquid pectin

Pulverize and then liquefy the strawberries and rhubarb in a blender. Using either a jelly bag or two layers of cheesecloth, gently squeeze out 3-1/2 cups of juice and put it in a saucepan, mixing with the sugar, and then bring to a rolling boil. Add the pectin and allow to boil vigorously for *one minute only,* remove from heat, and immediately pour into hot sterile jars, leaving 1/4 inch of headspace. Process five minutes in a boiling water canner. Yield: 5 half-pints.

Apple Jelly

- 5 lbs apples
- 5 whole cloves
- 1/2 tsp cinnamon
- 8 cups water
- 8 cups sugar

Wash the apples and cut them in quarters, and put them in a covered casserole pan with the eight cups of water and spices. Put in the oven at 225 degrees overnight. In the morning, strain through cheesecloth or a jelly bag and collect the liquid. Add it to the cooking pot one cup at a time, simultaneously adding one cup of sugar for every cup of liquid. Heat to a rolling boil, stirring constantly, and check with a candy thermometer until it is boiling at 220 degrees. Immediately pour into hot sterilized pint or half-pint jars, tighten the lids finger-tight, and process for five minutes in a boiling water canner. Yield: 8 half-pints.

*

The same techniques covered in the recipes above can be used successfully with other fruits. For fruits high in natural pectin and acid, use the second recipe as a guide, and use the first recipe as a guide for fruits lacking pectin. For fruits that lack both pectin and acidity, use the first recipe as a guide but add 1-1/2 tsp of lemon juice per cup of liquid. Jams are made the same way except the entire fruit is pulverized and used, rather than just the juice.

Brined Pickles and Kraut

Pickling preserves food by raising its level of acidity. It is used for foods that are not naturally acidic enough to be safely canned using a boiling water method. The two methods most widely used are lactic acid fermentation in brine, and infusing with vinegar.

Brine fermentation is most often used with cucumbers to make kosher-style dill pickles, but it is also used to make sauerkraut. Many other vegetables—like collard greens—can also be processed this way, but since I've never tried it myself, I can't guarantee the results will be tasty! There are three very important aspects of doing brine fermentation. First, keep everything clean. Second, use only plain salt with no additives whatsoever, or all sorts of cloudiness and discolorations will result. (Regular salt contains anti-caking agents that will make the brine cloudy as well as iodine that will inhibit proper fermentation. Use canning salt!) Finally, pay close attention to the correct procedure, or your pickles will be soft and possibly even slimy.

Brine fermentation can take several weeks. It is also temperature sensitive and works best at temperatures ranging from 55 to 75 degrees. Before starting brined pickles, make sure you have both the time and the space to leave the containers undisturbed for a while. You should only use glass, nonchipped enamel, or food-grade plastic containers for fermentation. Under no circumstances should you consider using a metallic container because the product will become contaminated and possibly even poisonous. Don't use old-fashioned wooden barrels because sterilizing them is practically impossible. Start off with well-cleaned containers and well-washed produce.

Brined Dill Pickles

- 5 lbs of 3- to 4-inch pickling cucumbers
- 3 heaping Tbsp whole pickling spice
- 8 heads of fresh dill (1/3 of a bunch)

- 3/4 cup white (distilled) vinegar
- 1/2 cup pickling salt
- 5 pints (10 cups) of clean pure water

The proportions of salt, vinegar, and water in this recipe are not approximations—measure them exactly! You can double or quadruple the recipe if you keep the proportions the same for a larger batch of pickles. Put half of the pickling spices and a light layer of dill in the bottom of a clean food-grade plastic pail or pickling crock. Put in the cucumbers. Mix the remaining dill and spices with the salt, vinegar, and water and pour over the cucumbers. If the amount of liquid isn't enough to come about two inches above the cucumbers, make more liquid from water, salt, and vinegar according to the same proportions. Take a clean plate and place it on top of the cucumbers so they are held completely under the brine. The plate may need to be weighted down with a second plate. Cover the container loosely with plastic wrap covered with a clean towel held on with a couple of bungee cords tied together around the container like a big rubber band. Try to keep at room temperature—certainly no warmer than 72 degrees and no cooler than 60 degrees.

Uncover and check the pickles for scum once a day. Use a clean spoon to scoop off any scum, then put the towel back on. This should be the only time the pickles are uncovered. After three weeks, check the pickles by removing one from the container, cutting it lengthwise, and tasting it. If it is translucent and tastes like a good dill pickle, you are ready to can the pickles. If not, wait another week and try again.

Once the pickles are ready, remove them from the brine and pack into cleaned and cooled glass jars with a couple of heads of dill added to each jar. Take the brine, pour it into a large saucepan, and bring it to a boil, then pour it over the pickles in the jars, leaving 1/4-inch headspace. If you run out of brine, make additional brine from 4 pints of water, 1/4 cup of salt and 2 cups of vinegar raised to boiling. (Again, proportions are exact rather than approximate—use measuring cups!)

Put the lids on finger-tight, and process 10 minutes for pints or 15 minutes for quarts in a boiling water canner. Yield: 10 pints.

Sauerkraut
- Cabbage
- Canning/pickling salt

Any sort of cabbage can be used for this recipe, but larger heads tend to be sweeter. Remove any damaged outer leaves, quarter the heads, and remove the hard cores, then weigh the cabbage on a kitchen scale. Weighing the cabbage is important because the weight determines the amount of salt to use—3 Tbsp of salt per 5 pounds of cabbage. Shred the cabbage into slices of about 1/8 inch thickness, and using clean hands thoroughly mix the cabbage with the salt. Put the mixture into a five-gallon food-grade plastic container a little at a time and use a clean potato masher to mash the mixture until enough juice has been squeezed out of the cabbage that at least one or two inches of juice are above the cabbage by the time all the cabbage has been added.

Fill and seal a noncolored food-grade plastic bag with a mixture of 6 Tbsp salt and one gallon of water, and put this on the cabbage to weigh it down and keep it completely submerged, then cover the top of the container with plastic wrap. Keep the container at room temperature, and in four weeks, your sauerkraut will be ready. Just like with the brined pickles above, check daily for scum and remove any that you find. Once the kraut is ready, pour it in a large pot (or a portion of it at a time depending on the relative size of your pot) and heat while stirring to 190 degrees as indicated by a candy thermometer. Do NOT let it boil. Pack into clean canning jars and add brine to leave 1/4 inch of headspace, and process in a boiling water canner for 15 minutes for pints or 20 minutes for quarts. Yield: depends on how much cabbage you use.

Quick Process Pickles

Quick process pickles rely on vinegar for their acidity rather than fermentation, so they are faster and easier to make. (And you needn't worry about scum!) The vinegar used to make pickles lends its own character to the pickles, so be cautious about using flavored vinegars such as red wine, cider, or balsamic vinegar unless specifically required in a recipe. When the type of vinegar isn't mentioned in a recipe, use white distilled vinegar. The preservation process relies on a certain specific amount of acid, so always use vinegar that is 5% acidity.

Bread and Butter Pickles
- 4 lbs cucumbers, washed but not peeled
- 3 thinly sliced medium onions
- 1/3 cup of canning salt
- 4 cups distilled vinegar
- 3 cups sugar
- 2 Tbsp mustard seed
- 1 Tbsp + 1 tsp celery seed
- 1-1/2 tsp turmeric
- 2 tsp whole black pepper

Slice the cucumbers 1/4-inch thick and the onions as thinly as practical. Combine all of the ingredients except the cucumbers and onions in a large sauce pot and bring to a simmer (not a boil!). Add the cucumber and onion slices, and bring to a very light boil before turning down the heat to low. Pack the slices into jars and then fill with pickling liquid to 1/4 inch headspace, and put the lids on the jars finger-tight.

For the most crisp pickles, pasteurize by placing the jars in water deep enough to be at least 1 inch over the top of the jar lids that is kept at 180–185 degrees (check with a candy thermometer) for 30 minutes. Alternately, you can process in boiling water for 10 minutes for either pints or quarts. Allow to sit six weeks before using for the development of full flavor. Yield: 4 pints.

Vegetables

Vegetables (other than tomatoes) are not acidic enough to be canned using the boiling water method. Instead, they must be processed in a pressure canner for a fairly long period of time. The process is essentially the same for all vegetables, the only difference being in the processing time. For larger vegetables, cut into pieces so that there is at least one dimension less than 1/2-inch thick, bring pieces to a boil in water (to which 1/2 tsp of salt per quart can optionally be added), pour hot into clean jars allowing the right amount of head space, put on the caps finger-tight, and process for the time specified in Table 19. You might consider using a little sliver (1/2-inch × 1-inch) of kombu kelp instead of salt. Kelp enhances the flavor of canned vegetables because of the natural glutamaic acid that it contains.

Generally, the pressure canning methods employed with vegetables destroy a good portion of the vitamin C, so I recommend freezing instead. Regardless, the macronutrient and mineral values of vegetables remain intact after canning, so it is worthwhile if you don't have a freezer or reliable electric service.

Meat

Meat is usually better vacuum sealed and frozen, but where the electrical supply is unreliable or too expensive, canning meat is a viable alternative. Because canning times and temperatures for meats are significant, most vitamins that can be destroyed by heat, especially vitamin C, are destroyed in the process. On the other hand, both the protein and mineral value is unaffected, so as long as you have plenty of vegetables in your diet, canned meat isn't a problem.

While the USDA says that putting raw meat into jars and then processing it is safe, it is my opinion that the flavor suffers. So I recommend that all meats first be soaked for an hour in a brine made with 1 Tbsp salt to a gallon of water and then at least lightly browned in a little vegetable oil until rare and then packing into the jars. Once the meat is packed into the jars, the jars should be filled with boiling water, meat broth, or tomato juice to leave the amount of headspace described in Table 19. Most people prefer 1/2 tsp of salt added per pint, but this is optional. Put on the lids finger-tight, and process for the appropriate length of time. You can season meats before canning them, but avoid sage because the prolonged high temperatures can cause bitterness. Also, any meat broth you use *shouldn't contain flour, corn starch, or any other thickening agent* because under pressure canning conditions, thickening agents congeal and make it impossible to get all of the air

properly evacuated from the cans, and the risk of spoilage is increased.

Soups, Stews, and Other Mixtures

When canning anything that is a mixture of more than one ingredient, the time and headspace requirements from Table 19 that are the longest and largest for any of the ingredients apply. So if, for example, a mixture of carrots and peas were being canned, the processing time and headspace requirements for peas would be used since those are the greatest. The same warning about thickening agents regarding meats applies to stews as well.

Buffalo Stew
- 4 lbs buffalo stew meat cut into 1-inch cubes
- 12 medium red potatoes cut into 1/2 inch cubes
- 5 medium yellow onions, diced
- 2 lbs of carrots sliced 1/4-inch thick
- 2 stalks celery
- 1 Tbsp cooking oil
- 1 tsp salt
- 1/2 tsp ground black pepper
- 1 tsp thyme
- 1 clove garlic
- 3 quarts water

Get the three quarts of water boiling in a large saucepan and brown the stew meat in oil in the bottom of another large saucepan. Add all of the spices and vegetables to the meat, stir thoroughly, cover, and allow to cook down for five minutes. Then pour in the three quarts of boiling water slowly and carefully, and bring everything to a boil. Put into jars leaving 1 inch of headspace, and process in a pressure canner for 75 minutes for pints or 90 minutes for quarts. Yield: 9 pints.

Freezing

Like canning, freezing has its pros and cons. In its favor is that it is easier and quicker to freeze vegetables and meats than it is to pressure can them, and the resulting product is usually closer to fresh in terms of quality. Some things, like broccoli, are just plain inedible when canned but perfectly fine when frozen. The downside is that when freezing an appreciable amount of food, a large freezer is required—which isn't cheap. Figure at least $300 for a new one at current market price. Also a consideration is the ongoing ever-increasing cost of electricity. And, if you are in an area prone to long electrical outages, you could lose the entire contents of your freezer if you don't maintain a backup power supply of some sort. So you'll have to weigh the advantages and disadvantages. We have a reliable electric supply and not a lot of spare time at my house, so we do a lot of freezing.

I used to freeze in regular freezer bags from the grocery store or wrap things in freezer paper. No more! Now, the only method I use, and the only method I recommend, is vacuum sealing. Vacuum sealing consistently yields a superior product that keeps up to five times longer, so it is what I'll describe.

Getting a Sealer

I got my first vacuum sealer at a Boy Scouts yard sale, complete with instructions and a bunch of bags, for $3. Evidently, people often purchase sealers thinking they will be handy and use them once or twice, and then they end up in the yard sale bin. It may not be practical to wait around for a sealer to show up at a yard sale while harvest season comes and goes—but it never hurts to look.

There is another big reason why these sealers end up in the yard sale bin: the price of bags. The name-brand bags at the store that carry the same name as the sealer you buy will cost over $0.50 each. You don't have to do a lot of math to see that spending that much on just the bag to store a product (like broccoli) that you could buy frozen at the store for $0.99 isn't a winning proposition. I'll give you some solutions to that problem in the next section.

There are two suitable sealers on the market in various configurations available at department stores—the Seal-a-Meal and the FoodSaver. I've found both to be adequate, though you will find the FoodSaver a bit more expensive. I prefer the Seal-a-Meal since its design allows it to work better with a wide variety of bags. These are light-duty home-use units. They work fine for the amount of freezing that I do for the carbohydrates and vegetables for a family of three because we tend to freeze in relatively small batches of 10 or fewer packages at a time. Heavy-duty commercial units are available—but you should hold off on these until you see if the less expensive home-use units will meet your needs. Certainly they will work fine as you ramp up for the first couple of years.

Bags

As mentioned earlier, the name-brand bags for sealers are expensive—sometimes even more than $0.50 apiece. Luckily, you can get around this problem a number of ways. First, keep an eye out for the sealers and bags at yard sales. Second, use plastic rolls instead of premade bags because by cutting them to size for what you are freezing, you will use a lot less and save money. Finally, you can buy bags and rolls from brands other than those made by the manufacturer of your sealer. Two sources come to mind. First, a number of manufacturers make less expensive bags and/or rolls including Black and Decker, FoodFresh Vac-strip, and Magic Vac. These usually cost less than half of what the other bags do. Second, check the Internet. There are eBay stores dedicated strictly to vacuum sealers that offer good deals and also Web sites dedicated entirely to getting good prices on bags, such as vacuum-sealer-bags.com. With these resources in hand, you will see the superior properties of vacuum sealing become financially viable.

The Freezing Process

Freezing is a six-part process that requires harvesting, blanching, cooling, drying, sealing, and freezing. First, since no form of food preservation can actually improve the quality of food, harvest as close to freezing time as possible, and thoroughly clean the produce. Hose it off with the garden hose outside first, then put it in a big bucket to soak that contains two tablespoons of salt per gallon of water to draw out any insects. Then cut it up as needed, rinse out the salt, and weigh it into portions using a kitchen scale. For vegetables, figure 4 ounces per person. So for a family of four, you'll want your bagged portions to be about 16 ounces, or 12 ounces for a family of three.

⊗ Weighing produce for consistent portions helps with menu planning.

Next comes blanching. Blanching serves to inhibit the enzymes that destroy the quality of food in storage. There are two common methods—placing the produce in boiling water for a period of time, or steaming it for a slightly longer period of time. Both methods work, but I recommend steaming because it preserves more of the vitamin content of the food. The blanching time varies depending on what is being frozen (see Table 18).

When the allotted blanching time has passed, the produce should be dumped into a bucket of ice water so that it is cooled down immediately. (I slip a metal colander into the bucket first so that it holds the produce and makes it easy to retrieve.)

Leave the produce in the ice water for the same amount of time as it was being blanched,

⚙ This steam blancher is just one of many steamers available.

⚙ Cooling down the produce in ice water after blanching.

Table 18: **Blanching Times**

Produce	Water Blanch	Steam Blanch
Artichoke, globe	7–10 min	Not recommended
Artichoke, Jerusalem (chunks)	5 min	7 min
Asparagus spears	3 min	4 min
Beans, lima, butter, edamame	3 min	5 min
Beans, string	4 min	6 min
Beet roots, sliced 1/4"	12 min	Not recommended
Broccoli	4 min	4 min
Brussels sprouts	4 min	6 min
Cabbage, shredded	2 min	3 min
Carrots	3 min	5 min
Corn (on the cob)	10 min	Not recommended
Corn (whole kernel)	5 min	7 min
Greens of all sorts	3 min	5 min
Parsnips, sliced	2 min	3 min
Peas, shelled of all sorts	2 min	3 min
Peppers	3 min	4 min
Potatoes, sliced/cubed	5 min	7 min
Turnips, diced	3 min	4 min

then take it out and put it between a couple of superclean, dry, and fluffy towels to pat dry. You have to do this when vacuum sealing otherwise the large water content gets in the way of making a good seal.

Once the produce has been dried, it is placed into bags and sealed. After the bags have been sealed, put them into the freezer in various locations so that they will freeze more quickly. Come back and rearrange them in 24 hours.

For some vegetables, particularly potatoes, and Jerusalem artichokes, discoloration can be a problem. This is easily solved by adding one tablespoon of citric acid or two tablespoons of lemon juice per gallon of water to the ice water being used to cool the vegetables after blanching.

Meats and fruits aren't handled the same way as vegetables. Usually, meats are frozen raw, though I find that they freeze better if first soaked in a light brine (one tablespoon salt/gallon) to draw out any blood and then patted dry. The reason for drawing out the blood is so it doesn't interfere with vacuum sealing. Another

⊗ Sealing with a vacuum sealer preserves freshness longer.

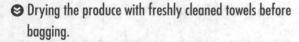
⊗ Drying the produce with freshly cleaned towels before bagging.

way to accomplish the same thing (which I do with ground meats) is put the meat in a regular zipper bag and put it in the freezer overnight, then remove it from the zipper bag and immediately seal it in a vacuum bag—the frozen juices then won't interfere with sealing. With wild game such as squirrel or deer, I recommend soaking for an hour in a light brine, as that removes some of the "gaminess" from the meat.

Fruit is best frozen in a sugar syrup like used when canning. Once the sugar is dissolved in the water, you can add 1/4 teaspoon of vitamin C or 2 teaspoons of lemon juice per pint of syrup to prevent darkening. Slice or dice the fruit and put it in a can or freeze jar or suitable plastic container and then cover the fruit with syrup, leaving one inch of headspace to allow for expansion in the freezer.

Dehydrating

Drying food is one of the oldest methods of food preservation. By removing most of the moisture from foods, enzymatic action and microbial growth are retarded, and the food will keep for a long time. Food loses more nutritional value from drying than from freezing, and dehydrated foods will seldom reconstitute with water to look like appetizing fresh produce. But even at that, dehydrated products make a conveniently stored, tasty, and healthy addition to soups, stews, and sauces. When my daughter was little, I used to powder mixed dehydrated vegetables in a blender and stir that powder into her spaghetti sauce so she'd get a mix of vegetables without knowing it. She also loves dehydrated apple rings as a snack, and other dehydrated fruits make a great addition to oatmeal in the morning.

Just like vacuum sealers, dehydrators run the gamut from inexpensive units available at department stores costing less than $50 all the way to commercial-sized behemoths. I recommend starting with a small model that includes a fan and thermostat since that will be easy and trouble free. You can always switch to a more expensive commercial or even homemade unit later. (Dehydrators lend themselves easily to homemade solutions, and literally dozens of free designs—including solar designs—are available on the Internet just by doing a Web search that includes the terms "homemade" and "dehydrator.") You can use a dehydrator for fruits, vegetables, and meats, though the process for the three is somewhat different.

Vegetables destined for the dehydrator need to be cut in slices no more than 1/4 inch thick and blanched just as though they were going to be frozen. This helps them dehydrate better and keep longer. Fruits should also be sliced no more than 1/4-inch thick and then dipped in a solution containing one tablespoon lemon juice per quart of water before being put in the dehydrator. Fruit shouldn't be blanched. Every dehydrator is different in terms of its drying characteristics, so use the drying times and temperatures recommended in the literature that comes with your particular model.

Meats, especially ground meat and poultry, are problematic because dehydrating is not the same thing as cooking, and the temperature seldom gets high enough to ensure pathogen destruction. This becomes an issue because bacterial contamination of these meats is common, so failure to thoroughly cook them can result in serious illness or even death. There are some jerky mixes available at department stores that are specifically formulated to deal with potential contamination of ground meats through the use of nitrites. If you choose to use one of these mixes, follow the directions precisely! Outside of this exception, I don't recommend making jerky or dried meat from either ground meats or poultry. Other meats—like beef steak/ roast, venison, buffalo, and so forth—are perfectly fine.

Most jerky recipes are for raw meat. In recent years, a number of universities have done studies and concluded that the practice can no longer be considered safe and that meat for jerky should be precooked in a boiling marinade. With the foregoing in mind, then, here is my general-purpose jerky recipe.

Brett's General-Purpose Jerky

- Start with prefrozen and partially thawed beef, buffalo, moose, venison, and so on. Trim away any visible fat and slice meat into uniform 1/4-inch-thick slices across the grain.

- Create marinade in a saucepan by combining 2-1/4 cups of water, 3/4 cup teriyaki soy sauce, 1/2 tsp of liquid smoke, and a dash of Tabasco sauce. Raise to a gentle rolling boil.

- Putting only a few strips of meat in at a time, boil a few strips in the marinade until uniformly gray then remove from the marinade with tongs and place on the drying rack of the dehydrator. Repeat this process until all of the meat strips have been used.

- Dry according to manufacturer's directions, or at a temperature of 140 to 150 degrees for six or more hours.

- Test to see if the jerky is done by taking a piece off the dehydrator, letting it cool to room temperature, then bending it. If it cracks but doesn't break, it is done.

Root Cellaring

Root cellaring is one of the best methods of preserving certain foods, including onions, cabbage, potatoes, carrots, parsnips, and apples, among others. The key to success at cold storage is establishing conditions conducive to long storage life, and these conditions include darkness, certain temperatures, and particular ranges of humidity.

Many things can be preserved via root cellaring for some small period of time ranging from days to a couple of weeks, while others can be preserved for times ranging from several weeks to several months. Invariably, food that can be stored only for a short time is better preserved via some other method. This includes all brassicas except late cabbage, asparagus, beans, sweet corn, cucumbers, summer squash, lettuce, tomatoes, eggplant, spinach, melons, and peas.

Other foods, though, can be preserved in a root cellar for extended periods assuming proper temperatures and humidity are maintained. Unfortunately, these aren't the same for all crops, but thankfully we don't have to be too fine-grained in our specification because, in general, crops that do well in a root cellar fall into broad categories.

Everything but onions and garlic will do well with humidity ranging from 85% to 95%. Onions and garlic require humidity ranging from 50% to 75%. All fruits store best at temperatures as close to 32 degrees F as possible, and almost all vegetables as well, except for late potatoes, which do best at 35 degrees F to 40 degrees F.

So, in general, cold storage requires an environment that is humid, dark, and close to 32 degrees F without going under. The real question becomes how to create and maintain such an environment in homes that were not designed with root cellars.

If you have a cellar of any sort, a portion of it can be turned into a root cellar simply be walling off a corner, insulating the walls thoroughly, providing some sturdy shelves up off the floor, and installing some ventilation that will allow cool air to enter near the floor (PVC pipe is good for this) and warm air to exit near the ceiling. You'll want a thermometer so you can keep an eye on the temperature and shut off or limit ventilation if it starts to sink too low. (This may or may not be a problem depending on where you live.) If humidity is insufficient, you can add a humidifier.

Most produce should be placed in open-weave baskets and kept up off the floor and shouldn't be piled deeply as the pressure from the weight of produce on the lower layers could cause premature rotting. Fruits should be stored only one layer deep and, if possible, individually wrapped in tissue and not touching other fruit. Carrots and parsnips should have the tops snapped off and then be buried in dampened clean sand in a box sitting on the floor.

If you don't have a basement, you could bury a drum in the ground or build an external root cellar. For more details on how to build root cellars, check out the book *Root Cellaring* by Mike and Nancy Bubel.

Table 19: Canning Times and Methods

Food	Packing Method	Head-space	Canning Method	Time for Pints	Time for Quarts
Apples (sliced)	Hot packed	1/2"	Boiling water	20 min	25 min
Applesauce	Hot packed	1/2"	Boiling water	15 min	20 min
Asparagus	Hot packed	1"	Pressure (10 lbs)	30 min	40 min
Beans (dry)	Hot packed	1"	Pressure (10 lbs)	75 min	90 min
Beans (shelled lima)	Hot packed	1"	Pressure (10 lbs)	40 min	50 min
Beans (snap)	Hot packed	1"	Pressure (10 lbs)	20 min	25 min
Beef, lamb, pork, venison, and bear (strips, cubes, ground, or chopped)	Hot packed	1"	Pressure (10 lbs)	75 min	90 min
Beets (sliced)	Hot packed	1"	Pressure (10 lbs)	30 min	35 min
Berries (all types)	Either	1/2"	Boiling water	10 min	15 min
Carrots (sliced)	Hot packed	1"	Pressure (10 lbs)	25 min	30 min
Cherries	Fresh packed	1/2"	Boiling water	20 min	25 min
Cherries	Hot packed	1/2"	Boiling water	10 min	15 min
Corn	Hot packed	1"	Pressure (10 lbs)	55 min	85 min
Fish	Fresh packed	1"	Pressure (10 lbs)	100 min	Don't use quarts
Fruit purees	Hot packed	1/4"	Boiling water	15 min	20 min
Greens, spinach, chard, kale, collards	Hot packed	1"	Pressure (10 lbs)	70 min	90 min
Jams and jellies	Hot packed	1/4"	Boiling water	5 min	Don't use quarts
Meat stock (any nonseafood meat with seasoning)	Hot packed	1"	Pressure (10 lbs)	20 min	25 min
Peaches, pears, plums, and nectarines	Fresh packed	1/2"	Boiling water	25 min	30 min
Peaches, pears, plums, and nectarines	Hot packed	1/2"	Boiling water	20 min	25 min
Peas (shelled)	Hot packed	1"	Pressure (10 lbs)	40 min	40 min

Food	Packing Method	Head-space	Canning Method	Time for Pints	Time for Quarts
Peppers (hot/sweet)	Hot packed	1"	Pressure (10 lbs)	35 min	Don't use quarts
Pickles (fermented)	Fresh packed	1/2"	Boiling water	10 min	15 min
Pickles (quick process)	Hot or fresh	1/4"	Boiling water	10 min	15 min
Potatoes (1/2" cubes)	Hot packed	1"	Pressure (10 lbs)	35 min	40 min
Poultry, rabbit, or squirrel with bones	Hot packed	1-1/2"	Pressure (10 lbs)	65 min	75 min
Poultry, rabbit, or squirrel without bones	Hot packed	1-1/2"	Pressure (10 lbs)	75 min	90 min
Pumpkins and squash (pureed)	Hot packed	1"	Pressure (10 lbs)	55 min	90 min
Rhubarb	Hot packed	1/2"	Boiling water	10 min	10 min
Sweet potatoes (cubed)	Hot packed	1"	Pressure (10 lbs)	65 min	90 min
Tomatoes (acidified)	Fresh packed	1/4"	Boiling water	40 min	50 min
Tomatoes (acidified)	Hot packed	1/4"	Boiling water	35 min	45 min

20

Selling Your Produce

The mini-farm gains its first economic advantage through growing enough food to reduce family food bills. During the first two years of mini-farming, it is likely that the family will use all that can be produced. But in the third and subsequent years, it is quite possible to both reduce food bills and sell enough food to replace a job when the two economic aspects are added together. Growing enough food to reduce food bills is easy, but the idea of selling produce looks like a bear at first glance. And, certainly, it *is* a bear if you anticipate trying to persuade the local branch of an international conglomerate supermarket chain to buy your products. It is unlikely to work, and even if it did, it would be a bad idea because you'd be positioning yourself in competition with global corporations using massive economies of scale and below market rate labor, so you wouldn't make any money.

It is important to understand that just as there are areas in which a mini-farm is at a disadvantage compared to agribusiness, mini-farms have notable strengths that provide a competitive edge as well.

The hottest agricultural niche right now is organic produce. The organic label has caught on to such an extent that even major department stores are offering it. The problem is that along with this positive interest in chemical-free produce, major corporations have gotten into the act and have started to squeeze the small farmers out of the market.

But all is not lost. Large-scale agribusiness organics suffer from many of the same problems as conventional produce—especially problems associated with shipping long distance, picking produce before it ripens, and selecting varieties for shipping characteristics rather than flavor. This is where the small farmer has an insurmountable edge over the competition, because the small farmer can specialize in varieties selected for taste and provide naturally ripened produce that hasn't lost its nutrient content from sitting in a warehouse for two weeks.

Locally grown organic heirloom vegetables and herbs are extremely attractive to locally owned superettes, convenience stores, restaurants, and natural food stores, not to mention the neighbors!

There are other advantages that come from the fact that mini-farms operate on a small scale. A mini-farmer can talk to the owner of a local health food store or restaurant and strike a deal to grow specific crops. A large warehouse can't do that. The mini-farmer can also grow labor-intensive crops that resist automation and where the attention of the farmer can net a superior product. In addition, specialty crops can be selected. Specialty crops, like purple potatoes or exotic lettuces, make no sense at a large agribusiness scale but will find a ready market through farm stands, local stores, and restaurants. The "Biggest Little Farm in America" uses this approach to earn $238,000 on just 1/2 acre of land.[51] Considering all of this, it is no surprise that the number of small farms is increasing at a rate of 2% per year and is likely to continue increasing at that pace for as long as the next 20 years![52]

Sales to stores would, of course, be at wholesale rather than retail price. This cuts the profit margin but has the advantage of a ready market. Restaurants and neighbors—through delivery to the restaurant or setting up a farm stand—represent retail pricing. The downside is that getting business from restaurants can be difficult, and farm stand sales are uncertain, but the benefit in terms of higher profit margin merits consideration.

Folks who are likely to consider mini-farming may have difficulty seeing themselves as salespeople, but selling your produce is very different from other sorts of sales. First, you are selling something you have created with your own hands and in which you have pride. Second, you are selling something of incomparable quality. Finally, instead of trying to create an artificial need, you are selling something that everybody needs already. As a result, it is something that can be approached with a sense of personal integrity in the spirit of a truly mutually beneficial transaction.

Approaching a local restaurant owner or the proprietor of a small health food store is not difficult because you already have something that these folks want: superior vegetables from a local supplier. There is marketing and public relations value in using vegetables from a local source, and local produce has superior taste and nutritional quality because long-distance shipping is avoided. The key is simply to present a proposal

---

[51] Macher, R. (1999) *Making Your Small Farm Profitable*

[52] Ibid

that eliminates risk on the part of the owner while advancing mutual benefits.

The largest risks for the local restaurant and health food store are lacking supply when it is needed and purchasing goods that either cannot be sold or would hurt their reputation. This latter concern is allayed by providing samples and consistently delivering the highest-quality goods. The first concern requires a little thought.

As a single small farm, a mini-farm doesn't have the scale to protect against crop losses, freak hail storms, and the like. In spite of the best intentions, a mini-farmer really can't promise unfailing supply. Likewise, a restaurant or store of even small size would sell far more produce than a mini-farm could supply in the best of seasons.

The solution is to make it clear to the customers that the intent is to provide no more than 20% of their needs, so their current relationships with larger suppliers remain intact. In this way, you will be able to sell all that you can produce, and your customer has no risks. This straightforward technique works extremely well.[53]

Organic and Certified Naturally Grown

Organic produce grown without chemical insecticides, fungicides, or fertilizers commands a premium price about 40% higher than

---

[53] Bartholomew, M. (1985) *Ca$h from Square Foot Gardening*

conventional produce. It therefore stands to reason that organic production should be strongly considered simply from a marketing perspective, not to mention for the health aspects.

The use of the term *organic* to refer to food products is regulated by federal law under the National Organic Program. The gist is that if the gross income from produce is less than $5,000 annually, a farmer can use the term to refer to products as long as they are truly grown using the standards of the program. If the gross income is greater than $5,000, then significant fees apply for certification, and a great deal of paperwork is required. The fees are generally on a sliding scale—meaning "the more you make, the more they take."

A mini-farm is likely to start out making less than $5,000 in gross sales yearly, so using organic labeling from the beginning is perfectly feasible; once that threshold is crossed, the funds for certification can be considered a cost of doing business. Even at that, it pays to shop around for a USDA-accredited certification agency whose fees don't gobble up all the profits! Many state departments of agriculture are accredited by the USDA, and this is the least expensive route.

An alternative to the expense of the National Organic Program is Certified Naturally Grown, a voluntary program that follows the same guidelines but has no associated fees. Certified Naturally Grown is oriented toward small local producers and features rigorous inspections offset by streamlined paperwork requirements. My own farm has been Certified Naturally Grown.

Taxes and Accounting

It should go without saying, but I'll say it anyway because it is important: Keep all of your paperwork, receipts, and so forth in order, and file your taxes properly on time. It is possible that by following the rules, you actually make minimal money after accounting for expenses, but it all must be properly accounted for or you'll ultimately have an unfortunate encounter with the IRS. There are a number of special deductions and rules applicable to farmers, and the IRS has a Web site dedicated to explaining these.

Outside of tax matters, careful accounting is important to your bottom line. As a small business, you need to know what you should be growing because it earns you a profit and what you should stop growing because it is losing you money. The only way to do this is to keep track of your income and expenses down to a crop-by-crop basis.

21

Putting It All Together

Especially if you are new to gardening or farming, the preceding chapters may seem to contain an overwhelming amount of information about a million things that you have to keep track of all at once in a delicately orchestrated dance: crop rotations, cover cropping, insect and disease prevention, seed starting, planting dates, and so forth. In a sense, it *is* finely choreographed, but there is a way to deal with all of this so that everything falls in place: Start small.

The easiest way to get the hang of all this while gaining some benefit and keeping expenses in line is to start a small garden composed of only three 4-foot × 25-foot raised beds—a mere 300 square feet. Within that space, all of the techniques described in this book can be practiced and fine-tuned to the individual circumstance, and minor mistakes are easily corrected. Also, and I am not kidding, by using intensive agricultural methods, you will easily grow more vegetables in 300 square feet than most people do in gardens seven times the size. Your problem won't be with gardening—it will be with storing everything it produces!

To give you an idea, in one 4-foot × 14-foot bed from April through September, my family harvested 22 pounds of broccoli, 8 pounds of cauliflower, 16 pounds of cabbage, 90 pounds of tomatoes, 23 pounds of pole beans, 40 pounds of cucumbers, and 15 pounds of potatoes, not to mention onions, beets, carrots, spinach, and Swiss chard in prodigious quantities. That is just from 56 square feet—so imagine what you can do with 300 square feet!

The point here is to start at a small and easily managed level while you get the hang of things and then expand from there. Expand as you gain confidence and ultimately start a small commercial enterprise as well.

The Garden Year

I count the garden year as beginning in fall, and I believe that you should as well. Fall is when all the activity from the prior season draws to a close with all of the garden refuse and leaves finding their way into the compost pile and cover crops being planted for the winter. Because things are somewhat rushed in the spring, fall is the best time to dig new beds and expand the space in use.

Through early winter in the northern United States there isn't really much to do except plan the garden and look through seed catalogs while staying warm. Now is the time to decide what you will grow and order the seeds. If you wait until spring to do this, you will be too late since many plants—like onion seedlings—need to be started in late winter to be ready to plant in the spring. Chilly fall and winter evenings are likewise a good time to separate out and prepare your own seeds from the prior season's harvest.

By the time late winter arrives, it is time to start seedlings for onions, leeks, chives, and many herbs. Shortly thereafter, the cole crops get started along with annual flowers. Then come the tomatoes and peppers. Around this same time, the onion and brassica are being planted out, followed shortly by seeds for spinach and lettuce. Soon, carrots, beets, peas, turnips, and parsnips get planted. After the last frost date, the tomatoes, peppers, corn, and beans get planted, followed by squash. About the time the tomatoes are planted out, it is time to start seedlings for the fall planting of broccoli. And you will be harvesting the long-growing winter cover crops like winter wheat and vetch for the grain and to put on the compost pile.

You get the idea: Gardening doesn't start on the last-frost date. Instead, it starts in the fall! If you start in the fall and follow the timing charts in this book, you will most definitely collect a tremendous amount of food even if you start small.

Help Around the Corner

For a variety of reasons—lifestyle, economics, philosophy, and you name it—small farms are springing up all over. Many of these new farmers are first-generation farmers, and they have already encountered a lot of what you will be experiencing. Unlike other industries in which everybody jealously guards trade secrets, farmers come together to help each other out. As a result, there are many initiatives filled with people ready and waiting with advice and wisdom that would otherwise require a PhD to obtain.

Such resources can be found on the Internet via a simple keyword search and via links from Cooperative Extension Service Web sites. Here in

New Hampshire, there are a number of farming organizations—including one sponsored by the state—intended specifically for beginning farmers! Similar groups exist all across the country.

Speaking of the Cooperative Extension Service, every state has at least one so-called land grant university. These universities were originally established under the Morrill Acts of 1862 and 1890 with primary missions to teach agriculture, classical studies, mechanical arts, and military tactics. The Hatch Act of 1887 established agricultural experiment stations at these universities to advance the state of agricultural science, and the Smith-Lever Act of 1914 established the Cooperative Extension Service to disseminate the data gained at the experiment stations. As a result, there is a branch of the Cooperative Extension Service associated with a land-grant university in every state; many of these services have branch offices in every county within a state.

The Cooperative Extension Service can provide, either in person or via publications or Web sites, a wide array of information. The available information ranges all the way from how to safely can foods at home to the specific varieties of apple trees that will grow best in your area. The amount of research and information available via the USDA, various state departments of agriculture, and Cooperative Extension Services is impressive and represents a valuable resource.

State governments also have their own agriculture departments under various names. These departments often have research grants available. Some do organic certification far less expensively than private organizations; many administer a plethora of programs designed to enhance the progress of agricultural endeavors in their respective states. They also, of course, publish a lot of regulations, which also should be examined, particularly regarding handling of livestock, creation of value-added products in the kitchen, sale of seeds, and so forth.

A number of private, semiprivate, and quasi-governmental agencies have a lot of information available as well. Baker Creek Heirloom Seeds has a bulletin board where people help each other with ideas and advice. The National Sustainable Agriculture Information Service offers a number of informative workshops and symposiums. Ecology Action offers self-teaching modules by mail order. Regional organic growers associations also hold workshops and annual events for information and networking.

So there are a lot of places to turn for help and advice—most of them at minimal or no expense. Millions of dollars are spent every year to establish the infrastructure that will help make you successful, so it makes sense to take advantage of it all.

The Final Analysis

Starting a mini-farm can provide you with the safest and most nutritious food available while saving more on the food budget year after year. The superior nutrition combined with outdoor exercise will make everyone healthier, and the economic benefits of selling excess production can enable any number of personal or family goals.

This book is a tour of everything you need to know to get started, but don't stop here! Go to the bibliography for a list of other recommended books. Knowledge is power in that it increases your odds of success in any endeavor.

From the Markham family to yours, we wish you all the best!

PART II
Getting the Most out of Your Vegetables

22

Soil and Fertility

In *Mini Farming: Self Sufficiency on 1/4 Acre,* I spent several chapters discussing soil and fertility in depth. The reason is because proper soil management and fertility practices are the foundation upon which everything else is built to make mini-farming an economically viable enterprise rather than merely a hobby. Optimum soil leads to reduced problems with pests and diseases, supports higher yields with greater density, creates more nutritious food and allows you to spend less money and effort on getting more food.

In this chapter, I am going to summarize what you need to know, plus add a bit more information. This summary should be enough to get you started, though it doesn't substitute for the in-depth knowledge in *Mini Farming: Self Sufficiency on 1/4 Acre.*

Raised Beds

I recommend planting in raised beds for a number of important reasons. Raised beds that have been double-dug and enriched with finished compost retain water while properly draining so that oxygen levels in the soil are optimal, nutrients are bound in a living symbiotic matrix for release to plants as needed and soil temperatures allow for early working. Furthermore, the close spacing of plants in a raised bed increases yields over use of row gardening while growing closely enough together to shade out weeds.

Beds are also useful for practicing crop rotation on a small scale. Every crop has slightly different requirements and places slightly different demands on the soil as well as enhancing it in different ways. Probably the single most dangerous thing that can be done, in terms of pests and disease, is growing the same crop in the same place year after year. By doing this, diseases and pests build up until they are ultimately beyond control. Rotating crops between beds substantially reduces pest and disease problems.

In general, beds should be placed near each other, but with enough space for walking between them. The space between the beds can be sod/grass, crushed stones, bark mulch or practically anything else. Usually, sod/grass is not a problem, and that is what is between my beds. However, these can serve as a reservoir for diseases such as botrytis and a breeding ground for wireworms while providing easy access to slugs, so if disease problems are experienced or wireworms start doing serious damage, using (untreated) bark mulch or straw between the beds to suppress grasses may be wise. Also, if any grass isn't mowed regularly, it can grow over into a bed. Next thing you know you'll be pulling grass out of your beds by the handful.

Composting

Composting is the key to preserving and enhancing the fertility of the soil. The law of conservation of matter says that matter cannot be created or destroyed. Without getting into the physics of matter/energy systems, in practical terms this means that the elements in a plant came from the soil,

and unless those elements are put back into the soil, a mini farmer will find it necessary to purchase outside inputs such as fertilizer. Thus, if the foliage of a tomato plant has taken phosphorus from the soil, and that plant is simply discarded, the phosphorus will need to be replenished from an outside source. But if instead that plant is composted, the phosphorus can then be returned to the soil via the compost and thereby reduce the need for an outside source of phosphorus.

Compost is a complex and literally living substance made from the aerobic decomposition of organic matter. Other than volatile elements such as nitrogen, all of the essential elements added to the pile as part of the composted materials are retained. But, in addition, the process of composting breaks down poisons, destroys both human and plant pathogens, generates a wide array of beneficial soil organisms that help plants get the most from the nutrients in the soil and even produces antibiotics for combating diseases.

Composting, therefore, is absolutely crucial from an economic perspective because of the way it reduces the need for fertilizers; it also serves to passively prevent a whole host of pest and disease problems. The importance of composting cannot be over-emphasized. You should be adding at least four cubic feet of finished compost to every 4'x8' bed annually.

pH

pH is a measure of how acidic or alkaline the soil is. It is important because plants generally have a certain range of pH preference for optimal growth and because the pH of the soil actively affects which microorganisms will thrive in the environment and how readily the nutrients contained in the soil can be used by plants. The pH is measured on a scale from 0 to 14. Zero (0) is highly acidic, like battery acid; 14 is highly basic like lye, and 7 is neutral.

Many sources list a pH preference range for each plant, but these sources often differ in the details. For example, one source will list the preferred pH for tomatoes as 5.8 to 6.5, whereas another will list it as 6 to 7. The simple fact is that you don't need to be that detailed, as with only a very few exceptions, plants grown for food in gardens will grow well with a pH ranging from 6 to 7. True, a cucumber can grow at a pH as high as 8, but it will also grow at 6.5.

Because pH corrections can take months to show results and because the constant rotation of beds between crops makes it impractical to customize the pH of a bed to a given crop, it makes sense to test each bed individually, and correct the beds to a uniform pH of between 6 and 6.5. The exceptions are that the beds used for potatoes should have the pH lower than this, and the beds used for brassicas (such as cabbage and broccoli) should have extra lime added to the holes where the transplants are placed. These practices will be specifically covered in the chapters pertaining to those particular plants.

In most of the country, the soil pH is too low and needs to be raised to be within an optimal range. Correcting pH using lime can be problematic in that it takes several months to act. Though the gardening year should start in the fall, along with any soil corrections so the lime has time to react with the soil; the reality of life is that the decision to start a garden is generally made in the late winter or early spring. Thus, the farmer is stuck trying to correct pH within weeks of planting instead of months.

However, with a bit of creativity and use of alternate materials, both short and long term corrections can be made to pH.

There are many liming materials available for this purpose, but only four I would recommend: powdered lime, pelleted lime, dolomitic lime and wood ashes. Others such as burnt and hydrated lime act more quickly, but are hazardous to handle and easy to over-apply. If you choose to use these latter products, please follow package directions closely.

Pelleted lime is powdered lime that has been mixed with an innocuous water-soluble adhesive for ease of spreading. It acts no more or less quickly than the powdered product, but costs more. Lime can take as long as a year to take full effect, but will remain effective for as long as seven years.

Dolomitic lime contains magnesium in place of some of the calcium. In most soils in the U.S. (excepting clay soils in the Carolinas), its use for up to ¼ of the liming is beneficial to supply needed magnesium with calcium. It is used at the same rate as regular lime, takes as long to act, and lasts as long.

Wood ashes are a long-neglected soil amendment for pH correction. They contain a wide

Measured pH	Sandy	Sand/Loam	Loam	Clay and Clay/Loam
4	5.5	11	16	22
5	3	5.5	11	16
6	1.25	3	3	5.5
7	None	None	None	None

Pounds of lime required to adjust the pH of 100 square feet of bed space.

array of macronutrients such as potassium and calcium but also contain elements such as iron, boron and copper. They act more quickly in correcting soil pH, but do not last as long. Wood ashes are applied at twice the rate of lime for an equal pH correction but should not be applied at a rate exceeding five pounds per 100 square feet. So, in effect, wood ashes are always used in conjunction with lime, rather than on their own.

The pH scale is a logarithmic value, similar to a decibel. As such, the amount of lime needed to raise the pH from 4 to 5 is greater than the amount of lime needed to raise the pH from 5 to 6. Furthermore, the effectiveness of lime is strongly influenced by the type of soil. So the accompanying table reflects both of these factors. The numbers represent pounds of powdered limestone per 100 square feet. For wood ashes, double that number, but never exceed five pounds per 100 square feet in a given year. Wood ashes can seldom be used exclusively as a pH modifier. Rather, they are best used when mixed with lime.

One further note about lime. A lot of sources say you shouldn't apply fertilizer at the same time as lime because the lime will react with the fertilizer and neutralize it. To some extent, this is true. However, lime stays active in the soil for as long at least seven years, so the fertilizer will be affected anyway. As long as both are thoroughly incorporated into the soil, don't worry. In addition, these concerns largely pertain to inorganic fertilizers such as ammonium nitrate. When the fertilizers are organic, and constituted of such compounds as blood meal or alfalfa meal, the adverse effect of the lime is considerably reduced.

Though excessively alkaline (e.g. a pH higher than 6.5) soils are rare in the United States, they exist in a few places such as the Black Belt prairie region of Alabama or can be accidentally created through excessive liming.

Correcting an excessively alkaline soil can be done using a variety of substances, including elemental sulfur (known as flowers of sulfur), ammonium sulfate, sulfur coated urea and ammonium nitrate. These latter methods are seen to be best practices in industrial agriculture, but they are excessively concentrated and can hurt the soil biology, so aren't recommended for a mini farm aiming at sustainability.

Some authorities also recommend aluminum sulfate, but the levels of aluminum, if the pH ends up changing, can be taken up by the plant and can become toxic to both plants and animals. So I recommend either straight flowers of sulfur (if growing organically) or ammonium sulfate (if you don't mind synthetic fertilizers). In practice, the amount of ammonium sulfate required to lower soil pH a given amount is 6.9 times as much as sulfur, so you'll likely use sulfur for cost reasons.

Sulfur works by combining with water in the soil to create a weak acid. This acid reacts with alkalies in the soil to form water-soluble salts that are leached from the soil and carried away by rains. Because it creates an acid directly, it is

Measured pH	Sand	Loam	Clay
8.5	4.6	5.7	6.9
8	2.8	3.4	4.6
7.5	1.1	1.8	2.3
7	0.2	0.4	0.7

Pounds of sulfur needed to adjust the pH of 100 square feet of bed space.

easy to overdo sulfur, so it should be measured and added carefully, then thoroughly incorporated into the soil. It takes about two months to reach full effectiveness, but results should start to manifest in as little as two weeks.

Ammonium sulfate works by virtue of the ammonium cation combining with atmospheric oxygen to create two nitrite anions (negatively charged ions), two molecules of water, and four hydrogen cations (positively charged ions). These hydrogen cations are the basis for acidity, and they will then acidify the soil.

So, how do you measure your pH? You can use a soil-testing kit or a pH meter. The cost of pH meters for home use has dropped considerably in recent years, with accurate units selling for as little as $13. Simply follow the directions that come with your individual meter for measuring each bed.

Macronutrients

Macronutrients are generally defined as being nitrogen, potassium and phosphorus, as these are the elements that are required in greatest quantity by plants. To these, I also add calcium, magnesium, sulfur, carbon, hydrogen and oxygen. These latter three are supplied by water and the atmosphere so they won't be further considered here except to note that proper aeration of soils allows beneficial bacteria access to oxygen. Furthermore, avoid walking on beds to prevent the soil from being compacted. Raised beds in general, due to being higher than their surroundings, usually don't have a problem with becoming waterlogged, which helps keep water from forcing out the oxygen that these beneficial microorganisms need.

Most soils in the U.S. are acidic and require lime for optimum growing. Adding lime also adds sufficient calcium automatically. Furthermore, those few soils in the U.S. that are alkaline are usually made so from the high natural limestone content of the soil. So, in general, calcium levels should be fine.

The major problem you will see that involves calcium is blossom end rot. Blossom end rot is caused by uneven uptake of calcium, usually due to extreme variations in rainfall. Usually this can be avoided through properly thorough watering. There are also some commercial preparations on the market that contain a readily absorbed calcium salt called calcium chloride that are effective.

In general, if you are using dolomitic lime for at least a portion of your lime needs, your soil will not be deficient in magnesium. However, the soil chemistry of competing cations such as magnesium and potassium is complex, and a plant could end up deficient even though there is sufficient elemental magnesium in the soil. Magnesium can become unavailable if potassium is present in a severe excess, or if the organic matter that forms the biological colloid that makes magnesium available to the plant is present in insufficient amounts.

A clear symptom of magnesium deficiency is often observable in seedlings that have been held too long in nutrient-poor starting mixes before being transplanted: interveinal chlorosis (the green turns yellowish between the veins) of older/lower leaves, often combined with curling leaf edges that have turned reddish brown or purple. If this symptom manifests, the deficiency can be corrected in the short term by adding Epsom salt (magnesium sulfate) at a rate of eight ounces per 100 square feet. This form of magnesium is easily absorbed by plants. However, the deficiency should be addressed in the long term by adding sufficient levels of compost to the soil, and using dolomitic lime.

Sulfur is an important constituent of amino acids—the core building blocks of DNA and life itself. As such, the primary source of sulfur in the soil is organic matter. Soils rich in organic matter through composting hold onto sulfur so it can't be leached out and convert it to the sulfate form needed by plants a little at a time as needed. However, even the most meticulous composting won't replenish all the sulfur lost because what we eat is seldom composted. So sulfur, in some form, should be added annually.

Elemental sulfur is not a good choice for this task unless it is already being used to alter the pH of the soil. In its elemental form, particularly in soils that aren't rich in organic matter, it isn't available to plants as a nutrient. Sulfur is best added in the form of either garden gypsum (calcium sulfate) or epsom salt (magnesium sulfate). It can be added at the rate of five ounces per 100 square feet every year for either product.

Phosphorus is a constituent of the enzymes essential for energy production within cells. The primary source of phosphorus in soil is from plant and animal wastes, in which it exists in an organic form not immediately accessible to plants. The phosphorus is converted as needed to an inorganic phosphate form that is usable by plants via microorganisms in the soil. This is, overall, the best method of maintaining soil levels of phosphorus because most of the phosphorus is held in reserve until needed and can't be leached out of the soil by rain.

The process of microorganisms converting phosphorus into a usable form is temperature dependent, and it is not at all unusual for spring transplants to suffer from deficiency because of this, even though there is adequate phosphorus in the soil. This is a condition that is better prevented than corrected, and can be done by simply using a good liquid fish fertilizer at the time of transplant and every week thereafter until soil temperatures are consistently above 55 degrees.

You should also test your beds for phosphorus. Numerous test kits are available, and they all work fine when used according to the directions in the kit. If your soil is deficient, you should add phosphorus in the form of bone meal in preference to rock phosphate. Bone meal is broken down slowly in the soil, so you should test your soil and add it at least five weeks prior to planting. The amount you'll need to add depends on the results of your soil test, and the instructions will be in the testing kit.

The reason why rock phosphate should be avoided is because it is high in radioactive substances that can be taken up by plants. In fact, one of the primary dangers of smoking is the radioactivity of the smoke, which is a result of tobacco being fertilized with rock phosphate. Tobacco is part of the same family of plants as peppers, eggplant, tomatoes, potatoes and many other garden edibles. So if you don't want to be eating radioactive substances, rock phosphate is best avoided.

Potassium is abundant in most soils, though usually in forms not readily available to plants. These unavailable forms are converted by the microbial life in the soil into forms that plants can use as the plants require it. Though potassium is required for life, its deficiency is not as readily noted as other essential nutrients. Plants are smaller and less hardy than they would otherwise be, but this might not be evident unless compared side-by-side to the same plant grown in non-deficient soil. Therefore, use a test kit to determine if there is any deficiency.

Both the Rapitest and LaMotte testing kits will provide **pH**, **nitrogen**, **phosphorus** and **potassium** levels and recommendations.

Conscientious composting practices that return crop wastes to the soil are the primary source of potassium in a mini farm. This is, however, inadequate as the potassium removed in crops that are consumed or sold can't be returned in this fashion, so a certain amount of potassium will need to be supplied.

Nearly all plant materials contain usable levels of potassium, so occasionally supplementing your compost supply with an outside supply of compost will help maintain your levels of potassium. Alfalfa meal, usually used as a source of nitrogen, also contains potassium. Wood ashes, discussed earlier as a way of lowering pH, also contain substantial amounts of potassium along with other minerals. Greensand, a mineral originally formed on the ocean floor, is also a source of potassium along with micronutrients. The same applies to kelp, seaweed and fish meal. Depending on the results of soil testing, these materials can be used in any combination to supply potassium that is removed from the soil by crops.

Nitrogen is a primary constituent of amino acids and the DNA within plant cells. Though we live in an atmosphere that is roughly 78 percent nitrogen, this form of nitrogen is inert and not useful to plants. In nature, the nitrogen is converted into a usable form through a bacterial process known as nitrogen *fixation,* that is usually done through rhizobium bacteria that live in symbiosis with the roots of legumes. This is why cover cropping is so important (as explained in *Mini Farming: Self Sufficiency on 1/4 Acre*). A proper cycle of cover cropping and crop rotation can reduce the need and cost of outside sources of nitrogen.

Deficiencies in nitrogen show themselves quickly in the loss of green color, starting with the oldest or lowest leaves on the plant. Because the rate at which nitrogen in the soil can be made available to plants is affected by temperature, this deficiency is most often seen early in the season when soil temperatures are below 60 degrees. There may be enough nitrogen in the soil, but the bacteria can't keep up with the demand of the crops. It is better to prevent this problem than correct it, and early plantings should be supplemented with a liquid fish fertilizer until well established and soil temperatures are sufficient to support natural nitrogen conversion.

Just as with most other nutrients, composting should be your first source of maintaining soil fertility. But because you can't compost crops that you eat or sell, and because nitrogen losses in composting can be as high as 50 percent, you will need to add nitrogen as it is removed by crops. Good crop rotation with legumes and legume cover crops can help as well; sometimes this is enough. But often nitrogen needs to be added, and a soil test can tell you how much you need.

Sources of nitrogen include compost from an outside source, various fish, feather, alfalfa, cottonseed, blood and bone meals, well-rotted

Wood ashes, sea minerals and borax are sources of micronutrients for your beds.

manure from chickens and other animals, etc. I like using diverse sources in order to also include as many other micronutrients as possible. Because we keep chickens, the chicken manure added to our compost pile dramatically reduces our overall need for outside sources of nitrogen, but to an extent this comes at the cost of feed for the chickens. In terms of dollar cost, however, this works in our favor as the eggs are more valuable than the feed, so the manure is free.

Micronutrients

A large array of minerals have been identified as being essential for human health, and more are being discovered all the time. So far, the following are known to be needed: potassium, chlorine, sodium, calcium, phosphorus, magnesium, zinc, iron, manganese, copper, iodine, selenium, molybdenum, sulfur, cobalt, nickel, chromium, fluorine, boron and strontium.

These can only be acquired through the food we eat. We can get them through plants, or through animals that have eaten plants. But ultimately, they have to enter plants through the soil. Thus, deficient soils, even if the plants seem perfectly healthy, ultimately lead to problems with human health.

Because industrial farming doesn't have human health as its goal; farm management practices have led to a long-term decline in the mineral content of foods. A number of studies have shown that in just a thirty-year period, the content of vitamins and minerals in foods have declined by anywhere from 6 percent to 81 percent.[1,2]

There are a number of elements needed by plants that are needed in small quantities, and are thus described as micronutrients. Overall, due to over-farming, these are deficient in agricultural soils because they were never restored as they were depleted. Only a handful of plant micronutrients are officially recognized: boron, chlorine, copper, iron, manganese, molybdenum and zinc. That is because severe deficiencies of these elements usually give clear adverse symptoms in plants.

However, as plants are the start of our food chain and humans require far more than just these seven minerals, soil deficiency in any mineral needed for human health should be avoided as its disappearance from plants means we don't get enough in our diet.

Composting to maintain the fertility of the soil and retain these elements is important. To a degree, as described in *Mini Farming*, these elements can also be added in small quantities to your beds. This is easy to do with elements such as calcium or iron that can be easily obtained, but more difficult with fluorine or strontium. And even if these are available, you may be missing something we haven't learned about yet.

[1] Bergner, Paul (1997), *Healing Power of Minerals, Special Nutrients, and Trace Elements* (The Healing Power), ISBN-13: 978-0761510215.
[2] Marie-Mayer, Anne (1997), "Historical Changes in the Mineral Content of Fruits and Vegetables."

The easiest way to make sure the soil has all of the trace elements needed is the periodic addition of ocean minerals. Over the ages, rain and erosion have moved a great many minerals that would ordinarily be on land in abundance into the sea. Over-farming without replenishment has exacerbated this problem. Though I am able to go to the seashore and collect kelp from the beach for my own compost, this is seldom practical for most people. What I recommend as a solution for the most robust and nutritionally complete plants possible is the periodic addition of a small quantity of ocean minerals.

In essence, seawater contains, in varying amounts, every known element save those made artificially in nuclear reactors. In 1976, Dr. Maynard Murray published a book entitled *Sea Energy Agriculture* in which he highlighted the results of numerous studies he had made from the 1930s through 1950s on the addition of ocean minerals to agricultural land. Though his book was published some time ago, I have discovered that in growing beds side by side, those treated with sea minerals do, in fact, produce obviously healthier plants.

The big problem with using ocean water directly is obvious: you can't grow plants in salt water because it kills them. In fact, one of the practices of ancient warfare was to sow your enemies' fields with salt so they wouldn't be fertile. Fortunately, only a small quantity is required, and when package directions are followed not only is there no harm, but plants become more healthy and more resistant to insects and diseases. It is also fortunate that on a mini farm, the amount of sea minerals required is tiny, so even a ten-pound bag of sea minerals from various sources will literally last for years. (I use five pounds annually.) There are a number of companies offering sea minerals such as GroPal, Sea Agri,

Sea Minerals from Arkansas and others. The key is that each offering is a bit different, so be sure to scale the package directions appropriately.

The one micronutrient that I don't believe sea minerals provide in sufficient quantity is boron. You'll see boron deficiency in hollow stems for broccoli and hollow or grey centers of potatoes. The amount of boron required is tiny, and can be derived from borax. Use extreme caution because borax in higher concentrations is an effective herbicide that will leave your beds sterile for years if it is dumped on them indiscriminately. Sufficient borax can be added with one tsp dissolved in one gallon of water and used to lightly sprinkle over a single 4' x 8' bed before a regular watering. Once a year is plenty.

Conclusion

Healthy plants require healthy soil. Use of composting practices will help reduce the need for outside inputs plus provide optimum soil health for suppression of diseases. Raised beds allow for more aerated soil, higher levels of production, and the use of less fertilizer overall. Ideally, the process of amending beds for pH range and nutrient deficiencies will start in the fall; at a bare minimum start as soon as the soil can be worked in the spring. Cover cropping and crop rotation fill out the mix to create the most healthy soil possible, thus making whatever crops you grow more productive. I have only given basic information in this chapter, so for more in-depth knowledge of bed construction, double-digging, composting and soil fertility practices such as biochar, please see *Mini Farming: Self Sufficiency on 1/4 Acre*, in which several chapters are devoted to covering these subjects in depth.

Asparagus

23

No, asparagus is not poisonous! Well, the berries made by the female plant are poisonous, but the rest of the plant isn't. And the compounds that make urine smell ... different ... to the 22 percent of the population who are able to detect it are perfectly safe. In addition, it is a nutritional goldmine, rich in folic acid, antioxidants, minerals, and even vitamins E and C. No wonder it was cultivated by the ancient Greeks, Egyptians and Romans.

The asparagus in stores is sold by the pound, so sometimes it is sold when old and the stems have turned woody (so it weighs more). In terms of usable portions, it is quite expensive. Organic asparagus, even frozen, sells for $7/lb at my local supermarket. If there were ever a compelling argument for growing your own asparagus, the price and quality of what can be found at the supermarket should be enough.

Though it takes a few years to get established, asparagus is easy to grow and can be eaten fresh, frozen, dried for use in soups, and even canned using a pickling method so that it will keep for years. Once you have a bed of asparagus started, if you properly care for it, it will last twenty to thirty years.

Selecting the Right Variety

Asparagus is one of the few dioecious species of plants grown in gardens, meaning that a plant is either entirely male or entirely female, rather than combining both male and female attributes within the same flower or plant as is seen with tomatoes. All asparagus variants grow just fine anywhere in the country, so they should be selected based on your own tastes. Popular open-pollinated varieties include Mary Washington, Argenteuil (also known as Precoce D'Argenteuil) and Conover's Colossal. Though there are hybrid male-only varieties available as crowns (i.e., bare-root plants), I'd encourage growing one of the open-pollinated varieties from seed because of the ease of seed-saving so that if anything ever happens to your bed, you can re-create it instead of relying on a company that may have gone out of business.

Starting Asparagus

Asparagus is easy to start from seed. Start it indoors six weeks before last frost, and plant it out when you plant out your tomatoes. Because some of the seeds are male and some are female—and only the male plants produce substantive shoots—start twice as many plants as you think you'll need. Transplant them in two rows in your bed, six inches apart. The next year, cull all the female plants but the two strongest, leaving these so that you can produce seed. Then cull the weakest of the male plants until you have plants every 12" to 18" in each of the two rows in the bed.

Planting Asparagus

Asparagus can be grown from either seed or bare-root plants known as "crowns." The primary difference is that crowns are an already-established plant, and will produce useful shoots a year earlier than growing from seed. Whether growing from seed or crowns, you should keep in mind this is a pretty permanent planting, and the bed should be prepared accordingly.

The single most important aspect of an asparagus bed is drainage. Wet feet, that is, waterlogged roots, are the death of asparagus. Raised beds are an important tool in this regard, but make sure the raised bed isn't located in an area of the yard that gets flooded. The second most important consideration is soil pH; asparagus prefers a soil as close to neutral as possible. Thus, because of the long time frames needed for lime to work, an asparagus bed should be prepared and pH correctives added in the fall prior to the transplanting of crowns or seedlings in the spring. The third most important consideration is light; asparagus needs at least six hours of direct sunlight daily. Fourth, beds should be four feet wide, and 1.5' long for each plant; so when growing six plants, you'll need a bed 4' wide and 8' long. (Make sure the long side faces south for greatest sun!)

Finally, the bed should have plenty of reserve fertility. This is accomplished by double-digging, incorporating properly aged compost into the bottom of the trenches, working even more compost—a good 4"-6"—into the top of the bed. This can all be done in advance. Then, a month or so before planting, add trace minerals and then use organic sources to correct any deficiencies in major nutrients. The use of organic sources is especially important with asparagus

Asparagus growing through the straw mulch used to suppress weeds.

because you can't just till more stuff into the bed later (remember: asparagus takes three years to produce, and the plants last as long as twenty years). Anything added later will just be mixed with compost as a top dressing. The annual spring top-dressing should be five cubic feet of compost per 4'x8' bed. You should mix 3 lbs of wood ash, 1 lb of lime, 2 lbs of bone meal, 2 lbs of alfalfa meal and 1lb of blood meal into the compost before application, and then cover with a 2" matting of clean straw.

There is one other very important thing you need to know about asparagus: it loves arsenic, sucking it up like a vacuum cleaner, and will give it to you. Arsenic is not a problem unless your bed is in an old apple orchard that was treated with arsenic as an insecticide, but the one thing you absolutely must avoid is pressure-treated wood that has been treated with arsenic compounds anywhere near your bed. All you have to do to keep your asparagus safe is keep pressure treated wood away, and don't try to grow it where arsenic was used heavily in the past. This is absolutely no joke—it is entirely possible for someone who disregards this advice to munch an asparagus stalk and then quite literally flop over dead.

Weeds

Because an asparagus planting is long-term, weed problems can accumulate and quickly overwhelm the plants. Furthermore, because the crowns that produce the shoots tend to grow upward, weed control via hoe can inadvertently damage them. The standard protocol for dealing with weeds in asparagus beds is to use flame weeding, mulching or other (non-herbicidal) means to keep weeds away from the bed. Grasses are especially invasive, so don't let any get close enough for the seeds to fall into the bed. Apply 2"-4" of compost yearly to the bed, and cover that with 2" of clean straw to smother weeds. Pull any weeds that still manage to grow by hand before they produce seed.

Diseases

Asparagus is vulnerable to a number of root-rot diseases, but these are highly unlikely to manifest in an asparagus bed situated as described earlier. It can also be affected by botrytis mold spread from grasses, but proper weed control as earlier described will prevent this. There are also some viral diseases that can kill off asparagus. These are believed to be spread by aphids, but are extremely rare in home-grown beds as opposed to commercial situations where acres upon acres of asparagus are grown. All you have to do is create a well-drained raised bed, control weeds and control aphids when/if they appear, and you'll have no disease problems.

Pests

Asparagus aphids are very rarely an issue because a wide array of natural predators such as ladybugs keep them in check. If you find a large population of aphids (they will hide under the bracts of the leaves), they can be effectively controlled with two applications of insecticidal soap a week apart.

Asparagus beetles are more of a threat. These are usually metallic blue or black and a quarter of an inch long, though some orange species exist. The adult asparagus beetle does little direct damage, it is the offspring that are a problem. The eggs appearing like black specks hatch into green to gray worm-like larvae as much as 1/2" long that eat voraciously. The defoliation weakens the plants.

Primary control of asparagus beetles is to cut down all asparagus foliage at the end of the season when it has turned yellow/brown and add it to the compost pile. This denies the beetles a place for offspring to overwinter. During the season, just vigorously shaking the foliage will dislodge the larvae, and because they will be unable to climb back up the stalk, they will dehydrate and die in the soil.

Harvest

If grown from transplanted seedlings, allow asparagus to grow without harvesting anything for two years. This will allow the foliage to store energy in the crowns that will enhance their ability to survive over the winter. If grown from transplanted crowns, allow them to grow without harvest for the first year. Then, the first year you harvest, only harvest the stalks that appear for one week. In subsequent years over the next twenty or thirty years, you can harvest stalks for a full six weeks as they appear in spring. Then let the rest of the stalks grow out into full plants to replenish the crowns.

Harvest of asparagus isn't all at once. You'll see a stalk here and a stalk there. The stalks should be cut with a sharp non-serrated knife just below ground level when they are no more than 8" tall. (Much bigger and they get woody.) Put an inch of water in the bottom of a wide-mouth canning jar, and put the stalks in the water in your refrigerator until you have enough of them to cook or preserve. They'll keep just fine for a couple of weeks this way.

Save asparagus spears upright in water in the refrigerator until ready for use.

Saving Seed

Collect the ripe red berries from the female plants, bring them inside, and let them dry out on a paper plate. Next, crush the berries and winnow out the seeds. Keep the berries out of reach of children as the attractive red berries are poisonous, and as few as seven of them might send someone to the hospital.

Preservation and Preparation

Asparagus can be kept fresh in the refrigerator for a couple of weeks if the bottom ends are in water, or it can be blanched and then dehydrated or frozen. Pickling works extremely well with asparagus. Even though it is technically feasible, I don't recommend pressure canning because the resultant mush is vile in my opinion. For fresh eating, asparagus can be eaten raw, steamed or stir-fried with excellent results. Frozen packages can be cooked in the package in the microwave if vented to prevent explosions.

Pickled Asparagus
Ingredients:

60 asparagus spears
1/2 cup coarse salt
1 gallon cold water
3 1/3 cups distilled white vinegar
1 1/3 cup sugar
2 teaspoons coarse salt
2 teaspoons mustard seed
1 tbsp dill seed
1 yellow onion, sliced into rings
4 cloves of garlic

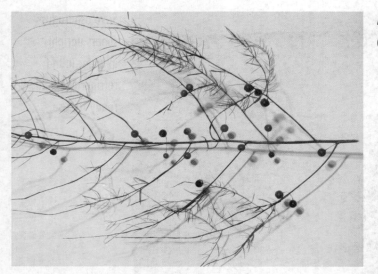

Asparagus berries are easy to collect for seed-saving, but don't let children have them.

Procedure

1. Clean the asparagus, cut 1" off the bottom and then cut the spears 3-1/2" long so they will fit upright in the canning jars while leaving 1" to the top. Put the cut spears in a large bowl, add ½ cup of coarse canning salt (sea salt is fine too), and then cover with water for two hours. After the two hours, drain and then rinse the asparagus, and pat it dry.
2. Clean and sterilize four wide-mouth pint canning jars and lids.
3. Combine the vinegar, sugar, 2 teaspoons of salt, dill seed, mustard seed and onion in a saucepan over medium heat. Bring to a slow boil, then turn down to a simmer.
4. Pack the asparagus spears upright and tightly in the jars. Add a clove of garlic to each jar, then pour in the pickling liquid to within ¼th inch of the rim.
5. Adjust the two piece lids and process in a boiling water canner for 10 minutes.

These can be enjoyed fresh from the jar, as a garnish, or as a tasty addition to salads.

Asparagus

Ingredients:

20 fresh asparagus spears
1 lemon
1-1/2 Tbsp butter
2 cloves garlic

Procedure:

1. Wash and dry asparagus spears, cutting off the bottom one inch. Cut the lemon in half, setting aside one half for later. Mince the garlic cloves. Preheat the butter in the pan over low-medium heat.
2. Add the garlic to the butter and stir-fry until slightly browned.
3. Add the asparagus, and stir-fry until tender.
4. Squeeze the juice from ½ of the lemon over the asparagus in the pan
5. Cut the remaining half lemon into thin slices.
6. Serve the asparagus with the lemon slices as garnish.

Delicious!

Asparagus fresh from the garden makes this simple dish a culinary delight!

24

Beans

Beans are one of the most versatile vegetables grown in the garden. They can be used to replenish nitrogen in the soil, eaten as green beans, and made into everything from soups and stews to tofu. They are also one of the most evocative in terms of cultural imagery, with the cowboy carrying his supply of dried beans on a lonely trek, and even little odes having been composed in honor of the ... music ... we often make after eating them.

The variety of beans available crosses species and is truly amazing, with literally hundreds of varieties available from traditional cultures and more modern breeding. There are seed companies that offer over a hundred varieties! But despite this diversity made possible by dedicated seed savers, the reality is that most beans available in the supermarket are from only a handful of varieties, and fully 85 percent of the soy crop in this country has been subject to artificial genetic modification to convey traits such as herbicide resistance.

Furthermore, beans are very commonly over-cropped and adding insult to injury, supplies of dried beans are sometimes several years old. Unless you know a farmer and can get them fresh, the best way to have a decent bean is to grow it yourself. Luckily, they are among the easiest to grow of all garden crops.

Variety Selection

Beans can be divided into categories in various ways, but for most mini farmers they can be categorized in terms of growing habit (bush beans versus pole beans) or culinary use (green beans versus dry beans). But they can also be divided even further to include Lima beans, cow peas (aka "black-eyed peas"), yard-long beans and more. As they grow well anywhere in the country, the biggest concern is the farmer's personal taste.

When beans are grown fresh and compared, you soon discover a tremendous difference in flavors and textures that is not evident in supermarket fare. A green bean is definitely not just a green bean! There is a big difference in flavor between the Blue Lake and Old Homestead varieties. You may even find that, like in my family, different family members prefer the taste of different varieties. What I encourage you to do is grow more than one variety each year, and keep trying out new varieties while continuing to grow favorites you've discovered along the way. A mix of green and dried varieties is best for menu diversity throughout the year.

Rather than tell you exactly what to grow, instead I'll list some of the varieties that I've grown and enjoyed in each category as a starting point for your own investigation.

Blue Lake, Green Pole: There are many variants of this, some of which offer a wide array of disease resistance. Blue Lake pole beans used to be the dominant bean grown for commercial processing, and it definitely holds up well to canning and freezing. Blue Lake is very mildly flavored and thus ideal for picky eaters who might not otherwise like green beans.

Kentucky Wonder, Green Pole: This is a a very productive pole bean that will produce 8" long beans as long as you keep it harvested. It seems to never stop! Kentucky Wonder is also very versatile in that, if you allow the beans to mature into a dried bean instead of harvesting while green, they make an excellent dry bean for baking and soups. It is also a good freezing bean with a very distinctive flavor.

Top Crop, Green Bush: If you want to put a lot of beans away, you'll find the production impressive. The plants grow up to 2' tall, and start producing beans about fifty days from planting.

Jacob's Cattle, Dry Bush: This is my favorite dry bean. Not only is it tasty, but it is productive and grows really well on the outside edges of the corn patch. It is easy to harvest and a very attractive white bean with purple splotches.

Black Turtle, Dry Bush: In my wife's opinion, the best choice for bean soup recipes. It has an assertive but excellent flavor and very good cooking qualities. It isn't as productive as some varieties, but more than makes up for that with its flavor.

Henderson's, Bush Lima: Lima beans are a little tricky in terms of timing the harvest. You want to catch them when they are big, but before they start to mature. Henderson's has a very defined "Lima bean" flavor with a hint of butter. Shelled out, they steam nicely.

Soil Preparation

Beans don't grow well in acidic soil, so the bed where you plan to grow beans should be corrected to a pH of between 6 and 6.5 well in advance of planting. Enrich the soil with compost, and make especially sure of sufficient potassium and phosphorus. If the soil is a bit low in nitrogen, that's okay as long as you use a bacterial inoculant when planting as the beans will make their own nitrogen.

Planting Beans

Beans can be planted anytime after the last expected frost date for your area by planting the seed 1" deep directly in the soil. If average soil temperatures are under 60 degrees, though; germination will be poor. Though beans can be productive over a period of several weeks, they eventually stop producing, so for a longer harvest you should plant beans in two phases, with the first phase being about a week after the last expected frost date when soil temperatures are above 60 degrees, and the second phase being three weeks later. In most of the United States, this is sufficient to give yields until fall. If you live in an area with a growing season of 120 days or longer, you can also plant a third phase in another three weeks.

Beans will generally grow fine with or without any inoculant; however, in order to maximize their utility in a crop rotation based on their ability to fix atmospheric nitrogen into the soil, an inoculant should be used. This will also increase yields.

A little bit of inoculant goes a long way. What I do is put the bean seeds I will be planting in a jar, mist them with a bit of water, add a couple of teaspoons of inoculant and gently swish them around until they all have some inoculant on them. Then I plant them about 1" deep.

With bush beans, I plant them 5" apart in all directions. With pole beans, I plant them 5" apart in one row 6" away from the frame on the North side of the bed. Pole beans can grow as much as 9' tall, which can be pretty inconvenient for harvesting. You can either make your trellis so it slants away from the bed and put a 6' support on the top of the leaning trellis, or prune the bean vines as they reach the top of a conventional trellis. Either way will work.

Weeds, Pests and Diseases

Weeds are seldom a problem with bush beans grown in beds because the beans sprout and grow quickly and the leaf cover they provide effectively shades out weed competition. All you need to do is keep any grass growing around the bed trimmed, and make sure the bed is prepared and weed-free prior to planting.

The two major pests you'll likely see in beans are bean beetles and Japanese beetles. Japanese beetles start as grubs in your lawn (or that of your neighbors). If you have a lot of property so there is a good buffer with your neighbors, treating your entire lawn and beds with milky spore disease can be a good preventative after the disease has become established in a couple of years. Japanese beetle traps are pretty controversial as a pest control measure, because some studies show that they attract more beetles than they trap and will likely bring in beetles from the neighbors. They work well for me, though, when placed downwind of the garden at least 100' away.

Japanese beetles" attract each other. So one way to keep them controlled is to simply pick them off by hand into a small bucket of soapy water. (The soap lowers the surface tension of the water so the beetles sink and drown rather than floating on top where they will climb up the sides of the bucket and fly back onto your beans.) If you keep

The dense foliage of closely spaced beans shades out weeds.

them picked off daily once they are noticed, you'll likely prevent the problem all together. They can also be controlled by organic sprays such as pyrethrin used according to package directions, but this is a last resort as such sprays are expensive.

Adult bean beetles overwinter in the debris from the prior year's bean crop. So cleaning out your bed at the end of the season and composting the plants is an important preventative. Bean beetles look like slightly larger than average lady bugs with a bronze cast. They lay masses of yellow eggs on the undersides of the leaves which hatch into spiny yellow grubs about 1/4" long. Both the adults and the grubs eat everything but the veins in the leaves of the bean plants, and they eat voraciously. Except in the cases of large-scale monocropping, bean beetles can be controlled by cleaning up the prior year's plants, smashing any egg masses or grubs found under the leaves, and flicking the adults into a bucket of soapy water. In the extremely rare cases where they can't be controlled by these measures, the grubs can be controlled with insecticidal soap or light horticultural oil (be sure to get under the leaves) and the adults can be controlled with neem oil preparations. The most effective control I have found for potato beetles is an organic bacterial

poison called spinosad used according to label directions.

Disease is seldom a problem with beans in a properly managed mini-farm environment because crop rotation and debris removal control most likely diseases. If you have a problem with sclerotinia (which looks like a white mold), switching to pole beans will likely solve the problem.

Harvest

Dry beans need to stay on the bush or vine until they are tan/brown, dry and brittle. Once they have reached that stage, pick them into a bag, then break open the pods and allow the beans to settle to the bottom. Discard the large debris and pour the beans into a large bowl. You'll notice a lot of smaller debris, but this is easily discarded through a process known as winnowing.

It takes a bit of practice to get the hang of winnowing, but the idea is simple. The beans are heavier than the debris, so if the beans mixed with debris are poured into another bowl from a height while the wind (either natural or artificial via a fan) is blowing, the debris will be blown away and the debris-free beans will be alone in the second bowl. I have found this works best using a fan on medium speed a couple of feet away, and pouring from a distance no greater than three feet. Using this method, you only have to pour from one bowl into the other a couple of times to have perfectly clean beans.

Once the dry beans have been winnowed, set them aside in an uncovered bowl for a few weeks for the moisture to dissipate, giving them a stir with your hand once in a while. Then store them in an airtight container in a cool, dark place.

Black turtle beans in a bowl after winnowing.

Green or "snap" beans are best harvested as soon as they are large enough to use. If you keep the plants picked clean and don't allow the beans to start maturing, the plants will keep generating flowers and beans for a few weeks. Incidentally, plants grown like this that are not allowed to set seed fix the most nitrogen into the soil. Harvest the beans in the afternoon when the plants aren't damp to avoid spreading diseases, and store them in a bag in the refrigerator for up to a week until you have enough beans to eat or preserve.

Seed Saving

In the case of dry beans, simply using the ones you have stored for food is sufficient if you intend to use them the next year. Otherwise, you'll want to dehydrate them a bit. To save seed from green or snap beans, treat them like dry beans. Allow at least twenty plants to grow to mature their pods into the dry-bean stage (making sure that is the only variety of beans you are growing at the time!), and then winnow like dry beans.

Preparation and Preservation

Green beans can be kept in a plastic bag in the refrigerator for up to a week. After that, they can be pickled, canned, or blanched and then frozen or dehydrated. They are best steam-blanched for four minutes, cooled in ice water for another four minutes, and then frozen. But that is simply my own preference, and many people like green beans that have been pickled as dilly beans, preserved via pressure canning or reconstituted from dried form into stews and casseroles.

Old Fashioned Green Beans

Ingredients:

1 lb fresh green beans with the ends removed and cut into 1" pieces
1 small onion
3 tsp butter
1/4 cup of water
1/2 tsp salt
dash of pepper
1 chicken bouillon cube (use good stuff, not the bouillon that is mostly MSG or salt.)

Procedure:

Cut the onion into slices and sauté in the butter until soft. Stir in the beans, then add the water, salt, pepper and bouillon. Crush the bouillon with a fork or spoon until it is dissolved. Cover and cook until the beans are crisp-tender.

Beets and Chard

Beets and chard (also known as Swiss chard) are variations of the same *beta vulgaris* species commonly descended from a sea beet that grows wild around the Mediterranean. Though beets are grown for their roots and chard for their leafy greens, the greens of both are edible. Beets, beet greens and chard are an absolute nutritional powerhouse. The roots contain glycine betaine, a compound shown to reduce homocysteine levels in the blood. Homocysteine levels are predictive of coronary artery disease, peripheral vascular diseases and stroke, so beets are definitely a case where cleaning your plate is a good idea!

In addition to this, beets supply minerals such as manganese, magnesium and iron, as well as B vitamins such as niacin, pantothenic acid, pyridoxine and folates. Beet greens and chard are also an excellent source of vitamin K, which plays a role not just in blood clotting, but also in bone formation and limiting damage to brain tissues. They also contain vitamin C, beta carotene, zeaxanthin, lutein and a host of other important antioxidants.

That's all well and good but . . . are they tasty? Absolutely! And, even better, they are among the easiest crops to grow on your mini farm.

Variety Selection

Given properly prepared soil, beets and chard can be grown practically anywhere in America that plants will grow. I've never tried a variety of either that wasn't delicious, though you'll find over time that certain varieties may grow a little better or taste a little better in your specific location. I'll give you a list of my favorite varieties, and I think you'll find them well-suited, but please don't limit yourself to just my suggestions.

Beets: Bull's Blood, Early Wonder, Cylindra, Detroit Dark Red

Chard: Ruby Red, Rainbow (a/k/a 5 color silverbeet), Fordhook Giant

Soil Preparation

Beets and chard grow best in deeply dug, rock-free soils rich in organic matter that have a pH between 6.5 and 7.5. The beds should be fertilized normally, though adding a teaspoon of borax (mixed with something like bone meal or wood ashes for even distribution) per thirty-two-square-foot bed is a good idea because beets are sensitive to boron deficiency. One major problem with germination of beets and chard is that soil can crust over the seeds, leading to plants being trapped underneath the crust. This will cause uneven stands with different rates of maturity. To solve this problem, make sure there is plenty of well-finished compost in the soil.

Starting and Planting

Beets and chard can be grown as both spring and fall crops. During the heat of the summer when temperatures climb above 80 degrees and stay there, they'll become bitter and tough. Chard can be harvested at practically any stage, but beets aren't usually ready for harvest before 50-60 days. On the other hand, chard and beets don't germinate well at soil temperatures below 50 degrees. In my area, the best time to plant is a month before last frost. This is late enough that the soil is sufficiently warm, but early enough that the beets are at harvesting size before the summer heat makes them tough.

Beets and chard can be succession planted, but in my experience this works best in the fall because the cooler weather during the later development of the beets keeps them sweeter, whereas a second spring crop of beets can be hit-or-miss depending upon the summer weather. For fall planting, plant your first crop about seven weeks before first frost and your second crop about four weeks before first frost.

It is entirely possible to transplant beets and chard that are grown inside first as seedlings. Though this is seldom done on a commercial scale because of the care required to avoid damaging the taproot and the tightness of the timing; on the scale of a mini farm, transplanting can improve production by allowing the grouping of more uniformly sized seedlings, thereby preventing plants that sprouted earlier from shading out those that sprouted later. Simply start the seeds inside in soil blocks two weeks before the seeds would usually be sown outside.

Whether using seeds or transplants, space your planting at 3" in all directions for beets and 4" in all directions for chard. During the spring planting, plant them about 1/2" deep and keep the planted area evenly moist until germination. If a crust forms, use a standard kitchen fork to lightly break up the crust no more than 1/8" deep.

You can fit a lot of beets into a bed when planting at 3″ intervals.

Because the seeds often contain seeds for multiple plants, about a week after germination you'll want to go back and thin out the extras. Save the thinned plants—roots and all—for a delicious salad green.

Weeds, Pests and Diseases

Because the plants are spaced so closely together, once they start growing they will shade out most weed competition (provided the bed was weed-free at the start). What few weeds remain should be carefully pulled by hand.

Beets and chard seldom have pest or disease issues that are economically important on the scale of a mini farm, though in commercial monocropping with inadequate rotation quite a few pests and diseases are problematic. Cleaning up debris at the end of the prior season, rotating crops between beds, mowing the lawn and keeping grasses and weeds out of the beds are usually sufficient measures to avoid problems.

Leaf miners and other beet-specific pests spread from nearby weeds that are botanically related, such as lamb's quarters, and the more generalized pests such as leaf-hoppers and carrion beetles migrate from tall grasses nearby. The diseases either accumulate in the soil from growing a crop in the same place year after year, or are transmitted by pests. So 95 percent of the time, just doing basic mini farm maintenance will prevent any problems. Those few that remain, if they become economically threatening, can be controlled with organic sprays such as neem oil and used according to label directions.

Harvest

Chard and beet greens can be harvested as soon as they appear, but should be allowed to grow to at least a couple of inches before picking. Don't harvest more than a couple of leaves from beets intended to produce roots, as doing so would reduce the yield. With chard, harvest the outside leaves first as they get large enough, and then the next layer of leaves will continue to grow. Keep harvesting like that in succession and the chard will produce for three weeks or more. As the beet greens or chard are harvested, you can store them in a plastic bag in the refrigerator for up to a week until you have enough to prepare or preserve.

Though it varies somewhat with the variety of beet, in general, beets should be harvested when they are no larger than 2″ in diameter. If you wait longer than that to harvest (and especially if you

New beets can be planted for fall as soon as the spring crop is harvested for maximum productivity.

wait until the heat of summer is intense), they tend to get woody. When harvest time comes, grab the leaf stalks just above the root and pull the beets out of the ground. Cut off the leaf stalks two inches above the root and set aside the leaves for eating, and then hose all the dirt off the beets outside. Let them dry for a bit, and then prepare or preserve as desired.

Seed Saving

Beets and chard are biennials, meaning they produce seed in their second year of growth. (Some varieties of chard will produce seed in their first year.) South of Maryland, you can mulch the plants with 6" of straw at the end of the season and they'll produce seed in the second year. North of Maryland, you'll need to cut off the tops, store the roots indoors overwinter and then put the roots out again in the spring. They will produce a flower stalk four feet long.

Beet pollen is very mobile, so if you are saving seed, make sure you have only one variety of beet or chard in flower in your garden. Beets and chard are also subject to inbreeding depression, so you should have at least twenty plants in the flowering and seed-setting population.

To harvest the seeds, cut the stalk when most of the seed pods have turned brown and hang inside upside down for two or three weeks. Then, use your hands to strip the pods from the stalk into a bag, break up the pods so the seeds fall to the bottom of the bag, and discard the larger debris. You can separate the seeds from the smaller debris using the winnowing method described in the chapter on beans. Then, dry the seeds using a desiccant such as dried silica gel for a couple of weeks, and store in an airtight container in a cool, dark place.

Preparation and Preservation

Beet greens and chard can be stored in a plastic grocery bag in the refrigerator for up to a week prior to fresh use or preservation. Both beet greens and Swiss chard contain oxalic acid. Though the oxalic acid is not present in sufficient quantities to be problematic for most people, if anyone in your family is prone to kidney stones you can prepare them in such a way as to reduce the amount of oxalic acid. Cook the greens by boiling them in

Chard and Beet Greens are easily preserved by freezing.

a couple of inches of water until wilted, and then discard the water and eat the greens.

Greens are best preserved by blanching for two and half to three minutes, cooling in ice water for four minutes, drying and then vacuum sealing for the deep freeze. Unfortunately, they don't stand up well to pressure canning and they don't reconstitute well from dehydrating. Even so, I dehydrate many greens so that I can later reduce them to powder in the food processor and blend that powder into spaghetti sauce and soups for an added nutritional boost.

If not properly prepared, beets literally taste like the soil in which they were grown. The outer layer of the beet, known as the "skin" needs to be removed. Once the skins have been removed, the beets can be sliced, rinsed lightly, and then used in your recipes. This can be done by peeling the beets with a peeler, or by roasting and/or boiling the whole beets until tender and then slipping the skin off after plunging them into cold water. This latter method is best as it gets the entire layer that absorbed the flavor of the soil. When boiling beets this way, leave about an inch of the stalk at the top and don't remove the root at the bottom. The loose dirt should be removed prior to boiling, and this can be accomplished using a high-pressure stream of water from a garden hose outside or by washing them off thoroughly in the kitchen sink and using a vegetable brush if needed.

Beets can be stored whole for as long as three months by cutting off the tops, leaving only 1/2" of stem, and layering the beets in damp sand or peat moss in a container with a tight-fitting lid. The container should be stored in a cool place—preferably just slightly above freezing. Though beets can be frozen, the results aren't impressive. Pressure canning them reduces them to an indistinct mush. The best long-term storage methods for beets are dehydrating and pickling.

Once the skins have been removed from the beets, they can be sliced uniformly, steam blanched for four minutes and then dehydrated until hard. Beets dehydrated this way will reconstitute just fine for soups and stews.

Pickled Beets

Ingredients:

6-8 lbs of beets with the skins removed, sliced uniformly

1 lb onions, skins removed and sliced thinly

1 thinly sliced lemon (rind and all, remove seeds)

4 cups of vinegar (either white or cider vinegar, 5 percent acidity)

2 cups of water

2 cups of sugar

1-1/2 tsp pickling salt

1 Tbsp ground cinnamon

1/2 tsp ground cloves

1 tsp ground allspice

Procedure:

Cook beets and remove skins. Slice uniformly. Slice the onions and the lemon, and combine with the sliced beets. Prepare a syrup with the remaining ingredients and bring just barely to a boil. Add the sliced beets, onions and lemon to the syrup, bring to a simmer and hold at a simmer for 15 minutes. Pack the vegetables into hot sterilized jars and then pour in syrup leaving 1/4" head space. Adjust the two-piece caps and process in a boiling water canner for 10 minutes. Yield: 8—10 pints of pickled beets.

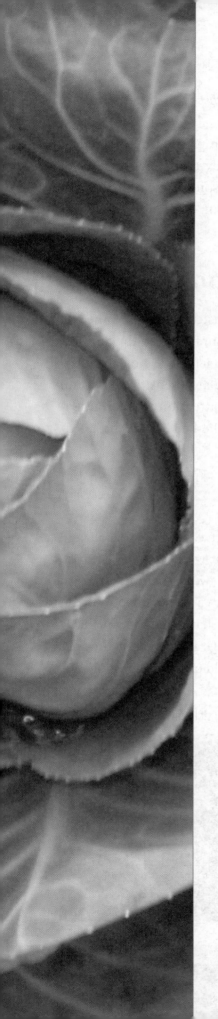

26

Cabbage, Broccoli, and Cauliflower

Broccoli made the news during the administration of President George H. W. Bush because he said he didn't like it. But since that time, broccoli, cabbage, and cauliflower have made the news dozens of times in a more positive sense, indicating that the elder statesman might want to re-examine his palate and plate. These delectable delicacies have been in the news quite often for their cancer-fighting benefits.

Cabbage, broccoli, cauliflower and other plants in this family all produce sulforaphane, a potent anti-cancer compound. Along with this, they are rich in fiber, vitamins, minerals, anti-oxidants and more. But the primary reasons they are featured in more meals at my house than any other vegetables is they are not only delicious, but easy to preserve in an appetizing state and incorporate into meal planning.

Variety Selection

Most varieties of cabbage, broccoli, and cauliflower will grow just fine in most parts of the country if grown during the right time of year. However, because they are a cool-season crop that is frost-hardy, they tend to do better in the north. As long as the maturation date is no more than sixty days longer than the growing season (and most mature much more quickly), that variety can be grown in your area.

My favorite varieties of cabbage are Early Jersey Wakefield and Golden Acre. Both are early maturing and form a compact head with excellent sweet flavor. My favorite varieties of broccoli are Atlantic and Waltham 29. Both of these varieties produce a lot of side shoots once the main head is cut and have a classic broccoli taste. I usually plant Atlantic in the spring and Waltham 29 in the fall. I've had best results in my area with the Early Snowball variety of cauliflower. Cauliflower is vulnerable to earwigs, and we have a lot of them! A quick-growing cauliflower gives the best odds of a harvest with minimal insect damage.

The foregoing are simply my current preferences and will necessarily reflect my own tastes as well as climate and soil. These are excellent varieties for starting your exploration, but you shouldn't limit yourself.

Soil Preparation

Soil pH should be adjusted to 6.5, and the soil should be generously amended with compost and as-needed for sufficient levels of all nutrients. Broccoli in particular is sensitive to boron deficiency, so pay close attention to micronutrient supplementation. The bed should be weed-free prior to planting.

Starting

For spring crops, start cabbage, broccoli and cauliflower indoors eight weeks before last frost, and plant outside three weeks before last frost. Broccoli and cauliflower can be planted out a bit later if desired without harm, but if you delay transplanting the cabbage it might not produce as large a head as it would otherwise produce.

Broccoli produces side shoots after the main head has been cut.

Insufficient boron causes hollow stalks in broccoli.

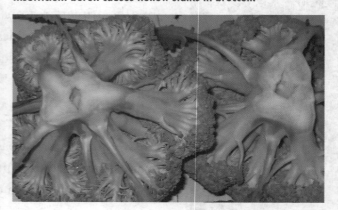

Broccoli grows well closely spaced.

For fall crops, the timing of planting is a bit more complicated, but easily understood. Mark the date of first fall frost on your calendar, and then mark the date thirty days after. Now, count backwards the number of days to maturity for that variety, count back another ten days to make up for diminishing sunlight, and mark that day on your calendar. That is the day you put your transplants in the ground. Now, count backwards five weeks from that date and mark that date on your calendar. This is the day you start the seedlings inside for your fall planting.

So, given my first fall frost of September 6 and Atlantic broccoli maturing in 62 days, my projected date of harvest is October 6th. The transplants should be put into the beds 62+10 days beforehand, on July 26. The seedlings should be started indoors five weeks before that date, on June 21.

This technique, incidentally, is suitable for any frost-hardy crop grown in fall such as kale, kohlrabi and mustard greens.

Planting

Broccoli, cabbage, and cauliflower get pretty big, but they can nevertheless be spaced closely in the beds. Doing so helps to shade out weed competition. In fact, it is very rare for me to have more than a couple of weeds in a bed of these vegetables. So space the plants every 12"-18".

This will allow you to fit as many as thirty-two plants in a single 4'x8' bed.

Early in the season, the availability of nitrogen in the soil is not reliable because the soil temperature may be too cool for microorganisms to work. Because cabbage, broccoli and cauliflower are heavy feeders, you may see signs of nitrogen deficiency almost immediately in the form of older leaves turning yellow. This is easily prevented by watering spring transplants heavily every couple of days with fish fertilizer until they are well-established and danger of frost is past.

Weeds, Pests, and Diseases

As long as the bed was prepared and weed-free prior to planting, with these large-leaved vegetables planted so closely together, most weeds will be shaded and have difficulty growing. While the plants are small, you can remove weeds between them with careful use of a stirrup hoe; once they are larger you can easily hand-pull any weeds encountered.

As with other crops, the best approach to pests and diseases is prevention through crop rotation and proper sanitation. Especially when growing in raised beds that prevent waterlogged roots and with properly adjusted soil pH, most disease problems simply will not occur.

Cabbage, broccoli and cauliflower are subject to a few likely pests. Chief among them in common are cabbage loopers. These are the small green worm-like larvae of a nondescript moth with mottled gray and brown coloration. The moths lay eggs either singly or in groups of as many as six on the underside of leaves. When the leaves hatch, the green larvae grow quickly as they consume three times their body weight in vegetable matter daily, leaving a slime of fecal matter in their wake. They have a distinctive "looping" style of locomotion.

Since these pests seldom eat the crowns of broccoli or cauliflower and only rarely bore into the heads of cabbage, on the scale of a mini farm their economic impact is usually small and they can be adequately controlled by hand-picking. (I feed mine to the chickens who consider them a rare delicacy!) If, however, infestation becomes a serious risk, they can be controlled with a Bt (*Bacillus thuringiensis*) preparation used according to label directions. Cabbage loopers have a lot of natural enemies, and among them is the nuclear polyhedrosis virus (NPV). If you are observant and you find any whitish cabbage loopers hanging limply from vegetation, they are dying from NPV. If you can collect them in a can, wait a few hours for them to die, and then mash them up into a water-based spray; any

cabbage loopers that eat the coated vegetation will die from NPV in about a week.

Cabbage root maggots can be a problem with early plantings, particularly if immature compost has been added to the beds. These are the larvae of a fly that looks similar to an ordinary house fly. The tell-tale symptom is plants that look wilted even though they are thoroughly watered. The easiest prevention is to plant no more than three weeks before last frost and never use immature compost. Diagnosis is easy: when you pull up a stunted and wilted plant, there will be little white grubs all over the roots. This problem is best prevented by later planting and using only well-matured compost; once you have the problem I have found that it can be solved if caught early by drenching the roots of affected plants mixtures designed to solve this problem. If the root damage from the maggots wasn't too extensive, the plants will re-establish themselves and thrive.

Earwigs can be a real nuisance, especially with cauliflower, but also to a lesser extent with cabbage. Earwigs are harmless to humans (they can inflict a minor but harmless pinch with their abdominal pincers) but are a nasty-looking brown creature about 3/4" long with prominent pincers on their abdomen. They hide in the heads of cauliflower or in the leaves of cabbage and do tremendous damage from the inside-out that may go undetected until harvest. I have found no organic sprays that are truly effective in dealing with earwigs, though non-organic carbaryl/Sevin will work. They can be prevented by surrounding beds with dry gravel, and they can be trapped by placing damp loosely rolled newspaper near problem areas overnight and disposing of the newspaper in the morning.

Clubroot is a disease of cabbage-family crops that has symptoms similar to cabbage root maggot infestation: the plants are wilting in spite of adequate water. This disease cannot thrive at a pH exceeding 6.8, so it can be prevented by mixing a handful of lime into the soil in the hole you make for transplanting.

Other common diseases such as alternaria, black leg, black rot, downy mildew, turnip mosaic virus, and others can be controlled through conscientious composting of plant residues, rotating which beds are planted with cabbage-family plants, keeping weeds far away from beds and not working in the beds during wet weather. If these measures are insufficient, you can pre-treat seeds (which may harbor some of these diseases) by immersing them in water at 122 degrees F for five minutes prior to planting, and downy mildew can be treated by spraying with one tablespoon of baking soda mixed with a gallon of water.

Harvest

There's more art than science in determining when to harvest cabbage. The heads should be harvested when they reach full-size for that variety, but before the heads crack. In general, there's no such thing as harvesting too early; it is better to be safe than sorry.

The harvesting time frame for broccoli is likewise limited. You want the broccoli to reach its full growth, but you don't want the buds to start flowering. (The flowers are, however, perfectly edible.) Cauliflower should be harvested when the curd is still firm, and before it becomes grainy-looking. The key here is your observation skills. As the florets and curd get larger, examine them daily for any signs of florets opening or the curd getting grainy. Harvested heads can be kept in the refrigerator in a plastic bag for up to a week until enough have been accumulated for cooking or preservation.

When harvesting cabbage, broccoli and cauliflower, use a sharp knife and cut at an angle. In the case of both broccoli and cabbage, you will likely get many individual florets growing on the broccoli plant that can be harvested over the next couple of weeks for use in salads, or several mini-cabbages that taste delicious when steamed.

Seed Saving

Cabbage, broccoli, cauliflower and other plants in the same family such as kale and kohlrabi can all interbreed. As their pollination is via wind and insects, maintaining purity requires that only one variety be allowed to flower for seed production at any given time.

To save seed for broccoli, just don't harvest the heads from twenty or more plants in close proximity. Allow them to flower, and soon they will develop seed pods. Once the pods have turned tan/brown, strip them from the plant into a bag,

A perfect broccoli crown ready for harvest.

break up the pods, remove the larger debris and then winnow out the smaller debris and dehydrate using silica gel.

Both cabbage and cauliflower are biennial, meaning they produce seed in the second year. In the Southern parts of the U.S. where winter temperatures seldom fall below 20 degrees, cabbage and cauliflower can be mulched with hay over the winter, and cleaned off in spring. In parts of the country where the temperature stays lower than that in the winter, you'll need to bring in the plants to overwinter in a cool (35-40 degree) and dark place, such as an unheated basement. To do this, dig up twenty plants from the fall crop, and store them in damp dirt in five gallon buckets. When spring comes, plant them outside again. To help the cabbages form a flower stalk, use a sharp knife to cut an X in the head. Once cabbage and cauliflower have bolted, they are processed just like broccoli.

The high likelihood of cross-breeding among this species makes it difficult to save seeds from more than one variety in any given year, but the seeds stay viable for five years when properly stored, so if you time your seed saving right, you can stay well-supplied with all the seed you need without danger of cross-breeding.

Preparation and Preservation

With the root and outer leaves removed, a head of cabbage will keep in the refrigerator for two weeks if wrapped tightly in plastic wrap. Broccoli and cauliflower will keep for a week in a tied plastic bag until you've accumulated enough for use or preservation. All three freeze just fine when cut into 1-1/2" chunks. For freezing, cut into chunks, blanch for four minutes, cool in ice water for four minutes, remove excess water, seal, and freeze.

Cabbage (as well as kale, collard, and turnip greens) can be turned into sauerkraut via lactic acid fermentation, and cabbage, broccoli and cauliflower can be successfully pickled in pint jars using vinegar. Broccoli and cauliflower turn to mush when pressure-canned, but cabbage holds up okay. Pack blanched cabbage pieces into pint jars, cover with hot water leaving 1" of head space, and process for forty-five minutes. Cabbage that has been blanched and dehydrated does fine in winter stews, but broccoli and cauliflower don't dehydrate well.

If you discard the stalks of broccoli after cutting off the florets, you should consider using them to make broccoli-slaw instead. To make broccoli-slaw, peel off the outer layer of the stem and then julienne the rest of it. Broccoli-slaw sells in the produce section for as much as $5 for a 12-ounce bag. I like adding broccoli slaw to regular salads.

Baked Cauliflower

Ingredients:

> 1 large head of cauliflower cut into 1" pieces
> ¼ cup olive or walnut oil
> 1 tsp garlic powder
> ½ tsp salt
> ¼ tsp ground black pepper

Procedure:

Preheat oven to 450 degrees. Cut up the cauliflower and place in a large bowl. Add the oil and spices, and mix thoroughly until

Broccoli can be fried, baked or steamed as in this photo.

uniformly coated. Put the coated cauliflower in a roasting pan arranged in a single layer. Bake for twenty minutes until crisp on the outside, but fork-tender.

Pickled Cabbage

Ingredients:

1 gallon of chopped cabbage

2 large onions, diced (optional)

½ cup coarse non-iodized salt

4 cups sugar

4 cups vinegar

1 ½ cups water

2 Tbsp mixed pickling spices

1 spice bag

Procedure:

Combine the cabbage and onion in a large bowl, mix together with the coarse salt, cover with plastic wrap and allow to sit in the refrigerator overnight. In the morning, flood with fresh water to remove the salt, and drain. Combine the sugar, vinegar and water in a large pot, add the spices well tied in the spice bag, and bring to a simmer for 5 minutes. Add the drained cabbage to the pot, stir thoroughly, and bring to a gentle boil for 5 minutes. Remove and discard the spice bag. Pack into sterilized pint jars and process in a boiling water bath canner for 10 minutes.

27

Carrots and Parsnips

My mother always told me that carrots were good for my eyes. That's certainly true, as the beta carotene they contain is a precursor for important compounds that assist with vision. But carrots also contain appreciable amounts of vitamin K, vitamin C, folate, potassium and manganese. Parsnips are a member of the same botanical family, but being white they lack carotenes. Nevertheless, they make up for that lack with added amounts of vitamin E, twice the folate of carrots, and B vitamins. For some reason, parsnips aren't as popular as carrots, but as they are both calorically and nutritionally dense; if you find them appetizing they merit equal growing space to carrots in a self-sufficiency enterprise.

Variety Selection

There are very few varieties of **parsnips** available, and these include Harris Model, Hollow Crown, All American and Half-Long Guernsey. All are long-season varieties that are planted in the spring and harvested after the first fall frost.

The varieties of carrots available number in the hundreds and encompass an endless array of colors, lengths, widths and tastes. These range from the tiny Thumbelina carrot that is literally no bigger than your thumb all the way through the multi-colored Cosmic Purple carrot. In general, carrots fall into a few broad categories. These include Imperator-type varieties that are long and tapered, Nantes that are cylindrical and high in sugar but don't keep well, Danvers with a high fiber content and good keeping qualities, and Chantenay types that are short and wide, and so better-suited for heavy soils. Even though most carrots you'll find in the supermarket are Imperator-type carrots; these are usually among the least tasty varieties. We eat a lot of carrots. The primary varieties that I grow are Saint Valery, Scarlet Nantes and Danvers Half-Long, though I usually plant some purple carrots such as Dragon for variety. The Saint Valery carrots are 12" long and as much as 3" in diameter— real monsters. They store well, have a high germination rate for carrots and therefore tend to be quite productive. Scarlet Nantes carrots are blunt-tipped and about 7" long. They are reddish, sweet and almost core-less. They are a great variety for juicing. Danvers Half-long grow well in tough soils, are about 7" long and are a favorite at markets.

Soil Preparation

Carrots and parsnips require a soil that is deeply dug, cleared of stones, light and with a pH of 6.5-7.5; though they will grow at a pH as low as 6.0. They prefer a soil that is rich in phosphorus, potassium, calcium and micronutrients, but go very easy on the nitrogen. Wood ashes as a form of potassium are well-loved by carrots and parsnips. When preparing the bed, use about half the nitrogen-bearing fertilizer that you would for other crops. Also avoid any form of fresh manures, especially animal manure. Carrots and parsnips will taste just like the manure and your entire crop will be a loss. You should ideally add *fully matured* compost in the fall to beds destined for carrots in the spring, because freshly added or immature compost will inhibit germination as well as causing deformities in the shape of the carrots. The deformed carrots are perfectly safe to eat, but not marketable. Stones will also cause deformities. Again, this isn't a problem in terms of edibility or flavor, but will make the carrots less marketable and more difficult to store.

Planting

Carrots and parsnips are among the slowest germinating crops in the garden; this slow rate of germination can be problematic because weeds will likely sprout first, and there is difficulty in maintaining optimum levels of soil moisture long enough for the seeds to sprout. They also don't like being thinned as they are very fragile when young, and should therefore be planted at optimum spacing from the beginning.

These crops should be planted three weeks before last frost or when soil temperatures are above 50 degrees at a 4" spacing in all directions. Parsnip seeds aren't too difficult to handle, but carrot seeds are small. If you find them difficult to handle, there are several seed companies that sell carrot seeds that have been encapsulated in an innocuous substance that will break down once the seeds have been watered. These encapsulated seeds are the size of a BB and much easier to handle. Alternately, you can have someone with smaller fingers take on the task.

In spring plantings, the seeds should be planted no more than 1/4" deep because the lower temperatures will make germination take longer, and the fragile seedlings will have too much difficulty breaking through the soil if they are planted more deeply. For late summer plantings, they can be planted more deeply.

Carrots and parsnips take a long time to germinate, but this is very much temperature dependent. At a soil temperature of 42 degrees, they take 51 days to germinate. At 50 degrees, they take 17 days to germinate, but at a soil temperature of 59 degrees, they require only ten days. Only six days are required at 72 degrees, but germination rates at temperatures higher than that decline. Use of a soil thermometer to time your planting can help a great deal with these vegetables.

After the seeds are planted, you should water twice daily using a fine mist until the seedlings are well established. Once they are established, a weekly deep soaking providing the equivalent of an inch of water is sufficient.

The one growing problem you may encounter with carrots is green shoulders. If they grow up out of the ground, the tops of the carrots will turn green and they will become bitter. If you see carrot tops poking up out of the ground at all, hill them with some dirt and it won't be a problem.

Weeds, Pests, and Diseases

Weeds are a real problem with carrots and parsnips because even if the bed is seemingly weed-free at the time of planting, the long period of germination can give weeds a head start. With the seedlings in such a delicate state, weeding at an early point can be too disruptive.

There are a lot of ways to handle this. If you time your planting for a soil temperature of 59 degrees, then germination will take only ten days. Another approach often cited in gardening literature is to soak the seed bed and then lay a board over it to seal in the dampness and deprive potential weeds of light. No doubt this works in some cases, especially with sandy soils, but in my case the soil adheres to the board and when the board is lifted, the seedlings come with it. You can also solarize the bed by giving it a good soaking a couple of months before planting and covering with closely stapled clear plastic until time to plant. This will raise the temperature of the top two inches of the soil high enough that weed seeds will be unable to survive. What I do is go over the bed slowly with a flame weeder just prior to planting, and disturb the soil as little as possible while putting in the seeds. This only kills seeds in the top 1/4" of soil, but it works well enough and is quickly accomplished. While I am at it, I use the flame weeder to get all the weeds and grasses growing along the edges of the beds.

Though, theoretically, there are a lot of potential pest and disease problems with carrots; on the scale of a mini farm, if you are practicing crop rotation and cleaning up debris at the end of the season, you really only have two pests of concern: wireworms and carrot flies.

Wireworms are the larvae of click beetles, and are usually a problem when growing in areas that were previously sod, or are abutted by sod. Thus, they are a common problem with mini farms in particular, because raised beds are usually located in areas that were previously used for growing grass. Wireworms burrow into many edible

Wireworms are easily identified but not easily controlled.

root crops including carrots, parsnips, potatoes and more.

If you surround your bed frames with a mulch that smothers out grasses such as a thick layer of bark or gravel, that will help diminish populations over time. Turning up the soil in the beds a couple of days prior to planting will encourage birds to eat them. Also, when we turn the soil, we scan it for wireworms and other grubs, and feed them to our chickens. You can also bait the wireworms by burying some pieces of cut potato attached to a skewer (for ease in locating) two to four inches under the soil surface. Pull up the skewers twice a week and dispose of the wireworms. If you put the skewers into the beds intended for root crops a week prior to planting and keep them in place until a week after germination, damage from wireworms will be reduced considerably. Figure on one skewer per four square feet of bed space.

Carrot flies are the other likely pest. Carrot flies look like a regular housefly, except they are more streamlined. Often, you won't see them. Once attracted by the smell of the foliage of parsley, carrots, celery, parsnips and related plants, they fly in and lay eggs in the soil at the base of the plant. When the eggs hatch, the grubs burrow into the roots and ruin them. Unfortunately, you won't find the problem until you harvest the roots and start cussing.

An important aspect of preventing carrot flies is to avoid anything that injures or disturbs the foliage. Bruised foliage is a powerful attractant. Luckily, when spaced so closely together, the plants will usually shade out any weeds, so the primary cause of bruised foliage—weeding—can be avoided. If you must weed, do so carefully.

Another trick that works surprisingly well is to attach some wooden stakes to the corners of the bed, and wrap a 2' high section of clear plastic around the bed, stapling it to the stakes and the edges of the bed. Carrot flies seldom fly any higher than 18" from the ground, so the plastic baffles them and they move on to easier pickings.

Finally, carrot flies (and some less common pests such as carrot weevils) don't like wood ashes. If you use wood ashes when you prepare the bed, and water the bed every couple of weeks with a mixture of two tablespoon of wood ashes per gallon of water, they will be deterred.

Carrots grown in a box with a landscape fabric bottom to outwit wireworms.

Harvest

Carrots and parsnips can be harvested at any stage, however the balance of bitter turpenes and sugars favors the turpenes when harvested early. Parsnips are best left until after the first hard frost, as this sweetens them. Carrots, on the other hand, should be harvested no more than two weeks later than the specified maturity date of that variety, as letting them sit in the ground too long can make them fibrous.

To harvest carrots or parsnips, water thoroughly to make the roots easier to pull; grasp the foliage as close to the root as possible, and pull while giving a slight twist. If the tops break off, you can use a digging fork or hand shovel to dig around the affected roots and lift them out gently. Cut off the tops 1/4" above the root and immediately place in the compost pile. Let the roots sit out in the sun for a couple of hours for the dirt to dry, then dust it off with a soft brush. Carrots should be washed immediately prior to use.

Seed Saving

Carrots and parsnips are biennials, meaning they produce seed in their second year. During their first year, they store energy in the root. If allowed to stay in the ground over the winter, they will sprout in the spring, sending up a seed stalk with a beautiful flower called an umbel that is identical to Queen Anne's lace. In fact, Queen Anne's lace is a wild carrot from which our domesticated varieties are derived, and it will interbreed freely with garden carrots.

Because wild carrots are so widely distributed and this family is insect-pollinated, isolation techniques are recommended for saving carrot seed, though they aren't necessary for parsnips. In addition, inbreeding depression can be a problem, so ideally seeds will be saved from a population of at least twenty plants.

Carrot flowers can be impressively large.

Bag the umbels (using a spun polyester material such as what you can buy as a floating row cover) when they have not yet flowered to keep insects from getting to them. You don't have to bag all of the umbels, just one from each plant that you will be using for seed. Once the umbels have flowered, use a horsehair or camel hair brush to cross-pollinate. The technique is straightforward: every day for two to four weeks once the flowers have formed, remove the bags from as many flowers as you can keep free of insects at one time. Gently rub the brush over the flowers in each umbel, going back and forth so that all flowers of each umbel have been touched. Replace the bags, then remove the bags from another set of umbels and continue until all of the umbels have been processed.

Once the umbels have matured, cut them from the plant and allow them to mature indoors in a cool, dry place for another two weeks. The seeds can be stripped from the umbels by rubbing with your hands and separated from the chafe by winnowing.

Preparation and Preservation

Carrots and parsnips can be stored whole for a few months in moistened peat moss or clean sand. The tops are cut 1/2" above the root so they don't suck the moisture out of the roots. They can also be blanched for four minutes and then either cooled, dried and frozen or dehydrated. If dried thoroughly, they can be stored in the refrigerator in a sealed bag for a couple of months.

Carrot and Parsnip Pickles

Ingredients:

- 1 pound carrots
- 1 pound parsnips
- 3-1/2 cups vinegar
- 1-1/2 cups sugar
- 2 tsp ground cinnamon
- 1 tsp ground allspice
- 1 tsp sea salt or other non-iodized salt
- 1/2 tsp ground cloves

Procedure:

Quarter the carrots and parsnips lengthwise and cut into spears 3-1/2" long. Pack into clean pint jars. Combine the remaining ingredients in a saucepan, and bring to a light boil for 5 minutes. Pour this into the jars, completely covering the spears and leaving 1/2" headspace. Adjust the two-piece lids and process in a boiling water canner for 15 minutes.

Lemon Dill Carrots

Ingredients:

- 1 pound of carrots
- 1 lemon
- 3 Tbsp walnut oil (butter can be substituted)
- 1/2 tsp dried dill weed

Procedure:

Preheat oven to 350 degrees. Cut the carrots to uniform thickness, coat thoroughly with walnut oil, then add one quarter of the zest of the lemon and all of its juice (making sure to remove any pits) and uniformly cover with dill weed. Spread in a single layer in a covered (it is important that it be covered!) baking dish. Bake for 30 minutes or until fork-tender.

This dish is enhanced with dill fresh from the garden.

Corn

28

Corn is one of the biggest commercial crops in the country, being used to make everything from corn starch baby powder to ethanol for vehicles. Unfortunately, it is also one of the most genetically modified. Depending upon the State in which it is grown, between 79 percent and 95 percent of all corn grown in the United States is genetically engineered.[3]

There is sufficient debate regarding the safety of such crops that the European Union currently bans importing or growing genetically engineered corn for human use. Whether they are safe or not I cannot pretend to know with certainty. Much of the data pertaining to its dangers seems rather alarmist, but the data pertaining to its safety is from biased sources. Perhaps the strangest development in this debate is the adoption of Federal laws that preempt State laws requiring that products containing genetically modified crops be labeled.[4]

Thus, other than the laws that ban the use of genetically modified seeds in USDA Organic produce, there is no way to know whether what

---

[3] USDA Economic Research Service (2010), Adoption of Genetically Engineered Crops in the U.S.: Corn Varieties.
[4] Lasker, Eric (2005), *Federal Preemption and State Anti-"GM" Food Laws.*

you are eating contains genetically engineered organisms.

As I have mentioned, I find the data pertaining to the safety or harm of genetically engineered corn rather murky. Other than buying expensive organic-labeled products, the only way to assure the corn you eat is free of genetically engineered attributes is to grow it yourself.

Varieties

Corn is a staple of the human diet in many places, and as a result many variations of corn have been created for different uses. Flour corn can be ground into a fine flour. Flint is used to make coarse corn meal. Dent corn is used in animal feeds and industry. Pop corn is used to make (you guessed it) popcorn. But the type of corn most commonly grown by home gardeners is sweet corn.

Of the many varieties of flint corn available, Floriani Red Flint is one of the most productive open-pollinated varieties available. Grain yield is roughly five pounds per 4'x8' bed. Blue Hopi is an heirloom variety with a distinctive blue color and fantastic flavor, though it is slightly less productive at four pounds per 4'x8' bed.

Sweet corn falls into three categories based upon genetics: Normal Sugary (Su), Sugary Enhanced (Se) and Supersweet (Sh2). These genes determine how much sugar is in the kernel and how long the sugar will stay in the kernel before turning to starch. All of the genes that result in sweet corn are recessive traits that spontaneously arose in flint or dent corn. As a result of the recessive quality of these traits, sweet corn should be separated from field corns that may be pollinating at the same time by at least 400 yards. Otherwise, the kernels of the sweet corn won't be sweet.

Su sweet corns are the oldest varieties of sweet corn. Nearly all available open-pollinated varieties of sweet corn have this genetic profile. Examples of popular open-pollinated varieties include Golden Bantam (yellow), Country Gentleman (white), Stowell's Evergreen (white) and Double Standard (bicolor). Common hybrids with Su genes include Early Sunglow (yellow), Silver Queen (white) and Butter and Sugar (bicolor).

Su sweet corn needs to be kept well away from Sh2 sweet corn, but can be grown near Se sweet corn and vice versa. Harvest timing is critical, and it should ideally be processed within thirty minutes of harvest, as the sugar starts turning to starch the second the ear is picked from the stalk. Even so, Su varieties deliver a classic corn taste, and hold up well to being blanched and frozen on the cob.

Se sweet corn has even more sugar than Su corn; so much so that it can keep at high quality for two to four days after harvest if refrigerated. Although some projects for producing open-pollinated Se varieties are underway,[5] all commercially available Se varieties are hybrids. Se corn has excellent taste, but is comparatively delicate so it doesn't stand up well to processing. It is better for fresh eating. Popular Se varieties include Kandy Korn (yellow), Argent (white) and Precious Gem (bicolor).

Sh2 sweet holds its sugar content for as long as ten days after harvest, and is thus ideal for truck-shipping and display in supermarkets. In addition, though more ideal for shipping than eating,

---

[5] The Organic Farming Research Foundation has funded a project to create two open pollinated, sugary enhanced sweet corn varieties. Joseph's Garden in Paradise, Utah, is undertaking a similar effort.

the kernels are tougher, and so stand up better to rough handling. All commercially available Sh2 varieties are hybrids, and they must be separated from Se and Su types to avoid developing starchy kernels. Popular Sh2 varieties include Challenger (yellow), Aspen (white) and Dazzle (bicolor).

Though there are a staggering number of varieties available, for mini-farming I recommend sticking to Su and Se varieties because they are more tolerant of planting depth and soil temperature variations. For seed-saving, you are limited to open-pollinated varieties that, so far, are entirely Su strains. I recommend Floriani Red Flint or Blue Hopi for corn meal, and Golden Bantam or Stowell's Evergreen for sweet corn; these are beginner recommendations and through experimentation you'll likely find other varieties that you like.

Soil Preparation

Corn is a seriously hungry plant, requiring plenty of food, light and water for optimal production. In addition, it is shallow-rooted, a fact that makes proper soil management all the more critical. Corn prefers a pH of 6.0 to 6.5, and lots of organic matter tilled throughout the top six to eight inches of soil. It is a heavy feeder and in agribusiness production is typically treated with high-nitrogen fertilizers three times during the course of the season. However, this is because the artificial fertilizers they use are highly soluble, and they pay little attention to maintaining high enough levels of organic matter in the soil to hold onto those nutrients. A properly prepared bed won't need additional fertilizer to produce great corn.

To prepare a bed for corn, add at least six cubic feet of mature compost per 48 square feet of bed and mix it into the top six to eight inches of soil. Adjust the pH to somewhere between 6.0 and 6.5 using lime. Add micronutrients in the form of sea mineral solids at the manufacturer's recommended rate. Amend the soil using organic fertilizers based upon a home soil test for nitrogen, phosphorus and potassium. Finally, to provide additional both slow and fast release nitrogen, add ten pounds of alfalfa meal and two pounds of blood meal per forty-eight-square-foot bed, in addition to what you have already added based upon soil test. The compost will work with the nutrients to hold them in the soil so rain won't wash them out, and make them available to the corn as the plant requires. Using this method, I have never needed to add fertilizer during the season.

Starting and Planting

Corn can be temperamental about planting depth, temperature, water levels and more, especially when dealing with hybrid Sh2 varieties. But even Su varieties can suffer from staggered germination, seeds rotting in the ground before they can sprout, and other woes.

Though this solution certainly won't work on the scale of the agri-giant Monsanto, for a mini-farm it works extremely well: instead of planting your seeds in the ground, start them indoors one week before last frost. Then, plant out your corn seedlings at one-foot spacing in all directions one week after last frost. This allows you to skip all these problems and have a nice, uniform stand of corn.

If you don't want to do this, then plant your seeds 1" deep spaced 12" apart one week after last frost, and water daily until they sprout.

Also, if you follow my practice of planting beans with corn, wait until a week after the corn seedling have emerged before planting the beans. Otherwise, the beans will sprout first and shade out your corn.

Corn is wind-pollinated and strongly outbreeding. Pollination is necessary to produce kernels on the ears. Planting the corn so closely spaced is generally sufficient to yield adequate pollination, but just to be sure, once the pollen-bearing tops have grown, I reach in and gently shake a few corn plants every once in a while to distribute the pollen.

Weeds, Pests, and Diseases

In agribusiness production on the scale of hundreds of acres and where harvesting is mechanized, weeds are a serious problem for corn. Mass spraying with herbicides is practiced, and genetically modified corn that is immune to the herbicides is planted. Fortunately, on the scale of a mini farm, weeds can be controlled with little effort. If you clear the bed of weeds before planting, a weekly hand-weeding or use of a stirrup hoe between plants is sufficient.

Though in commercial mono-cropping there are a lot of pest problems, in a properly run mini farm where crop sanitation and rotation are practiced; there are only a couple of notable pests that are easily controlled. Japanese beetles can defoliate the corn and thus reduce productivity. Japanese beetles are a ubiquitous lawn grub. If you have a lot of property so there is a good buffer with your neighbors, treating your entire lawn and beds with milky spore disease can be a good preventative once the disease has become

established in a year or so. Japanese beetle traps (available at hardware stores) can work well, but they must be placed downwind of the garden at least 100' away.

Japanese beetles attract each other. So one way to keep them controlled is to simply pick them by hand into a small bucket of soapy water. If you keep them picked off daily once they are noticed, you'll likely prevent the problem all together. They can also be controlled by sprays such as pyrethrin and used according to package directions, but this is a last resort as such sprays are expensive.

The other notable pest is corn ear worm. This is the larva of a large but rather nondescript moth. Though it will attack nearly anything edible in the garden, including tomatoes, broccoli and lettuce, it is primarily a risk for corn because the damage it has done is not visible until harvest. Because the moth can't overwinter north of Maryland, it tends to be more consistently damaging in the South, though winds blow it well up into Canada.

The moth lays its speck-sized eggs on corn silk. The hatched eggs produce a tiny worm that crawls down the silk into the ear, and burrows its way in. It grows as it eats and by the time it is done it can be a good three inches long. Often, it will not be immediately detected because its head resembles a kernel of corn and it will have bored through the cob and put its head in place of a corn kernel. It can be a bit unsettling when an ear of boiled corn is chomped, and you pull away with a worm dangling from your mouth! Sometimes the worm simply eats along the outside of the ear. Almost always, it eats some of the silk, which prevents kernels from being pollinated and growing.

Damage from corn ear worm can be substantially reduced with a critically timed application of Bt (*Bacillus thuringiensis*) mixed with corn oil from the supermarket and using liquid lecithin (available at health food stores) as an emulsifier. Mix one heaping tablespoon of liquid lecithin and three level tablespoons of Bt (in this case, Dipel DF) with one quart of corn oil. Mix thoroughly. Apply 0.5 ml of the mixture to each corn tassel. I use a small syringe (without the needle) that I picked up from a veterinary supply company to measure the amount accurately. Apply it to the corn tassel, and distribute it evenly by hand.

The oil can adversely affect pollination but is extremely effective in controlling ear worm damage during the crucial stage. There is a short five to eight day window when it can be applied with minimal impact on pollination and still achieve good control. If you observe your corn carefully, that time period starts 57 days after the start of silk growth, or 34 days after the silk is fully grown.

This sort of observation may not be feasible. But all is not lost! You can also judge when to apply the oil by waiting until the tips of the silk have just barely started to turn brown and wilt. If you peel back the husk from an ear of corn, you'll discover that silk is only attached to less than the top inch of kernels.

This is the optimal method as it provides greatest control with minimum use of materials. However, it might not be practical. Especially if you are raising a substantial amount of corn, the process can quickly become tedious. If this is the case, you can deal with the problem by using a Bt or spinosad preparation according to label directions, and thoroughly spraying the corn once a week using an ordinary garden sprayer starting once the silk has formed. The water-based spray will have no adverse effect on pollination and as long as you don't skip, adequate control will be maintained.

Though corn is vulnerable to about a dozen diseases of commercial importance in large-scale farming, within the format of a mini-farm in which soil fertility is properly maintained, crops are rotated among beds and crop debris is composted, none of them are likely to be an issue at all. Likewise, many of the diseases that manifest in agribusiness production are the result of damage to the corn stalk or ears from machines. As mini-farming methods don't use machines, this won't be a problem. If in spite of good cultural practices you encounter disease problems, switching to a hybrid Su corn for future plantings will likely take care of them.

Though it isn't a pest or disease problem per se; lodging of corn hurts productivity in large-scale production and can certainly be a problem on a mini farm. Lodging is defined as stalk breakage below the corn ear, and it is usually caused by severe winds or weather. Because corn is grown in beds on a mini farm, lodging can be entirely eliminated by using deck screws to screw some four foot uprights to the corners of the bed and running some stout string that is resistant to UV degradation around the bed and through holes drilled near the top of the uprights.

Harvest

Field corns such as dent and flint corn are harvested at their dry stage. Harvest as soon as the green husk fades to tan by holding the corn stalk in one hand, and pulling the ear down with the other while twisting slightly. The ears should be shucked immediately, meaning that the husks and as much silk removed as possible. Then the husked ears should be hung in bunches out of the weather where there is good air circulation for a month or more. Once the kernels are well dried, the kernels can be removed from the cobs by shelling. On a small scale, you can remove the dry kernels from the ears by wearing gloves (so you don't get blisters) and rubbing two ears together and twisting the cob in your hands. Collect the kernels and allow to dry further. On a larger scale, you can use a simple hand sheller, or a manually operated mechanical sheller. Mechanical shellers are operated with a hand crank and are pretty fun to use. My cousins and I used to shell corn for my grandfather using a mechanical sheller, and we thought it was a lot of fun. As he had never told us to do it, we never realized it was supposed to be work.

The timing of sweet corn harvest is a bit more tricky. If you harvest too early, the kernels are imperfectly formed and there is insufficient sugar. If you harvest too late, it becomes starchy and hard. To complicate matters, especially with open-pollinated varieties, not all the ears mature at once. This is one reason why hybrids are used in large-scale farming—they allow all of the corn to be harvested in one session. Nevertheless, all of the ears of open-pollinated sweet corn can be harvested within a week of each other.

Corn will mature at a different rate each year, depending on temperature, amount of sunlight, and the amount of water it receives, so the "days to harvest" given in the seed catalog is an approximation. Start checking the ears twenty-one days after silk has appeared. When the silk has turned brown and started to dry, feel the ears to see if they are firm. If so, gently separate some of the

When the silk has turned brown and started to dry, check your sweet corn for ripeness.

husk midway down the ear, and puncture one of the kernels with your thumb. If the juice is clear, the corn isn't ready yet. If the juice is milky, it is time to harvest. If it is creamy, then the corn is over-ripe. All is not lost with slightly overripe sweet corn because at that stage it is perfect for canning.

To harvest, remove the ears using the same technique as for field corn, but leave the husks on. Store at a cool temperature, preferably in a refrigerator until used to help slow down the

Sweet corn should be shucked and used as soon as possible after harvest.

conversion of sugar to starch. With Su varieties, use or preserve within a few hours. With Se varieties, you have 2-3 days. With Sh2 varieties, you have a week.

Seed Saving

Corn is a strongly out-breeding plant, meaning that it is subject to inbreeding depression if a large number of plants aren't used as the breeding pool. In the case of corn, so many plants are needed that it may not even be feasible to save seed at a small scale. You need at least 200 plants, from which you cull any that are clearly inferior or off-type. Because corn is wind pollinated and readily crosses with all other varieties of corn, if you are trying to maintain pure seed it should be separated from other corn by at least a mile, but preferably more.

The seeds of field corn are harvested as described above in the section on harvesting. In order to save seed from sweet corn, treat it like field corn and allow the ear to reach maturity rather than harvesting at its milk stage. I recommend shelling all of the corn into a large container, mixing it thoroughly so that seeds are saved from as many unique plants as possible, and taking a random sample of at least a quart from the container as seed. The dried corn that isn't used for seed can also be ground into corn meal.

Preparation and Preservation

Dried corn should be stored in an airtight container in a cool, dry place. Ideally, that container will be free of oxygen in order to prevent pests. There are a lot of ways to do this. One way is to put a metal plate on top of the corn and place an amount of dry ice (solidified carbon dioxide) on the plate. Because carbon dioxide is heavier than air, as it vaporizes, it will supplant all of the oxygen in the container. When the dry ice is almost gone, put the lid on the container. Another way is to use an airtight metal container, put a very stable heat-proof plate on top of the corn, put an unscented candle on it, light the candle and close the lid. Though this won't remove all the oxygen, it will alter the oxygen/carbon dioxide proportions sufficiently to be inimical to animal life. You'll need to re-light the candle each time the lid is opened. Flint and dent corn can be ground into truly excellent corn meal using a hand grinder with proper burrs such as the Corona grain mill.

Sweet corn is ideally prepared within a few hours of harvest to prevent the conversion of sugars to starches. The most popular way to eat sweet corn is on the cob. The corn is shucked, and the ears are boiled for twenty minutes or so. I prefer to slather mine with enough butter and salt to make a cardiologist wince, but there are plenty of other toppings. Corn on the cob can also be grilled. Peel back the husk but leave it attached, remove the silk, coat the kernels with plentiful olive oil, put the husk back and tie closed with cotton string. Then grill, turning frequently, on a medium-hot grill for fifteen to twenty minutes. If you don't want to bother with the husk, wrap the shucked ears in aluminum foil and use butter instead of oil.

Sweet corn can be frozen either on or off the cob. Blanch for four minutes, cool for four minutes, dry off the water, and put in freezer bags from which the air has been evacuated. Off the cob, it can also be dehydrated following blanching. Corn holds up to pressure canning pretty well, especially if harvested a couple of days late.

Canned Corn

Ingredients:

2 pounds of husked corn on the cob per pint
salt
water

Procedure:

Husk the corn and remove the silk. Use a sharp knife to cut the kernels from the cob. Place the kernels in jars, add (optionally) 1/2 tsp salt per pint or 1 tsp per quart, ladle boiling water over the corn in the jars leaving one inch of head space, and then process in a pressure canner at ten pounds of pressure for 55 minutes for pints, or 80 minutes for quarts.

Fresh Corn Salsa

Ingredients:

5 ears of fresh corn
1 jalapeño pepper
1/2 pound of tomatillos (preferred) or tomatoes
1 red pepper, chopped small with membranes removed
1 small onion, sliced thinly
1 lemon
1/2 tsp ground coriander
1 Tbsp chopped fresh cilantro
water

Procedure:

Husk the corn and cut the kernels from the cobs. Remove membranes and chop the jalapeño pepper finely. Chop up the tomatillos after removing the husks. Add all of the ingredients to a frying pan, squeeze the juice of the lemon into the mixture, add enough water to prevent scorching, and bring to a light boil over medium heat. Stir frequently for 5 minutes, and then remove from heat. Put it in the refrigerator to cool, and then stir in the cilantro before serving. Note: this is a fresh salsa and is not intended for canning as it isn't acidic enough to be canned safely.

29

Cucumbers

Cucumbers are in close competition with tomatoes as the quintessential vegetable announcing the joy of summer. Eaten alone, as part of a salad or as a pickle, cucumbers lend a distinctively fresh and wholesome flavor to any meal. A member of the gourd family along with gourds, melons and squash, cucumbers were originally cultivated in India, and spread from there to ancient Greece, Rome and eventually to France where they graced Charlemagne's table.

Cucumbers contain caffeic acid and vitamin C, as well as being a good source of molybdenum, vitamin A, fiber and folate in the diet. Their silica content is good for the skin, and they have been used as a cosmetic for hundreds of years to reduce puffiness in and around the eyes either sliced or as a paste.

Variety Selection

In general, cucumbers are classified as *slicers*, *picklers* or *burpless*, though at the right stage of development their uses are interchangeable to some degree. Slicers are usually long and straight, and are intended for fresh eating. Picklers usually grow no longer than four inches, and have been bred specifically for their quality as pickles. Burpless cucumbers are supposed to be more easily digested without burping when eaten fresh, but as I've never had a problem with either slicers or picklers causing burping, I can't say with certainty that burpless cucumbers solve the problem.

When growing in raised beds, space is an issue. Cucumbers are usually a vining crop, though some bush varieties have been introduced. In general, bush varieties aren't very productive. Using raised beds, the best space efficiency is gained by growing vining varieties on a trellis on the Northern one foot of a bed, and using the rest of the bed for growing a shorter crop such as lettuce or carrots. Trellised cucumbers also tend to grow straighter.

One additional complication in choosing cucumber varieties is bacterial wilt disease, spread by cucumber beetles. There are very few resistant cultivars, but if you run into trouble with this pest and the accompanying disease, your best bet may be to switch to a variety of cucumber that is resistant.

Pickling and slicing cucumbers ready for a salad.

Among slicers, good vining varieties include Muncher, Marketmore 76, Tendergreen Burpless and Straight 8. My favorite vining picklers are Homemade Pickles and Boston Pickling Improved. If you have difficulty with cucumber beetles carrying bacterial wilt disease, you might want to consider the hybrid pickler County Fair which has demonstrated resistance to bacterial wilt disease in controlled studies.

Soil Preparation

Cucumbers like fertile, well-drained soils with lots of organic matter. Add at least 5 cubic feet of compost per 4'x8' bed, adjust the pH to between 6 and 7, and amend for NPK as indicated by a soil test. Cucumbers like trace minerals, so make sure these are added as well. Organic fertilizers are well-matched to cucumbers as continuous harvest creates long-term needs for fertility. Organic fertilizers buffered with plenty of compost are a recipe for impressive success with cucumbers, and also reduce the uneven growth spurts that make cucumbers more vulnerable to disease.

Starting and Planting

Cucumbers can be grown either from seed or from transplants. I prefer to start the seeds indoors a week before last frost, and then plant them out a week after last frost to give them a head start. If you prefer direct seeding, wait until a week after last frost, put the seeds in soil 1/2" to 1" deep and water thoroughly daily until the seedlings emerge.

As mentioned earlier, cucumbers are most productive and most space-efficient when trellised. A six foot trellis is sufficient. Plant

Growing cucumbers on a trellis makes them straighter and saves space.

cucumbers spaced 8"–12" apart in a single row along the Northern one foot of a bed. As the seedlings grow, train the vines onto the trellis. Once they have a foothold on the trellis, you'll only have to train the occasional errant vine.

Weeds, Pests, and Diseases

Plant cucumbers in a weed-free bed and weed by hand weekly. Once established, cucumbers will outgrow most weed problems, but you want to get the weeds out anyway so they don't set seed and create a problem for future crops.

Cucumbers are vulnerable to three major pests: leaf miners, aphids and cucumber beetles.

They also are vulnerable to squash bugs and squash vine borers, though they aren't a preferred food for those creatures. (For more information on these latter two pests, please see the section on squash.) Leaf miners are the larvae of a small yellow and black fly. The eggs are laid on the upper surface of the leaf, and the hatched larvae burrow through the leaf, leaving tracks. When ready, they cut a semi-circular hole on the underside of the leaf, and drop to the ground to pupate. Usually, leaf miners pose little or no economic risk to cucumbers. Crop rotation and cleaning up debris are sufficient to keep them at bay.

Various species of aphids affect nearly every soft plant in existence. They suck out the plant juices and excrete a sticky honeydew that serves as food for ants and fungi. At low levels of infestation, aphids aren't usually an economic threat, but at higher levels they can weaken and stunt plants. Aphids are tiny oval creatures about 1/16th of an inch long when full grown. Some have wings and some don't. They can be controlled with insecticidal soap or a light horticultural oil applied to tops and bottoms of leaf surfaces and along the stem.

Cucumber beetles are a serious threat because they carry bacterial wilt disease. They can do serious feeding damage as well, with adults feeding on fruit, flowers, stems and foliage and larvae feeding on the roots. But overall, bacterial wilt disease is their greatest threat because the disease kills the plants outright. Organic control focuses mainly on prevention because botanical insecticides are only moderately effective at best, especially given that all it takes to kill a plant is a single bite. Because cucumber beetles overwinter away from the garden, feed on a variety of wild

Cucumber beetles are the most-feared pest of cucumbers as they carry bacterial wilt disease.

plants and trees until cucurbits are available and can be carried hundreds of miles on high altitude wind currents; crop rotation and composting debris are not as effective in controlling them as controlling other pests.

Some people grow cucumbers for decades and never encounter a cucumber beetle, while another farmer less than a mile away can suffer serious infestation year after year. You never really know unless you encounter them. If you encounter them, here are some strategies for their management:

Grow resistant varieties. Only two resistant varieties exist as far as I know: County Fair (a pickler) and Saladin (a European greenhouse slicer). Use transplants instead of seeds to get a head start. Use floating row cover (well-anchored) to exclude the beetles until the first flowers appear. If you use this strategy, you should thoroughly weed the bed and then flame the soil before transplanting, as opening up the row cover

to weed will defeat its purpose. Use aluminum foil or mylar (you can get this cheap as a so-called "emergency blanket") as a mulch because studies show this sort of mulch can reduce pest levels below the threshold of economic damage.[6]

Once you see cucumber beetles on your vines (they often hide in the flowers), it's too late for any organic sprays to have much of an effect. Plus, those sprays (particularly those containing pyrethrin) would likely be far more toxic to bees, and bees are critical pollinators for cucumbers.

Other than bacterial wilt, the most likely disease you will see in cucumbers is powdery mildew. Powdery mildew is caused by a fungal spoor taking root on (usually) the underside of the leaves. It appears like baby powder, and is often accompanied by a yellowing of the upper side of the leaf opposite the fungus colony. As the

[6] Diver, S. & Hinman, T. (2008), *Cucumber Beetles: Organic and Biorational Integrated Pest Management.*

Powdery mildew is preventable and curable.

disease progresses, it can spread to the upper sides of leaves and even (although rarely) to the fruit. Powdery mildew infections, if uncontrolled, will cause the death of the associated leaves and poor quality fruit.

Conditions favoring powdery mildew development are high humidity, shade, and poor air circulation. It overwinters in crop debris, so even though the spoors are widespread, risk of reinfection can be diminished through sanitation. Likewise, the variation and species of powdery mildew fungus is usually specific to a given family of plants, so crop rotation will help. So growing cucumbers on trellises for better air circulation and locating them in full sun, along with crop rotation and sanitation will go a long way toward prevention.

Another thing to consider, because a lot of resistant varieties of cucumber are available, is planting a variety of cucumber that is resistant to powdery mildew. Examples include Marketmore 76 and Tendergreen Burpless among others.

Once an infection is noted, immediate treatment can eliminate the problem. Because development of fungicide resistance has been observed in many variations of powdery mildew, I recommend a fungicide cocktail approach. The fungicides used in organic production, particularly bicarbonate and horticultural oils, have the potential to harm or kill garden plants. So during this treatment regimen, please make sure the plants are well-hydrated, and test bicarbonate and horticultural oils on a single leaf first and wait

a day to assure no harm is done before making a wider application.

Use a pressure sprayer to spray the plants and leaves, making sure to get the undersides of the leaves, with a solution *Bacillus subtilis* (such as Serenade™) according to label directions. Wait two days, then spray with light horticultural oil mixed according to label directions and to which you have added one tablespoon baking soda (sodium bicarbonate) per one gallon of water. Spray to the point of run-off. Wait three days, and then repeat the cycle. Continue repeating the cycle until no powdery mildew remains, and then spray every other week with the *Bacillus subtilis* preparation.

Harvest

Cucumbers should be harvested when they have reached the size for the particular variety grown and well before they have started to turn from green to yellow. Keep a watchful eye for cucumbers that manage to hide among

Cucumbers will look like this due to uneven watering. Assuring the equivalent of 1" of rain weekly will prevent this.

the leaves while they ripen, because once a cucumber on a particular vine starts ripening, that vine will stop producing new fruit. To pick a cucumber with minimal damage to the vine, gently hold the cucumber with one hand, while using a pair of scissors in the other hand to cut the stem.

Saving Seed

Cucumber seeds are saved via the wet method. Allow a couple of cucumbers on each vine to grow to maturity—meaning they grow large, yellow and soft. Leave these on the vines until they are dead from frost, and then bring them in to ripen out of direct sunlight for another couple of weeks. Slice the cucumbers open lengthwise, and scoop out the seed mass into a plastic cup. Add some warm water, stir, and allow to sit for five days. At the end of five days there will be mold growing on top. Give it a swirl, and the bad seeds will float while the good ones will sink. Empty out the water, discard the mold and bad seeds, and rinse the good seeds thoroughly. Dry the

good seeds with a paper towel, and then allow them to dry on a screen until they are brittle. You can dehydrate them further using a silica gel desiccant. Store in a sealed container in a cool, dry place away from sunlight.

Preparation and Preservation

Cucumbers keep best at a humidity of 95 percent and temperature of 45 degrees. In practical terms, this environment doesn't exist in most homes. For short term storage—five days or less—putting cucumbers in sealed bags in the refrigerator works well. For longer storage, up to two weeks, wrap each cucumber individually in plastic wrap and store in the refrigerator. That is the effective limit of how long cucumbers can be stored fresh, but they will keep for several years as pickles using any of a number of available recipes. They neither freeze nor dehydrate well, though you can freeze them with moderate success if you bake them first at 350 degrees for thirty minutes.

Sesame cucumber salad is a quick and delicious summer dish.

Sesame Cucumber Salad

3 slicing cucumbers
1 tsp sesame seeds
1 Tbsp sesame oil
1 tsp soy sauce
1/2 tsp salt
1/4 of a lemon

Peel the cucumbers and cut into chunks. Add salt and stir thoroughly. Squeeze the lemon over the cucumber and mix. Mix the remaining ingredients together, then pour over the cucumber and mix thoroughly. Serve chilled.

30

Greens

The term "greens" includes any plant whose leaves are eaten as food, including cabbage, kale, collard greens, beet greens, chard, spinach and lettuce. But it also includes a wide array of under-appreciated leaf vegetables rich in nutrients that you can seldom—if ever—find in the store. Examples include orach, lettuce, mustard, garden purslane, water cress, garden cress and corn salad just to name a few. Greens are eaten both raw and cooked, depending upon culinary tastes.

Some of the plants in this category are covered in other chapters, such as chard. In the case of plants where I've given more detailed information in another chapter, that more specific information should be preferred. Nevertheless, greens have enough in common in spite of their diversity that a chapter dedicated to their general growth and properties is useful, especially given that having separate chapters on orach and lettuce would be wasteful.

Leafy greens are a nutritional powerhouse that combine high nutrient density with compounds that lower the risks for serious diseases such as cancer and atherosclerosis. Some work better raw, and some work better cooked. But in either state, leafy greens in many cases literally contain more vitamins than a vitamin tablet from the store. As a mini farmer, you have the ability to eat these greens as fresh as humanly possible, along with growing a diversity of greens unavailable in stores. You'll discover amazing taste sensations.

Growing Greens

By definition, greens are grown for their leafy vegetation. As such, they require a substantial amount of nitrogen. As key dietary sources of everything from minerals to Omega 3 fatty acids, they should be provided with soil rich in compost and properly managed for trace nutrients. Most greens grow best in cooler weather and are grown from seed. Raised beds are ideal as they allow the soil to be worked earlier in the spring, thereby extending the season while preventing over-saturation with moisture.

With the exception of collards and kale which should be started from seed in the same manner as cabbage and transplanted at a spacing of at least twelve inches, greens are usually harvested in two stages: early in their growth as salad greens that are eaten raw, and later in the season as pot greens that are steamed, boiled or fried. In order to accommodate this, greens are usually sowed as closely together as an inch. They are harvested as they grow, leaving an increasing amount of spacing between plants until all that is left are the plants being grown for pot greens.

Often, so-called "mesclun" mixes are sowed. Mesclun mixes contain seeds for a variety of greens that have different tastes and textures. Common mixes contain lettuces, arugula, endive and chervil; but quite a few also include mustard, chard, spinach and sorrel. You can buy these pre-mixed, or mix your own.

To grow mesclun mixes or use the dual-harvest method described; put narrow furrows in the soil of the bed spaced four inches apart. Sprinkle the seed in the furrows at about a one-inch spacing, and then cover the seeds with soil and water thoroughly daily until they sprout. Start harvesting when plants are four inches tall, and do so in a fashion that will leave increasing spaces between what remains. This way you can harvest baby lettuce and mature lettuce from the same planting, or both small mustard greens for salad and large mustard greens for steaming.

Pests and Diseases

The most troublesome pest of greens, especially milder greens, is the slug. Slugs gobble holes in the vegetation, leaving a slimy trail in their wake. They can be large or small, and seem to be able to work their way through the smallest crevasse. Luckily, there are a lot of ways to deter slugs.

Caffeine is deadly to slugs. Spread coffee grounds around plants that the slugs like, and as they crawl across the grounds they will absorb the caffeine through their bellies and die. As a bonus, coffee grounds are a good nitrogen-containing organic fertilizer.

Corn meal is also deadly to slugs, as well as being an attractant. Put a few tablespoons of corn meal in a jar, and lay that jar on its side near plants requiring protection. The slugs will crawl into the jar, eat the corn meal, and die.

Beer is an extremely effective lure. You can fill a container 75 percent full of beer, bury it so the lip is at ground level, and provide it with a canopy of some sort to keep out rain and debris. Slugs will crawl in and drown (my wife uses cleaned cat food cans for this trap).

Slugs are physically delicate creatures. Sand, egg shells and similar substances will cut them severely, causing them to dehydrate and die.

Outside of this, all you need to be concerned about are grasshoppers, leaf hoppers and similar insects migrating from nearby vegetation. These can be avoided by keeping the lawn trimmed near the beds. Diseases are not a problem so long as you practice crop rotation and sanitation.

Purslane

Though purslane is often considered a weed, I grow it every year in my garden. It contains more Omega 3 fatty acids than any other land plant[7], and is also a rich source of vitamins A and C, as well as pigment-based anti-oxidants. The leaves, stems and flowers can be eaten raw, steamed or fried. When harvested in the morning, it has a tangy apple-like taste; when harvested in the afternoon it has a sweeter and more grass-like taste. If you are eating a diet free of starches that are used as thickeners keep in mind that purslane has mucilaginous properties similar to okra that make it a good thickener for soups, stews and gravies. Blanch it, dehydrate it, and then turn it into a powder in your blender. Use the powder as a thickener in place of corn starch or flour.

Sow purslane seeds directly after danger of frost has passed. If you let it go to seed, it will regrow every year in that spot in your garden. The bed where I originally planted purslane has been used to grow greens, corn, carrots and more, yet

Purslane is delicious fresh and makes a good thickener for soups.

purslane now grows there every year with no effort.

Corn Salad

Like purslane, corn salad is often considered a weed; it can be an invasive weed in corn and wheat fields. It is delicately flavored, and rich in vitamins E, C, A, B6, B9 and Omega 3s. It is best when harvested before the flowers appear, and is best raw in salads, though it can be good when steamed lightly for about four minutes. It can be sown in late fall for an early spring harvest, or in early fall for a late spring harvest. It is an ideal crop to grow late in an unheated hoop house. Germination is slow at 10–14 days. Plant thinly—one seed per inch—and use the thinned plants in salads. Leave at a final spacing of 4" and harvest the entire rosette.

Orach

I grow Red Orach every year mainly for the colorful zest it adds to salads. It is best when sowed

---

[7] A. P. Simopoulos, H. A. Norman, J. E. Gillaspy and J. A. Duke. (1992) "Common purslane: a source of omega-3 fatty acids and antioxidants." *Journal of the American College of Nutrition*, Vol 11, Issue 4 374-382.

early in the spring and the young leaves harvested and eaten like young spinach. Sow seeds every two inches. As they grow, thin out to eight inches between plants and eat the thinnings.

Lettuce

Lettuce (also known as Claytonia) is native to North America and was called lettuce because it was used extensively by Gold Rush miners as a source of vitamin C to prevent scurvy. It tastes more like spinach than lettuce, and some consider its taste superior to both. It can be eaten either raw or gently steamed. If you have difficulty growing spinach, consider lettuce instead as it grows more easily. Lettuce will grow year round in a greenhouse, hoop house or cold frame. Plant directly in the spring at 1/2" spacing, thinning out to six-inch spacing as the plants grow.

Mustard

Mustard is a culinary delight, and this fact is demonstrated in the dozens of varieties available reflecting every size, shape and flavor imaginable. Sow in the early spring, harvest the small leaves for salads and then use the larger leaves for steaming and stir-fries. The pungent character in the fresh leaves is diminished by cooking. The seeds can be harvested as a spice for pickling. A single cup of raw mustard greens has almost double the U.S. RDA of vitamin A, and 500 percent of the RDA of vitamin K. It is high in folate and a number of other important vitamins and minerals too. As a member of the same family as broccoli, it also contains a number of cancer-fighting compounds. And, it happens to be delicious, so I grow a lot of it.

Plant the seeds directly in the ground every six inches as early as the ground can be worked in the spring, and then every week thereafter for the next month so you have a continuous harvest until it bolts. Once the mustard bolts, let it go to seed if you plan to use mustard seed in pickle or other recipes. Collect the seed pods by stripping them from the plant when brown, break up the delicate pods and separate the seeds by winnowing.

Cress

Cress grows both wild and cultivated, both in the form of watercress along stream banks and in the form of dry land cress in fields and gardens. Cress, watercress particularly, has shown a number of anti-cancer properties, including the ability to inhibit the formation of blood supply to tumors. It is tangy and peppery, and usually eaten raw—though it can also be steamed or boiled. It is best harvested before it goes to seed. Starting in the spring and every two weeks thereafter until fall, plant the seeds for cress directly, spaced every two inches.

Sorrel

Sorrel is a member of the dock family, and contains sufficiently high levels of oxalic acid that it could cause poisoning if eaten in large quantities. Thus, its tangy leaves are best eaten young as small additions to salads for variety rather than as a main-course pot herb when fully grown. Sorrel grows best in light shade but will tolerate full sun. It is a hardy perennial, so if not dug up or killed it will come back every year from the roots. Directly seed at twelve inch spacing. These plants spread, so growing them in a raised bed is a good idea.

Rich in folate and vitamin K, spinach is a super-food.

Arugula

Arugula (also known as rocket) has an assertive, peppery taste. Its young leaves are often used in mesclun mix for salads, and its older leaves as pot herbs. Starting in mid spring and every three weeks thereafter until summer, sow the seeds two inches apart. Harvest by pulling up the plants and cutting off the roots.

Endive

Endive is a member of the chicory family that has bitter leaves that promote salivation and appetite. It is an excellent source of fiber, vitamins A, C and K and folate and other vitamins and minerals. Endive can be started indoors for a head start, or it can be directly seeded. Space the plants at eight inch intervals.

Chervil

Chervil is a member of the same family as parsley and has a distinctive yet mild flavor. It is used in mesclun, but also as an herb in French cooking. Chervil is best started indoors four weeks before last frost, and transplanted at eight inch spacing once the danger of frost has passed.

Leaf lettuces pack a more powerful nutritional punch than iceberg lettuce.

Spinach

Spinach is, for all practical purposes, a superfood. A single cup of cooked spinach contains 2/3 of the RDA of folate, 25 percent of the RDA of calcium, 300+ percent of vitamin A and over 1,000 percent of the RDA of vitamin K. It is indeed powerful stuff. And for such good medicine, it is also quite tasty harvested young in salads or steamed when older.

Sow spinach six to eight weeks before last frost. I recommend "broadcast" seeding in a bed, such that there is approximately one seed per inch. As the plants start growing, thin to a three-inch spacing while using the thinnings in salad. You can also grow a fall crop by using the same method, starting six weeks before the first expected frost in fall. Spinach will grow up until hard frosts.

Lettuce

Lettuce has a reputation for being nutritionally vapid, but this only applies to the common iceberg lettuce found in stores. When growing your own, you can grow any of dozens of varieties of cos (also known as romaine) lettuce, leaf lettuce and butter lettuce; all of these pack a greater nutritional punch than standard iceberg lettuce. Two cups of romaine lettuce deliver 58 percent of the RDA of vitamin A, 45 percent of the RDA of vitamin C, and a substantial dose of vitamins" as well. The array of textures, tastes and colors available in lettuce is unequaled in any other leaf vegetable. My favorite varieties are Parris Island Cos, Buttercrunch and Lollo Rossa.

Lettuce can be directly seeded, or planted out from transplants grown indoors. I do both. I grow the headed varieties such as romaine indoors, and plant them out about six weeks before last frost so they have time to grow a large head. I sow the leaf varieties directly starting eight weeks before last frost and every two weeks thereafter until last frost. I make little furrows six inches apart across the beds, sprinkle seed in the furrows at the rate of one seed per inch, and lightly cover. I harvest the plants for salads until they reach a final spacing of six inches and allow those to grow into full heads.

Greenery Broth (a base for soups)

Ingredients:

1 head romaine lettuce, chopped
1 small onion, chopped
3 sticks of celery, chopped
2 cups of purslane, chopped
1/2 tsp salt (optional)
8 cups of water

Procedure:

Chop up the ingredients while the salted water is coming to a simmer in a medium pot. Add the ingredients, return to a simmer, cover, and allow to simmer for another hour. Strain out the greens and reserve the liquid as a soup base. This is surprisingly good!

Herbs

31

A few years ago I ran out of oregano, so I headed down to the supermarket to buy some. Talk about sticker shock! The good stuff in the glass containers was selling for $10/ounce! That's when I decided that I needed a bed full of herbs.

Herbs are, of course, used in naturopathic medicine. But for my purposes, I use them a lot in cooking to add taste and variety. Being oriented toward self-sufficiency, what I don't want to do is make the guys who own the grocery store rich in the process. I'd rather keep that money in the family budget while simultaneously making sure my herbs are fresh.

It isn't likely that you'll be growing your own nutmeg, cloves or cinnamon. For those, you'll remain beholden to the supermarket for the foreseeable future because the conditions required to grow them aren't favorable. But other common herbs such as basil, thyme, rosemary, sage, parsley, dill, mint, lovage and more can be grown easily at home. Some, in fact, are perennials or self-seeding annuals that will become established and return every year with little to no effort required.

Another benefit of growing your own herbs is variety. Down at the store, basil is just basil and thyme is just thyme. It is a standardized commodity product. But when you start looking through seed catalogs, you'll discover dozens of varieties of common herbs, each with subtle (or not so subtle) differences in color, flavor, aroma and texture. In one catalog I receive, there are two pages dedicated just to different varieties of basil. With this variety available, you can literally grow herbs that cannot be purchased at any price.

In addition, fresh herbs are simply amazingly tasteful and fragrant. Some of the finest dishes I prepare include herbs such as rosemary, thyme or dill that I have literally taken directly from a bed to the kitchen. The dimensions these add to taste are impossible to describe and have to be experienced to be understood. Dried herbs are good, but not as good as something harvested fresh. Some of the compounds responsible for the tastes and smells of fresh herbs are volatile at low temperatures, and they are lost in the drying process. So even though drying your own herbs is a great thing that will save a lot of money over time, it is the culinary experience of access to fresh herbs that will get you hooked on growing your own.

I grow most of my herbs in one 4'x8' bed. Most herbs aren't bothered by bugs so rotation isn't an issue, and those that aren't perennial often self-seed. Some herbs, mints in particular, seem to harbor ambitions for world domination, so pulling up the excess every year as part of bed maintenance is a good idea.

Basil

Basil is an essential herb in Italian cooking, salad dressings and pesto; it also goes well in broiled or roasted meats and stews. There are many varieties of basil available. For pesto, try Genovese or Napoletano. For a real treat, try one of the red varieties like Red Rubin. As a spice for dressings, try Lemon Basil or Fine Verde. Basil can be directly sown after last frost at 4" spacing and then thinned to 8" spacing or it can be started indoors three weeks before last frost and then transplanted at 8" spacing.

Borage

Borage has cucumber-flavored leaves that go well in salads, and its blue flowers are a nice edible garnish. Sow the seeds directly at 4" spacing after last frost. Once they have sprouted, thin to 8" spacing. Borage's greatest value may lie in its non-culinary benefits. Its flowers are a bee-magnet, and they will draw beneficial pollinators to your garden and thereby improve crops as diverse as cucumbers and okra. Inter-planted with

Chopped borage leaves go well in salads.

tomatoes it will repel tomato horn worms; some gardeners claim that they improve the flavor of tomatoes. Dried and powdered borage leaves make a very worthwhile addition to meat stews, making them more savory.

Chives

Chives have a mild onion flavor that goes well in everything from omelets to mashed potatoes. Chives are perennial and can either be directly seeded starting three weeks before last frost or started inside six weeks before last frost and transplanted at a final spacing of eight inches. The grass-like leaves are snipped as needed, or they can be dried for convenient use. The purple flowers are edible and make a wonderful garnish for salads.

Cilantro/Coriander

The leaves of this fresh herb are known as "cilantro" and the seeds are known as "coriander." Cilantro is used in salsas and other spicy dishes, giving them an air of cool freshness to offset the spice; coriander seeds are used in curries and roast poultry. Cilantro is directly seeded

Fresh cilantro contributes a sense of freshness to salads and salsas.

starting four weeks before last frost at a spacing of three inches. It becomes bitter when temperatures start averaging over 75 degrees. For culinary use, the seeds should be heated in a dry hot pan until the scent is notable, then cooled and ground with a mortar and pestle.

Dill

Dill is obviously used in pickles, but it is also used to spice fish, salad dressings, cooked vegetables and more. I enjoy chewing on a sprig of dill as I work in the garden. Both the foliage and the seeds can be used. It will re-seed itself every year, making for a bountiful supply. I grow "Mammoth" dill, but other common varieties include Dukat and Bouquet. It can be directly seeded starting a month before last frost, or started indoors two months before last frost and transplanted. Thereafter, it will re-seed itself impressively.

Fennel

Fennel has a flavor like anise or black licorice and is popular in Italian cooking; it is also used for flavoring fish, lamb and pork. The seeds are used as a spice, the leaves and flowers are used in salads, and the bulbs can be cooked as a root vegetable. Fennel re-seeds itself so aggressively it could become invasive; be merciless when culling unwanted volunteers. Directly seed at four-inch spacing.

Garlic

An entire book can be written about garlic. It is one of the most popular herbs in all forms of cooking, and dozens of varieties are available. Garlic falls into two broad categories: hardneck (also known as "stiffneck") and softneck. This differentiation is based upon whether or not the particular variety of garlic creates a flower stalk. The flower stalk, if allowed to grow, becomes hard, thus giving the garlic a hard neck. The flower stalks, also known as *scapes*, if cut young, make an excellent stir-fry vegetable. Cutting the scapes also makes the garlic more productive. Softneck garlic has a more flexible neck, and once harvested, those necks can be braided together to hang the garlic.

Best soil conditions are the same as for onions. Though garlic can be planted in spring, it is less productive. Likewise, even though all cloves of garlic will grow, the larger the clove you plant, the larger the bulb it will produce. So garlic is best planted in the fall around the first frost date for harvest the next year. Plant the cloves with the root side down, two inches deep at six inch intervals in all directions, and then mulch heavily with straw to assist survival through the winter. If you live in a very cold place like Maine or Minnesota, you may need to plant the more winter-hardy hardneck varieties.

When you see the foliage starting to die back, stop watering your garlic. Once the bottom leaves are brown, it is ready to harvest. Don't just try to pull it up by the dead foliage. Instead, loosen the soil by inserting a digging fork six inches away from the garlic and levering up the soil. Then dig out the bulbs. Brush off any dirt, leave the tops attached, and let it cure by drying in a shady well-ventilated place away from rain. After curing, you can remove the tops and store in the dark in mesh bags. Softneck varieties can keep for as long as eight months, but hardneck varieties will only keep for four months.

All garlic varieties can be successfully pickled in vinegar for long-term storage, and can likewise be blanched for four minutes and then frozen or dehydrated. (Once dehydrated, you can make your own garlic powder by putting the dehydrated garlic in a blender.) Though it is a popular practice, I would discourage putting fresh garlic cloves in olive oil for storage, as this provides good conditions for growth of undetectable botulism. In fact, people have died as a result. In 1989 the FDA issued the following statement about fresh garlic in olive oil:

"To be safe . . . garlic-in-oil products should contain additional ingredients — specific levels of microbial inhibitors or acidifying agents such as phosphoric or citric acid. . . . Unrefrigerated garlic-in-oil mixes lacking antimicrobial agents can permit the growth of *Clostridium botulinum* bacteria with subsequent toxin production without affecting the taste and smell of the products. Toxin production can occur even when a small number of *Clostridium botulinum* spores are present in the garlic. When the spore-containing garlic is bottled and covered with oil, an oxygen-free environment is created that promotes the germination of spores and the growth of microorganisms at temperatures as low as 50 degrees Fahrenheit."[8]

Lemon Balm

Lemon balm makes a pleasant tea, but is also a welcome addition to mushroom and asparagus dishes, as well as sauces and marinades for fish and meats. It is a perennial herb that will overwinter throughout most of the continental United States. The seeds won't germinate below 70 degrees, and can be started indoors and then transplanted, or sprinkled outdoors but not

---

[8] The FDA Memo on Garlic-in-Oil Preparations, 4/17/1989.

Like lemon balm, lemon verbena contributes a citrus and savory essence to marinades.

covered, and then watered frequently until they sprout.

Lovage

Lovage's unique celery-like flavor goes well in all sorts of stews and stuffings while adding new possibilities for salad dressings, herb butters and fruit dishes. Lovage will grow to be about six feet tall and comes back every year, so you only need one plant. Start a few seeds indoors about six weeks before last frost, and then transplant the best one outside on the North side of your herb bed. Lovage is best used fresh; the dried herb is marginally useful although blanching and freezing works pretty well. In place of the dried herb, you can use the seeds year-round. They are a bit sweeter than the leaves, but otherwise carry the same excellent flavor.

Marjoram

Marjoram is a close relative of oregano, it is more mild and sweet, complementing practically any meat dish. Although it is a perennial herb in its native regions, it is somewhat cold-sensitive and won't survive the winters in the Northern parts of the country. All is not lost, however, because it can be successfully grown as an annual by starting the seeds inside six weeks before last frost and putting out the transplants just after the last frost. Transplant at a spacing of twelve inches. The herb is harvested by cutting a section of growth and hanging it upside down in the shade until dry.

Mint

There are many mint varieties available, ranging from the common spearmint, catnip and peppermint to more exotic mints with flavors such as lemon and chocolate. Mint is best started indoors six weeks before last frost, and then planted outside at twelve inch spacing after last frost. It is a hardy perennial that will come back year after year throughout the continental United States. Its flowers attract bees in abundance, and it can self-seed to the point of becoming invasive if you don't keep an eye on it and ruthlessly cull invaders. In most mint varieties, the greatest concentration of flavor is in the top five to seven inches of growth. Snip that completely—stem and all—near midsummer, hang upside down in a shady but well-ventilated place to dry, and then use the leaves as seasoning, in tea, etc. Mints, in general, can attract cats.

Mustard

Growing mustard and harvesting the seed is covered in the chapter on greens. The seeds are used as a spice, both in whole form when making

This chocolate mint makes excellent teas but will take over the beds if you allow it!

pickles, and ground as an addition to practically anything that can be cooked. It is especially good when used as a flavoring for boiled cabbage, but likely the biggest attraction for purposes of self-sufficiency is the ability to make your own pre-pared mustard, so I'll include a recipe at the end of this chapter.

Oregano

Oregano is a perennial that is more cold-hardy than its cousin marjoram, and will overwinter well throughout the continental United States. It should be started indoors six weeks before last frost and then transplanted outdoors at a spacing of 12" sometime after last frost. Don't cover the seeds because they need light to germinate. Oreg-ano is known as the essential Italian herb, but it goes well with almost everything. I like to add a small amount to portabella mushrooms fried in butter. Oregano is best harvested before the

plant flowers. Cut a stalk all the way down to the ground to encourage a bushy habit. You can then hang it upside-down to dry in the shade away from weather and then strip the leaves, or strip the leaves from the stem directly for fresh use.

Parsley

Everyone has seen parsley used as a garnish, and many swear by parsley as a remedy for hali-tosis, but by far my favorite use is an ingredient in vegetable juices that I make with my juice ma-chine. I use a half pound of carrots, two stalks of celery and a handful of parsley to make the juice. The parsley makes the juice taste fresh and vibrant. There are two primary types of parsley: flat-leaved and curly-leaved varieties. Though some claim one variety to taste better than the other; I think they are both quite good.

Parsley is hard to start from seed. To start it, put the seeds in the freezer for a week, then put them in a wet paper towel sealed in a zippered plastic bag overnight before planting inside. They will take nearly a month to germinate. Once they have been established for a couple of weeks, transplant them outside at a spacing of twelve inches. Harvest by cutting entire stems back to the ground to encourage more growth. It is best eaten fresh, but it can be quickly blanched (one minute) and dehydrated as well.

Rosemary

Rosemary is a perennial herb best known for its use in poultry seasoning, but it is also useful in marinades and vegetables. Though it is sup-posedly only winter-hardy through zone six, my rosemary comes back every year in the more chilly zone five. Rosemary is most easily started as a purchased plant from a nursery or from a cutting taken from an established plant; it is nevertheless possible to start from seed using the same method as described with parsley. The germination rate is very low, so plant five times as much seed as you think you'll need. Put out the transplants at eight inch spacing two weeks before last frost. Harvest rosemary by cutting healthy branches, tying them together and hanging them upside down out of the weather until dry.

Sage

The uses of sage overlap those of rosemary; I have found that in marinades for various meats, one spice will be better than the other. Like rosemary, sage is most easily started from a nursery plant or a cutting, but it can be started from seed using the same method as with parsley with difficulty. Space plants at twelve-inch intervals, and don't harvest the first year. In subsequent years, harvest healthy branches that are hung upside-down inside to dry. Sage is also excellent in stews when used fresh from the plant.

Tarragon

There are two varieties of tarragon: Russian and French. The French variety (*Artemisia dracunculus*) is more flavorful but seldom produces seeds, and therefore must be started from a cutting or purchased from a nursery. The Russian variety (*Artemisia dracunculoides*) can be started from seed, is more prolific and has a milder flavor. Both are superb as flavorings for various species of white fish, as well as for making herbal vinegars for salads. Sow Russian Tarragon seeds

Sage will reward you abundantly year after year.

indoors six weeks before last frost, and plant out shortly after last frost. You'll probably only want or need one plant, as it grows to be two feet tall and two feet wide.

The leaves don't smell like much when growing, but once harvested the flavor starts to concentrate. The heat of cooking releases even more flavor, so it is easy to over-use tarragon. Tarragon can be used fresh, it can be dried on a dehydrator, or the sprigs can be sealed in airtight bags and frozen.

Thyme

A classic and essential herb, thyme lends its flavors to dressings, vegetables and meats alike. Thyme is a perennial, though different varieties have different cold tolerance, so make sure the variety you choose will overwinter in your area. Sow the seeds indoors six weeks before last frost, and then transplant shortly after last frost at eighteen inch spacing. Early in its life, thyme grows slowly, so weed control is important. Also, for its first year, don't harvest from the plants. From the second year and thereafter, harvest around midsummer, just before it blooms, or just as it is blooming. Cut off the top four or five inches, and dry it inside in the shade.

How to Make Mustard

The prepared mustard available in the store is made from vinegar, water, mustard seed, salt,

turmeric and other spices such as garlic. Each of these ingredients serves a particular purpose due to the nature of the active ingredients in mustard seed.

Just as the irritant substances in onions and garlic are released by mechanical damage to the cells of the bulbs, the distinctive tastes and smells of mustard seed are released by mechanical damage to the seed. Likewise, applying heat to the damaged mustard seed inactivates the compounds, so the degree of spiciness of mustard can be controlled by the amount of heat applied.

There are three types of mustard seed: the milder white/yellow mustard used in American mustards, the tangier brown prevalent in

This creeping **thyme** is featured in homemade salad dressings.

European mustards and the fiery black that predominates Asian cuisine. For your first experiments with making mustard, I recommend using mostly yellow and a bit of brown.

For processing, whole mustard seed should be soaked overnight in water. Once it has soaked, process it with the soaking water in a blender. Just as-is, the properties of the mustard would dissipate in a few days. Wait ten minutes or so, and then add the vinegar and process further in the blender. Salt is also needed to fix the qualities of the mustard, and anywhere from one teaspoon to two teaspoons is used per cup of product. The turmeric is used for imparting a yellow color. The reason why the famous "Grey Poupon" mustard lacks the distinctive fluorescent yellow color of American mustard is because it lacks turmeric. Turmeric lends a taste all its own, so if you are used to American-style mustards you'll want to add this ingredient as well. Freshly made mustard is unbearably bitter, but this bitterness will disappear once it has been refrigerated for twenty-four hours. I have only provided one recipe, but by explaining the process, you can branch out to create your own.

Down-Home Mustard

Ingredients:

1/3 cup water
1/2 cup wine vinegar
1/2 cup mustard seed, yellow and brown
2 tsp salt
1/2 tsp turmeric
1/2 tsp garlic powder

Procedure:

Soak the seeds in the water overnight at room temperature. Dump in the blender, and blend until it is smooth enough for your purposes. Add the remaining ingredients, blend thoroughly, and then dump into a sealed container. Store in the refrigerator, and allow to sit at least a day before sampling.

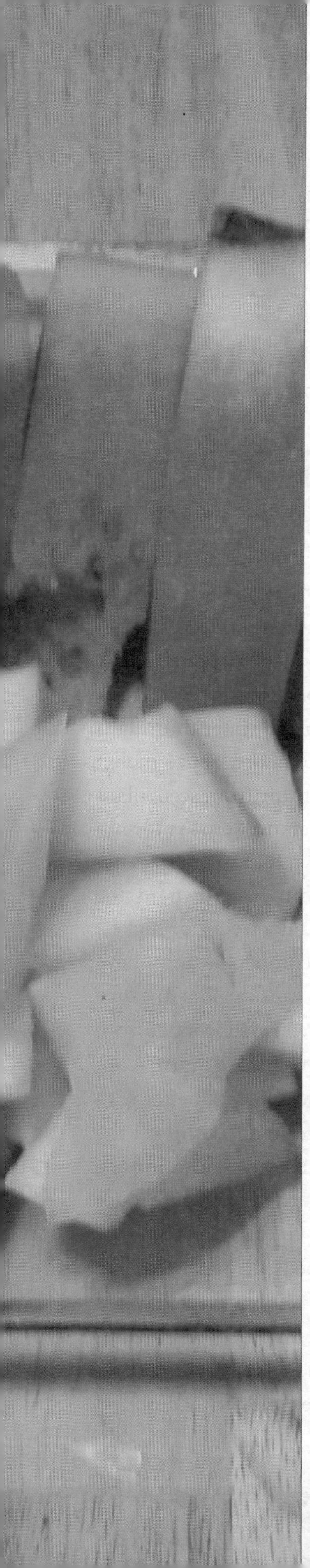

Melons

32

The quintessential taste of summer is the melon. Whether it be watermelon, honeydew or cantaloupe, melons just seem to concentrate summer's essential sweetness. And even though they are nature's candy, they are very healthful as well. Watermelon contains citrulline, an arginine precursor that relaxes blood vessels and indirectly supports nitric oxide synthesis.[9] It likewise contains a great deal of lycopene, known to help prevent prostate, breast and lung cancer. Cantaloupe is so tasty that it is hard to believe that a single cup contains more than the RDA of both vitamins A and C.

Melons are members of the same family as cucumbers and squash, and there are likely a hundred varieties around the world. Many are eaten fresh, but just as many are pickled as condiments or used to make preserves.

In the United States, we typically think in terms of three melon variations: watermelons, cantaloupes and honeydew. In reality the melon with netted skin that we in the United States call a "cantaloupe"

---

[9] Nitric oxide synthesis is necessary for achieving and maintaining erections. Studies show that watermelon can assist in that regard. *Science Daily,* July 1, 2008, "Watermelon May Have Viagra-Effect."

is a muskmelon, *Cucumis melo var. reticulatus.* True cantaloupes, *Cucumis melo var. cantalupensis*, have scaled rinds and are much more common in Europe than in the United States. Honeydew, crenshaw and casaba melons are *Cucumis melo var. inodorus.* But all variations of *Cucumis melo* can interbreed with each other, so if you are growing them for seed, you will need to practice isolation techniques to keep seedlines pure.

Watermelons are *Citrullus lanatus* and will cross with other watermelons and citron, but not with any other melons grown in the United States.

Variety Selection

Plants that make fruits require sun to make them, so melons in particular tend to be long-season crops with some requiring more than 100 frost-free days—preferably warm days. Particularly if you live in the Northern parts of the country, you should choose a variety that will produce ripe fruit within your growing season with some room to spare.

Another consideration is disease resistance. Watermelons are pretty much resistant to bacterial wilt, but all varieties of muskmelon are susceptible. Powdery mildew and mosaic virus can pose a problem with melons, but resistant cultivars are available.

In New Hampshire, I have successfully grown Moon and Stars and Sugarbaby watermelons, and Hale's Best and Green Machine melon varieties.

Soil Preparation

Like other members of the cucumber family, melons prefer fertile, well-drained soils with lots of organic matter. The use of raised beds assists with drainage. Add at least three cubic feet of compost per 4'x8' bed, adjust the pH to between 6 and 7, and amend for NPK as indicated by a soil test. Melons use a lot of nitrogen, so make sure to combine nitrogen sources that release both quickly (such as blood meal) and slowly (such as alfalfa meal) when amending the soil.

Starting and Planting

Melons can be grown either from seed or from transplants. I prefer to start the seeds indoors a week before last frost, and then plant them out a week after last frost to give them a head start. If you prefer direct seeding, wait until a week after last frost or until soil temperature is 65 degrees, put the seeds in soil 1" deep and water thoroughly daily until the seedlings emerge. Space melon plants at one per foot. If planting from seed, plant two seeds every foot and then use scissors to snip off the least strong of the two that sprout.

Melons, theoretically, can be grown in the Northern one foot of a bed on a trellis for highest space efficiency—just as cucumbers— and I have successfully done this with muskmelons by supporting the growing melons with a sling made from old washed nylons (aka panty hose). It turned out to be labor intensive, and would work better with true cantaloupes because those don't slip off the vine. What I recommend instead is planting the melons six to twelve inches back from the South side of the bed, allowing the vines to trail along the yard or the area between beds. I mulch the area covered by vines with grass clippings (or hay can be used) and set boards under the growing melons to keep them off the ground. The Northern portion of the bed can be planted with other crops.

One thing to consider is planting trellised cucumbers on the North side of a bed, free-running melons on the South side of the bed, and closely spaced bush beans treated with inoculant down the center for a continuous supply of nitrogen.

Melons tend to have shallow root systems. Considering their need for water, it is important to establish the deepest root systems possible. To this end, then, watering should be only weekly unless the weather is abominably hot; the watering should be extremely thorough each time it is done. Use a rain gage, and in any week where less than an inch of water was received, give them an inch of water on top of what they already have. If an inch or more of water was received that week, you can let it pass as long as the vines look okay.

Weeds, Pests, and Diseases

Melons are fast-growing once they get started and tend to shade out weed competition, so weeds aren't usually a direct problem, but they can be an indirect problem as a reservoir of disease organisms and a hiding place for pests. It is practically impossible to weed efficiently around melon vines without risk of harming the vines, so mulching is the best option. In my own mini-farm, I usually use grass clippings because they are abundant and free and return their elements to the soil. But if you have trouble getting melons to ripen within your season, I recommend killing two birds with one stone by using black weed barrier that suppresses weeds while allowing water and air to penetrate.

Once watermelon plants have grown to have ten leaves or more, they are immune to the bacterial wilt disease transmitted by cucumber beetles. Even so, if present in large numbers they can decrease the vigor of the plant through the mechanical damage of feeding, and their larvae can hurt the roots, causing the vines to wilt and die. Planting nasturtiums around the stems of watermelons can help prevent the adults from laying eggs around the stem and thus prevent root damage, but once adult numbers are noticeable, chemical controls may become necessary. Natural alternatives include using a fine clay product called Surround™.

Muskmelons are not immune to bacterial wilt and, in fact, are almost as susceptible as cucumbers. The most effective natural way of dealing with cucumber beetles spreading bacterial wilt to muskmelons is to seal them up tightly under floating row covers until the flowers appear.

Aphids can sometimes spread from surrounding vegetation to melons in sufficient quantities to pose a risk to the plant. If this happens, two applications of insecticidal soap spaced five days apart will usually get rid of them.

Other than bacterial wilt, the next most likely disease to be encountered is powdery mildew. Powdery mildew starts on the underside of the leaf and then spreads. It can become a serious problem if conditions are shady. If you have a problem with bacterial wilt, resistant varieties of melon are available, and you should grow resistant varieties in future seasons.

Once an infection is discovered, fast treatment can eliminate the problem. Because development of fungicide resistance has been observed in many variations of powdery mildew, I recommend a fungicide cocktail approach. The fungicides used in organic production, particularly bicarbonate and horticultural oils, have the potential to harm or kill garden plants. So during this treatment regimen, make sure the plants are well-hydrated, and test bicarbonate and horticultural oils on a single leaf first and wait a day to assure no harm is done before making a wider application.

Use a pressure sprayer to spray the plants and leaves, making sure to get the undersides of the leaves, with a solution *Bacillus subtilis* (such as Serenade™) according to label directions. Wait two days, then spray with light horticultural oil mixed according to label directions and to which you have added one tablespoon baking soda (sodium bicarbonate) per one gallon of water. Spray to the point of run-off. Wait three days, and then repeat the cycle. Continue repeating the cycle until no powdery mildew remains, and then spray every other week with the *Bacillus subtilis* preparation.

Harvest

Timing the harvest of watermelons is sometimes seen as a black art, where only those initiated to the secrets of the unique sounds melons make when rapped can make such determinations. Most certainly, with watermelons, a very experienced person can do so. But you can also tell by looking for three signs: the curly tendril opposite the stem of the melon has turned brown and/or died, the spot here the watermelon was touching the ground has changed from white to

This watermelon shows yellow instead of white where it was touching the ground, and so it is ready for harvest.

The netting is well defined and it slipped from the vine easily, indicating ripeness.

yellow, and the rind of the melon has become a bit less shiny. The stem to the watermelon should be cut with a sharp knife to harvest. It should never just be pulled.

Muskmelons should be harvested when the netting is well defined, they are fragrant, and there is a bit of "give" when the blossom end is pushed. A ripe muskmelon will also slip easily from the vine when pulled. If it is stubborn, it isn't ripe yet—give it another couple of days. Muskmelons are harvested by pulling them from the vines.

Over-ripe watermelons, incidentally, will explode. When I first started growing watermelons, I had no idea how to tell when they were ripe, so I just let them grow until the vines they were on were dead, then I brought them in the house. For some reason, I also suffered under the notion that they would keep for a long time sitting out, just like squash. So I brought in some 30+-pound melons, put them on the kitchen table, and let them sit for a couple of weeks. One day when I was in the living room, I heard a "thud" reminiscent of a sledgehammer hitting something. I ran into the kitchen to find a most impressive mess all over the table, chairs, floor, walls and more. You have been warned!

Seed Saving

Melons are insect-pollinated, and if pollinated naturally, only one variety should be grown, or it should be isolated from other varieties by at least 1/4 mile. The seeds are ready when the melon is ripe to eat, and they are best collected using the wet method. Put the seeds and a bit of the pulp into a large plastic cup, add a cup of water, stir and allow to sit for three days. At the end of three days, clean off any scum and discard any floating seeds. Then, wash and dry the seeds that remain, and dry them over a dessicant for a week before storing in a dark, cool place in a sealed container (see *Mini Farming* for more information on dessicants).

Preparation and Preservation

Melons don't keep long—maybe a week at room temperature or two weeks in the refrigerator tops. Preparation consists of just slicing it up and eating it!

You could dehydrate melons, but as they are mostly water you wouldn't get much after the dehydrating process. Muskmelons can be cubed and frozen with some success, but watermelon won't come out well at all.

The only effective way to make sure excess melons don't go to waste is to turn them into preserves, pickles, sorbets or even wines. The good news is that even in such states, many of the preserves still retain important nutritional components such as vitamins and antioxidants.

That makes me happy because watermelon rind pickles have been my favorite since childhood!

Muskmelon Ice

Ingredients:

- 4 cups cubed muskmelon
- 2 cups water
- 1/2 cup sugar
- 2 Tbsp fresh-squeezed lime juice (don't use the bottled kind)
- 1/4 tsp vanilla extract
- 1/8 tsp cinnamon

Procedure:

Place all the ingredients in a blender and process until smooth. Pour into clean ice cube trays and allow to freeze. Once frozen, store the cubes in sealed freezer bags. To serve, put the cubes into the blender and break them up, or just put them in a bowl and use the edge of a spoon to eat them a little at a time.

Watermelon Rind Pickles

Ingredients:

- 4 quarts of cubed watermelon rind
- 4 quarts of cold water
- 1 cup coarse sea salt
- 9 cups of sugar
- 4 cups of distilled (white) vinegar
- 4 cups of water
- 2 lemons, thinly sliced
- 4 tsp whole cloves
- 8 cinnamon sticks broken into one-inch pieces

Procedure:

Remove the pink flesh and the outermost green rind from the watermelon, and cut the remaining rind into 1-inch cubes. Add the 1 cup of sea salt to the 4 quarts of water to make a brine, and pour this over the cubed watermelon rind in a large bowl. Allow to sit for 3 hours, then drain and rinse. Put the drained cubes into a large pot, add just enough water to cover, and bring to a simmer. Simmer for 10 minutes, then drain and set the cubes aside.

Make the pickling brine by putting the spices in a spice bag, and adding the bag to the mixture of vinegar, water, sugar and sliced lemon in a medium pot. Bring to a boil, then reduce to a simmer and stir occasionally for half.

Pack the rinds into pint jars, add one of the pieces of cinnamon from the spice bag, cover with hot pickling brine leaving 1/2" of head space, and process for 15 minutes in a boiling water canner. Allow to sit a month before consuming.

Onions

33

I have it on good authority that, without onions, food would still exist in some form or fashion, but it would hardly be an exaggeration to state that *good* food would be rare. Onions lend their unique flavor and pungency to everything from spaghetti sauce to chicken soup. And along with flavor, they have so many health benefits that even the World Health Organization recognizes them as a medicinal treatment and preventative for chronic diseases.

Onions are well known as a preventative for atherosclerosis, and when used regularly the fibrinolytic substances they contain suppress the platelet aggregation that can give rise to heart attacks. Several studies have shown that eating as little as half an onion a day reduces the risk of stomach cancer by 40 percent.

Given proper care and conditions, and using intensive spacing methods, you will easily reap over 180 onions from a single 4'x6' bed. The trick lies in the proper care and conditions, along with selecting the right variety for your purposes—so that's what this chapter is all about.

Selecting the Right Variety

Onions can be categorized in a number of different ways. There are bulb-forming and non-bulb-forming onions, sweet and pungent varieties, multiplier onions and seed-bearing onions, and that's just for starters. For now we're just going to discuss the common bulb-forming and seed-bearing onion that people usually grow in their gardens or buy in stores.

This onion, typified by the red, white and yellow varieties in the grocery store produce department, can be divided into short-day, long-day and intermediate-day onions based upon how much sunlight they need to receive in order to properly form a bulb. Long-day onions require 15+ hours of sunlight, intermediate-day onions require 12-13 hours of sunlight and short-day onions require only 9-10 hours of sunlight.

The number of hours of sunlight your garden receives at mid-summer is determined by your latitude. Though it may be counter-intuitive, the closer you are to either the North or South Pole, the greater the hours of sunlight you'll see at midsummer. In practice, this means you can grow a long-day onion in latitudes greater than 40 degrees. In latitudes less than 40 degrees, you'll grow an intermediate-day onion. Short-day onions are used in areas with mild winters and are planted in the fall for a spring harvest.

Not everyone walks around with a globe in their back pocket, but there's an easy rule of thumb for the United States. If you are on the East Coast, 40 degrees runs through Newark, NJ, and Pittsburgh, PA. If you are in the Midwest, it runs through Columbus, OH. If you are in the Great Plains it runs through Lincoln, NE, and Denver, CO. If you are on the West Coast, it runs about 100 miles north of Sacramento, CA.

The choice of intermediate-day or long-day onion is made for you based upon where you live, but there are still other considerations including taste and keeping qualities. When it comes to storage ability, Northern growers have a definite advantage. As a general rule, the more pungent a variety, the better it keeps, and long-day onions usually (but don't always) store better than short-day onions. The following table is far from exhaustive, but lists some common and heirloom onion varieties that are successful in home gardens.

Keeping Qualities	Short Day	Intermediate Day	Long Day
Good for storage	Red Creole	Long Yellow Sweet Spanish, California Early Red	White Sweet Spanish, Yellow Sweet Spanish, Walla Walla, Brunswick, Stuttgarter
Best for fresh eating	Bermuda, Grano, Granex, Torpedo, Excel	Yellow Globe, Long Yellow Globe, Candy	Ailsa Craig

Common onion varieties for your location and intended use.

Starting Onions

Onions usually require a long season, so it is a good thing that they are not terribly sensitive to frost! You can start or plant onions in three ways: from seed, from transplants, and from bulbs.

In areas such as Southern California, Georgia, Florida or Alabama, you can plant seeds in the fall for harvest in the spring. And, in fact, this is exactly what growers of the famous Vidalia onion do. The Vidalia onion is not its own unique variety, but is rather a Grano or Granex onion that is sweet due to the unique conditions of the soil in that region combined with being grown from seed over the winter months. So if you live in a warmer climate, it could be worthwhile to experiment with growing onions from seed. However, if you live in a cooler climate, you will find that planting onions from seed, even as early as possible in the spring, will give very small bulbs. In this case, you can plant the seeds closely together and use the resultant sprouts, once they are the size of a pencil, as "bunching onions." These are a delightful addition to salads and soups.

In order to form a bulb, onions need to gather a lot of energy from the sun; outside of very warm areas, will need a head start in order to form a bulb. Thus, onions are typically planted as either bulbs (knows as "sets") or transplants. Onions grown from transplants usually have the best keeping qualities, so if you are growing onions for storage, this is definitely the way to go. Onions should be started indoors approximately twelve weeks before last frost, and the sets planted outside about six weeks before last frost. This gives them the head start they need to form a good bulb. The seeds can be started within a wide temperature range—anywhere from 65 to 80 degrees; once they have sprouted, try to keep them cooler at around 60 degrees for best growth.

Onions can be started indoors from seed. This technique usually grows the best onions.

Many find growing onions from bulbs to be more convenient, and this can easily be done. Simply sow seeds close together in a small patch of ground about six weeks before last frost. Then, about three or four weeks after midsummer, pull the plants when the bulbs are no more than 3/4" in diameter. Discard the largest ones or use them for pickling or salads because they will go to seed early if planted. Lay your sets out in the sun (but protect them from rain) for 7 to 10 days to cure, then remove the dry tops and store just as you would an onion for eating. Come spring, six weeks prior to last frost, plant them out at their optimal distance for the expected size of that particular variety of onion.

Planting Onions

Soil for onions should already be corrected for the major macronutrients (nitrogen, phosphorus and potassium) before planting. Raw manures and the like should be strictly avoided, and only very well matured compost employed. This is the case, incidentally, for all root crops that come into direct contact with the soil, because fresh manures draw pests, leach nutrients and worst of all lend their flavor to what is grown in them.

The compound in onions that makes them pungent is a sulfur compound. Therefore, onions can be made sweeter by depriving them of sulfur. This, however, can make them keep poorly and be more susceptible to pest damage because sulfur is a crucial element in certain amino acids that are a part of DNA structure. This is why you can only get the famously sweet Vidalia onion during a short time of the year—the low sulfur soil in which it is grown makes it a very poor keeper. Thus, you can make sweeter onions by depriving the soil of sulfur, but you do so at the expense of keeping quality.

Potassium and phosphorus are particularly crucial for onions, and should be present in sufficient quantities prior to planting. If needed, they can be added later in the season as a side dressing in the form of ashes, greensand, bone meal, etc. Nitrogen, as a key constituent of amino acids, is likewise needful and should be present at adequate levels at the beginning of the season. However, it should not be added later in the season, as doing so will delay or otherwise inhibit the formation of bulbs in favor of excessive top-growth. This is where slow-release organic forms of nitrogen such as alfalfa meal have a definite advantage over chemicals easily washed from the soil.

Onions taste better when grown in sweeter (i.e. less acidic) soils with pH between 6 and 6.8. Lime in either pelleted or powdered form should be applied well in advance of the season because it takes months to affect the pH of the soil. So it is best applied in the fall. If, come spring, the soil pH is still too low, you can use a mixture of lime (which acts slowly) and wood ashes (which act quickly) to raise the pH. These should be mixed into the top 6" of soil very thoroughly as ashes contain potassium hydroxide (wood lye) which can be highly corrosive and therefore toxic to plants in heavy concentrations.

Weeds are the Nemesis of Onions

Early in the season, onions' greatest vulnerability due to their slow growth is being choked out by weeds—particularly grasses. This is especially problematic as distinguishing between an onion and blades of grass can make weeding difficult. As a result, onions are definitely a case where applying the proverbial "ounce of prevention" is wise.

For beds that will be growing onions, soil solarization as covered in the chapter on weeds is a very effective strategy. This requires some

advanced planning because solarization is most effective in July and August when the sun is at its hottest. So you'll need to know in advance which bed you'll be using for onions.

The following step-by-step strategy will allow you to effectively prevent weed problems without need for chemicals. As an added bonus, as part of a bed rotation combined with solarization, nutrients will be more available and diseases will be suppressed.

- Previous Spring: Grow a spring crop such as broccoli that is harvested in midsummer.
- Previous Summer: Harvest the spring crop.
- Mix in amendments, then smooth out the bed so it is nice and flat.
- Water the bed very thoroughly with the equivalent of 2" of rain.
- Cover with 6 mil thickness plastic attached to the bed with staples. Leave plastic in place until late August.
- Late August: Remove the plastic and sow with a cover crop.
- Early Spring: Harvest cover crop and add to compost pile.
- Cover with dark breathable landscape fabric.
- When the transplants are ready, cut Xs in the landscape fabric and plant them in the Xs.
- Cover the landscape fabric between plants with straw and water thoroughly.

Diseases: Rare but Preventable

Though not typically a problem for home gardeners, onions are vulnerable to a number of fungal and bacterial diseases that can be spread via soil; most notable among these diseases are

Well-controlled weeds make for happy onions.

sclerotinia, botrytis and pink root. Primary prevention for these is crop rotation, with pre-solarizing also being a great help.

Sclerotinia of onions shows up as small dark brown spots on the blades that can expand to kill the entire blade while infecting others. The organism responsible is *Sclerotinia homoeocarpa*, which is the same organism that causes dollar spot on turf grasses, which are its primary host.[10] Using bark mulch or similar mulching to prevent

grasses between and around growing beds will help prevent inoculation.

Botrytis infection looks like small white or yellow spots on the blades of the onion where cells have died. These spots appear sunken. Successful infection will usually bring about the death of the tops of the onions in as little as a week. Though botrytis spoors are ubiquitous, the most common source of infection is debris from the prior year's crop where the spoors have over-wintered.

In industrial agriculture where onions are grown on a large scale and often re-planted in the same fields year after year, crop losses from

[10] Saharan, G. & Mehta, N. (2008) *Sclerotinia Diseases of Crop Plants: Biology, Ecology and Disease Management.* ISBN: 978-1-4020-8407-2.

botrytis can approach 50 percent annually. However, on the scale of a mini farm, simple preventative measures can keep you from ever seeing it. The conditions that favor development of the mold are cool and wet weather, particularly later in the season. However, this factor alone is insufficient to cause infection. Botrytis spoors require a wound in the onion in order to enter. All you need to do in order to prevent botrytis is the following:

- Rotate so that onions aren't grown in the same bed more often than once every four years,
- clear and compost all crop debris at the end of the season so spoors have nowhere to overwinter,
- avoid disturbing the onions during damp or wet weather, and
- respond to the rare pests of onions that can cause breaks in the leaves leaving them vulnerable to infection.

Pink root is common in industrial agriculture, but something you will hopefully never see. It manifests in dead onions that die back as though affected by drought, and the bulbs are shriveled and pink. Pink root infestation is ubiquitous in poorly drained soils with low levels of organic matter and nutrient deficiencies that have been used to grow onions or other susceptible crops for year after year. The fungus responsible, *Pyrenochaeta Terrestris*, is only weakly pathogenic, and if it is infecting your onions, you are doing something wrong.

Using the mini farming method, by growing in raised beds your soil should be well drained, and by using plenty of mature compost for organic matter, rotating crops and amending soil as needed for proper nutrient levels, your onions should be practically invulnerable.

Onion Pests

Most insects don't like to eat onions, and for good reason: when onion tissues are injured, they release a compound that, when mixed with water, produces sulfuric acid. This is why cut onions make your eyes water. But just as there are some intrepid souls who can eat even the most pungent onions as though they were apples; there are a couple of insects who seem not to notice the onion's natural defense mechanism.

Thrips are a common garden pest. They are tiny, with the winged adult being no more than 1/10 of an inch long. Damage from thrips can be two-fold. First, in the direct damage they can do to the crop, but most importantly the cuts they make provide an entry for botrytis. A thrip infestation combined with a week of cold, wet weather can spell doom for the whole crop. They plant their eggs—anywhere from 10 to 100 of them—in the leaves, and when the eggs hatch, the larvae can do considerable damage to the host plant. Thrips are not unique to onions and eat practically anything grown in the garden, so crop rotation won't help.

Prevention requires a combination of cover crop selection, vegetation control, proper soil fertility and garden hygiene. Clearing crop debris at the end of the season to reduce overwintering populations of thrips is crucial. Their eggs won't survive the composting process. Using a mulch between and around beds to keep extraneous vegetation away will also reduce thrip populations. Thrips have a preference for wheat and rye, so if a cereal grain is anticipated as a cover-crop choose oats instead. Finally, many studies have shown that inadequate levels of calcium as well as trace minerals predispose thrip infestation, so adequate lime plus the addition of sea minerals would be wise. Likewise, excess nitrogen is a risk factor, so maintaining optimal fertility of the soil will ward off this pest.

If all efforts at prevention fail, and severe crop damage is likely or occurring, a number of natural insecticides, such as Hot Pepper Wax™, are effective against thrips. Be certain to follow label directions including safety precautions.

The other likely pest problem is onion maggots which are the larvae of a fly that lays its eggs near the roots of the plant. The first symptom you'd likely see, as the flies stay hidden, is wilting plants. When you dig them up, you'll find onions that are a rotten and putrid mess. Once an area is infested, it will likely remain so. Meticulous hygiene in debris removal, solarization and application of parasitic nematodes will help, as will avoiding white onion varieties because these are most susceptible. But of these, removal of onion debris, including making sure no onions are left in the ground, is the most important. Overwintering onion maggots need onions for their survival, and removal of onion debris and burying it deep in the compost pile will substantially reduce their population.

Harvesting Onions

An onion can be pulled and eaten at any stage, but for purposes of storage and marketing, they should be harvested when mature. Onions are mature when the tops of 80 percent of them have weakened, turned brown, and flopped over. When this happens, go ahead and bend over the remaining tops, and then allow the onions to remain in the ground until the next sunny day five to ten days away. When harvest day comes, pull up the onions in the morning, and leave them outside in the sun until evening. This will kill the little rootlets at the bottom of the bulb. Then bring the onions out of the weather into a place that is shaded, protected from rain, and with good air circulation. Leave them for a couple of weeks, turning every couple of days. This yields a fully cured onion of the best keeping quality for its variety.

Preparation and Preservation

Whole onions should be stored either braided or in mesh bags with good air circulation in a cool, dark, dry place. Don't let them freeze. Onions can be frozen raw (without blanching) by peeling, quartering, and placing in freezer bags from which as much air as possible has been removed. Onions can also be successfully dehydrated with or without blanching, but are likely to discolor unless first dipped in a bowl containing one cup of water to which either a tablespoon of lemon juice or a 250mg vitamin C tablet has been added. The discoloration is harmless and doesn't adversely affect the quality of the onions. Onions can also be pickled in vinegar for preservation using water bath canning; they will turn into a shapeless blob if pressure-canned.

Onions play a key role in food preparation generally, and are prepared in every imaginable way ranging from breaded onion rings to creamed pearl onions.

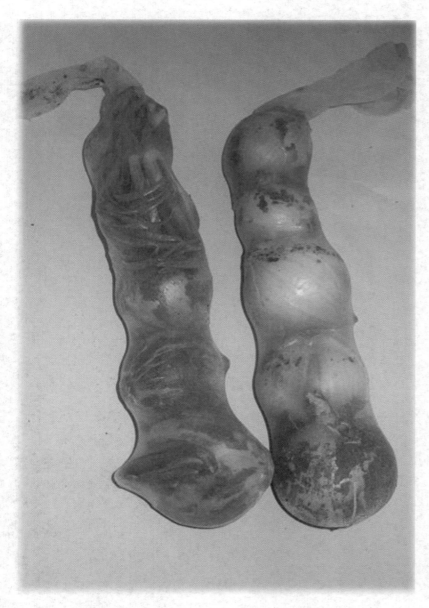

The onions on the left have sprouted because they were allowed to freeze.

Dilled Salad Onions

Ingredients:

3 lbs onions, sliced thinly
1-1/2 cup vinegar
1-1/2 cup sugar
3/4 cup water
1 Tbsp salt
1-1/2 tsp dill weed

Procedure:

Peel the onions and slice thinly. Pack into sterilized pint jars. Bring the remaining ingredients to a boil, and use the resulting pickling mixture to pour into the pint jars leaving 1/2" of head space. Process in a boiling water bath canner for 15 minutes.

Peas

Sometimes kids aren't impressed by peas, but they will likely enjoy classic dishes such as peas with carrots, peas with pearl onions, split pea soup and more. Naturally, peas fresh out of the garden are far superior to the canned peas from the supermarket, with a bursting sweetness that makes them almost like candy. In addition, peas are high in fiber, protein, vitamin C, vitamin K and a variety of phytonutrients that make our mothers' advice to eat them quite wise.

Another great thing about peas is that, being legumes, they improve the soil by fixing nitrogen from the air. So using peas (as well as other legumes such as beans) as part of your bed rotation will reduce the need for nitrogen fertilizers.

There are a great many types of peas, representing not just varieties of a given species, but two different species. Garden peas (also known as English peas) that are removed from the pod for eating, and snap peas and snow peas whose pods are eaten, are members of the species *Pisum sativum*. These peas are a cool-weather crop started in the spring once soil temperatures reach 50 degrees. Split peas are dried peas that have been mechanically split after the shell has been removed.

Cowpeas, also known as peas, are members of the species *vigna unguiculata*; they are adapted to warm seasons and near-drought conditions. Peas are usually prepared from a dried state in a fashion identical to dried beans.

Variety Selection

In order to select a variety, you need to determine the type of pea you want to eat. Do you want snow peas for Asian cooking? Sugar snap peas? Shelled garden peas? Split peas for soup? Black-eyed peas?

Among garden peas, my favorites are Laxton's Progress #9 and Little Marvel. These are short vines—no more than 18"—that can be very easily trellised around the edges of a bed.

There are now a large variety of sugar snap peas available. My pick of the bunch is a variety known simply as Sugar Snap. These grow a massive six-foot vine requiring a trellis like pole beans.

Flat-podded snow peas are popular in Asian cuisine, and my selection in this category is Oregon Giant. The vines are three feet long, and the pods are harvested while still flat.

I grow the same variety of peas that my grandfather grew, because I haven't found any varieties I like better. The Black Crowder Cowpea makes an extra-long pod that is easily shelled. At first, the peas are purple but they become black when dried.

Soil Preparation and Planting

Peas prefer deeply worked and well-drained soils with a pH of between 5.8 and 7. You should check macronutrient levels with a soil testing kit and amend as needed with appropriate organic additives. Organic matter is not as important for peas as with other crops, but adding one or two cubic feet of compost per 4'x8' bed would still be a good idea as it would supply micronutrients; as well as biological content that will help assure the success of the inoculant.

Like beans and other legumes, peas perform best when the seeds are treated at planting time with an inoculant containing nitrogen fixing bacteria. The bacteria turn nitrogen from the air into a form usable by peas and other plants, as well as assisting with the symbiotic bacterial interface that provides other nutrients to the roots. I put my pea seeds in a pint canning jar, moisten slightly, and then add a heaping tablespoon of inoculant to the jar. The pea seeds are planted after they are swirled around in the jar so they will be evenly coated with inoculant.

Garden, sugar and snow peas should be planted in the spring as soon as the soil can be worked. This is because the heat of summer shuts them down. If you happen to have apple trees, I have found that the optimal time for planting peas corresponds to the proper time for spring pruning. Otherwise, a soil temperature of 50 degrees is a good guide.

Unlike garden peas, cowpeas are very vulnerable to frost, so they can be planted at the same time as other crops that are susceptible to frost.

Seeds for peas and cowpeas should be planted more deeply than is immediately evident. Usually, seeds are planted at a depth of double the size of the seed, but peas are best planted two inches deep. This is necessary to establish a sufficient root system. If they are planted more shallowly, the plants will be more vulnerable to drought and weaker generally.

Every variety grows a bit differently. Some only grow a vine that is 18 inches long, so they are easily

Three rows of peas trellised in a single bed.

vines are more delicate, you have to be more careful when weeding. For this reason, I like to get off to a good start by pre-sprouting weeds where peas will be grown, followed by flaming. This way, hand weeding won't be required until the vines are strong and well established.

Pre-sprouting is a straightforward process. You cover a bed with clear plastic in early spring so that it heats more rapidly than it would otherwise, thereby inducing weed seeds to sprout. Two weeks is enough. Once that is done, you can dispose of the weeds by hand pulling, using a stirrup hoe, tilling or flame weeding. Flame weeding offers the advantage of bringing up no new seeds. But if the bed needs tilling anyway, the best approach is to till the bed (adding any needed amendments) before the plastic is employed.

Crop rotation between beds and composting all crop debris at the end of the season goes a long way toward keeping disease and pest problems in check. Fusarium wilt and powdery mildew are the most likely diseases to be encountered. Fusarium wilt can be diagnosed by the symptoms: the leaves start browning at the bottom of the plant, and then the disease progresses along the vine's length until the plant is dead. Powdery mildew is aptly named, because it appears as a white, powdery mold on the leaves and other plant parts. Thankfully, a large number of pea varieties are

trellised on a few branches stuck in the ground. (Traditionally these are the branches pruned from fruit trees, though anything other than poison sumac will do fine.) Other varieties might grow as tall as six feet, requiring a more extensive trellis similar to that used for beans. The shorter varieties of peas can be grown around the perimeter of the garden without shading other crops; however, the taller varieties can be grown on the North side of a bed to avoid shading other crops. Peas should be planted at a two-inch interval.

Weeds, Pests, and Diseases

Peas are more vulnerable to weeds than many of their other legume cousins, and because the resistant to these diseases. Just check the seed catalog when ordering your seeds, and if you have experienced these problems in the past, select resistant varieties.

Though other pests such as Japanese beetles will feed on peas, the primary pests likely to cause difficulties are cutworms, aphids and slugs.

If you walk out to inspect your garden one morning and find a young seedling snipped off at ground level just as neatly as if it had been done with scissors, you'll know you have a cutworm. The next night, that particular cutworm will get a different plant. Cutworms are little caterpillars about an inch and a half long, usually colored in a motley fashion so that they blend in with the soil. After making a meal of your seedling, the cutworm will usually burrow down into the soil no more than four inches from the seedling and make its bed during the day in preparation for the next night. So if you dig around the cut seedling, you'll dig up the cutworm. My chickens like them, so I save them in a jar along with other grubs, wireworms and so forth, and feed them to the grateful poultry.

Cutworms can be largely—though not entirely—prevented by timing your planting so that at least two weeks have passed after tilling other organic materials into the ground. For example, if you are cutting a cover crop and tilling it into the ground, wait at least two weeks after incorporating the cover crop before planting the next one, as the fresh organic matter attracts the cutworms.

One thing I have often seen recommended is the use of cardboard collars. This does work, but it can be time-consuming if you are trying to protect 50 plants. There is also a matter of timing in that a cutworm can feed on anything from a new sprout to a transplant as big around as a pencil.

The stems expand as the plant grows. So rather than attaching collars directly to plants, it is more efficient to surround them with a wall at the time the seed is planted or the transplant is put in the ground. For this purpose, I use scissors to snip paper towel or toilet paper tubes into 1-1/2" sections. You push them into the ground about 1/4" around the seed, seedling or transplant and you're all set. Eventually they'll become soggy and start to decompose, but by then danger from cutworms will have passed.

I've mentioned aphids in connection with many plants, and that's because they affect practically every plant to some degree. In most cases their numbers are insufficient to create a problem, so they can be ignored. But if their numbers become too great, they will weaken the plants they infest and predispose those plants to mold or other diseases. If aphids are a problem, they can be dispatched with insecticidal soap sprayed twice, four days apart. Make sure to get under the leaves and along the stems.

Harvest

Garden peas are somewhat like corn in that their sugars will turn to starch if left too long, so the timing of harvest is important. The key is to catch them when they are fully expanded yet immature. Once the pods have started to become round, pick a pod and sample the peas raw every day. The pods on the bottom become ripe first, followed by those on the middle of the vine three days later and those toward the top another three days later. So you'll get three harvests. At the third harvest, just pull up the plant and add it to the compost pile. Once garden peas are harvested, they should be shelled

Garden peas should be shelled and used within a couple hours of harvest.

and either eaten or preserved within a couple of hours because from the moment they are picked, their sugars start converting to starch.

Unlike garden peas, the vines of sugar snap peas and snow peas will continue to grow and produce new blooms and pods so long as they are kept harvested. The pods closest to the root are ready first, and once those are ready count on harvesting every other day until the vines stop producing. Snap peas are harvested when they first start to fatten, but they still snap like a green bean. If you let them stay on the vine longer, the pods will become fibrous and inedible. If this happens, don't despair—just treat it like a garden pea. Snow peas are harvested at an even earlier stage—when the pods are still flat and the peas inside make little

lumps no larger than a BB. (The diameter of a BB, incidentally, is 0.177 inches.) Once harvest is started, they need to be harvested daily to keep any pods from becoming overly mature.

Snow peas and sugar snap peas can be stored in a plastic bag in the refrigerator for as long as two weeks without deterioration.

Any of the peas discussed so far can be used as a dried split pea for soup-making. All you need to do is leave the pods on the plant until they turn brown and you can hear the peas rattling when you shake the pod. Pick the pods, and set them aside either in the sun or in a well-ventilated place for a couple of days. Then, split open the pod by pressing on the seam and remove the peas. You can split the peas as you go along by using a thumbnail and the work progresses pretty quickly. It's the sort of thing you can do if forced to watch a bad movie on television with a family member. Put the peas in a large bowl and allow to sit out for a couple of weeks to dry, mixing with your hand every once in a while. Then, store them in an airtight container in a cool place away from sunlight.

Cowpeas or black-eyed peas are treated the same as split peas. Harvest when the pods are brown and you can hear the peas rattling when you shake the pod.

Preparation and Preservation

As I explained above, garden peas should be shelled and then eaten or preserved as soon as possible after harvest to preserve their sweetness. Split peas and cowpeas should be harvested when the pods are brown. Shell, and then allow them to dry before being stored in an airtight container. Sugar snap and snow peas can be sealed in a plastic bag and kept in the refrigerator for up to two weeks without loss of quality.

Garden peas, sugar snap and snow peas are all at their best fresh, but freeze very well. Steam blanch garden peas for two and half minutes or edible-podded peas for four minutes. Dump them into ice water for an equal amount of time to cool, dry them, and then seal in freezer bags with as much air removed as possible.

Sesame Snow Peas

Ingredients:

1 lb snow peas
1 Tbsp sesame seeds
2 Tbsp canola oil
1 Tbsp toasted sesame seed oil
2 tsp soy sauce
1/2 tsp ground ginger
4 green onions, chopped small
2 carrots, julienned

Procedure:

Prepare the snow peas by pinching off the stem end and pulling the strings down the pod. (Strings may not be present depending upon pea variety and timing of harvest.) Toast the sesame seeds in a dry pan, stirring constantly over low heat for 5 minutes. Set the toasted sesame seeds aside. Bring a large skillet to high heat, add the oils, then add the remaining ingredients. Keep in constant motion so nothing burns (peas burn easily due to high sugar content) until the peas are a bright green and slightly tender. Then add the soy sauce, put in the sesame seeds, give everything another good stir and then transfer to a heated dish for serving.

35

Peppers

Native to Mexico, South America and Central America, peppers have become an important ingredient in cuisines worldwide, both in the form of sweet peppers and hot peppers. The peppers available in the store represent only a tiny fraction of the range of this versatile fruit, and growing your own peppers is an ideal way to experience the array of flavors available. A cup of ripe sweet peppers contains two days' supply of vitamin C and more than a days' supply of vitamin A, along with a goodly dose of vitamin B6, fiber and important antioxidants.

Peppers can be divided into two broad categories: sweet and hot. Sweet peppers carry two copies of a recessive gene that inhibits the production of the capsaicin and closely related compounds that give hot peppers their bite. Many sweet peppers have been bred, and the standard blocky bell pepper is the one with which most people are familiar, though there are many other sweet pepper cultivars that have a wide array of shapes, flavors and colors.

Hot peppers either lack the gene that inhibits capsaicin, or have only one copy of the gene. Because the gene is recessive, with only one copy (rather than two), capsaicin production is not inhibited. Open-pollinated hot peppers always lack the gene altogether, but in some hybrids there is only one copy. Once capsaicin production is enabled, however, there are other genes that modulate the amount that is produced in a given variety of hot pepper as well as genes that have the effect of creating different flavors and colors.

The degree of hotness of a pepper is measured in either Scoville Heat Units or ASTA pungency units. The Scoville Heat Units are a measure of how much an alcoholic extract of the dried pepper must be diluted before it is just barely detectable by a panel of five tasters; the larger the number, the hotter the pepper. ASTA pungency units are derived through use of High Performance Liquid Chromatography (HPLC) to measure the absolute amount of capsaicinoid content. Most people are familiar with the Scoville Heat Units, and in my personal opinion, because there are

This little yellow pepper is mildly hot.

elements to taste outside of just a specific set of related chemicals, SHUs are a better measure of a person's likely subjective reaction.

The peperoncini peppers on a Greek salad and the pimentos stuffed into olives usually have fewer than 200 Scoville Heat Units, so they are pretty mild. Banana peppers will have up to 500 SHUs. Jalapeño peppers will have more than 2,500 SHUs. The world's hottest pepper is the Naga Viper, with more than 1,300,000 SHUs.

Variety Selection

Peppers are indigenous to warm zones with long growing seasons, though over time varieties have been selected that will do fine in cooler zones with shorter seasons. So the most important aspect of a cultivar to consider is its growing season. Keep in mind that there are two maturity dates for peppers: one for green peppers, and another for ripe peppers. Usually a catalog listing will give the number of days for green peppers and then specify an additional number of days for those peppers to ripen. Especially if you plan to save seeds, you want to choose a variety whose time to a mature and fully ripened fruit is at least ten days less than the length of your growing season. My area only has ninety-six frost-free days on average, so I have to pick varieties that are ripe in eighty-six days or less.

Another consideration is whether you prefer peppers that are sweet or hot and whether the peppers are for use in salads, salsa, frying or other specific uses.

Because my mini farm is in the Northeast, my particular choices might not be the best for other parts of the country, so you can use these as a starting point only for your own experimentation:

A frying pepper awaiting my frying pan.

I grow Jimmy Nardello's both for frying and drying, Ozark Giant or California Wonder for salads, and Black Hungarian as a hot pepper for salsas and spice. This latter is about half as hot as a jalapeño and has a nice smoky flavor.

Starting and Planting

Peppers should be started indoors seven weeks before last frost, and planted out a week after last frost after they have two sets of true leaves. They germinate slowly at lower temperatures, so use a heat mat when growing seedlings indoors to achieve the best temperature of 70 to 80 degrees. In addition, make sure to keep the fluorescent lights to within an inch of the leaves so the stems are stocky and strong. In order to avoid bacterial leaf spot (unless you are planting a variety of pepper that is resistant to that disease) the seed should be pre-treated via the method described in the section on weeds, pests and diseases.

Prepare the bed for the peppers by correcting the pH to between 6.0 and 6.5, thoroughly incorporating three cubic feet of finished compost or well-rotted manure per 4'x8' bed. Correct the soil for the major macronutrients, and then add an additional two pounds of bone meal per 4'x8' bed.

When transplanting, sprinkle a tablespoon of Epsom salt (magnesium sulfate) into the hole that will receive the transplant and mix it into the soil. Space transplants at 12"-18". Water transplants daily for the first week, and then make sure they get the equivalent of an inch of rain every week in the form of a deep soaking rather than multiple shallow waterings.

Weeds, Pests, and Diseases

Because peppers are spaced a good distance apart, if you make sure the bed is weed-free before planting, weeds can be either handpicked or controlled by carefully using a stirrup hoe.

Bacterial leaf spot (BLS) is an economically important disease of peppers that has caused failure of entire crops. It starts with water-soaked spots on leaves that turn brown. Subsequently, the affected leaf may turn yellow, wither and die. The reduced foliage reduces yield and delays fruit maturity, and the spots can affect the peppers as well. It is spread primarily via infected seeds, though once the infection is present it will inhabit the soil and can be spread from plant to plant, especially in wet conditions, via hand contact. Once an infection is noticed, it can be controlled and kept from spreading by applying copper sulfate as indicated on the package. If you run into trouble with bacterial leaf spot, keep in mind that crop rotation and thoroughly cleaning up crop debris at the end of season are the best preventatives. If that is insufficient, seed pre-treatment and growing resistant cultivars will help.

Seeds can be pre-treated with scalding water to kill the bacteria. Unfortunately, this is a delicate process because the bacteria are inside the seed, so anything that would kill the bacteria would adversely affect the vigor of the seed as well. Ideally, this would be accomplished using laboratory equipment such as stirring hotplates and so forth, but the gear to do that would easily cost $400. Thankfully, there is another way that is a lot less expensive. The only gear you'll need that you may not already have is a high quality laboratory-grade thermometer such as the Fischer Scientific 14-983-15B.

Procedure: Seed Pre-Treatment

Equipment:

3 large Styrofoam coffee cups

1 fitted lid for one of the coffee cups

1 saucepan holding 8 cups of water

1 quart jar of cool water, uncovered

2 ice cubes

1 laboratory grade thermometer with a Fahrenheit scale

1 clean handkerchief, cut in four squares—use one of the squares

2 rubber bands

1 large nut

Procedure:

1. Nest two of the coffee cups together and set the lid next to them. These are for the hot water.

2. Fill the other coffee cup 2/3 with cold water and add the two ice cubes.

3. Twist the nut into a pocket in the square of handkerchief, and secure with a rubber band. Put the seeds in an adjacent pocket formed similarly, and secure with the other rubber band.

4. Bring the water in the pot to a temperature of exactly 122 degrees F. Test by swirling the water with the thermometer and then observing the reading. If the temperature goes higher than that, turn off the burner and add cool water a little at a time, stirring each time until the temperature is exactly 122 degrees.

5. Pour the water from the pot into the two nested cups until 2/3 full.

6. Add the handkerchief and assure it sinks.

7. Attach the lid.

8. Wait 25 minutes.

9. Remove the handkerchief from the hot water, and put it in the cup containing ice water, and leave it there for another 25 minutes.

10. Removed the handkerchief, unwrap the seeds, dry them on paper towels and plant as usual.

Phytophthera root rot, also known as "chile wilt" occurs throughout the United States but is most economically important in irrigated fields. The conditions that give rise to it—"wet feet" or waterlogged soil—simply do not exist in raised beds. Furthermore, as it is caused by a microorganism, standard sanitation and rotation practices will keep it even further suppressed, so you are unlikely to ever encounter this problem on your mini farm.

There are about twenty other bacterial and viral diseases that could theoretically infect your peppers, but just as with phytophthera, standard mini-farming practices will make most of them a theory rather than a fact. The one exception is Tobacco Mosaic Virus" (TMV). TMV can be present in the tobacco in cigarettes, and it is easily transmitted by hand to peppers, tomatoes, potatoes and other plants in that family. If anyone who touches your plants smokes, uses snuff, etc. make sure they wash their hands thoroughly before touching the plants. Other viruses, such as Tobacco Etch Virus, and Pepper Mosaic, are transmitted by aphids. If you keep aphids controlled, the lawn mowed and border weeds well away from your garden, these are an unlikely problem.

Aphids are a pest of all pepper species. Because of their role in transmitting diseases in peppers, you want to keep them under control. Aphids are a small, soft-bodied insect, green for camouflage, and they are usually kept controlled by natural predators. You can often prevent them by growing a bed of something they really like, such as marigolds, at some distance from the crop you are trying to protect. (This is called a *trap crop*.) But if they become prolific, you can keep them controlled by spraying weekly with a dilute solution (one tablespoon/gallon of water) of pure soap such as Dr. Bronner's or a specific insecticidal soap.

Slugs can also be an issue. You'd think, especially with hot peppers, that slugs would avoid them, but evidently they have no taste and will eat foliage and the peppers alike. Ground up egg shells combined with coffee grounds (renewed every couple of weeks) will create a deadly barrier around your pepper plants. The coffee grounds are poisonous to them and the egg shells cut their skin so they dehydrate. Other ways to deal with slugs are explained in Chapter 3: Greens.

Root knot nematodes are microscopic roundworms that can affect many garden plants including peppers. Symptoms include wilting and loss of productivity. When the plants are pulled, the roots have little nodules that can be as big as a pea, though they are usually smaller. Root knot nematodes prefer sandy soils low in organic matter, so if you use plenty of cured compost to start with, they won't likely become a problem. Use plenty of compost, practice crop rotation, pull up and compost old pepper plants and you won't have troubles.

Pepper maggots are the larvae of a fly with green eyes and a yellow head that is the same size as an ordinary housefly. The females use an ovipositor to punch a hole in the surface of the pepper, laying a tiny egg that grows into a white-yellow larva a bit under half an inch long. The larva eats inside the pepper, burrows back out, falls to the ground and then pupates in the soil. The injury to the fruit opens it up to diseases, and the insides become discolored. Pepper maggots aren't a problem for thin-skinned hot peppers, but tend to adversely affect sweet bell peppers. Keep in mind that you can grow peppers for years without seeing a pepper maggot and then suddenly have an entire crop wiped out. Remedies are the usual: sanitation and rotation. Sanitation in the form of burying old/dead/rotting peppers deep in the compost pile is particularly important because it is the scent of rotting peppers that draws the adult flies.

Harvest

Peppers can be harvested at any stage, though hot and sweet peppers alike have more sweetness and flavor when harvested fully ripe.

Each pepper plant has what is called a "fruit load." This is the maximum number of peppers that the plant can sustain given its foliage and root system. Once a plant has reached its fruit load, it will cease to flower or produce new fruits. In general, then, it is best to harvest some early fruits while green to make room for more peppers, and to allow some of these latter peppers to stay through full maturity and ripening.

Peppers vary in color as they ripen. Some ripen to orange, and others to red or even purple. A good rule of thumb is the less green you see on the pepper, the more ripe it is. Once they start to lose their green color, they ripen quickly—sometimes in just a day or two. Peppers start to lose quality quickly once fully ripe, so keep an eye on them and harvest when ready. Letting a pepper stay on the plant overlong will not improve its flavor. If you are planning to can or pickle your peppers, they maintain their crispness better when harvested a day or two prematurely.

The stems of pepper plants are brittle and delicate. You can harvest peppers, especially when ripe, just by lifting up the fruit and the fruit stem will separate from the plant easily enough. But when the peppers are green, this happens with difficulty and there is possibility of breaking the plant stems. So I use a pair of garden shears to cut the fruit stem with minimal disturbance to the plant.

As noted previously, hot peppers contain an oily substance called capsaicin. Capsaicin can wreak havoc with mucus membranes at even low concentrations, and burn or blister skin at higher concentrations. In fact, law enforcement officers use the substance to disable people resisting arrest, so it is pretty powerful stuff. When harvesting hot peppers, resist any urge to scratch your nose or rub your eyes. If your skin starts to

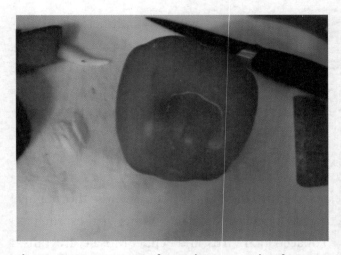

These striations occur most often on hot peppers, but if you see them harvest immediately so the pepper isn't over-ripe.

burn, you can remove the capsaicin from your skin (but NOT eyes, nose, etc.!) with rubbing alcohol. Internally, milk can be helpful.

Seed Saving

Peppers are both self-fertile (meaning they will self-pollinate from the male and female parts inside the same flower and that they are receptive to their own pollen), and can be insect pollinated. All peppers are the same species, so they will interbreed freely. If you are planning to save seed, you either have to practice isolation techniques or grow only one variety of pepper. Isolation is as simple as covering the flower with a bag made from spun polyester. (Floating row cover is made from spun polyester; this is plentiful and cheap.) Cover the flower before it opens and gently shake the plant a couple of times a day to encourage self-pollination. Once a fruit starts to form, remove the bag, but mark that pepper as one that will be used for seeds.

Pepper seeds have greater vigor and higher germination rates if the peppers from which they are taken are allowed to become over-ripe. So allow the marked peppers to mature for an extra week or two after becoming fully ripe.

Seeds are collected by cutting open the pepper and removing them. Put the seeds, separated from any internal membranes, on a paper plate and allow to dry for a month. Then dehydrate further over a silica gel desiccant and store in a sealed container in a cool place away from sunlight.

Preparation and Preservation

Peppers can be eaten raw or cooked. They will keep in the refrigerator for one or two weeks in sealed plastic bags, and can be pickled, canned, dehydrated and frozen.

For freezing and dehydrating, first blanch the peppers in water (two minutes for rings, three minutes for halves) or steam (three minutes for rings, five minutes for halves) and then cool in ice water for several minutes. Then the peppers can be blotted dry and either frozen in evacuated freezer bags or dehydrated and stored in airtight jars.

Un-pickled peppers must be pressure-canned. But pickled peppers can be canned in a water bath canner. In either case, the process of canning makes the skin tough, so the skin is best removed. The skin is removed via a process known as "blistering." This consists of heating the skin, thereby causing it to become easily removed. You can do this in the microwave, oven or frying pan. To use the frying pan method, cut off the top and bottom of the peppers, split them lengthwise and remove the seeds. Heat the pan to medium. Put the split peppers in the pan skin-side down until the skins start to blister. Allow the peppers to cool, and then peel off the skin.

Though it varies with the variety of pepper, sometimes you can skip blistering by steam blanching the peppers for four minutes first, which sufficiently softens the skin. You can try it both ways and note the difference. In general, if I am cutting up the peppers small for a relish, I blanch them, but if I am leaving them long, I blister them.

Pickled Peppers

Ingredients:

8 lbs peppers, cleaned, seeds removed, sliced lengthwise and blistered or blanched

7 cups vinegar (5 percent acetic acid. Either cider vinegar or distilled vinegar is fine.)

1–1/3 cups water

2 Tbsp pickling salt

3 Tbsp sugar

2 cloves of garlic

1 tsp peppercorns

1 tsp whole coriander seeds

Procedure:

Prepare the peppers. (They can be hot, sweet or a mix.) Combine the remaining ingredients in a large saucepan to make the brine, bring to a boil, and allow to simmer for 10 minutes. Pack the peppers into sterilized jars leaving one inch of head space, then fill the jars with brine leaving 1/2 inch of head space. Adjust the two-piece caps and process in a boiling water canner for 10 minutes. Makes 8–9 pints.

Potatoes

36

Originating in the Andes mountains and spread throughout the world by European explorers, potatoes have become a staple crop throughout the world. In fact, though you are unlikely to find potatoes at a Chinese or Indian restaurant, China and India are the world's first and third ranked producers of potatoes respectively. Potatoes are calorically dense, easy to grow, delicious and packed with vitamin C, potassium, vitamin B6 and fiber.

Potatoes also contain what is called resistant starch. This is starch that can't be broken down into sugars by enzymes in the small intestine, and is instead fermented in the large intestine. Research indicates that this resistant starch helps in the synthesis of important short-chain fatty acids and acts as a probiotic encouraging the growth of beneficial bacteria in the colon. Potatoes, especially purple and red ones, contain a substantial amount of antioxidants as well.

Because of the glycemic index[11] of potatoes and the growing problem with weight management in the United States, there are many who would counsel not to eat potatoes (or any other concentrated

---

[11] Glycemic index is a measure of how much a person's blood sugar levels are raised by eating the food. The higher the glycemic index, the more (or more quickly) the blood glucose level is raised.

carbohydrate such as grains or breads) for reasons of health. This subject is fiercely debated by experts, and I'm not about to definitively address the issue in a book on gardening. Instead, I will point out that the glycemic index of a potato is influenced by the variety grown, where it is grown and even how it is prepared.

Potatoes are a member of the nightshade family, and the foliage and fruits of potato plants are poisonous, containing a number of toxic compounds. Solanine is the toxic compound most likely to be a concern for humans.

In general, the actual tubers of potato plants contain a safely low concentration of solanine. However, there are two circumstances where this may not be true. If potatoes are exposed to light their skin starts to turn green and solanine concentrations within the tuber increase rapidly. Do not eat any potatoes with green skin! If you live in South America, there are some wild closely-related species that have toxic tubers. If you grow potatoes from true seed in such an area, be sure to use isolation practices. Otherwise, the plants grown from the true seed could yield a toxic potato. This is not an issue in the United States or Europe as toxic wild potatoes don't grow in those areas.

There is also some concern about acrylamide—a suspected carcinogen in tobacco smoke. The problem is that acrylamide is formed in carbohydrate-rich foods when they are cooked[12] and can provide a level of acrylamide exposure similar to smoking. If this is a matter of concern for you, two things can be done to lessen the amount of acrylamide derived from

eating potatoes. First, do not eat stored potatoes once they have become soft. This softness comes from the starch turning to sugar, and the higher sugar content leads to higher acrylamide formation on cooking. The second is to cook potatoes by boiling and then cool them for consumption. This decreases the amount of acrylamide formed and simultaneously increases the amount of beneficial resistant starch.

Variety Selection

Though there are literally thousands of varieties of potatoes, only a few dozen are commercially available. The primary consideration in choosing a potato cultivar is the purpose for which the potatoes will be used. Different varieties of potatoes have different amounts of starch as well as different ratios of amylose and amylopectin. High levels of starch create qualities desirable in a baking potato, high levels of amylose are best in mashed potatoes and higher levels of amylopectin allow for better boiled potatoes for potato salads. All of these characteristics are different for each variety of potato, so it is best to select a variety suitable for the end use.

Potatoes are also susceptible to a number of diseases including late blight, scab, verticillum wilt, potato viruses, blackspot and more. For most of these diseases, resistant varieties have been bred. If you have difficulty with a given disease, look in the seed catalogs to see what resistant varieties are available.

Starting and Planting

Potatoes can be started either from tubers or true botanical seeds. By far the most popular

---

[12] Tarake, E. et. al. (2002) *J Agric Food Chem.* 2002 Aug 14;50(17):4998-5006.

	Baking	Mashed	Salad
Early/New Potatoes	All Blue, Purple Viking, Red Gold	German Butterball, Mountain Rose, Red Gold	Red Pontiac, Nicola, Sangre
Main Crop	Burbank Russet, Gold Rush, Katahdin	Burbank Russet, Kennebec	Yukon Gold, Yellow Finn, La Ratte

method is using the tubers. The eyes that form on potatoes are a small plant that, if planted in soil and allowed to grow, will turn into a full potato plant that will grow more potatoes.

Potatoes can accumulate many blights and viral diseases that can be passed in the tubers. For this reason, using potatoes from the supermarket is a very bad idea. Will it work? Usually it will. I've done it. But just because I've done something foolish and gotten away with it doesn't mean it should be emulated. The fact is that potatoes in the supermarket are not screened for diseases and

These potatoes are ready for planting.

using them as seed stock can be a recipe for crop failure.

There are a great many sources for certified seed potatoes. These are grown in isolation and tested for diseases. You can use them on your farm with a high degree of confidence that you aren't importing something nasty.

In terms of productivity, certified seed potatoes are usually superior to true botanical seed. Seed potatoes are cloned from the most productive plants available to the seed producer, whereas the results of heterosexual reproduction in true seed never reproduce either parent's characteristics exactly. So using seed potatoes that have been certified disease-free from a reputable supplier is generally most productive in the short term.

Nevertheless, I recommend growing potatoes from true botanical seed because most of the potatoes commercially available are from just a handful of cloned varieties representing a tiny segment of genetic diversity that leaves our food supply far more vulnerable than it should be to unknown pest and disease threats. True botanical seed gives and preserves the greatest genetic diversity, giving greater odds of maintaining a crop in the face of unknown future hazards. Furthermore, it gives you the ability to save your own seeds to cut costs and increase self-sufficiency.

Potatoes grow best in loose soil that is rich in organic matter, so mix in two to four cubic feet of well-finished compost per 4'x8' bed. Don't use immature compost or fresh animal feces as these can suck certain nutrients out of the soil as well as imparting off-flavors and potential human pathogens to the crop. Furthermore, fresh manures can cause unsightly scab on potatoes. Potatoes will grow fine in soils with pH as low as 4.8, and in fact these lower pH levels inhibit the fungus that causes scab, so skip the lime. Beyond that, if you add micronutrients (including boron) and correct the soil levels of macronutrients using appropriate organic amendments, you'll be fine. Potatoes also need soil to be well drained, but using raised beds solves that problem in advance.

Potatoes are a cool weather crop and should be planted around a month before the last frost. This is important, as the productivity of potatoes falls in 90 degree weather, and 95 degree weather may even kill the plants. So get started early!

If you use true botanical seed rather than seed potatoes, start those seeds indoors ten weeks before last frost so they can be planted outside at four weeks before last frost. Plant twice as many seeds as you think you'll need because germination rates on true seed aren't very good. If using certified seed potatoes, set them in a warm window for a week in advance of planting to help them break dormancy. Small- and medium-sized seed potatoes can be planted whole, but large ones should be cut into sections such that there are at least two buds in each section. Allow the cut potatoes to scab over in the open air for a day before planting. Plant either the seed potatoes or the transplants grown from true seed at 18" intervals in all directions. If your beds are so narrow you can only fit in two rows at that

distance, you can space the seed potatoes or transplants at one foot lengthwise and allow two feet between those rows. Plant the transplants as you would any other, and put seed potatoes two to three inches underground.

When the plants have grown to six inches, mound the dirt over them and let them grow some more. This will maximize the total number of potatoes grown from each plant. There are limits to this: the plants need foliage to make tubers, and the more stem you put underground, the less foliage there is to make tubers. I have tried mounding potatoes as much as two feet high, and have found their productivity to be no greater than in instances where I have planted the seed potatoes two inches deep in a six inch trench, and then filled in the trench with more dirt once the potato plants had grow up above the edge of the trench. You can continue mounding up until the plants start to flower, at which point new tubers stop being produced.

Potatoes need sufficient water to prevent hollow tubers and to grow them to optimal sizes. The equivalent of one inch of water weekly is sufficient.

Weeds, Pests, and Diseases

Potato vines grow quickly. Planted as closely as I've recommended, all you need to do is make sure all the weeds in the bed are pulled prior to planting, and the vines will shade out competition in short order. All that will remain is keeping weeds at the edge of the bed pulled before they set seed. Potatoes have a few pests. Colorado potato beetles are pretty much a given anytime you plant potatoes. Wireworms can be a serious problem, especially in areas that

Colorado potato beetles are an important pest of potatoes.

abut or were previously grass. These two are the most likely to be of economic importance, but you can also experience damage from flea beetles, aphids and cutworms.

Colorado potato beetles and their larvae eat the foliage of potato plants. A single female can lay hundreds of eggs, so if left unchecked just a couple of beetles can devastate a crop in a couple of weeks. When the beetles are done with the potatoes, they may also jump to any tomato or eggplant plants they can find. The adult beetles are up to 3/8 of an inch long, bright yellow or orange, and each wing has five distinct brown stripes. They lay yellow eggs underneath the leaves in clusters of thirty, which hatch in a few days. The larva are reddish-orange with a row of black spots on each side.

In practice, because of their high fecundity, natural predators are almost always insufficient to keep potato beetles in check even using the best practices. The only alternatives available are to grow a resistant variety of potato (such as King Harry, Dakota Diamond or Elba) or spray them with something that will kill them.

Adult potato beetles overwinter just under the ground so in large-scale operations the practices of flaming, plastic trenches and similar physical controls have an aggregate effect that can mitigate the need for spraying when combined with crop rotation involving fields separated by long distances. Unfortunately, in a small scale operation like a mini farm, crop rotation doesn't give enough separation. And, if you flame the beds in which potatoes were previously grown, the beetles arrive anyway from alternate natural hosts such as horse nettle or woody nightshade (two common weeds). Thus, if resistant varieties aren't grown, we are left with spraying.

When spraying for Colorado potato beetles, I use mixtures designed for this purpose. I carefully add them according to the concentrations specified by the manufacturers to achieve a perfect result. Pyrethrin is a contact poison highly toxic to bees, so spray it at dusk once all bees have left your plants to avoid hurting them. Its effects last a couple of days before it is rendered harmless through fresh air and sunshine.

Some organic poisons come from the roots of tropical plants. They needs to be ingested to work properly. Certain varieties of these poisons target adult beetles to keep them from laying more eggs and stop them from doing damage, though you need to be aware that they will also kill any larvae. Spinosad is a bacterial toxin derived from a unique bacteria found in a rum distillery in the 1980s. It has to be ingested and is especially toxic to larvae. It takes a couple of days to kill the larvae, but they stop feeding immediately. I have found full control with only two sprayings a week apart.

Wireworms are a serious problem for potatoes as well as carrots, parsnips, beets, Jerusalem

This stackable frame with a landscape fabric bottom allows potatoes to be progressively hilled and excludes wireworms.

artichokes and practically any other edible root save those in the onion family. They will also damage directly planted corn seeds. They will be in soil that was previously lawn or is near lawn. Grassy cover-crops such as rye will likewise attract them. Rotations with crops they don't like, such as mustard or onions, have no practical effect in reducing their presence.

Up until soil temperatures reach 60 degrees, as many as a quarter of wireworms are two or three feet underground—far deeper than you will dig. But once the soil temperatures are that high, the preponderance of the wireworm population will be in the top one foot of soil. Though poisoning them is the modus operandi in industrial agriculture, the poisons used are among the most toxic imaginable and often require special permits for use as some of them, such as chlorpicrin

and methyl bromide are chemical warfare gases usable as weapons of mass destruction. Others, such as carbofuran and imidacloprid, are systemic insecticides that are absorbed into the plant tissues of the treated crop, which is a valid cause for concern.

Obviously, I'm not going to encourage this approach on a mini farm. What I do, as part of preparing a bed for potatoes or any other root crop, is dig through the soil looking for wireworms with a fine-toothed comb. As I find them, I put them in a jar, and when I'm done, I feed them to the chickens. Also, prior to planting I turn the chickens loose in the yard. They inevitably forage through the beds pulling weeds and eating various bugs, including wireworms. This is not 100 percent effective, but over time it has reduced crop damage to tolerable levels.

With potatoes, another very viable approach is to grow them in containers. As long as there are holes in the bottom (blocked with a water-permeable barrier that will exclude wireworms) to allow for drainage, growing them in containers such as five gallon buckets is entirely feasible and works well.

Potatoes are susceptible to several economically important diseases, including early blight, late blight, scab, and black leg. Black leg is not a problem in raised beds because they provide adequate drainage to prevent the disease. The most important weapon against the other diseases is crop rotation such that the same bed is not used to grow anything from the nightshade family (potato, tomato, pepper, eggplant, etc.) any more often than once every four years. Spoors also overwinter in crop debris and culled potatoes; crop debris and culled potatoes should be routinely buried deeply in the hottest section of the compost pile.

Early blight affects potatoes and tomatoes. It is caused by *Alternia solani,* and shows up first on the lowest leaves of the plant; it can ultimately kill the entire plant and adversely affect the tubers. It starts as a small, sunken brown spot on the leaf that expands. Usually, there is more than one such spot. As the spot progresses, the leaf turns yellow, then brown, and dies. In my experience, this disease will also affect cabbage-family crops once it is in the soil, so make sure to rotate crops such that nothing in either the nightshade or cabbage family is grown in that bed for four years to help deny it a host.

One thing that can help with this, as the fungus usually affects leaves rather than stems, is to grow your potato vines on a trellis and remove any leaves within one foot of the ground. This minimizes opportunities for the fungal spoors to be splashed up onto the lower foliage by rain or watering. I have also completely avoided this problem by planting my potatoes in an established living clover cover crop.

If all else fails and early blight visits your potatoes anyway, you can spray with a *Bacillus subtilis* based preparation used according to label directions starting as soon as the infection is noticed, and this will usually control the disease.

Like early blight, late blight also affects tomatoes. Late blight is also known as potato blight, and was the disease responsible for the Irish potato famine. The water-soaked areas on the leaves that serve as the first symptom usually escape notice, but those areas then turn brown and as the leaf dies, it turns black. The spoors are washed from the leaves into the soil where they infect the tubers. Warm, wet weather favors its growth and you may see gray hairy mold growing under affected leaves in humid weather. Crop rotation is very important to prevent this disease, and because the spoors overwinter on potatoes left in the soil, plants growing in cull piles and so forth, meticulous sanitation is equally valuable.

Yet, in spite of the best rotation and sanitation, some of the spoors may blow in to your beds; if they take hold, it can be a serious problem. Sprays are more effective as preventatives than curatives, and those with greatest utility in that regard are copper sulfate and *Bacillus subtilis*. A program of regular spraying at least once every fourteen days, with particular attention to getting the undersides of the leaves, is generally effective. Copper can accumulate in the soil and reach toxic levels, so I would generally recommend using the

Bacillus subtilis instead; it is also more effective. If you see signs of infection in the plants, you can mix both together as the mixture is synergistic. If you grow a large crop of potatoes and you see some of them are affected, you can cut off the affected plants immediately and burn or thermophilically compost them. This will often stop the spread of infection.

Potato scab is another fungus. It leaves unsightly scab-like blemishes on the surface of potatoes, but doesn't pose a risk to the plant overall and the potatoes, once peeled, are perfectly edible. Even so, it makes the potatoes unsaleable. The best preventative is to grow the potatoes in beds where the pH is lower than 5.2; the fungus that causes scab doesn't survive well below that pH but the potatoes will do just fine. This, however, may not be practical as crops are rotated between beds and most crops prefer a pH of 6 or higher. If lowering the pH that much is not practical, a rotation of at least three years substantially diminishes scab. Using plenty of

The symptoms of early blight when it starts on the lower leaves are distinctive.

compost to enrich the soil provides competitive organisms that diminish the incidence of scab even further.

Harvest

As long as they are not green, which indicates the presence of poisonous solanine, potatoes can be harvested at any stage. Early or so-called "new" potatoes can be harvested a week after the potato plants start to flower. New potatoes do not keep well, so they must be used soon after harvest. If you are careful, you can gently dig around under the plants with your bare hands and take a few new potatoes and leave the plants otherwise undisturbed. The potatoes that remain will continue to mature.

Or, you can pull up entire plants and dig around. Because the soil in my beds is uncompressed and practically ideal, I can harvest with my hands and nothing more than a garden trowel. If your beds aren't yet at that point, you can use a digging fork. Stick it in the dirt twelve to sixteen inches from the base of the plant, making sure to insert it as deeply as possible, and then lean back using the digging fork as a lever until the tines emerge from the soil. Do this along one side of the plants, and then along the other side, and then dig out the potatoes with your hands.

This same technique is applicable when harvesting fully mature potatoes. Fully mature potatoes have a toughened skin and are more suitable for long-term storage. Potatoes are mature when the foliage starts to die back later in the season. In my area, that is usually late August.

Mature potatoes harvested this way should be harvested in the morning, laid out in the sun to dry, and then turned at mid-day for even sun exposure. After that, the dirt can be brushed off with a large clean paint brush, and the potatoes can be stored.

Seed Saving

If you use tubers to start your potatoes, you are best off not trying to use your own tubers as seed potatoes except in an emergency, because as I mentioned earlier, a number of diseases will tend to accumulate and within just a couple of years you are likely to have seemingly intractable disease issues. So if you use tubers, you should order or otherwise obtain certified seed potatoes every year.

I have previously discussed using true botanical potato seed as the only practical way for a mini farmer to save potato seeds at all without concentrating diseases. So if total self-sufficiency is your goal, using true seed—even if productivity may be a bit less—is the way to go.

If you are going to grow your potatoes from true seed, it would be best to start by ordering true seeds rather than tubers. You shouldn't use just any old potato variety as a starting point for collecting true seed. Many commercial strains of potatoes (though the breeders will not say which ones for trade secret reasons) have beneficial characteristics such as disease resistance that have been imparted through crosses with wild potato varieties that have toxic properties that are reliably suppressed in the first generation hybrids which are cloned for certified seed potatoes, but would **not** be reliably suppressed in the next generation grown from true seed. Growing random poisonous potatoes probably wouldn't be a big hit with the family.

In theory, if you have the facilities to measure solanine content, you could select the plants from that second generation whose tubers were non-poisonous, pull the other plants, and ultimately create a variety that bred true without potential for poisonous potatoes. But in practice, it is a lot easier to stick with heirloom varieties provided as true seed.

There are very few sources for true potato seed that you can use to start. One unlikely but very productive place to get a small quantity of seed for research purposes is the USDA Germplasm Repository at www.ars-grin.gov/npgs/orders.html. Another source is New World Crops (www.newworldcrops.com). Some other sources can be found by using an Internet search engine, but these are mostly private individuals and seed savers.

Potatoes are an outbreeding plant, and as such you want to grow at least twenty potato plants to avoid inbreeding depression. Then, collect the berries from those plants that were the most resistant to diseases and pests, excluding berries from the runts or those that seemed particularly susceptible to problems. (Warning: when ripe, the berries smell appetizing but are poisonous to eat. Keep out of reach of children!) Put the berries in a blender with a cup of water, and process just enough at low speed to break up the berries and free the seed. Dump that into an open container to ferment for a couple of days, then pour off the water, rinse the seed, and let it dry for a few days on paper towels before dehydrating over a dessicant and storing in a cool, dark place in a sealed container.

Within just a few years you will end up with your own strain of potatoes that grows optimally in your location and soil and that has also accumulated robust multiple-gene resistances to a variety of diseases and maybe even a pest or two.

Preparation and Preservation

Mature potatoes last longest in locations that are cool (42 to 50 degrees), dark, and humid with good ventilation. They should be checked weekly and any rotting potatoes removed before the rot spreads to other potatoes. In these conditions, the potatoes will remain sound and free of sprouts for up to 140 days; the specific time will vary with the particular potato. Commercial storage facilities with computer-controlled storage conditions can keep some potatoes as long as 210 days, but you are unlikely to create such perfect conditions at home.

New potatoes—those that have been harvested before the plant starts to die back and have not been sun cured—can't be stored this way as they go bad quickly. The alternative for both new and mature potatoes is freezing. To freeze potatoes, wash, dry, chop into slices or fries no more than 1/4" thick, water blanch for four minutes, cool in ice water for five minutes, pat dry, and then seal in freezer bags excluding as much air as possible.

Potatoes can also be dehydrated. Wash the potatoes, cut into 1/8-inch-thick rounds, water blanch for eight minutes, cool in ice water for fifteen minutes, pat dry, and dehydrate according to the recommendations of the manufacturer of your dehydrator. The results can be stored in air-tight jars for a year or more, and if you are ambitious can be ground into a powder for making your own instant mashed potatoes.

Oven French Fries

Ingredients:

Non-stick cooking spray
Several large baking potatoes

Procedure:

Wash and dry the potatoes and pre-heat the oven to 450 degrees. Cut the potatoes into 1/4" strips. Spray liberally with the non-stick cooking spray, season as desired, and place flat in a single layer on a non-stick baking sheet in the oven. Cook for 25 minutes, turning over after the first 10 minutes for even browning.

37

Squash

Squash have been cultivated starting more than 8,000 years ago in the Americas, and are now grown in almost endless variety in every region on the planet that supports agriculture. Their culinary uses extend from soups and salads to even pies, so their popularity is understandable.

In a culinary sense, squash are divided into two categories: summer squash (including zucchini, patty pan and yellow) and winter squash (including acorn, hubbard, butternut, spaghetti, pumpkins and others). But in a botanical sense, squash are divided into four distinct species. Hubbard and buttercup squash are *Cucurbita maxima*; Cushaw squash are *Cucurbita mixta*; butternut squash is *Cucurbita moschata*; and acorn squash, pumpkins, zucchini and other squash are *Cucurbita pepo*.

All varieties of squash are rich in fiber, vitamin C and carotenes that exert a protective influence against cancers. Squash also provide useful amounts of folic acid, omega-3 fatty acids, pantothenic acid, vitamin B1, vitamin B6 and niacin. With the exception of hubbard squash (because the woody seed capsule is generally too tough) all squash seeds are edible. The seeds are high in minerals such as zinc, manganese, phosphorus and iron, and studies have shown pumpkin seeds to reduce the symptoms of BPH (benign prostatic hypoplasia).

Variety Selection

The three most important things to consider in selecting varieties of squash to grow are the types of squash your family prefers to eat, the length of your growing season and disease resistance. Most supermarkets carry a variety of squash year-round and summer squash seasonally. You can try various types to find out what you and your family prefer. Growing season is not generally a consideration for squash as they are harvested early, but some squash require a growing season well in excess of 100 days. The time to maturity for squash is measured from the time the seed is planted, so if you start your squash inside three weeks before planting out as a transplant, you can often squeeze a variety of squash into your season that otherwise wouldn't have enough time.

Powdery mildew is quite common in all varieties of squash, and is the only disease for which a wide variety of resistant cultivars is available. If you have serious economic impact from powdery

Zucchini and squash are prolific and grow in a short season.

Starting and Planting

In typical gardens, squash seeds are planted directly in hills or rows. However, both to maximize productivity in terms of season extension and to get a head start against pests or diseases, I recommend starting them indoors two weeks before last frost and putting out the transplants a week after last frost.

Optimum soil pH is between 6.5 and 6.8, though squash will grow satisfactorily at pH levels as low as 5.5 if the soil's fertility is otherwise optimal. Squash grow best with even soil moisture. Uneven moisture can cause blossom end rot and malformed fruit. As rain is unpredictable, the best way to assure the most even moisture uptake possible is to establish deep root systems and provide a great deal of organic matter in the soil. This can be accomplished by adding at least five cubic feet of compost per 4'x8' bed so that the organic matter will buffer and hold moisture, and through deep watering equivalent to one inch of rain at least once a week, but twice weekly in hot weather. Using raised beds will help to compensate for over-watering due to heavy rains by allowing excessive moisture to drain.

Squash require full sun so the bed location should be optimally located for minimum shade. Some squash varieties, notably yellow, patty pan and zucchini, grow on bushes. These should be spaced at two foot intervals throughout the bed. Others, such as acorn squash and pumpkins, grow a long vining system.

For smaller squash varieties such as acorn squash, it is fine to put your transplants at 1'

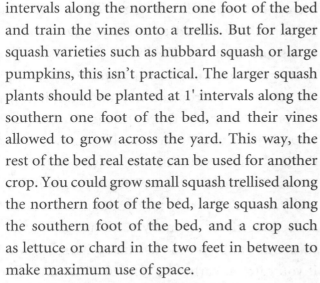

Small squash can be trellised on the north side of a bed.

As you can see, even larger winter squash grow fine on a trellis.

intervals along the northern one foot of the bed and train the vines onto a trellis. But for larger squash varieties such as hubbard squash or large pumpkins, this isn't practical. The larger squash plants should be planted at 1' intervals along the southern one foot of the bed, and their vines allowed to grow across the yard. This way, the rest of the bed real estate can be used for another crop. You could grow small squash trellised along the northern foot of the bed, large squash along the southern foot of the bed, and a crop such as lettuce or chard in the two feet in between to make maximum use of space.

If the vines for larger squash are allowed to grow across the yard, you won't be able to control grass and weeds in that area that could serve as a reservoir for pests and disease. To cut down

on weeds and the pests/diseases they carry, that area can be heavily mulched with grass clippings, hay, or something similar.

Squash will also grow well planted in between corn stalks as long as you space the corn a bit wider than usual. It is also one of the very few plants that will do fine in companion plantings with onions.

Weeds, Pests, and Diseases

Weeds can sap nutrients, block sunlight and give a safe-haven to pests and diseases. Bush-type squash are planted far enough apart that a stirrup hoe, used shallowly once a week, can deal with the weeds. Weeding is likewise easy on smaller squash that are trellised, but the squash vines that are allowed to grow across the yard outside of the beds really need to be mulched under the vines to control weeds as using a hoe or weeding by hand just isn't practical. Lots of materials can be used for mulch. I use grass clippings because they are free. Some studies indicate that using very shiny mulch such as aluminum foil or mylar may help deter cucumber beetles; these should be placed on top of a regular mulch because all by themselves they won't hold back weeds.

The most common disease of squash is powdery mildew. This appears as a white or gray powdery-looking mold that results in deformed and dead leaves. It spreads rapidly and can wipe out a plant or even several plants within a few days of emerging. Prevention is better than attempting a cure, and the best preventatives are growing resistant varieties, planting in full sun, and avoiding nighttime watering. If the disease still takes hold, remove affected leaves and discard in the trash. (Make sure that the tools you use to cut off the leaves are disinfected after each cut by dipping in a 1:10 bleach solution before being used on other leaves or plants.) If that fails to halt the progress of the disease, try a milk and baking soda spray composed of one pint of milk and three teaspoons of baking soda for every gallon of spray. Spray twice weekly, being sure to get both the tops and bottoms of the leaves.

Other important diseases of squash include bacterial wilt, anthracnose, angular leafspot and mosaic viruses. All of these are either spread by pests that can be controlled, overwinter in the previous year's crop refuse, or both. So the most important preventative measures are crop rotation, cleaning up debris at the end of each season, and controlling pests.

Bacterial wilt is spread by cucumber beetles and organic control is quite difficult which is one reason organic squash varieties (pumpkins especially) from the U.S. are hard to find. Preventative measures include giving seedlings a head start through transplanting instead of sowing seed directly, covering the plants with floating row cover until the blossoms appear so they can produce at least some mature fruit before succumbing, planting trap crops that are more attractive than those being grown and that have been treated with a non-organic insecticide, and using organic insecticides such as pyrethrin mixed with canola oil or diatomaceous earth prophylactically. In non-organic gardens carbaryl applied regularly according to package directions from the moment of seed emergence is effective.

Anthracnose fungus overwinters in crop debris and in seed collected from infected fruit. It usually starts as yellow spots on older leaves, but especially in warm damp weather it can quickly spread to affect younger leaves, stems and fruit. As the disease progresses, the spots get larger and turn brown, followed by the vine dying. Crop rotation and cleaning up the prior year's debris are the most important steps to prevent anthracnose. If your seed is of dubious origin, you can treat it with hot water as described in the chapter on peppers, but this will substantially reduce germination rates so start three times as many seedlings if you do this. Once anthracnose has made itself known, if you catch it early you can cut off and throw away infected leaves—this may prevent further spreading. Thereafter, spray neem oil according to package directions every seven to ten days as a preventative, making sure to get the undersides of leaves. Once the disease is clearly actively spreading, Soap Shield[13] **copper** fungicidal soap will control it if used quickly, as will Bordeaux mixtures of **copper sulfate** and **lime**.

Angular leafspot overwinters in crop debris, so crop rotation and sanitation will effectively prevent it. Angular leafspot gets its name from the spots it produces on leaves; they are confined to the leaf area between veins. The spots start as water-soaked spots that later turn brown and develop tears. It spreads like wildfire in wet weather, and is spread by people working with the fruits, leaves and vines when they are damp. Prevention is better than cure, but if prevention fails a copper fungicide will usually work if used soon after detection. Copper fungicides, used excessively, can harm soil biology and the runoff can harm fish. So, again, a concentration on prevention is wise.

Squash are affected by both squash mosaic and cucumber mosiac, transmitted by cucumber beetles and aphids respectively. Cucumber beetle control has already been discussed in relation to bacterial wilt disease, and aphids can be controlled in a variety of ways. Insecticidal soap applied according to label directions is effective, as are the encapsulated natural pyrethrins. Garlic oil sprays will kill aphids, and most varieties of aphids can be deterred or killed with a tea made from potato or tomato leaves.

Squash (as well as cucumbers and melons to a lesser degree) are also affected by squash bugs. They suck the plant juices and inject a toxin that can weaken and kill the vines. Even worse, in four states (Oklahoma, Kentucky, Texas and Ohio) they have been found to transmit Cucurbit

Yellow Vine Disease virus. Squash bugs are about 5/8" long, dark brown or mottled with brown and gray, and hard-shelled. They are shield-shaped and make a disagreeable odor when crushed. They lay their orange-yellow eggs in clusters of twelve or more on the underside of leaves. Adult squash bugs overwinter in crop debris, under mulches and under boards. Avoiding mulches (other than hay, which seems to repel them) in beds that will be used for cucurbit family crops is a good idea, as is removal and composting of crop debris.

The best organic control of squash bugs is to cover the vines with floating row cover that is well-anchored so bugs can't sneak in from the moment the crop is planted until the first flowers emerge. This will at least reduce the time-frame available for them to do damage. You can try interplanting buckwheat to attract parasitic wasps that will prey on the squash bugs, but the results of this are marginal. Likewise, inter-planting with marigolds or nasturtiums may have some marginal effect. On the scale of a mini-farm you can pick off the bugs and put them in some soapy water and smash the egg clusters by hand. If infestation can't be controlled that way, some sprays used according to label directions can control them.

The larvae of squash vine borers burrow into vines and destroy the tissue, thereby killing any part of the vine beyond where they entered. The adult is a moth whose coloration often leads to it being mistaken for a bee or wasp. It lays small blackish pin-head eggs, usually along the six inches of a vine just above where it emerges from the soil. When the eggs hatch, the larvae burrow into the vine, growing as they eat until they are ultimately large enough that their burrowing physically disrupts the plant.

---

[13] Soap Shield is a registered trademark of Gardens Alive, Inc.

Squash bugs inject a poison into the vine.

Squash vines will put roots into the soil anywhere the vine is covered with soil, so one thing that will help diminish the damage from borers is burying parts of the vine as it grows so that the vine has a diversified source of nutrients and water. Another thing you can try is wrapping some aluminum foil around the bottom six inches of the vine so the moth has no place to lay its eggs or has to settle for a less damaging place.

Observing your plants daily, and particularly looking for "frass"—the sawdust-like leavings that borers leave behind them as they eat into the stems—can allow you to react before too much damage is done. If you catch it before the vine wilts, you can kill the borer in the vine by poking through it with a pin and leaving the pin in place. You can sometimes cut the stem along its length, extract the borer, push the vine back together where it was cut and bury the cut section in soil.

Industrial agriculture depends on insecticides sprayed on a regular schedule to kill the larvae as they emerge from the eggs, but they are seldom a large enough problem on a mini farm to justify default use of insecticides "just in case."

Particularly in summer squash, blossom end rot is a possibility. As the name of the condition implies, the blossom end of the squash simply rots. This is caused by uneven uptake of calcium due to variations in water availability such as two weeks without water followed by a sudden soaking rain. Often the first fruits of summer squash will have this problem and it is nothing to worry about. But overall the problem can be prevented by making sure the beds have plenty of compost to buffer the water supply and watering regularly (once a week in normal weather but twice a week if it is hot and dry) and deeply to the equivalent of an inch of rain each time.

Harvest

Summer and winter squash are harvested differently. Summer squash are harvested while still immature like cucumbers so the plants will continue to make new flowers and squash. For best flavor, yellow squash and zucchini should be harvested when no more than six to eight inches long, and patty pan squash should be harvested when no more than four inches in diameter. Once you allow a summer squash to mature, the plant stops making new ones, so make sure none escape your notice, which can easily happen under the heavy cover provided by squash leaves. A couple of times I've missed squash that easily grew to several pounds. Not only did the plant stop making more squash, but the large squash was not very tasty.

Winter squash, on the other hand, are harvested when mature and they are cured for longer keeping. In fact, in most cases the flavor of winter squash varieties improves over the first several weeks after harvest. Winter squash are harvested when they have developed full color and their rinds are hard enough that they can't be dented with a thumb nail and the rind has become dull-looking as opposed to glossy. Don't pull them off the vine or their keeping quality will be adversely affected. Instead, cut the vine using pruners or a sharp knife, leaving two or three inches of vine still attached to the squash. With the exception of acorn types, other winter squash should then be cured by leaving them in the shade at temperatures exceeding 80 degrees for five to ten days before storing.

Seed Saving

The biggest challenge with seed saving is that squash require bees or other pollinators to pollinate, and interbreeding between varieties within

Squash flowers are very attractive to bees and rely on them for pollination.

the same species is quite easy. If you want to save seed, I would recommend growing only one type of squash of a given species each year.

Cucurbita pepo: Yellow, zucchini, patty pan, acorn, spaghetti, common pumpkin

Cucurbita moschata: butternut, naples, kentucky field pumpkin, neck pumpkin

Cucurbita mixta: cushaw squash (looks like a pumpkin)

Cucurbita maxima: buttercup, hubbard, banana, Lakota

There is room for confusion, particularly with squash known as pumpkins, because there are many varieties of pumpkins, and the term encompasses squash from more than one species. Just to be on the safe side, when ordering seeds for squash, check the catalog to make sure what species it is.

Winter squash used for seeds should be taken three or even four weeks later than the squash would normally be harvested. Also, those squash that grow closest to the root of the plant are likely to produce seeds with the highest rate of germination. Scoop out the seeds, swirl around in a bowl of lukewarm water, dry off with some paper towels and allow to sit for a couple of weeks before drying further over a dessicant. Store in an airtight container in a cool, dark place.

Summer squash are treated identically. If you leave them long enough, they will get large and grow a tough rind. Once this rind is tough enough you can't dent it with your thumbnail, let the squash mature for another three weeks before harvesting.

Preparation and Preservation

Summer squash can be kept in a plastic bag in the crisper drawer of your refrigerator, but it will only keep for three to five days. Like corn, it is one of those vegetables best eaten or preserved soon after harvest. The best way to preserve summer squash is freezing. Cut off the ends, slice uniformly, water blanch for three minutes or steam blanch for five minutes, cool in ice water for five minutes, pat dry and then store in freezer bags with as much air excluded as possible.

Winter squash should be stored at a temperature of 50-55 degrees. Acorn type squash will keep for one or two months, butternut, turban and butternut squash will keep for two or three months, and hubbard squash for as long as six months. Storage life can be enhanced even longer if, after the fruits have been cured and before you store them, you wash the surface using a cloth dipped in soapy water (dish liquid is fine) that contains one part of bleach for every ten parts of soapy water. This kills many of the pathogens that would normally affect the squash, thus prolonging storage life. Check your stored squash frequently and discard those showing signs of rotting promptly so spoors don't spread to adjacent fruit. The optimal humidity for storage is 50 percent to 70 percent. Higher than that will decrease storage life due to increased rotting and lower than that will decrease storage life due to dehydration of the fruit. Don't store winter squash near apples as the ethylene gas that apples generate will cause the squash to rot.

The seeds of any edible squash (including pumpkins) can be eaten (though those of the largest varieties may be too tough), and they make a tasty high-energy snack. There are several ways to prepare them depending upon one's

The seeds of this acorn squash will make a nutritious high-energy snack.

preferences and health-consciousness. To preserve the healthful character of the oils in squash seeds, they shouldn't be cooked at a temperature higher than 170 degrees. On the other hand, cooking at higher temperatures is preferred by many because it results in a different taste. Seeds prepared either way will keep for a week if stored in an airtight container in the refrigerator.

To prepare in this fashion, clean the seeds by swishing them around in a big bowl of warm water, then strain them out of the water and dry them on paper towels overnight. Preheat your oven to 160-170 degrees, and spread the seeds in a single layer on a baking sheet. Bake for twenty minutes, use a spatula to flip the seeds, and then bake for another ten minutes.

To go all-out on snack food, clean the seeds as above, preheat the oven to 450 degrees, mix the seeds in a large bowl with canola oil and a bit of Adobo,[14] and then put in a single layer on the baking sheet. Cook for ten minutes, flip with a spatula, and then cook for another ten minutes.

Baked Acorn Squash

Ingredients:

2 acorn squash (will also work with butternut, buttercup, delicata, etc.)
4 Tbsp butter
1/4 cup packed brown sugar
salt and pepper to taste

Procedure:

Preheat oven to 400 degrees. Cut the squash in half lengthwise and remove the seeds. Cook the halves in a shallow pan with the cut side down for 30 minutes. Turn them with the cut side up, then add the butter, sugar, salt and pepper. Return to the oven and cook for another 30–40 minutes until a fork can be easily inserted.

Squash Casserole

Ingredients:

2 lbs squash (yellow, zucchini, patty pan or any combination)
1 beaten egg
2 cups of chopped tomatoes
1 onion, chopped
1 cup bread crumbs
2 Tbsp melted butter
1/2 tsp salt

Procedure:

Preheat the oven to 350 degrees. Slice the squash and cook in a bowl in the microwave for 5 minutes, stopping to stir at the halfway point. Thoroughly combine the bread crumbs, salt, beaten egg and tomatoes and salt thoroughly, then stir in the squash. Use the butter to grease a casserole dish. Dump all the ingredients into the casserole dish and bake for 45 minutes.

---

[14] "Adobo" in this case is a seasoning available in the Latin section of the supermarket. I use the Adobo con Cumin for this recipe.

38

Tomatoes

If there is any one thing that motivates more people to take up gardening, it is the desire to eat a tomato right off the vine. The tomatoes in the supermarket usually look perfect, but they taste unripe and have little flavor. Many people remember the taste of tomatoes right out of their mother's or grandfather's garden, and they know they don't have to settle for the unappetizing fare at the store.

Not only are tomatoes are a nutritional powerhouse rich in vitamins A and C along with various minerals and B vitamins, but study after study has shown that a diet rich in tomatoes is protective against a variety of cancers, including prostate and pancreatic. Other studies have shown that important antioxidants in tomatoes, such as lycopene, are present in greater quantities when the tomatoes are raised organically, so growing your own would be a tremendous benefit in more than just taste.

One thing you may find helpful in your quest for higher levels of self-sufficiency is how easy it is to make your own spaghetti sauce, salsa and even ketchup from your own tomatoes.

Variety Selection

There are literally hundreds of different varieties of tomatoes encompassing colors from yellow to purple, as well as variations in growing habits, disease resistance, early or late maturities and a range of taste that makes tomatoes the subject of tastings similar to wine. There is no way to even make a dent in all the varieties available, but there are a number of ways to make sense of them.

Tomatoes are either determinate, meaning bush-like, or indeterminate, meaning vine-like. Determinate varieties can be grown using just a short tomato cage, but indeterminate varieties will need a trellis to maximize their potential. Determinate tomatoes also tend to ripen more closely together, whereas the tomatoes on indeterminate vines will ripen at different times. For purposes of processing large numbers of tomatoes for spaghetti sauce or ketchup, determinate varieties are usually best, but for adding to salads throughout the summer or for drying in batches, you might find indeterminate varieties more convenient.

The maturity date for tomatoes listed in seed catalogs is based on the number of days since they were put in the garden as transplants. Usually, you will want tomatoes for both early in the season and later in the season, so you might grow a couple of varieties to have your harvest spread out.

Though in most respects tomatoes can be readily substituted for each other, there are differences in moisture content that make some tomatoes more suitable for sauces and other more suitable for fresh eating. For example, the Italian plum varieties tend to have a lower moisture content, so they don't have to be simmered as long to make a thick sauce.

Tomatoes come in a variety of colors ranging from white to purple. There are even varieties that remain green when ripe! In general, the tomatoes rated most highly in taste tests are pink, purple or black varieties. (These latter aren't really black. They have a complex darker color.) Examples include Pruden's Purple and Brandywine. However, your taste and opinion is the only one that matters.

In my garden, I usually grow an indeterminate cherry tomato for salad tomatoes all season, an early slicer for sandwiches and a late slicer for even more sandwiches, and a group of determinate paste tomatoes for sauce and salsa. I like Peacevine cherry for salads, Moskvich and Stupice for early season slicing, Brandywine and Pruden's Purple for late season slicing and Amish Paste, Black Plum and Plum for sauces among others. But those are just my own preferences!

Starting and Planting

Tomatoes are a warm weather crop and as long as they are supplied with sufficient water, the more sun and heat the better. This makes tomatoes a bit of a challenge for Northern growers, but breeders have put a great deal of effort into producing early tomatoes, especially in Eastern Europe. So with proper variety selection, tomatoes certainly belong in gardens across the continental United States.

If you've ever had tomatoes rot in the garden and been faced with dozens if not hundreds of volunteer plants the following year, you know that tomatoes can be directly seeded in the garden. Volunteers need to be ruthlessly culled because they can serve as a reservoir of disease (for both tomatoes and potatoes) that negates the value of crop rotation. Even so, putting seeds in the ground directly is not very reliable and in most of the country tomatoes could definitely benefit from a head start. Maturity dates given for tomatoes in catalogs assume the use of transplants started six weeks earlier, so a bit of math shows that sowing them directly from seed won't allow for enough time before frost sets in in the fall in most of the country. Start them indoors six weeks before last frost, and plant them out right after the last expected frost.

If you are growing indeterminate tomatoes, plant them spaced 18" apart in the northern one foot of the bed, and train them onto a trellis six feet tall. Prune the tops back once they reach that high. If you are growing determinate tomatoes, use the cheap wire tomato cages, and space them 18" to 24" apart. Ideally, these will be in a bed that has the long sides on the East and West so the tomatoes will benefit from sun on both sides of the bed.

The soil for tomatoes should be deeply worked, incorporating a lot of organic matter. I would recommend at least five cubic feet of compost per 4'x8' bed. The pH should ideally be in the 6.5 to 7 range, though closer to 6.5 is better for prevention of a condition known as yellow shoulder. Uneven uptake of calcium due to uneven uptake of water causes blossom end rot and splitting in tomatoes. The organic matter will help hold and buffer the water while using a raised bed will help prevent an overabundance.

Too much nitrogen can cause tomato plants to create lots of foliage but bland tomatoes. So when you add amendments in accordance with a soil test, use slow release nitrogen sources such as alfalfa meal, cotton seed meal and compost as opposed to sodium nitrate, urea or blood meal, and don't add any more than the soil testing indicates. If you mix a tablespoon of garden gypsum

Lay the stem horizontally when transplanting for maximum strength roots.

into the soil of the hole where you plant tomatoes, it will also help prevent blossom end rot.

Tomatoes will send down roots anywhere the stem is covered with soil. For the most robust root system and plants, put the tomatoes deep in the soil with the stem horizontal and only four inches of the plant above ground. As the plant grows, strip off the leaves that are within a foot of the ground, as this will help prevent a variety of blights and other diseases that start with infecting the lower leaves.

Weeds, Pests, and Diseases

Because tomatoes are planted with such wide spacing, controlling weeds via careful periodic hoeing is straightforward, and the foliage is often so plentiful at close spacing that much weed competition is shaded out once the plants are growing well.

Because tomato foliage is poisonous to most things, tomatoes only have a few notable pests; among these are hornworms, cutworms, flea beetles, aphids, whiteflies and root knot nematodes.

Aphids will always exist to some degree on tomato plants and they don't usually pose a problem, but if their numbers become too large they can weaken the plants. They can be controlled with a couple sprays of insecticidal soap. Cutworms will exist in any bed that has had fresh organic matter (such as cover crops or heavy weeds) cut and turned into the bed within a couple of weeks of planting. Protect the seedlings with cardboard collars four inches long and buried an inch deep in the soil when they are first planted, and you'll have no trouble.

Hornworms are such a unique creature that once you've seen one you'll never forget it. They have a prominent horn at one end, are as much as three inches long, and green with stripes and eye-like markings over their body. They gobble foliage extensively, even chopping off entire branches of the plant at times. You can pick these off and feed them to the chickens. I've never found more than a few of these in a single season, but if your plants are suffering from an extensive infestation, they can be controlled overnight with a single complete spraying with a *Bacillus thuringiensis* preparation used according to label directions.

Whiteflies are not usually a problem when using home-grown transplants; they often hitch-hike on plants purchased from nurseries or garden stores. In small quantities, these don't adversely affect the plant. In large populations they can leave a lot of honeydew on the plant that gives room for sooty mold to take hold. Sooty mold looks like a sooty coating on leaves and fruits. It

Tomato hornworms have a unique beauty, but they are voracious.

doesn't actually infect the plant, but rather lives in the honeydew on the surface. It isn't economically important unless it becomes so extensive as to block sunlight and photosynthesis. White-flies are ubiquitous in garden stores, greenhouses and the like because over the decades they have become immune to practically all insecticides. If you develop a substantial infestation of white-flies, about the only thing that will control them is a light horticultural oil. Don't use such oils during a drought or they can kill the plant.

Flea beetles resemble fleas. A few of them won't hurt anything, but if the populations are high they can defoliate and weaken the plants. If their damage crosses an economic threshold, they can be easily controlled with sprays designed for this purpose and used according to package directions.

Perhaps the most dreaded pest of tomatoes is root knot nematodes. These microscopic worms burrow into the roots causing knots that interfere with nutrient absorption and the full cycle of photosynthesis. The preparations used to control them on a commercial scale are breathtakingly toxic and expensive and thus impractical on a mini farm; they are better off prevented. Luckily, they can be prevented easily through crop rotation and sanitation. At the end of the season, pull out all plants including as much of the roots as you can and compost them. If you develop an infestation in a bed, I would recommend growing mustard in that bed for a couple of years, followed by onions the next year. Then try a crop such as beets that is susceptible to root knot nematodes and where the damage is easily seen to see if you've successfully abolished them. If not, go back to the mustard and onions for another couple of years.

A common but seldom recognized pest of tomatoes is the tomato russet mite. The symptoms start with the lower leaves turning brown and then moving up the plant with the stem taking on a bronze-like appearance. If they appear, you can control tomato russet mites with a commercial wettable sulfur preparation.

Diseases of tomatoes include fusarium wilt, verticillium wilt and mosaic viruses among others, though tomatoes can also be affected by potato early and late blight, manifesting identical symptoms to potatoes. The key to controlling diseases is crop rotation and sanitation. Only once have I ever had a problem with disease in tomatoes, and those seedlings were brought home from a nursery (purchased after an unexpected late and hard frost killed our seedlings). Otherwise, following the simple precautions of rotation, sanitation and keeping tobacco products away from the plants I've never had a problem.

Fusarium wilt affects all nightshade-family plants including tomatoes, eggplant, peppers and potatoes. Fusarium usually times its arrival for damp weather when there is already lots of full-sized green fruit on the plant, turning the leaves yellow. There seems to be no rhyme or reason to which leaves will be affected, and sometime it will infect one half of the leaves but not the other. Those leaves lose the power of photosynthesis, and the fruit doesn't get enough energy to ripen. Fusarium is a soil-born fungus that can be controlled by crop rotation. If problems persist, there are many varieties of tomatoes that are resistant, so if you choose a resistant variety it won't be an issue.

Verticillium wilt usually starts on the older leaves with the edges turning first yellow than brown. Unlike fusarium it doesn't kill the plant, but it definitely hurts productivity. Crop rotation and sanitation are your biggest preventatives; as the pathogen is soil-born I have found another solution. What I do is sow my tomato bed in clover, and grow indeterminate varieties trellised on the North side of the bed. The clover creates a dense ground cover that keeps rain from splattering fungus spoors from the soil up onto the leaves. I plant the transplants in the clover patch, take off the bottom leaves once they get big enough, and train them onto a trellis. For determinate plants where trellising isn't feasible, they tend to shade out the clover so the protection isn't as full, but a number of verticillium resistant varieties of tomato are also available.

There are many mosaic viruses, but they all have the same symptoms on tomatoes. The leaves develop a mottled appearance, wilt, and grow small—almost like a fern. The result is a plant that fails to thrive. Plants infected with such viruses should be discarded in the rubbish.

Now for the good news: your tomatoes will never suffer from this virus. The reason is because 99.9 percent of the time mosaic virus comes from tobacco in cigarettes where the gardener fails to wash his or her hands after smoking and then transmits the virus to the tomatoes. If you smoke, all you need to do is avoid smoking in or around your garden and wash your hands after smoking before touching tomato (or potato or pepper) plants and you will never see this.

Pinching and Pruning Tomatoes

As mentioned earlier, tomatoes can be divided into determinate and indeterminate types. Determinate plants only reach a certain size and do not require extensive pruning or a trellis; indeterminate plants, given proper conditions, will literally grow with no limits. Determinate plants only need a cage or a stake—though I much prefer cages. Indeterminate plants will grow adjunct stems at leaf axils in an infinite variety, and if left unchecked will outgrow practically any trellis and start creeping along the ground.

Because of soil-borne diseases, it is important to keep tomatoes off the ground. Thus cages for determinate tomatoes and trellising for indeterminate tomatoes are absolutely necessary. Pruning indeterminate tomatoes is an exercise in discretion; understanding why it is needed will help put it in context.

The more vegetative growth a tomato plant produces, the more of that growth will be shaded and thus consuming more sugar than it produces. Furthermore, the more vegetation, the more fruit clusters, the smaller the fruit, and the later it will ripen. Too much vegetation will also favor disease conditions due to the prolonged time required for moisture to evaporate from the leaves. There is an optimal trade-off between the number of stems and the size, and the number and speed of maturation of fruits. In most cases, this is just three or at most four adjunct stems.

How high up on the plant these stems grow is important. You don't want them growing from below the first fruit cluster because they will put too much strain on the root. You don't want them growing too high on the plant, because then they will be too weak to support fruits of their own. What I recommend is allowing a new stem to grow from the leaf axils immediately above the first, second and third fruit clusters, and ruthlessly pinching off any others.

In between the leaves and the stems (an area known as the axil) is where the new stems emerge. Once you see it growing small leaves, you'll know

Excess stems can be easily pinched off when they are small.

it is a new stem. These new stems are most easily removed by "pinching." Just grasp between your thumb and forefinger, and literally pinch it off. This method exposes the least amount of remaining tissue to disease. Sometimes, though, the plants get away from you and you'll have a stem three feet long before you realize it; such stems that can't be removed by pinching should be removed with the least tissue damage possible by using a razor knife in preference to tools such as scissors or pruners.

Indeterminate tomatoes should also be "topped." About a month before your first expected frost, you want to cut the top off of any growing stems. This will force all energy production to go into ripening the fruit.

Because damp conditions favor the spread of disease, never prune tomatoes when the plants are damp. And because diseases spread easily between plants, I recommend dipping any tools used in a 10 percent bleach/water solution after each cut.

Harvest

Tomatoes can be eaten at any time and size. Though green tomatoes contain small amounts of the poisonous alkaloid tomatine, no cases of poisoning have been reported from their consumption and studies indicate that the tomatine binds to cholesterol in the digestive tract, preventing absorption of both the tomatine and the cholesterol. In the concentrations present in green tomatoes, consumption has been shown to lower bad LDL cholesterol, inhibit certain cancers and enhance immune response.[15] So green tomatoes are safe to harvest and eat.

Even so, I much prefer my tomatoes ripe—especially for fresh eating—and I suspect most folks share my preference. Vine-ripened fruits are by far the most tasty, with those ripening indoors rating a very close second.

Timing the harvest is straightforward: pick the tomato when it has developed maximum color for its variety but has not become soft. There are two exceptions to this rule. The first is cherry tomatoes because of their tendency to split. Harvest these when the color has changed but before maximum ripeness to avoid splitting. The second is any variety of tomato that is prone to cracking. These should also be harvested before maximum color.

Problems with cracking can occur in any tomato that has been water-deprived for an extended period of time and then given an overabundance of water. Incorporating plenty of organic matter into the soil as a buffer to absorb and release water as needed will be helpful, as will growing in raised beds and making sure tomatoes are watered properly. But even with the best care, some varieties are prone to splitting as ripeness approaches, and these should be harvested before they crack.

---

[15] McGee, H. (2009), "Accused but Probably not a Killer," *New York Times*, July 18, 2009, ISSN 0362-4331.

Tomatoes harvested a little early will continue to ripen indoors. Ideally, put them in a closed paper bag at room temperature. A paper bag will retain and concentrate ripening factors such as the ethylene gas released by the ripening fruit that also triggers further ripening, but also keep the fruit from becoming water-laden and rotten as would happen with a plastic bag. You can hasten the ripening process by putting a ripe (but not overripe) banana in the bag with the tomatoes.

If you know a frost is coming and you have a lot of green fruits on your plants, you can either harvest the green fruits and use them in appropriate recipes or cut the vines and hang them upside down indoors in the dark. Surprisingly, a lot of the fruit will ripen.

Saving Seeds

Tomatoes usually self-pollinate. That is, the pollen fertilizes the ovum within the flower; sometimes before the flower even opens. To help this process, you can give your tomato plants a little shake now and then. Even though tomatoes are self-pollinating, they can also be cross-pollinated by insects, so maintain several feet of separation between plants of different varieties from which you want to save seeds. Also, use only open-pollinated or heirloom varieties for seed saving as hybrids will not make seed that re-creates the characteristics of the immediate parent.

When you save tomato seeds, you want to save them from the very best tomatoes on the very best plants. Pick the tomato slightly before it is fully ripe. If you wait until it is fully ripe it will hurt the germination rates of the seeds you save. Tomato seeds are processed using a fermentation method.

Cut the tomato across the equator, and use your clean fingers or a spoon to scoop the gelatin and seeds (but not the meat of the tomato) into a clean container. I use small plastic cups, but canning jars will also work fine. Add water equivalent to about half the volume of tomato gelatin in the cups, and swirl it around with a spoon. Cover the top with cheesecloth to keep out bugs, and set aside for two to four days until a mold starts growing on top. If four days have elapsed and there is still no mold, don't worry. Add water to the cups, swish it around, and pour off any mold or floating seeds. Rinse off with water a few times, and then spread the seeds on multiple layers of paper towels to dry. After about a week, put the seeds on a paper plate to dry further. After another week, you can dry further over a dessicant before storing for up to four years in a sealed container in a cool, dry, dark place.

Preparation and Preservation

If you wash and dry your tomatoes when you bring them in, they'll keep for a week without loss of flavor just sitting on the kitchen counter; longer if they are not yet ripe. They will keep for yet another week in the refrigerator, but at the cost of some loss of flavor and a sort of graininess being imparted to the flesh. Between the two methods you can save up your tomatoes for a couple of weeks (if you are saving for a batch of sauce).

Tomatoes can also be dehydrated, canned and even frozen. Though vegetables are usually blanched before dehydrating and freezing, this is not needed with tomatoes, though many prefer to remove the skin, and the procedure for doing so tends to blanch them a bit anyway.

Many recipes call for removing the skin from the tomatoes because especially when canned, the skin can become tough and a detracting annoyance in some dishes. Once you get the hang of removing the skin, it is easy. Bring some water in a pot to a gentle boil. Make sure it is deep enough to fully cover the tomato. Lower the tomato into the water on a slotted metal spoon. Leave it in the water until the skin starts cracking—about a minute—and then put the tomato in ice water for three minutes. The skin is then easily removed. Once the skin is removed, you can also remove the hard core from the tomato by using a simple apple corer. Once the tomato has been skinned and cored, you can cut it, remove the gelatinous portion containing the seeds, and either freeze directly in a freezer bag from which air has been excluded or dehydrate according to the directions that came with your dehydrator.

For making sauces, I don't bother with removing seeds, skins or cores. Instead, I boil up the tomatoes in a big pot until they are mushy and process them through a hand-cranked strainer that separates these portions out.

Canning tomatoes is a borderline proposition; that is, the pH of tomatoes is right on the borderline between foods that can be safely canned in a water bath and foods that require pressure canning. Most recipes in canning books specify the addition of an acidifying substance—usually commercial bottled lemon juice—as a means of lowering the pH sufficiently to allow for safe water bath canning. The reason they specify commercially bottled lemon juice is because it contains a predictable and standardized amount of citric acid. The problem is that the stuff usually contains potassium sorbate as a preservative. Even though as far as I know potassium sorbate is not harmful, it has been my experience that when used in products that are cooked it imparts off-flavors. So instead I recommend that you go on the Internet to any wine-making hobby store and order pure citric acid. Substitute 1/4 teaspoon of citric acid for one tablespoon of lemon juice, and you will achieve the same effect without imparting unintended off flavors. Also, keep in mind that if you add any other vegetable or meat to a tomato recipe (excepting salsa because salsa is actually a pickle), you will need to pressure can that product for the longest length of time for any of the ingredients. Failure to do so can result in botulism.

There are a host of recipes for relishes, salsas, chutneys and pies (for the adventurous) made from green tomatoes. Some like to slice them, dip them in egg and then seasoned flour, and fry them. All of these are wonderful.

Homemade Ketchup

20–25 lbs of tomatoes

3 cups vinegar

1 cup of chopped onions

1 cup of chopped sweet red pepper

1 cup sugar

1 clove garlic

2 tsp celery seed

1 tsp salt

1 tsp whole black pepper

2 tsp whole allspice

2 tsp mustard seed

1 stick of cinnamon

1/2 tsp cayenne pepper

Clean and weigh the tomatoes. I use a kitchen scale but for this quantity of produce you can use the bathroom scale. Cut them up whole and put them in a large pot with a little water to prevent scorching and add the onions, garlic, sweet peppers, celery seed, salt and cayenne pepper, cooking them over medium-low heat until they are mushy. While you are waiting on that, put the black pepper, allspice, mustard seed and cinnamon in a spice bag. Bring the three cups of vinegar to a simmer in a smaller pot, put the spice bag in the vinegar, and allow that to simmer for 20–30 minutes. Remove the spice bag and turn off the heat on that burner.

Once the tomatoes and other ingredients in the pot are mushy, carefully process them through a hand-cranked strainer. Clean out the pot, dry it, and then put the liquid that results from the straining back into the pot. Add the vinegar and sugar. Bring to a simmer for 30 minutes.

After this, you need to either simmer this while stirring for about 12 hours to get rid of the liquid, or put it in a large crock pot. I recommend the crock pot. Once the ketchup has simmered for about 12 hours and become thicker, fill sterilized pint jars leaving 1/4 inch of head space and process in a boiling water canner for 30 minutes.

Allow this to set for a couple of weeks before use for full flavor to develop. You'll be amazed at how good this is!

A strainer comes in handy for making large batches of sauce and ketchup for canning.

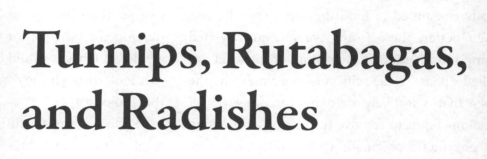

39

Turnips, Rutabagas, and Radishes

Some variants of turnips, rutabagas and radishes have been cultivated for hundreds and even thousands of years for good reason: they are versatile, nutritious and delicious! Both the roots and leaves of all three are edible, and can be cooked in a variety of ways. All three roots are high in vitamin C, folate, thiamine, niacin, and a number of essential minerals including potassium and copper. Their omega-3 to omega-6 fat ratio is 3:1 and they are a substantial source of cardio-protective dietary fiber.

But the good news continues into the leaves of these staple crops. The greens are strongly anti-inflammatory, and a single serving contains 350 percent of the RDA of vitamin A along with a whopping 1,050 percent of the RDA of vitamin K, a quarter of the days supply of vitamin E and calcium and valuable quantities of folate, copper, manganese and more. In essence, just like their closely related cousins broccoli and cabbage, turnips, rutabagas and radishes are a superfood.

Turnips were a staple crop for settling the American West because they keep well in root cellars while supplying vital vitamin C throughout the harsh winters. Turnips, and turnip greens in particular, tend to be more appreciated in the American South than in the rest of the country, but its taste and nutritional properties argue in favor of a place in the garden.

Eaten raw, a small slice of turnip, rutabaga or radish will share a characteristic pungency from the allyl isothiocyanate created by damage to the cells. These isothiocyanate compounds are a defense mechanism to keep herbivores from eating the plants, but in the small quantities normally consumed in food they are perfectly safe. Even better, these isothiocyanates and related compounds induce the production of what are called "phase 2 detoxification enzymes" in the liver that selectively detoxify carcinogens.[16] [17] Cooking tends to remove the bite by eliminating an enzymatic precursor to isothiocyanate formation, but studies indicate that this doesn't adversely affect the formation of detoxification enzymes.[18]

All of this means that turnips, rutabagas and radishes are potent cancer preventatives, and if your turnips have a sharp taste when raw, that just means they are good for you.

Variety Selection

Your local agricultural store likely only carries two varieties of turnip at most: Purple Top White Globe and Golden Ball. But if you look in the catalogs of heirloom seed companies, you'll find at least a dozen varieties from which to choose. As there are no particular diseases for which resistant varieties exist, your primary selection criteria is your own interests and tastes.

This same applies to rutabagas. At the agricultural store you'll be lucky to find even one variety, but you'll find at least half a dozen varieties in heirloom seed catalogs. Rutabagas are sweeter than turnips, and if your family hasn't developed a taste yet for this family of root vegetables, rutabagas would be a good place to start. Just look through the catalogs and find a variety that looks tasty.

Radishes are an entirely different proposition! With at least three dozen readily available varieties ranging from white to red to black and ranging in size from the size of your thumb to the size of an apple, you will find a lot of offerings that look nothing at all like the vegetable you associate with the word "radish." Initially, I would recommend trying a very common variety that looks familiar, such as French Breakfast. After that, though, you should branch out to try many different varieties.

Seeds for Purple Top turnips are readily available and they produce reliably.

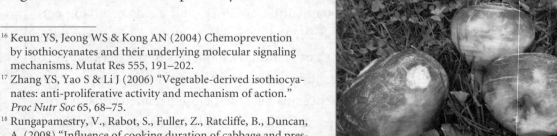

[16] Keum YS, Jeong WS & Kong AN (2004) Chemoprevention by isothiocyanates and their underlying molecular signaling mechanisms. Mutat Res 555, 191–202.

[17] Zhang YS, Yao S & Li J (2006) "Vegetable-derived isothiocyanates: anti-proliferative activity and mechanism of action." *Proc Nutr Soc* 65, 68–75.

[18] Rungapamestry, V., Rabot, S., Fuller, Z., Ratcliffe, B., Duncan, A. (2008) "Influence of cooking duration of cabbage and presence of colonic microbiota on the excretion of N-acetylcysteine conjugates of allyl isothiocyanate and bioactivity of phase 2 enzymes in F344 rats." *British Journal of Nutrition* (2008), 99, 773–781.

Starting and Planting

Turnips, rutabagas and radishes are grown from seed placed directly in the ground. Being brassicas they are somewhat cold-hardy and can be planted anytime the average soil temperature is 50 degrees or higher, but it is best to wait for a soil temperature of 55 for best germination. They will sprout in from one to five days depending on soil temperature. The seeds should be planted 1/2" deep. When planting turnips and rutabagas, the best technique for maximizing harvest is to space at three inches in all directions, and then come back in about forty-five days to harvest every other plant for greens and young roots. Leave the others to grow larger. Radishes can be spaced at two inch intervals though some varieties can grow as large as turnips so you should check the seed packet for the final thinning distance for the particular variety you are planting.

As with all root crops, deeply dug soil free of rocks will encourage the best growth. Plenty of finished compost (at least two cubic feet per thirty-two-square-foot bed) will encourage the proper biological environment. It is important that the compost be finished, however, as turnips, rutabagas and radishes are especially sensitive to the germination inhibitors present in unfinished compost. Maintaining a soil pH between 6 and 7 is optimal for these plants. The soil should have plenty of trace minerals, either from a wide variety of additives of biological origin or supplemented with sea solids. Boron is a key element for proper growth. Boron is contained in borax and constitutes 11.5% of its weight. You need 300-400 milligrams of boron per thirty-two-square-foot bed; 1-1/2 teaspoon of borax will supply just the right amount. (Use a real measuring spoon, don't "eyeball" it.) Borax is toxic to plants in concentrated form, so you should mix it thoroughly with some other powdery additive such as greensand or wood ashes and distribute evenly. The macronutrients should be supplemented as indicated by a soil test.

A higher quality crop with fewer pest problems can be assured by planting for a fall harvest. That is because once temperatures exceed 75 degrees and most certainly when you get 90-degree days, the quality of the roots suffers dramatically. Rutabagas shrink and become stringy, radishes become woody and turnips become just plain unpalatable. Rutabagas and turnips require 60–90 days to reach harvesting size. Even when planting six weeks before last frost in the spring you are in a race against hot weather on the one end while combating root maggots on the other. If, instead, you plant six weeks before your first expected frost, you will get rapid germination, the season for cabbage maggots will be past, and the roots will be maturing during cooler days. You'll appreciate the results.

Radishes mature much more quickly, sometimes in as little as three weeks. So these are a lot easier to plant as a reliable spring crop because you can have them planted and harvested before warm weather.

Weeds, Pests, and Diseases

Because of their rapid germination and prolific growth, if planted in a weed-free bed initially, weeds are unlikely to be an issue. What little weeding is required can be done by hand and will mostly be at the outside edges of the beds where the weeds can get light.

Turnips, rutabagas and radishes have good natural protection from predation and generally do not experience problems of economic importance on the scale of a mini farm so long as crop rotation and sanitation are practiced.

The only economically serious disease that is likely is clubroot, a disease that results in stunted roots unable to draw water so the plants wilt and die. This can be avoided by keeping the soil pH above 6 and preferably 6.5. Once clubroot is in the soil of a bed, you can't grow any cabbage family crops there for eight years, so it pays to do a pH test and adjust the pH if needed so this disease doesn't gain a foothold.

Most pests aren't keen on the peppery taste of these plants, but anything that affects broccoli or cabbage can theoretically come after your turnips if sufficiently hungry. If they do, just treat as described in the chapter on cabbage and broccoli. The only pest I have seen in turnips that poses a substantive threat—and it is completely preventable—is cabbage root maggots. Cabbage root maggots are the larvae of a fly that looks like a slightly smaller and more streamlined version of a housefly. They overwinter as pupae in the soil, and emerge at the time you'd usually plant seeds. Once the plants emerge, they lay eggs at the base of the plant that burrow into the soil and then eat the roots voraciously. With root vegetables you may not even know they have been affected until a very disappointing harvest.

Two factors disproportionately attract this pest. The first is rotting organic matter in the soil such as immature compost. The second is planting when the soil temperature is a little too cold. If you avoid immature compost, plant at an average soil temperature of 55 degrees and make sure you don't plant where cabbage-family crops were grown last year; this pest can be completely prevented by covering your bed with floating row cover once the seeds are planted. Remove the row cover once soil temperatures average 65 degrees and you are home free.

Harvest

You don't want turnips, rutabagas or radishes to wait too long in the ground as they'll get woody and their flavor will suffer. Once soil temperatures are averaging above 75 degrees they need to be harvested even if they are smaller than you'd like. Turnips for "bunching"—to be sold with greens and root together—should be harvested at a diameter of two inches. Those that will be "topped"—meaning that the roots will be sold or used without the greens—should be harvested at a diameter of three inches. If you are like me, you have seen so-called "turnips" in the produce aisle at the grocery store that are a solid five or six inches in diameter. These aren't turnips—they are rutabagas. Rutabagas should be harvested at four inches for optimum quality. The reason they are so large in the supermarket is because they sell on the basis of weight rather than quality.

Radishes can be harvested at practically any stage, so long as you don't let them wait more than a week or so after they have reached the mature size for the variety you are growing. After that, they tend to split and become less tasty.

Saving Seeds

Turnips, rutabagas and radishes are biennials that produce flowers and seed in their second year. Turnips and radishes are outbreeding plants subject to inbreeding depression if too few are grown for seed, and depend upon pollinators such as bees for pollination as they don't usually self-pollinate. Rutabagas are self-fertile and naturally inbreeding, though they will outbreed with the help of bees.

Radishes won't interbreed with other cabbage-family crops with the exception of other radishes. So only grow one variety of radishes for seed in any given year. Grow at least twelve plants for seed.

Turnips will interbreed with other turnips, broccoli rabe and Chinese cabbages. So only grow one variety of turnip (and no Chinese cabbage or broccoli rabe) for seed in a season. You should grow at least six plants for seed, but I would recommend an even dozen.

Rutabagas will interbreed with other rutabagas and with some varieties of turnip that are grown as livestock feed. Rape (a relative of mustard) can also interbreed with rutabagas, as well as Siberian kale. The species classification of rutabagas is a bit confused among various authorities, but they shouldn't interbreed with species of turnips you'll be growing. Again, to maintain genetic diversity, grow at least six plants but preferably a dozen.

Despite these differences, seed saving for all three is the same. In areas with mild winters, you can heavily mulch the roots in the ground to help them survive over the winter. In areas with harsh winters, the roots should be dug, foliage trimmed to two inches, and stored in peat moss at 95 percent humidity and temperatures between 33 and 40 degrees. In the spring, plant them in the ground at their original depth as soon as the soil can be worked.

The bulbs will leaf out and then grow a stalk around three feet tall. This stalk is somewhat delicate and I would recommend staking it. An amazing number of flowers will grow on the stalk and bees will seemingly congregate from miles around to have fun spreading pollen and fertilizing the plants. Harvest the seed pods once they turn brown. As they are fragile, I recommend stripping the pods into a plastic bag. The pods can then be broken up and the seed separated from the chaff through winnowing.

Let the seed set out in an open bowl for a couple of weeks, and then dry over a dessicant for a week before storing in a sealed container for up to five years in a cool, dark place.

Preparation and Preservation

Due to tradition, we think of rutabagas and turnips as something only eaten cooked and radishes as something only eaten raw. The reality is that these are interchangeable. Likewise, we eat turnip greens but neglect radish greens which are just as edible and delicious. Rutabaga greens are likewise edible. The greens, if dry, will keep in a bag in the refrigerator for a week. They can be steam-blanched for four minutes and then chilled in ice water, dried, and frozen in freezer bags from which all air has been excluded. Or they can be dehydrated after blanching and used as an addition to soups, stews, dips and sauces.

The roots store best in peat or sand with the leaves removed at 95 percent humidity and temperatures of 32 to 35 degrees. Summer radishes will keep for a month like this, but turnips, winter radishes and rutabagas will keep for several months this way.

In practice, it is hard to achieve such perfect storage conditions, which is why you will often find turnips and rutabagas in the supermarket to have been waxed. The wax prevents moisture loss for storage in less humid environments, and because the hot wax kills pathogens on the surface, it allows for long-term storage under less perfect conditions. To wax turnips and rutabagas, remove the tops and thoroughly wash and dry them first. (They must be thoroughly dried before immersing in wax or dangerous splatters of wax will occur.) Heat up regular canning wax in a pot on an electric stove or using a double-boiler if you have a gas stove. Using a slotted spoon, dip the vegetable in the wax and make sure it is thoroughly wet with the wax, then set aside on some paper bags for the wax to harden. Don't hold in the wax any longer than necessary to thoroughly coat with wax. Peel the wax and top layer of the vegetable and discard before eating.

Radishes, rutabagas and turnips also freeze well. Cut into uniform 1/2" chunks, water blanch for four minutes or steam blanch for six minutes, cool thoroughly in ice water for another five minutes, pat dry and then seal in freezer bags excluding air. You could also opt to dehydrate them for future use in soups or stews by following the directions of the manufacturer of your dehydrator.

There are a lot of ways to eat turnips and rutabagas. They can be boiled and mashed like potatoes, baked, cooked into stews and more. The greens can be eaten raw in salads, steamed, or boiled in the fashion of collard greens. I like to sauté them with olive oil and garlic.

Oven Roasted Radishes

Ingredients:

1 lb Radishes, cut uniformly in halves or quartered
1 Leek (mild onion can be substituted)
1 Tbsp Toasted sesame seed oil
1 Tbsp Canola oil
2 Tbsp Soy sauce

Procedure:

Preheat oven to 425 degrees. Wash and dry the radishes, and cut into uniform sections so they bake at approximately the same rate. Thoroughly coat the radishes with the toasted sesame seed oil and canola oil by mixing with your hands in a bowl, and pour into a baking dish. Put in the oven and set your timer for 20 minutes. Thinly slice the white portion of the leek, discarding the remainder. When the timer goes off, add the leeks and soy sauce to the radishes and mix thoroughly, then return to the oven for another 7 minutes. You'll never think of radishes as just a salad garnish again!

Oven roasted radishes will have you looking at radishes in a whole new light!

PART III
Tools and Techniques

40

Planting Guides and Seeders

Ah! The joy of planting! Your beds are prepared and ready to accept the seeds that will bring forth an abundant harvest, and the anticipation feels almost electric as you breathe in the smell of soil mingled with the scents of spring. You rush out the door eagerly with packets of seeds in one hand and a map of where everything will go in the other.

About an hour later, after you have painstakingly punched about 200 precisely spaced holes in the soil at two-inch intervals, your back is aching, your knees are dirty and the mosquitoes have come out in force. All you have done is poke holes and you still haven't even planted a seed, but when it comes to that the seeds are so tiny you can barely pick them out of your hand. You know placing the seeds in the holes will take forever.

Intensive agricultural techniques that involve close plant spacings are certainly space efficient, but as you slap another blood sucker off your forearm, you start wondering if it is worth it. The produce aisle at the supermarket is starting to look appealing.

Let's face it—as much as we may enjoy the fruits of our labor, on some days the details of mini-farming are sheer drudgery, and the initial planting of tiny and closely spaced seeds such as mustard and carrot is enough to make you think twice. Whenever I try to handle seeds that small, my fingers feel about six feet thick and as clumsy as an ox. It's frustrating. And how on earth am I supposed to precisely space all of the holes for those seeds? After poking a couple of hundred holes, I want to space them further apart just to make the task end more quickly, and nature doesn't reward shortcuts.

After thinking about these problems a bit, I developed a couple of solutions to making a lot of precisely spaced holes in your seedbed in a hurry, and have some methods for placing these seeds. This will help remove the drudgery and bring back the eager anticipation!

All-Purpose Fixed Planting Guide

Almost all seeds or transplants are spaced at multiples of two or three inches. That is to say plants are spaced at two, three, four, six, eight, nine, twelve or eighteen inches. This means

that with rare exceptions, **spacing** can be accommodated using fixed measurements of two or three inches.

An easy way to accomplish this is to take a piece of board, mark off two-inch intervals, and drill a long deck screw into each mark, leaving about an inch and a half protruding.

This board can be used to level the soil in a bed. It can also be used to tamp down the soil for a firm seed bed. Once the soil is leveled and tamped down, you can use the board to make hundreds of perfectly spaced seed holes in a hurry. To use it, lay it along the flattened soil in your bed, press the heads of the screws into the soil and wiggle it a bit. Now you have evenly spaced holes every two inches. If your seeds are spaced at four inches, just plant in every other hole. If they are spaced at six inches, then skip two holes after each one that is planted and so forth. So this board will work for spacings that are a multiple of two inches.

On the other edge of the board you can mark spacing at three inches, and this will work for spacings of three, six, nine, twelve inches and so forth. Using these two edges you can easily poke hundreds of perfectly spaced holes for seeds or transplants in just a minute.

Even better, the boards can also be used to make evenly spaced furrows for mesclun mix as well as evening out the soil in beds after mixing in soil amendments. After evening out the soil, you can use the flat side of the boards to pack down the soil a bit to make a picture-perfect seed bed prior to using the edge of the board to make the holes.

For this purpose, I would advise using 2"x4" stock between three and four feet long. Anything else will likely be either too fragile or too unwieldy. Once you have made the board, if you paint it with an exterior latex paint to protect it from the elements it will last for many years with just a touch-up of paint now and then.

Adjustable Planting Guide

The adjustable planting guide is the Rolls Royce approach to this problem. It is more flexible but can easily cost as much as $50, plus is more difficult to make. Nevertheless, I made one and I have to admit is works really well and that the larger head leaves a better hole for seeds. The materials that I have used in this case are just one way of accomplishing this task. Once you see how it works, you can do the same thing using other materials.

Materials:

1   6' length of 1/2" aluminum "U" channel
24   5/16" 18 thread bolts, stainless
48   5/16" 18 thread nuts, stainless

Tools:

Hack saw
Drill or drill press
21/64 drill bit
Combination square
Measuring tape
Metal scribe or sharp nail
Nail
Hammer

Procedure:

Cut the aluminum U channel to a 4' length, saving the 2' piece for other projects.

Mark a center line along the exact center of the length of the channel using the combination square and a metal scribe or a fine-point magic marker. Using the measuring tape, use the scribe to mark one inch intervals along the center line. Use the hammer and a nail to make a slight indentation at each intersection between the one inch interval and center line.

Drill a 21/64 inch hole using the drill or drill press at each indentation.

To use the adjustable planting guide, put a nut onto the bolt, leaving an inch of the thread protruding.

Put another nut into the U channel above the hole into which the bolt will be inserted. (The U channel fits the nut perfectly so no wrenches are needed.)

Screw the bolt into the nut through the hole in the U channel. Do this for whatever distance is needed. Adjust the bolts and nuts for proper depth and a snug fit.

To use the planting guide, place the properly spaced bolt heads on leveled earth and press to leave an indentation of the required depth. Then, lift and place the guide a suitable distance from the first row and repeat until done.

Putting Seeds in the Holes

Larger seeds, such as beans, peas, corn and so forth are easily handled and placed in the holes. But smaller seeds such as carrots, onions and lettuce can be challenging. It can be frustrating trying to pick up those seeds and place them in the beds one at a time. Usually, I use my daughter

with her small fingers for such chores, but when she isn't around other options are required.

Some seed producers have come up with pelletized seed to help with this. Carrot and lettuce seeds are surrounded by a coating that makes it easy to handle by hand or in automated seeders. The coating dissolves once the seeds are watered. This is a pretty good solution but so far it has unfortunately only been applied to a few vegetables. Luckily, there are some other solutions, though they all require some practice to master.

Seed spoons are tiny spoons formed in bright yellow plastic. You hold the seed in the cup of your hand, and use the other hand to manipulate the spoon. If you pick the right size (it comes with four sizes), every time you push the spoon into the mass of seeds in your hand, you will pull it back out with exactly one seed. Then you can easily put it where you wish. These cost less than a packet of seeds and work well.

Another option is a "Dial Seed Sower." This device holds seeds in a reservoir and you regulate the rate at which seeds leave the reservoir to slide down a slick slide by changing the seed size on the dial and lightly shaking the device. Once you get practiced at it, you can put exactly one seed of practically any size exactly where you want it.

Yet another option is a plunger-style hand seeder called the Mini-SeedMaster that looks like an oversized syringe. This takes a limited amount of seed into its canal at any given point in time and when held at a 45 degree angle it delivers seed from the reservoir to the soil with a depression of the plunger. I have found this works well with seeds like spinach and turnips, but not as well with the even smaller seeds such as carrot. Still, it allows planting a lot of chard in a hurry.

All of the foregoing devices are inexpensive in that they cost $10 or less. Considering that developing a bit of skill with them would easily repay their cost in time, they are a decent investment. At nearly $25, a vacuum hand seeder is a bit more expensive. This device uses a vacuum bulb with tips sized for the seeds you are planting. It allows you to pick up one seed at a time and deposit the seed where you'd like it. It requires a bit of manual dexterity, but once you get the hang of it you'll start using it for seeding your indoor transplants as well. It's a real time-saver.

41

Heated Water Platform

Here is the problem: you live in a climate where water freezes outside in the winter. Because your chickens don't appreciate trying to drink ice, you get a heated base and a metal waterer to set on top of it. But then you discover two problems: the base and waterer are too close to the ground so the chickens are slinging water everywhere, and the floor of the coop isn't level so when you put the waterer on the base, the water leaks out all over the floor and bedding material instead of being consumed as needed.

To solve this problem, here is a platform that you set the heated base upon, and then the waterer on top of that. The platform has adjustable legs so that it can be made level on any floor; the height can also be adjusted so that the chickens can still drink, but with minimal waste.

Materials:

1   1/2" plywood cut 17"x17"
2   1"x2" stock cut 17" long
2   1"x2" stock cut 15-1/2" long

4   2"x2" stock cut 5" long

20   1-1/2" deck screws

4   3/8" nuts

4   3/8" bolts 4" long

Epoxy

Outdoor latex paint and brush

Tools:

Carpenter or other saw for cutting wood

Drill or drill press (preferred)

1/8" drill bit

3/8" drill bit

9/16" spade bit

Driver for the deck screws

Combination square

Measuring tape

Procedure:

Cut the lumber to the specified dimensions.

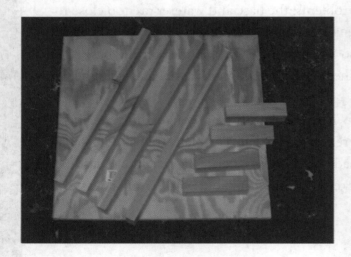

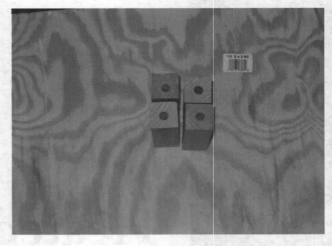

Drill 3/8" holes 3" deep in the center if the four 2"x2" pieces.

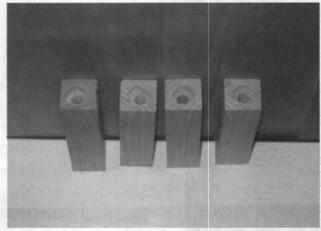

For each of the four 2"x2" pieces, use the spade bit to drill a flat 9/16" hole 1/2" deep centered on the previously drilled 3/8" hole.

Assemble the frame using the 1"x2" pieces as shown. Use one deck screw on each corner, pre-drilling each hole with the 1/8" drill bit to prevent splitting. The final dimensions of the frame should be 17"x17".

Attach the cut plywood to the frame using one deck screw centered along each side.

the nuts to the legs, taking care to avoid applying the epoxy to the bolts.

Attach the four 2"x2" legs by pre-drilling and using one deck screw. Attach to the 1"x2"x17" piece as shown.

Screw the bolts halfway through the nuts and set into the legs. Carefully apply epoxy to hold

Once the epoxy is dry, paint all surfaces of the platform. Once the paint is dry, center the heater and screw four screws into the top as shown to keep the chickens from pushing the heater off the platform.

42

Easy Trellising

Maximizing your productivity per unit area depends on making the best possible use of the space available. For many crops, including pole beans, indeterminate tomatoes, cucumbers, peas and vining squash, this means using a trellis. The problem with trellising on a mini-farm is that because of crop rotation, you might need a trellis for a particular bed one year but not for the next three. Because of this, portability and easy setup/take-down are important factors.

In Chapter 3, I discussed using electrical conduit cut into designated lengths for this task. And that certainly works well, except that the conduit can be difficult to cut, tends to rust where it contacts the ground, and requires a screwdriver for assembly. That system is good and if you are already using it, that's great! If you aren't already using electrical conduit, or just need to expand your trellising, you might consider the PVC pipe method I describe here.

PVC pipe is UV-stabilized so it handles the elements well. It doesn't rust, and the pipe fits tightly into the fittings without need for tools. Assembly and disassembly are as easy as using Tinker Toys™, only the parts are larger. In comparing PVC pipe to galvanized electrical conduit, the conduit bears weight better but the PVC is considerably less expensive. Comparing the two, even though PVC pipe would need support in more places, it is still less expensive.

To start with this system, buy ten pieces of 10'-long 3/4" schedule 40 PVC pipe. The first six pieces are cut into two pieces, one six feet long and the other four feet long. This gives you twelve uprights total: six that are six feet tall and six that are four feet tall. The remaining four pieces of pipe are each cut into two pieces 46-3/4" long and one piece 22-3/4" long. This will give you eight long cross-pieces and four short cross-pieces. You will also need a collection of fittings. You will need elbows for connecting the cross-pieces to the uprights at the ends of the bed, tees for connecting cross-pieces together and allowing for additional supports and side outlet elbows for running trellises around corners. You can get started with six of each. You can expand this system as needed by getting more PVC pipe

and fittings, and cutting the PVC to the specified lengths.

Just as with the system based on electrical conduit, the pipe slides down over 18" pieces of re-bar you have hammered straight into the ground at the ends of the bed and at four-foot intervals.

Four-foot intervals are required for most plants because PVC isn't as strong as electrical conduit. But if you decide to grow something extremely heavy, you can use the shorter cross-pieces and put more vertical supports using tees.

Place deck screws along the trellised side of the bed spaced every six or twelve inches as needed, and use these to anchor string or wire running between the bed and the cross-piece.

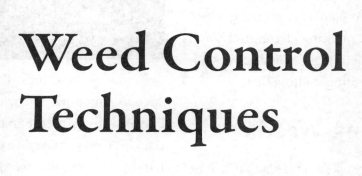

43

Weed Control Techniques

In general, weed control is easy using the methods I spelled out in *Mini Farming* because the beds are always growing something useful. During the growing season you have crops growing so densely as to shade weeds and off-season cover crops crowd them out. So theoretically weeds just have no chance.

But theory runs smack into reality when time constraints prevent planting a cover crop, weeds grow unnoticed along the edge of a bed then go to seed, or weeds manage to find sufficient light despite dense plantings. Another source of weeds is from the surrounding yard grass growing into your beds, and if you established your beds on previous grass, some of that may eventually grow through as well creating a weed problem.

Then again is the problem of self-seeding that is common with mustards and tomatoes that are allowed to go to seed. They can create dense stands of thousands of little plants in a bed that will be growing something else the next season.

Once upon a time I created a serious weed nightmare for myself by throwing some free fresh horse manure on one of my beds. I didn't realize how many weed seeds were in fresh horse manure that hadn't been composted; it took three seasons to finally get the resulting weeds in that bed under control. Now manures get composted before going on my beds!

So it's just a matter of time before you start having to deal with weeds. Sooner or later you will look at a bed in the spring with dismay realizing thousands of unwanted plants are growing where you intend to plant something else entirely, and I want to share some strategies for dealing with that problem or preventing it altogether.

Pre-Sprouting Weeds

This technique is very useful in beds that will be used for crops such as tomatoes or squash that are very susceptible to frost. The idea is to prepare the bed in early spring with any soil amendments or tilling that might be needed, and then just let it sit while all the weed seeds sprout. You can accelerate the sprouting of weeds by putting some clear plastic over the bed to trap heat for a week or so. Once they have sprouted, they can be pulled by hand or eliminated with either a hoe or a cultivator.

Use of a Stirrup Hoe

Stirrup hoes come in a number of configurations, but the one I use is shown here. Stirrup hoes are designed to travel just barely under the surface of the soil, anywhere from a quarter to half an inch, so they will sever weeds with their cutting edge as the hoe is drawn toward you. As you push the hoe away from you, it rides on top of the soil. This way, it gets weeds but doesn't disturb more deeply rooted plants that aren't

desired. In plantings that aren't very dense, such as tomatoes or corn, you can easily fit this between the desired plants with a bit of care. My daughter was amazed that using just this simple hand tool I was able to completely weed a bed in under a minute. Once you get the feel for a stirrup hoe, it is an exceptionally efficient device for controlling weeds.

The Manual Rotary Cultivator

The manual rotary cultivator is useful for controlling young weeds less than two inches high. It uses a series of interlocking rotating tines to grab the roots of weeds and pull them out. They

can be made as narrow as two inches for getting into tight places. In addition, they can be used to incorporate amendments into the soil to a depth of one and a half inches. If you put some elbow grease into it, it will go even deeper.

This device is moved back and forth across the area to be weeded with slight downward pressure. If the tines stop moving, it is because either a long root has become entangled or a stone has jammed the mechanism. Remove the obstruction and continue. Though this isn't quite as fast as a stirrup hoe, it is more flexible for tight spaces and works extremely well.

The Flame Weeder

These come in a number of styles from a couple of different manufacturers. I have a simple unit that accepts a standard propane tank, but there are larger models that require you to drag around a large cannister of fuel. For a mini farm something that size is overkill.

Flame weeding is very prevalent in organic agriculture for the obvious reason that it kills weeds without the use of poisonous chemicals. It also has the advantage of leaving the soil undisturbed. Often what happens with manual

methods of weed control such as hand-weeding, using a hoe or a cultivator is that more seeds are brought into a zone where they will sprout. Flame weeding leaves the soil untouched.

Even better, flame weeding can prevent weeds from sprouting by killing weed seeds in the top quarter inch of soil. This is very useful when preparing a bed for crops that are very susceptible to weeds like carrots or onions.

A flame weeder is like a giant propane torch. In daylight, the flame is invisible so exercise extreme caution. This device is a propane torch on steroids and it can cause severe injuries in addition to starting fires. Also, because the heat can be deceptive, do not use this in a bed containing live crops or you'll have a lot of unexpected dead crops the next day.

In spite of the fact it is called a flame weeder, you do not use this to incinerate weeds. All you do is aim at the weed from the distance specified by the manufacturer until the weed starts to wilt. That's all. That wilting is caused by the bursting of the internal cells of the plant and it's effectively dead. I have found that a lateral movement of about one foot per second allows sufficient time with my particular flame weeder, but you should follow the directions that come with your unit over mine.

Even with no weeds visible in a bed, you can use the flame weeder to sterilize the top bit of soil and delay weeds so delicate plants can get a head

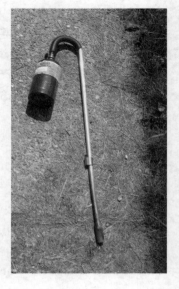

start. I go over the soil in the bed slowly from about a foot away until all of the soil has been covered.

Chickens Wreak Havoc on Weeds

They also wreak havoc on crops, so don't let them run loose in your garden at random or you'll have the most expensive eggs in town! But on a controlled basis, turning chickens loose in beds that need some weeding prior to the start of the season is a real winner. Chickens turn anyplace they run into a desolate moonscape devoid of living matter in no time flat, and they'll do the same for your beds. This sort of free labor helps them earn their keep, especially if you have a grouchy rooster like I have who is the terror of the county.

Solarization

Though not practical for large-scale operations, solarization is perfectly suited for mini-farming because it applies very easily to raised beds. The technique is straightforward. Weed the bed as well as you can, even out the soil, and then water it thoroughly with the equivalent of an inch or more of rain. Then put clear plastic over the bed, making as close contact as possible between the plastic and the soil. As the sun shines in through the plastic, the heat will be trapped in the soil of the bed, raising temperatures as high as 160 degrees. Temperatures this high will not only kill most weed seeds, but a great many pathogens as well.

If you leave the plastic in place for a couple of months, the top couple of inches of soil will be effectively sterilized. This is good in that it will kill pathogens and weed seeds, but bad in that beneficial organisms will be harmed as well. But because soil is a good insulator, organisms more than a couple of inches below the soil will survive just fine. If your bed has received generous compost all along, once the plastic comes off just a light tilling with a three-tined cultivator will be sufficient to bring the soil back to life.

PART IV
Making Wine

Markham Farm Private Reserve
283 Turnpike Road
New Ipswich, NH 03071

Apple Wine

- 2007 -

50/50
Cyser
mix

44

Overview of Winemaking

Anyone who has seen a wine critic on television can be a bit intimidated by the prospect of trying to make a wine that is even drinkable, much less enjoyable. Fortunately, Frederic Brochet conducted two studies using 57 wine experts at the University of Bordeaux in 2001 that will forever put the wine experts into perspective.[1]

In the first study, the experts were given two glasses of wine to describe, one being a white wine and the other a red wine. Unknown to the experts, both glasses were a white wine but the wine in one of the glasses had been dyed red. Not even one of the 57 experts at the University of Bordeaux could distinguish that the red wine was really white, and they even went on to describe the fake red wine as having characteristics associated with red wines such as "tannic notes."

In the second study, a cheap wine was put into bottles denoting both a cheap and an expensive wine. Same wine, different bottles. The experts described the wine in the expensive bottles as "woody,

---

[1] Downey, R. (2002), Wine Snob Scandal, *Seattle Weekly*, Feb. 20, 2002

complex, and round" while describing the exact same wine in the cheap bottles as "short, light, and faulty."

What this means is that you need not be intimidated by wine snobbery. All you need to do is make a sound product using good ingredients and proper methods, and as long as you put it in a nice bottle with a nice label and serve it in a nice glass it will be fully appreciated. Perception of the details really matters in the impression, so even if you performed your primary fermentation in a plastic bucket, don't you dare serve it in a plastic cup!

Winemaking is among the oldest methods of food preservation. In wine the levels of sugar in the original juice are reduced to make the juice unattractive to organisms that require sugar for growth, and the sugar is replaced with alcohol that makes the juice an inhospitable environment for most spoilage organisms. Meanwhile, many of the beneficial nutrients in the original juice are preserved, including vitamins and antioxidants. The yeast used to convert the sugar to alcohol also imparts a number of B vitamins to the mix.

Later, wine became an end in itself for which fruits were grown, and an entire culture and mythology have grown up around grapes, winemaking, and wine. What started as a method of preserving the essential nutrients of grapes and compensating for dangerous water supplies in an era when aseptic packaging and refrigeration did not exist has now grown into a multi-billion dollar global industry, and there are bottles of wine that can only be had for a cost exceeding that of a new car.

The term wine, in the purest sense of the term, applies only to the results of fermenting the juice of European vitis vinifera grapes. These are a species that is distinct from the grapes indigenous to North America, and only vitis vinifera grapes—and no other grape or fruit—have the right levels of sugar, tannin, acidity, and nutrients to produce wine without adding anything. Grapes grown in particular regions lend their unique flavors to wines named after them, such as Champagne; and wines produced by some wineries have even become status symbols, such as those produced by Château Lafite Rothschild.

Here, however, I am using the term "wine" to refer to country wines. That is, wines made from any fruit available and to which sugars, tannins, organic acids, spices, and other ingredients have been added to not only compensate for the areas in which the ingredients fall short of vitis vinifera grapes, but also to create their own experience of taste and smell.

Country wines are in no way inferior, and in fact being free of the constraints of traditional winemaking leaves you open to experiment broadly and create delightfully unique wines that are forever beyond the reach of traditional wineries. Home winemaking of up to 200 gallons annually is legal in the United States so long as you don't try to sell it. (If you try to sell it you will run afoul of the infamous "revenuers" who always get their culprit in the end.)

Americans drink nearly two gallons of wine per capita annually, meaning the consumption for a standard household is just shy of eight gallons. That's 40 bottles of wine. If you figure $12/bottle, that's nearly $500 per year. At that rate, and using fruit you either get inexpensively in season or free in your back yard, you will quickly recoup your investment in materials and supplies. In addition, homemade wines make excellent personal gifts; every year I give bottles to friends and business associates for holiday presents. The wine is always appreciated.

The technique of making wine is conceptually straightforward. The juice (and sometimes solids) of a fruit are purified of stray microbes and supplemented with sugar, acid, and other nutrients to make a must, inoculated with an appropriate strain of yeast, and fermented. The fermentation takes place in two distinct phases. The first phase, known as the primary fermentation, is very fast and lasts only a couple of weeks. The wine is then siphoned (a process called racking) into a new vessel and fitted with an airlock where it may continue its secondary fermentation for several months with a racking again after the first couple of months or any time substantial sediment has formed.

I'll explain the specifics of the equipment throughout this chapter, along with some of the nuances. For now, I want to convey that if you normally consume wine or would give wine as a gift, making your own quality wines is inexpensive, fun, and easier than most would believe.

There are places where you will be tempted to skimp or make do on the list of ingredients and equipment I am about to present, but let me encourage you to get everything on the list. Because the techniques I describe rely on natural ingredients whose constituents will vary, all of the testing equipment is necessary. The other equipment and ingredients are necessary to maintain sanitary conditions or make a quality wine. If you don't live near a store for wine hobbyists, there are a number of excellent sources on the Internet that can be located via a web search. To save on shipping, I'd recommend getting as much from one store as possible.

Winemaking Equipment
Primary Fermenter

The primary fermenter is a large plastic bucket made of food-grade plastic. It is sized at least 20% larger than the largest batch of wine you plan to make in order to keep the constituents of the vigorous primary fermentation from spilling out of the fermenter and making a mess you will not soon forget. The bucket should be equipped with a lid and gasket, and also have provisions for fitting an airlock. These are available in various sizes from beer and wine hobby suppliers. I'd recommend a two-gallon and a six-gallon bucket. Even though it is possible to get these buckets for free from restaurants, I would advise against it as most were used to hold something that was previously pickled using vinegar. You don't want vinegar organisms in your wine.

In general, the primary fermentation evolves carbon dioxide so rapidly that an airlock isn't strictly necessary. Furthermore, the first stages of fermentation require oxygen until the yeast cells multiply enough to reach a critical mass before the start of fermentation. Just plugging the hole in the lid with a clean cotton ball that allows air movement but blocks dirt, dust, and insects will suffice. (Replace the cotton ball if it becomes saturated with must.) Even so, I usually use an airlock after the first week.

It is possible for the smells and tastes of plastic to become infused into wine. This is not a concern for the primary fermentation because the wine is only in contact with the container for a couple of weeks. Also, you will have used a container of food grade plastic selected for its low diffusion which you cleaned thoroughly prior to use.

⊗ One- and five-gallon primary and secondary fermenters.

Secondary Fermenter

Because the wine stays in contact with the secondary fermenter for months or even years, this is best made of glass. You can also use specially made oak casks for long secondary fermentation, but these are very expensive and need special care and maintenance. So for now, I would skip the oak casks.

The glass vessels come in various sizes from one gallon up to five gallons. The smaller one-gallon vessels are just one-gallon jugs, and the larger three- or five-gallon vessels are glass carboys used on water coolers.

You will also see some plastic carboys available in winemaking magazines and from various suppliers. These are advertised as being made in a way that makes them impervious to the diffusion of the plastic into the wine, and they offer the advantage of being much lighter than glass so the shipping costs are lower. Nevertheless, plastic is harder to clean than glass, so I would not recommend these if glass can be obtained instead.

You will also need to get a special brush for cleaning your jug or carboy because the opening is too small for even the smallest hands and a regular bottle brush is too short and isn't bent for cleaning around the edges.

The fermentation that takes place in the secondary fermenter is long and slow. As the carbon dioxide is evolved more slowly, it is possible for air to be drawn into the vessel, especially if temperatures change. During secondary fermentation, you want to prevent oxygen from coming into contact with the wine, because oxygen adversely affects the quality of the wine by changing the character of some of the evolved organic compounds.

By fitting the hole in the fermenter with a stopper and an airlock, you will allow a protective blanket of carbon dioxide to cover the surface of your wine. You will need rubber stoppers with one hole in them that are sized correctly for your secondary fermenter. The airlock is prepared, put into the hole in the stopper, and then the stopper is placed in the hole at the top of the fermenter.

Because you will be racking your wine from one secondary fermenter into another, you need two secondary fermentation vessels.

One thing that people often overlook is a carrying handle. If you are making wine in batches larger than a gallon, those carboys are extremely heavy and difficult to handle. The handle that you order can be installed on a carboy and then removed to be used on another, so you only need one. They cost about $10 at the time of this writing and are well worth it as they make the task of handling carboys a great deal easier.

Airlocks

Airlocks are devices installed on a fermenter that allow gas to escape, but do not allow air to leak back in. They come in a variety of configurations, but all are filled with water or a solution of potassium metabisulfite. The airlock is filled to the level specified on the device, inserted in a one-hole rubber stopper and then attached to the fermenter. You should have at least two of these. The style you choose doesn't usually matter, but

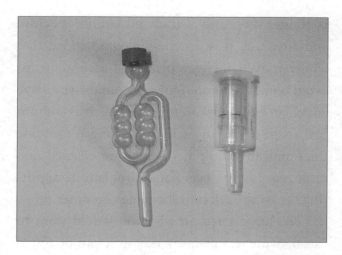

Two popular airlock styles. The one on the right is better if your wine is likely to experience swings of temperature.

components. Otherwise, it will accumulate debris attractive to fruit flies that carry vinegar bacteria and you will unwittingly start manufacturing vinegar instead of wine. The tubing is inexpensive and it is best to replace it after several uses.

if your wine will experience swings in temperature, avoid the type illustrated on the left because the liquid in it could be sucked back into the fermenter.

Racking Tube

A racking tube is a long two-part tube that is inserted into the wine and pumped to start a siphoning action in order to transfer the wine from one container into another. It has a knob at the bottom that directs the flow of fluid in such a way as to minimize the amount of sediment transferred in the process. You will also need five feet of plastic tubing to go with it. A stop-cock, which is a plastic clip that can be used to stop the flow temporarily, will come in handy when using the racking tube to transfer wine into final wine bottles for corking.

Racking tubes come in two sizes; one that is smaller and will fit into a gallon jug and one that is larger and will not. Get the smaller one initially as it will work for both gallon jugs and five-gallon carboys.

Always clean your racking tube and plastic tubing before and after use, and run a gallon of sulphite solution through it to sterilize the

Corker

Corkers are used to insert corks into wine bottles. As you've discovered if you have ever tried to put a cork back into a wine bottle, corks are slightly larger than the holes they are intended to fit. A corker compresses the cork enough for it to slip inside the bottle. Corkers come in many sizes and styles, but I would recommend a metal two-armed lever model which, although somewhat more expensive than the plastic models, does a better job and will serve you well for your lifetime.

Corks need to be soaked before insertion. You don't want to inadvertently transfer a spoilage organism on the corks, so I recommend boiling

Vinyl tubing and racking tubes sized for five-and one-gallon fermenters.

☯ I've had the corker on the left for eight years. The one on the right is just a toy.

the corks for 20 minutes and then allowing them to set in the boiled water for another 10 minutes before corking. This will make the corks pliable without contaminating them.

Another problem you may encounter is the cork backing out of the bottle after it was inserted. This is caused by the fact that the cork fits so tightly that the air in the bottle is compressed as it is inserted. The compressed air forces the cork back out of the bottle. You can solve this problem with a bent sterilized paper clip. Straighten the paper clip except for a hook that you leave for it to hang on the edge of the bottle's mouth. Insert the straight part into the bottle mouth and leave it hooked in the edge. Insert the cork as usual. The paper clip has allowed room for compressed gases to escape. Pull the paper clip out and you are done.

Wine Thief

A wine thief is a long tube with a special valve on the end that allows you to remove wine from a container very easily. Clean and sanitize it before and after use. It is generally recommended that wine removed not be returned to the container to avoid contamination. However, unless you have added an adulterant to the wine (such as sodium hydroxide for testing acidity), as long as the wine thief and any equipment used are cleaned and sanitized, I have never had a problem from putting the wine back into the same container.

The biggest reason why you would want to "steal" wine in this fashion is so it can be tested for specific gravity and acidity. I cover these tests and the required equipment extensively in the next chapters.

Nylon Straining Bags

These are fine-meshed nylon bags with zippered closures used to hold fruit for crushing in a fashion that allows you to remove the solids later with minimal mess. The bags can be cleaned, sterilized, and re-used many times. These come in very handy when making wines from crushed blueberries, cherries, and similar fruits. They come in various sizes in order to accommodate different sized batches of fruits and wine.

Wine Bottles

You will need wine bottles. Usually, light-colored wines are bottled in clear bottles and dark-colored wine in green or brown bottles. This is predominantly a social convention, though the darker glass serves the purpose of protecting the coloring matter in the wine from being bleached out by ultraviolet light and sunshine. Your wine should be stored well away from sunshine anyway.

Either way, you will certainly want to use real wine bottles that require a cork. Real wine bottles usually have a concave section at the bottom that allows for solid sediments to remain separate from the wine and have a top made to facilitate a perfect seal with a cork.

There is debate among experts over the use of plastic, screw-top caps, or genuine cork, and whether this has an effect on the long-term taste and quality of wine. In my opinion corks are best simply because they are easiest. Corks are inexpensive in quantity, easily inserted for a perfect seal using simple equipment, and will literally last forever if a bottle is stored on its side to keep it wet. Unlike the experts, I can't tell the difference between a wine stored in a corked bottle as opposed to one using a screw closure, but I recommend corking because it is easier and cheaper in the long run. Also, it just looks better, and the presentation of your wine is as important as any of its other qualities in terms of the reception it receives.

If you decide to make a sparkling wine, you will need to get bottles specifically for that purpose because ordinary wine bottles aren't rated for that pressure. You will also need special plastic corks and wire closures that will hold the corks in place on the bottle.

Wine bottles come in 375 ml and 750 ml sizes. You will need five of the 750 ml bottles or ten of the 375 ml bottles for each gallon of wine that you are bottling.

Consolidated Equipment List

The following list will make it easy to get everything you will need for the foreseeable future in one shopping trip. I priced this out with a well-known Internet beer and wine shop for $228.60 plus $63.22 for shipping by shop for for shipping, if you can find the gear lot price worth the trip. You could also save some mon by only getting the equipment needed to make one-gallon batches, and the equipment would only cost $134.75 plus $25.95 for shipping. These costs also don't take into account that it is often easy to get wine bottles for free. I get mine from a co-worker who works part-time at a bar. He brings me a few dozen empty bottles and I give him a couple bottles of wine yearly.

1	Five or six gallon plastic fermenter with sealing plastic lid and grommet
1	Two gallon plastic fermenter with sealing plastic lid and grommet
2	Five gallon secondary fermenters, preferably glass
2	One gallon secondary fermenters, glass jugs
1	Cleaning brush for carboys

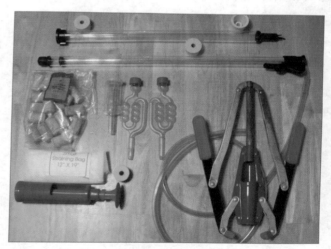

⊗ Airlocks, wine thief, racking tube, stoppers, corkers and other gear. These will give many years of faithful service if given proper care.

1	Carb... universal rubber stoppers with ...e hole
2	One-gallon secondary fermenters, glass
2	#6 rubber stoppers with one hole
4	Airlocks
1	Racking tube, sized to fit the one-gallon secondary fermenters, but will work with both
5 ft	Plastic tubing
1	Hose clamp
1	Wine thief
2	Nylon straining bags
1	Two-handed corker
36	Wine bottles
50	Corks

In addition to equipment, making country wines requires a variety of innocuous but nevertheless important additives. All fruits other than European grapes will require additional sugar in the form of either sugar or honey. Most fruits will lack sufficient acid, though without dilution a few may have too much. Likewise, most won't have sufficient tannin to give a properly wine-like mouth-feel. Of course, yeast will need to be added, and the fruits don't have enough nutrients on their own to sustain a healthy fermentation to completion, so nutrients will need to be added for the yeast.

Citric, Malic, and Tartaric Acids

Though most fruits contain more than one of these acids, citric acid is usually associated with citrus fruits, malic acid with apples, and tartaric acid with grapes. You can buy these mixed together as a so-called "acid blend," but they are inexpensive and I recommend buying them separately. This way, you can use the right acid for the fruit you are using or the character you want your wine to have and you aren't locked in to the formula of a given manufacturer. If you are using a recipe that requires "acid blend" you can make it yourself by thoroughly mixing an equal quantity of each of the three acids together.

The acidity of your must should be checked prior to the beginning of fermentation. Most often, acid will need to be added.

Grape Tannin

Tannins are responsible for the astringent taste of a wine. They are present in the skin and seeds of grapes, and so wines that result from conducting the primary fermentation with the skins and seeds will tend to have more tannin and have more astringency. White wines derived from pressed juice are therefore less astringent than red wines derived from fermenting with the skins.

Ingredients other than grapes can have more or less tannin content, and that content will vary based upon the amount of time whole fruit is left in the primary fermenter as well.

Pectic Enzyme

Pectic enzyme is needed to break down the pectins in fruits so they won't leave a cloudy haze in the wine. Grapes have enough pectic enzyme naturally, but all other fruits you are likely to use will need some help.

Fermentation Inhibitor

It can be difficult to judge when fermentation is completed. Early in winemaking it is also common for the home wine maker to be a bit impatient (and justifiably so!) for the finished product. The unfortunate side effect of bottling a bit too early is a wine bottle with a popped cork (and corresponding mess) or even a shattered bottle. Sometimes you can get lucky and just end up with a barely perceptible sediment and a lightly sparkling wine. In wine judgings, this is considered a defect in a still wine, but for home use it is a delightful thing. Still, if you want to make sparkling wines it is better to make them on purpose rather than accidentally, because their accidental manufacture is attended by some risk.

Potassium sorbate, a semi-synthetic preservative that inhibits fermentation, is added to wines as a stabilizer to prevent further fermentation. It is used in two instances. First, to absolutely guarantee an end of fermentation in wines that are bottled young. Second, to stop fermentation in wines that are intentionally sweet and the only thing inhibiting the yeast is the high alcohol content.

The positive is that potassium sorbate works well, is generally accepted as safe, and will give you good insurance against exploding bottles. It is seldom noticeable at all when used for young wines and white wines. The downside is that it can develop off-smells in some wines over a period of years. So if you are making a wine that you plan to keep for many years, rather than using potassium sorbate I would recommend bulk aging it for at least a year in a secondary fermenter to assure the end of fermentation prior to bottling.

Another method of ending fermentation is to add supplemental alcohol to the wine in the form of brandy (which is distilled from wine). This process is called fortification. Raising the alcohol level in the wine above the alcohol tolerance of the yeast (usually 20%) assures its dormancy. Fortification is used in the manufacture of port wines. Port wines are typically sweet and dark, though some dry and white ports exist. These sweet wines were stabilized for shipping purposes by racking them into a secondary fermenter that already contained enough brandy (about ¼ of the volume of the wine) to raise the alcohol level to 18% to 20%. This brought about a quick end to fermentation while retaining as much as 10% residual sugar. The stability of port wines can allow them to keep for decades.

Yeast Energizer

Yeast energizer supplies crucial nutrients for yeast that allow it to reproduce and do a good job of converting sugar to alcohol. Any wine made from anything but vitis vinifera grapes will need this. Yeast energizer usually contains food grade ammonium phosphate, magnesium sulfate, yeast hulls to supply lipids, and the entire vitamin B complex, of which thiamine (vitamin B_1) is the most important.

Sulfite

Sulfite is used to retard spoilage organisms and wild yeasts and as an antioxidant. Though it is possible to make sulfite-free wine, its use increases the likelihood of success for beginners, particularly when they are using real fruits instead of pasteurized bottled juices. Sulfite is even permitted in wines labeled as USDA Organic.

You should get two forms of sulfite. The first is potassium metabisulfite in the form of Campden tablets. Campden tablets are sized with the idea in mind of accurate dosing of wine and musts to purify must prior to initiating fermentation and help clear and preserve the wine later. The second is powdered potassium metabisulfite. In powdered form it is used to make sterilizing solutions for sterilizing equipment.

Yeast

Home winemaking has been popular so long across so many countries that there are literally hundreds of varieties of yeast available. Because covering them all would be a prodigious task, I want to cover some common yeasts that will be most generally useful for practically anything you'd like to try to turn into wine. Later, you can branch out and try the other excellent varieties of yeast that are available.

Red Star Pasteur Champagne

This is an excellent all-around yeast for making dry wines. It produces glycerol as well as alcohol, and this gives wines a nice mouthfeel. I particularly like using this yeast in wines containing apple, pear, and flower ingredients because it produces fresh aromas that match these ingredients. It works well at lower temperatures, even as low as 55 degrees, and tolerates up to 16% alcohol.

Red Star Montrachet Yeast

If you don't have much control of the ambient temperature of your must, this yeast is a good choice. It can work at temperatures ranging from 55 to 95 (though it does less well at the extremes than it does in the middle of that range), and produces less acetaldehyde than most yeasts. The aromas are nice, and with an alcohol tolerance of 15%, this yeast is well-adapted to making sweet port-style wines. I like using it to make blueberry and cherry wines.

Lalvin D-47

If you'd like to make a dry white wine starting from apples or pears, this is an excellent choice. Its temperature range is narrow—only 58 to 68—but that makes it perfect for fermentations that proceed in the house during the winter when homes are usually maintained precisely in that range. The sediment formed by D-47 is compact, which makes racking easier.

Lalvin ICV-D254

With an alcohol tolerance of 18%, ICV-D254 will ferment any practical must to dryness. This yeast ferments quickly, so you'll want to keep the temperature under 80 degrees to avoid foaming. You might want to keep the temperature even lower to preserve volatile flavor components because ICV-D254 creates a very complex and fruity flavor profile that really enhances the fruit character of a wine. This would be a good choice for blueberry wine.

Wyeast 4632 Dry Mead Yeast

Meads, also known as honey wines, are enjoying a resurgence in popularity. Many yeasts will work to make mead, but this yeast in particular creates flavor notes that have resulted in many award-winning meads. The temperature range is 55 to 75, but you'll want to stay as close to 65 as you can to maximize flavor production. Wyeast 4632 has an alcohol tolerance of 18% and will result in a very dry mead.

Consolidated Ingredient List

The following ingredient list will allow you to make many successful gallons of wine. As your experience expands, you may wish to adopt different materials and techniques; but most home wine makers find that this list is more than sufficient for their needs. In compiling this list, I went to two well-known online retailers of winemaking supplies, and in both cases the total cost was under $40. You can save $7 by omitting the Wyeast #4632 from the list.

4 oz	Citric acid
4 oz	Malic acid
4 oz	Tartaric acid
2 oz	Liquid tannin
½ oz	Pectic enzyme liquid
2 oz	Yeast energizer
1 oz	Potassium sorbate
100	Campden tablets
4 oz	Powdered potassium metabisulfite
2 pkt	Red Star Pasteur Champagne yeast
2 pkt	Red Star Montrachet yeast
2 pkt	Lalvin D-47 yeast
2 pkt	Lalvin ICV-D254 yeast
1 pkt	Wyeast #4632 Dry Mead yeast

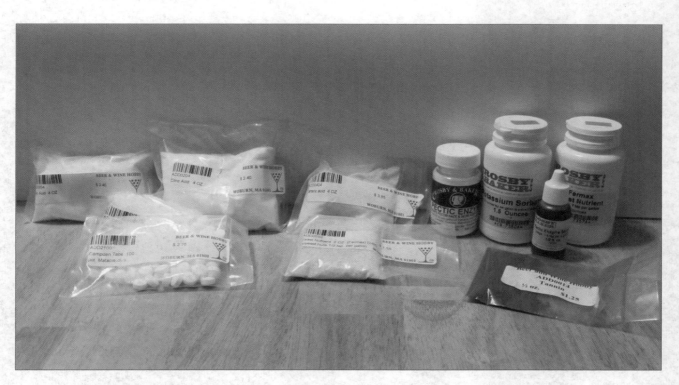

Important additives and adjuncts used for making wine. These are inexpensive and last a long time.

45

The Science of Wine

At its core, the theory of making wine (also beer and bread) is nothing more than the conversion of sugar into ethyl alcohol and carbon dioxide by the enzymes in yeast:

glucose → ethyl alcohol + carbon dioxide + energy

$C_6H_{12}O_6 \rightarrow 2(CH_3CH_2OH) + 2(CO_2) + Energy$

Using the foregoing formula based upon the molecular weights[1] of the compounds, 180 grams of glucose will be converted into 92 grams of ethyl alcohol and 88 grams of carbon dioxide. This means that the yield of alcohol, by weight, in a perfect fermentation is 92/180 or 51%, and that nearly half of the weight of the sugar is lost in the form of carbon dioxide gas.

The density of glucose is 1.54 g/cm³, so the volume occupied by 180 grams of glucose is 180/1.54 or 116.88 cm³. The density of ethyl

---

[1] The molecular weight of a compound is computed by adding the atomic weights from the periodic table of each constituent atom. The atomic weights of carbon, hydrogen and oxygen respectively are 12.0107, 1.00794 and 15.9994. So the molecular weight of glucose would be 6*12.0107 + 12*1.00794 + 6*15.9994. For ease of discussion I have rounded the results to the nearest gram.

alcohol is .789 g/cm^3, and the volume occupied by 92 grams of ethyl alcohol is 92/.789 or 116.6 cm^3.

In other words, even though nearly half of the mass of sugar is lost in the form of carbon dioxide gas, the volume of the solution stays so nearly the same as to be indiscernible without resorting to very precise measurements.

Furthermore, the percentage of alcohol in beverages is not measured by mass, but rather by volume. This means that the volume occupied by alcohol in a completely fermented solution will be nearly identical to the volume of sugar that was in the solution. So if you know how much sugar is in a solution before fermentation starts, you know how much alcohol could be produced in a completed fermentation.

As we discussed a bit in the last chapter, what happens over the process of making wine is a lot more complex than a simple conversion of sugar into alcohol, so I'd like to expand on that some more.

Sugar

Unless you are using vitis vinifera grapes, all of your wine musts will contain less sugar than is needed to make a self-preserving wine. The sugar content of common fruits (other than wine grapes) is insufficient. In order for a wine to be self-preserving without need for pasteurization or the addition of preservatives, it needs an alcohol content of at least 9%. In practice, because you may add water between rackings in order to fill air space, you'll want enough sugar to yield an alcohol content of 10% or higher.

⊗ Using the weight method of determining specific gravity.

Measuring Sugar Levels

Many winemaking books and pamphlets are full of recipes that specify a certain fixed amount of sugar for a given fruit. Such recipes rely upon the false assumption that the sugar content of a given fruit is the same no matter how close to ripeness it was when harvested, how long it has been stored, or even the variety of the fruit in question.

The key to getting the sugar right is using a hydrometer. A hydrometer looks a lot like a thermometer with a big bulb on the end. It measures the amount of dissolved solids in a solution by how far it sinks. There is a long stem and a scale, and the specific gravity is read where the liquid touches the glass. This is important because the surface tension of the liquid will give a false reading anywhere else, so be sure to read the value where the liquid is touching the glass.

I use a wine thief that doubles as a hydrometer jar. So I clean and sanitize the wine thief and hydrometer, and then give the hydrometer a spin as I put it into the liquid. Giving the hydrometer a spin is necessary because otherwise air bubbles could cling to it and give it false buoyancy that would give inaccurate readings.

Once you have your reading, you will need to correct it to compensate for the temperature of the must, because hydrometers are calibrated for 60 degrees. If the temperature is between 40 and 50 degrees, subtract 0.002 from the reading. If the temperature is between 50 and 55 degrees, subtract 0.001. If the temperature is between 65 and 75, add 0.001, and if the temperature is between 75 and 80, add 0.002. If the temperature is over 80, let it cool before measuring.

There is another method that I have never seen mentioned in books on winemaking, but I believe is superior even though it requires the use of math. The method is as follows:

Buy a jug of distilled water at the supermarket. Leave it at room temperature next to your primary fermenter so that it is at the same temperature (by doing this, you won't need to make temperature corrections later). Use a scale accurate to within 0.01 g to weigh an empty and dry 10ml graduated cylinder.[2] Then fill the cylinder with 10 ml of the distilled water and record that weight. Finally, empty the cylinder, and using a large sterilized syringe, fill the graduated cylinder to the 10 ml mark with wine must and

record that weight. When measuring volume, put your eye at a level with the markings on the cylinder and fill until the lowest part of the liquid is perfectly aligned with the 10 ml mark.

We now have three numbers. A is the weight of the empty cylinder, B is the weight of the cylinder filled with distilled water, and C is the weight of the cylinder filled with wine must. The equation for the specific gravity is: SG = (C-A)/(B-A). For example, my graduated cylinder weighs 37.65 g. When filled with distilled water it weighs 47.64 g, and when filled with a light sugar syrup it weights 48.57 g. SG = (48.57-37.65)/(47.64-37.65) or 1.093. Because both the distilled water and the must were weighed at the same temperature, temperature corrections aren't needed. Even better, the amount of must used for testing was truly tiny—less than an ounce. Discard the sample in the sink after testing.

Adjusting Sugar Levels

As I mentioned earlier, in order for a wine to be self-preserving, it should have at least 9% alcohol. The following table gives you the potential alcohol based upon specific gravity, and how much sugar is present in a gallon of must to give you that much alcohol if it is completely fermented by the yeast.

Because water may be added to the wine at some rackings—thereby diluting the alcohol—you should also aim for a starting specific gravity that exceeds 1.080, corresponding to 10.6% alcohol. Also, even though a particular strain of yeast might have a theoretical alcohol tolerance exceeding 20%, such yeasts will not thrive in musts containing enough sugar to make that

[2] I use the American Weigh AWS-100 scale. Complete with calibration weights it costs less than $20. Graduated cylinders are likewise ubiquitously available online for less than $10. Get a glass one rather than plastic. Large syringes are available from livestock stores and online for less than $3. You don't need the needle.

much alcohol. Higher levels of alcohol like that are achieved by fortification or by adding small amounts of sterile sugar syrup as existing sugars in the must are depleted. In order to avoid a fermentation failing due to excessive sugar levels, you should limit the initial specific gravity of your musts to no greater than 1.100, which corresponds to 13.6% alcohol. So, aim for a starting gravity between 1.080 and 1.100. In practice, I use 1.090 for almost all of my wines.

Almost all of your musts made from pressed or juiced fruits will contain insufficient levels of sugar to reach the minimum necessary alcohol content. Even though I am about to cover the math in more depth, the following shortcut equation will work fine:

Ounces of Sugar = (Desired S.G. – Measured S.G) x 360

If you decide to add honey rather than sugar, then multiply the amount of sugar needed by 1.3 to make up for the moisture content of honey. Ideally, you would use a scale for measuring sugar to be added; but if you don't have one, you can use measuring cups and allow for seven ounces of granulated sugar per cup.

For example, if you are making cyser from juiced apples and the measured S.G. of your must is 1.040 but you want a starting S.G. of 1.090, you first determine how much sugar is needed:

(1.090—1.040) x 360 = 18 ounces

Because you will be using honey instead of sugar, you'll multiply that by 1.3 to compensate for the moisture content of the honey: 18 x 1.3 = 23.4 ounces.

Specific Gravity	Potential Alcohol	Ounces Sugar Per Gallon Must
1.000	0.0	0
1.004	0.6	1.4
1.008	1.1	2.8
1.012	1.7	4.3
1.016	2.2	5.7
1.019	2.6	6.8
1.023	3.2	8.2
1.027	3.7	9.6
1.031	4.3	11.0
1.035	4.8	12.4
1.039	5.4	13.9
1.043	5.9	15.3
1.047	6.5	16.7
1.050	6.9	17.8
1.054	7.4	19.2
1.058	8.0	20.6
1.062	8.6	22.0
1.066	9.1	23.5
1.070	9.7	24.9
1.074	10.2	26.3
1.078	10.8	27.7
1.081	11.2	28.8
1.085	11.7	30.2
1.089	12.3	31.6
1.093	12.8	33.1

Specific Gravity Table.

Sometimes, you might want to start with a high-quality bottled juice to make wine. You can tell how much sugar is in the juice just by reading the label, and it usually amounts to anywhere from 30g to 50g per 8 fl. oz. serving. Your first task in that case is to do unit conversion. Let me illustrate with an example.

Fruit	S.G. Range	Fruit	S.G. Range
Apples	1.040—1.060	Blackberries	1.020—1.035
Blueberries	1.045—1.055	Currants	1.042—1.060
Cherries (sweet)	1.045—1.075	Cherries (tart)	1.040—1.070
Cranberries	1.015—1.020	Grapefruit	1.028—1.041
Lemon	1.025—1.050	Peach	1.030—1.040
Pear	1.040—1.045	Pineapple	1.045—1.060
Plum	1.045—1.055	Black Raspberry	1.030—1.050
Strawberry	1.020—1.040	Watermelon	1.030—1.040

Specific Gravity Ranges of Common Fruits.

I might have some 100% black cherry juice that I would like to turn into wine. It has 50g of sugar per eight-ounce glass. How many ounces of sugar does it have per gallon? A gallon is 128 ounces, so there are 16 eight-ounce glasses per gallon. So the total amount of sugar in a gallon of the juice is the amount in 16 eight-ounce glasses, or 16 x 50g = 800g. You convert grams to ounces by dividing by 28.35, so 800 g / 28.35 grams per ounce = 28.2 ounces of sugar per gallon. Looking at our table of specific gravities, we can see it already has plenty of sugar.

I may also have some organic concord grape juice that contains 40g of sugar per eight ounce glass. Doing the same math, (16 glasses x 40g)/28.35 = 22.6 ounces of sugar per gallon. That corresponds to only 8% alcohol, which is too low for a self-preserving wine. I want to bring it up to 12.3%, but to account for the increased volume from adding the sugar, I'll use the sugar quantity corresponding to 12.8% alcohol. So I need to add 33.1–22.6 = 10.5 ounces of sugar.

Sometimes using honey instead of cane sugar can give wine a really nice background flavor. When using honey as a substitute for sugar, just multiply the number of ounces needed by 1.3 to compensate for the honey's water content. Many cookbooks advocate oiling the containers used for handling honey. Do not do this, as you'll end up with a persistent oily layer in your wine. Instead, heat the honey by placing the jar and any handling tools in simmering water. That will make it easier to use without adding oil to your must.

To give you some idea of how much sugar would need to be added to the juices of various fruits, I have included a table listing some fruits and the range of specific gravities I obtained when testing different varieties. Keep in mind that this is just a guideline. Don't substitute use of this table for testing the specific gravity yourself because the particular fruits you use will be of different varieties, grown in other places, and harvested at different times.

Tannins

Tannins are complex polyphenols[3] produced by plants. In foods, they are bitter and astringent, and it is theorized that they serve to deter

---

[3] Phenol is a benzene ring compound with an -OH group on one of the carbons, making it an alcohol. Polyphenols are compounds composed of multiple phenol groups bonded together. The molecular weights of tannins range from 500 to more than 3000.

herbivores, though it is likely that they serve other purposes as well. Chemically, they can be divided into several categories, but they all have in common the characteristic that they are able to bind to proteins and precipitate them out of solutions.

Tannins are more present in the skins, seeds, and woody portions of plants. Hence, when red wine is made by fermenting the seeds and skins of the grapes, tannin is dissolved into the wine. The solubility of tannin is affected by the pH of the solution. Tannins are more soluble in neutral solutions than in acidic ones, and they are more soluble in alcohol than in water. So when a fermentation first starts, very little color and tannin is extracted but once some alcohol is produced, the extraction proceeds more rapidly. In addition, tannins are imparted to wines through aging processes that utilize oak barrels or the addition of oak cubes to the fermenter.

The ability of tannins to precipitate proteins has important implications for the aging of wines and beers. Precipitation refers to the dissolved tannins combining with dissolved proteins to form a compound that can't be dissolved. This compound, once formed, slowly sinks to the bottom of the vessel. When this happens, the astringent or bitter flavors imparted by the tannin are lessened and the haziness imparted by the protein is diminished.

Tannins are also chelators. That is, they combine with the ions (positively charged atoms) of metals in order to make them non-reactive. A major effect of tannins is that they combine with iron in such a way as to make it biologically useless to living things. Pathogenic bacteria love iron. They love iron so much that they invade the human body to get it.[4] One of the reasons why red wines keep so much better than others is because the tannins have tied up the iron, making the environment unattractive for pathogenic bacteria. Tannins also chelate magnesium, copper, and other metals, but do so without making the metals unavailable. This alters the taste by altering the nature of the compounds.

Ingredients other than grapes can have more or less tannin content, and that content will vary based upon the amount of time the whole fruit is left in the primary fermenter as well.

Unfortunately, because tannins encompass such a vast array of compounds, assessing the tannin content of a must is a devilishly complex exercise in experimental chemistry. If you are curious, please see *New Tannin Assay for Winemakers* by Moris L. Silber and John K. Fellman for the most accurate method using protein dye markers or the older (and more controversial) precipitation technique published by Hagerman and Butler in the *Journal of Agricultural Food Chemistry* in 1978.

Some fruits already have so much tannin that they should be diluted in order to make a drinkable wine, whereas others will require the addition of tannin to help pull proteins out of solution. I have included a table of common fruits that shows how much relative tannin they have, divided into low (less than 3 grams per liter), medium (3–4 grams per liter) and high (more than 4 grams per liter). If a juice is in the "low" category, add ½ teaspoon of grape tannin

---

[4] Ewald, Paul (2002), *Plague Time: The New Germ Theory of Disease*

Low Tannin	Medium Tannin	High Tannin
Apples, Bananas, Cranberries, Lemons	Blueberries, Blackberries, Cherries (sweet), Currants, Gooseberries, Grapes, Grapefruit, Passionfruit, Plums, Raspberries, Strawberries	Apricots, Blueberries, Cherries (sour), Guava, Kiwi, Mango, Oranges, Peaches, Papaya, Pears

Relative Tannin Content of Common Wine Ingredients.

per gallon. If a juice is in the "medium" category, add ¼ teaspoon per gallon. If it is in the "high" category, you will likely need to dilute the juice with water or a juice with lower tannin content to avoid making a wine that is too astringent to be enjoyable. If you have to dilute the juice anyway because of its acidity (later in this chapter), consider the diluted juice to be one category lower for purposes of tannin content.

Your fruits will certainly differ to some degree from those I used for testing and my testing method used my own home lab rather than a professional lab, so I recommend that you mix up your must and add half the tannins specified, and then take a clean spoon and actually taste the must. If it isn't giving you any "pucker effect" go ahead and add the rest of the tannin specified. A must that starts out tasty will likely turn into a tasty wine!

If you have a finished wine that for some reason has excessive tannin, keep in mind that some wines are at their best after being stored for several years, during which time the tannins slowly polymerize, combine with proteins or otherwise become less astringent. If that doesn't work, or you need to use a wine early, you can precipitate out the tannins using a combination of gelatin and kieselsol.

To use gelatin, use your scale to measure out one gram of fining gelatin (from a winemaking store), and mix that with two tablespoons of cold water in a clean coffee cup. Separately, put seven tablespoons of water in a glass measuring cup, and heat on high in the microwave for one minute. Add the hot water to the dissolved gelatin in the coffee cup, mixing thoroughly. Allow this to cool down to a temperature of 80 degrees, and then gently stir in two tablespoons per gallon of wine or the whole amount for five gallons. Leave it for two to five days before adding the kieselsol.

Whenever you use gelatin, it will impart some haze to the wine. This can be removed with kieselsol, a soluble silica gel. Soluble silica gel has an ionic charge that will attract uncombined gelatin and gelatin-tannin complexes. This will precipitate quickly. Use one ml per gallon of wine. Stir it in gently. Wait at least five days but not more than ten before racking the wine to leave the precipitated tannins behind. (Racking is explained in the next chapter.)

Acids in Wine

The acidity of wines is important because the organic acids help establish an environment favorable to yeast. They also combine over time

Fruit	Average Acidity in grams/liter	Primary Acids
Apple	6.5	Malic, citric, lactic
Banana	3	Citric, malic, tartaric
Blackberry	13	Malic, citric, isocitric
Blueberry	13	Citric, malic
Cantaloupe	2.5	Citric, malic
Cherry (sweet)	11	Malic, citric, isocitric
Cranberry	30	Citric, malic, quinic
Grapefruit	20	Citric
Grape	6	Tartaric, malic
Guava	12	Citric, malic, lactic
Lemon	40	Citric
Mango	3	Citric, tartaric
Orange	15	Citric, malic
Papaya	0.5	Citric, malic, ketoglutaric
Passion Fruit	25	Citric, malic
Peach	8	Malic, citric
Pear	4	Malic, citric
Pineapple	10	Citric, malic
Plum	6	Malic, quinic
Raspberries	14	Malic, citric, isocitric
Strawberries	10	Citric, malic
Watermelon	2	Citric, malic

Acidity of Common Wine Ingredients.

with alcohols to enhance flavor and smell, and they assist sulfite in sanitizing the must. Most importantly, they convey a taste of their own that balances the wine.

Depending upon the fruit you use, your wine must will already contain a combination of organic acids. Every fruit has some amount of citric acid, as citric acid is crucial to metabolism, but often a different acid is predominant and the combination of acids is unique for every fruit.

Each fruit also has a different overall level of acidity. Some fruits are so acidic (> 9 grams per liter) they cannot be used exclusively to make a wine must, and their juice must be diluted with either water or the juice of a less acidic fruit. The following table lists common fruits, their acidity as tested by titration and the primary organic acids in each fruit in decreasing order of relative quantity.

Measuring Acidity

Thankfully, unlike tannins, which are hard to measure, the overall acid content of wine musts is easy to determine. Wine musts contain a variety of acids, but it isn't possible for a home winemaker to separate these out and measure them independently. Because each of the primary organic acids has a different molecular weight (150.9 for tartaric, 134.1 for malic and 192.1 for citric), but a mole of each is neutralized by two moles of sodium hydroxide, what winemakers have standardized upon is interpreting the results of the tests as though the acid being neutralized were tartaric. Likewise, wine makers don't usually like to think in terms of moles, so the results are converted via a multiplier into the more familiar "parts per thousand." So acid measurements of wine must are provided in terms of TA (titrateable acidity) as tartaric in PPT (parts per thousand). This is the same thing as grams per liter, abbreviated as g/L.

The method of measuring the acid content is called titration, and it takes advantage of the fact that acids and bases neutralize each other. You might have observed this phenomenon as a kid by mixing baking soda with vinegar. The combination generated carbon dioxide gas initially, but after a while settled down and did nothing once either component was fully neutralized. We won't be using baking soda because we don't want to generate gas. Instead, we'll use a standardized solution of sodium hydroxide—otherwise known as lye.

The widely available acid test kits have a problem. That is, they rely upon the color change of an indicator (phenolphthalein) which turns pink when enough sodium hydroxide has been added. But if you are dealing with a pink, blue, or purple sample, ascertaining when it has changed color is really difficult. I recommend using an inexpensive pH meter[5] instead.

By using either an indicator that changes color when the solution has been neutralized or a pH meter, you can tell when enough base has been added to neutralize the acid. Because you know the concentration of the base you are using, the amount of acid in your test sample can be easily calculated. The calculation is as follows:

(Normality of Base) X (Volume of Base) = (Normality of Unknown) X (Volume of Unknown)

Because the calculations are just the arithmetic of converting molarity to grams per liter, I have designed the procedure below to take that into account, and use just a one-time multiplication.

Supplies

150 ml beaker
1 glass stirring rod
110 ml syringe
1 cup distilled water
1 container of 0.1N sodium hydroxide solution

Procedure

Wear safety glasses.

Use the clean syringe to measure 5 ml of wine must and transfer it into the beaker.

Clean the syringe and then rinse with the distilled water.

Fill the syringe to the 10ml mark with sodium hydroxide solution

Add the sodium hydroxide to the beaker 0.1 ml at a time. After each addition, stir the contents of the beaker and test the pH with the meter.

Repeat the previous step until the pH meter reads 8.3 or higher. Then stop.

Make note of the reading on the syringe.

The TA (tartaric) in PPT (or g/L) of your must is equal to 1.5 x (10—reading on syringe).

Clean, rinse, dry, and store your equipment.

Adjusting Acidity

Acids affect flavors and indirectly create new flavors in a maturing wine. When making wine, the acidity of a must needs to be adjusted so that it is high enough, but not so high as to make an unpleasant flavor. Though your sense of taste is

---

[5] I use the Milwaukee pH600. It costs about $20 from various vendors.

the final arbiter, there are some ranges of acidity that have been established by wine makers over time that can serve as a general guideline:

Dry White Wine: 7.0-9.0 g/L

Sweet White Wine: 8.0-10.0 g/L

Dry Red Wine: 6.0-8.0 g/L

Sweet Red Wine: 7.0-9.0 g/L

Dry Fruit Wines and Meads: 5.0-6.5 g/L

Sweet Fruit Wines and Meads: 6.5-9.0 g/L

Sherries: 5.0-6.5 g/L

Many country wines are blended. For example, you might make a blueberry wine that contains a fair amount of red grape concentrate. So consider the full nature and character of your wine in assessing which category of acidity is appropriate. In the case of a dry blueberry wine containing red grape concentrate, I'd be aiming for about 7.0 g/L.

If you find your wine is too acidic, no more than 2 g/L too much, you can reduce the acidity by adding potassium carbonate. Potassium carbonate has a molecular mass of 138.2, and tartaric acid has a molecular mass of 150.9. There are 3.79 liters in a gallon, and potassium carbonate removes one molecule of acid for every molecule of potassium carbonate added, so for every PPT reduction in acidity required, add 3.5 grams of potassium carbonate per gallon.

For example, if I have five and a half gallons of wine must as described above, it has an acidity of 8.2 g/L and I want an acidity of 7.0 g/L, the amount of potassium carbonate I would need to add is:

(5.5 gallons) x 3.5 grams (8.2 g/L−7.0 g/L) = 23.1 grams. Measure it with your scale for best accuracy.

For reductions greater than 2.0 g/L, I do not recommend adding potassium carbonate as it can impart undesired salty tastes. Instead, I recommend blending. You can blend with water or other juices with lower acidity. In general, you don't want to blend with too much water as that will reduce the flavor and increase the amount of sugar you'll need to add. Keep in mind that whatever fruit juices you use for blending shouldn't overpower the primary ingredient. This will require a bit of algebra.

Pretend I want to make blueberry wine. To that end, I have juiced some blueberries, and tested the acidity of the must at an excessively sour 11 g/L. I want 7 g/L. I am making 5.5 gallons of must.

There are 3.79 liters in a gallon. If my desired acidity is 7 g/L, then the total amount of acid in 5.5 gallons of must will be 7 g/L X 3.79 L/gallon X 5.5 gallons = 145.9 grams. My blueberry must contains 11 g/L of acidity, which works out to 11g/L X 3.79 L/gallon = 41.7 grams per gallon.

If I wanted to dilute the juice with water alone, it would be easy to determine how much blueberry must I could use by dividing the total amount of desired acid in 5.5 gallons of must (145.9 grams) by the number of grams of acid in a gallon of my blueberry must (41.7 grams). So 145.9 grams / 41.7 grams per gallon = 3.5 gallons. So to make 5.5 gallons of must with the proper level of acidity, I would use 3.5 gallons of blueberry must and make up the remaining two gallons with water. Because blueberries are very strongly flavored, this would likely work fine as long as we added tannin and sugar as needed.

Of course, we wouldn't have to use water. We could use watermelon juice instead! If one gallon of watermelon juice has an acidity of 3g/L, how much blueberry juice and water would we need to use?

The total acidity available from the watermelon juice is 3.79 L/gallon X 3 g/L X 1 gallon = 11.4 grams. The must requires a total of 145.9 grams, so the amount of acidity remaining is 145.9 grams–11.4 grams = 134.5 grams. If we divide that by the number of grams of acid per gallon of blueberry juice (41.7 grams) we get 134.5 grams / 41.7 grams per gallon = 3.22 gallons. That's close enough to three gallons plus a quart, so now our recipe is 3.25 gallons of blueberry juice, one gallon of watermelon juice, and the remaining (5.5 gallons–3.25 gallons–1 gallon) 1.25 gallons made up with water. As you can see, the math for blending to get the right acid levels isn't very difficult.

Usually, however, excessive acid is not the problem. The problem is more likely to be insufficient acid. This is especially the case with low or medium acid fruits that are fully ripened, and with fruits whose quantities need to be kept low due to high tannins such as cherries.

If I were making a cherry wine, because cherry is high in tannin, I would likely use half cherry juice and half red or white grape juice in my must. Because the result would be a red wine, I'd want the acidity to be at around 7.0g/L. In all likelihood, though, when I measured, I'd find the acidity closer to 5.5g/L.

To increase the acidity, you add acid directly to the must and stir it in. Winemaking shops make citric, tartaric and malic acids available, as well as an acid blend composed of equal parts of all three. The only place I can see acid blend being used is in meads (honey wine) that have no fruit component. Otherwise, what I recommend is the use of acids based upon the nature of the fruit.

Earlier in this chapter is a table that lists, in order of influence on taste, the primary organic acids present in a variety of fruits. For some fruits, the primary acid is malic, for others it is citric or tartaric. When correcting the acidity of a must whose primary character is that of a particular fruit, you should use the two most important acids for that fruit in a 2:1 ratio.

For example, if I am making an apple wine, the primary acids are first malic and then citric acid. When I add acidity to the must, I will add a blend of acids composed of two parts malic acid and one part citric acid.

Determining how much acid to add is straightforward. If I want my must to have 6.5 g/L acidity and it only has 5.0g/L of acidity, then I need to add 6.5 g/L–5.0 g/L = 1.5 g/L of acid. Converting that to gallons simply requires multiplying the result by the number of liters in a gallon, which is 3.79. So to increase the acidity of 5.5 gallons of must from 5.0 g/L to 6.5 g/L I would need to add 1.5 g/L X 3.79 L/gallon X 5.5 gallons = 31.3 grams of acid. In even numbers, then, I would add 20 grams of malic acid and 10 grams of citric acid.

There is a school of thought that citric acid should never be used in wine musts. The reason is because citric acid can promote acetification (i.e. the process of turning wine to vinegar) or can contribute to the development of diacetyl (buttery) flavors. Both statements are true. However, if you are scrupulous in your sanitation, acetification is not likely to happen and some wines could benefit from any diacetyl developed. That having been said, if you are concerned about this, you can substitute tartaric acid for citric acid, and by doing this you will increase the grape flavors in your wine.

Pectins

Pectins are long chains of carbohydrates composed of various sugars that form the cell walls of the fruits used to make wine. Pectins are responsible for turning the juices of some fruits into jelly. European grapes contain enough pectic enzyme—an enzyme that destroys pectin—to destroy that pectin so you end up with a clear fluid wine rather than a semi-solid gelatinous mass. Other fruits don't usually have enough of this enzyme naturally, which makes them excellent for making jelly but suboptimal for wine.

Pectic enzyme purchased from the winemaking store is used in small amounts to supplement the natural pectic enzymes in the must. Over time, this degrades the pectin and thereby either makes its sugars available for fermentation or precipitates the leavings into the bottom of the fermenter so they are left behind at the next racking. Therefore, pectic enzyme helps to produce clear wines.

You may recall that one reason most fruits and vegetables are blanched before freezing or dehydrating is that the high temperature of blanching inactivates the enzymes that cause the produce to degrade over time. The same will occur with pectic enzyme, so pectic enzyme should only be added to a must with a temperature under 80 degrees and the must cannot be reheated thereafter.

When making wines with no added sulfites or when making wines in which honey is the primary ingredient, it is common to heat the must in order to assure its sterility. Anytime heated ingredients are added to the must, the temperature of the must should be allowed to drop adequately before pectic enzyme is added. The container of pectic enzyme has instructions printed on the label for how much to add to your must, but this is a general direction. Some fruits require the standard amount, but some require double. The following table will let you see at a glance.

Enzyme According to Directions	Double Pectic Enzyme
Blackberries, Blueberries, Cherries, Nectarines, Peaches, Plums, Raspberries, Watermelon	Apples, Pears, Strawberries

Pectic Enzyme Requirements of Various Fruits.

Yeast Nutrient, Yeast Energizer, Thiamine, and Lipid Supply

During the reproductive phase of yeast in the must, the sheer volume of yeast that is created from a tiny packet is impressive. There will literally be millions of yeast cells per milliliter of must. All of this cellular budding and division requires core building blocks for protein and the other parts of a yeast cell. As with many important factors, though these are usually present in European grapes to a sufficient degree, they are lacking in practically all other primary ingredients for winemaking.

A wine can be made successfully in some cases without the addition of nutritional building blocks for the yeast, but adding those building blocks will go a long way toward stacking the deck in favor of a successful outcome.

You will see wine supply stores selling many supplements for yeast with names such as yeast nutrient and yeast energizer. There is no universal standard, and so the precise ingredients will vary with the supplier. In general, they will contain purified sources of nitrogen and phosphorus at a minimum, though many will also contain a variety of B-vitamins. Yeast nutrient

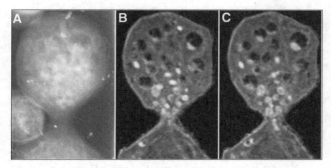

⊗ Yeast cell division requires proper nutrition.

usually contains only food grade ammonium phosphate, whereas yeast energizer will contain this along with magnesium sulfate, killed yeast, and the entire vitamin B complex; of which thiamine (vitamin B_1) is the most important. Sometimes you may see urea as an ingredient. If you do, don't worry. This is purified food-grade urea that supplies nitrogen for building proteins and it is perfectly safe.

I would recommend using yeast energizer in preference to yeast nutrient. But if you use yeast nutrient instead, at least add a 100% RDA thiamine tablet and a pinch of Epsom salt in addition for each gallon of must.

The cell walls of yeast also require lipids (fats), and such fats are in short supply in some wine musts—especially meads made predominantly from honey with little or no fruit. In such cases, you can use yeast hulls as an additive or a specialized additive that contains essential fatty acids such as FermaidK or Ghostex.

Sulfite

Some people who get headaches from drinking wine believe themselves to be sensitive to sulfites. Usually, however, they get headaches from red wine but not from white wine, both of which contain sulfites. So sulfites are not the issue.[6] This headache is called Red Wine Headache, and experts disagree widely on its true cause. Less than 1% of people are truly sensitive to sulfites which are found ubiquitously in lunch meats, dried fruits, and even white grape juice from the supermarket. Obviously, if you are truly sensitive to sulfites you should avoid them at all costs.

Sulfite is used so pervasively in winemaking and considered so essential that its use is even permitted in wines labeled as USDA Organic. Though it is possible to make wines without the use of sulfites and I have successfully done so, the odds of success for a beginner are greatly enhanced by using sulfites, especially if you are using fresh or frozen fruits in the must.

Sulfite is used in winemaking as a sanitizer to kill or inhibit wild yeasts and bacteria so you end up making wine instead of vinegar. It is also used to help clear wines during racking to arrest fermentation and to help prevent oxidation and consequent degradation of flavor.

Sulfite comes in many forms, but for our purposes two forms are important. The first is potassium metabisulfite in the form of Campden tablets. Campden tablets are sized with the idea in mind of accurate dosing of wine and musts to purify must prior to initiating fermentation and help clear and preserve the wine later. To use Campden tablets, do not just plunk them into the wine or must. Instead, use a cleaned and sanitized wine thief to remove four to eight ounces of must or wine, and put it into a sanitized glass. Thoroughly crush the requisite number of tablets, and add the powder to the must or wine. Stir to dissolve. Once the tablets are dissolved, add

---

[6] K. MacNeil, (2001) *The Wine Bible*

the must or wine back to the original container. For the initial sanitizing of a must, use two tablets per gallon of must. For protecting wine from spoilage and oxidation, add one tablet per gallon before racking.

The second is powdered potassium metabisulfite. In powdered form it is used to make sterilizing solutions for sterilizing equipment.

Make a gallon jug (a clean empty plastic water jug is fine) of sanitizing solution. To make the sanitizing solution, dissolve a measuring teaspoon of potassium metabisulfite powder in a gallon of water. You can use this solution repeatedly, and pour it back in the bottle after each use to rinse a fermenter or a racking tube until it loses its potency or becomes obviously dirty. If you keep the container tightly sealed when not in use, it will stay effective for a very long time. You can tell if it is potent by sniffing the solution. If the scent just barely tickles your nose, it needs to be replaced.

There are other sanitizers available and when you have become more experienced and confident, you can branch out and start experimenting. But sulfites are the easiest to use not only for the beginner, but also for the most prestigious of professional wineries.

Testing Sulfite Levels

It is very rare that you would need to test the sulfite levels in wine. Simply following the directions in this book will assure adequate but not excessive levels of sulfite for most purposes. However, there are instances where you'll want to know how much sulfite is in the wine. For example, if you plan to follow your secondary fermentation with a malolactic fermentation in order to reduce

perceived acidity, most malolactic cultures will be inhibited by sulfite levels greater than 20 ppm. So if you have been dosing regularly with sulfite between rackings, when you rack into a container to initiate malolactic fermentation, you should test the sulfite levels in your must, and reduce them if they are too high.

You can purchase sulfite test kits from wine equipment suppliers. These test kits use what is called the "Ripper" method and they work quite well with wines that are not strongly colored. With strongly colored wines, they give a reading that is too high because the compounds that impart color to the wine combine with some of the test ingredients making them inert. You can "guesstimate" the error by subtracting 10ppm from the results of the test, or you can do a more elaborate test on your own. I've detailed that test in the advanced techniques chapter.

To reduce sulfite levels, stir 3% hydrogen peroxide solution from the pharmacy into your wine and wait an hour. The amount you need is equal to 1 ml for every ppm reduction per gallon of wine. So if I have 5 gallons of must with a sulfite level of 33 ppm and I want to reduce the sulfite level to 15 ppm before adding a malolactic culture, I need a reduction of 33ppm−15 ppm or 18 ppm. The amount of 3% hydrogen peroxide solution to add is calculated like this:

(Gallons of wine) X (ppm reduction desired) = ml of 3% hydrogen peroxide solution to add

So 5 gallons X 18ppm = 90ml of 3% hydrogen peroxide solution.

Yeast

Yeast is the star of the show. Wild yeast naturally colonizes the surfaces of fruits, so sometimes crushed fruit, left to its own devices and protected from other organisms, will ferment all by itself. In fact, this is the case in certain famous wine regions where the wild yeasts inhabiting the area have co-evolved with the wine grapes. Though most wine yeasts are of the species *Saccharomyces cerevisiae*, there are hundreds if not thousands of variations of this species, some with dramatically different properties. The genome of wine yeast has over twelve million base pairs, making for substantial possibilities for variation.

In practice, wine makers do not rely on wild yeasts because the unpredictability can often result in serious failures or faults in the finished product. Instead, wine makers usually purify the musts of wild yeasts and bacteria by adding sulfite. Once the sulfite has been added, the must is stirred thoroughly and then allowed to sit for a day before a cultured wine yeast of known character is added.

Adding yeast to the must is known as pitching the yeast, though in reality little real pitching occurs because one- and five-gallon batches are relatively small. In batches of this size, the packet of yeast is just sprinkled as evenly as possible on top of the must in the primary fermenter. Do not stir. If you stir, it will take the yeast far longer to multiply enough to become active. You want the yeast to become active as quickly as possible because it is added after the sulfite has dissipated, so long lag times expose your must to a risk of spoilage by delaying the onset of production of alcohol.

Because yeast needs oxygen in its initial replication stage before fermentation begins, you should aerate the must by stirring it vigorously before pitching the yeast. Some wine makers put a sanitized fish tank aerator connected to an air pump into the must for an hour or so before pitching the yeast, but I have found a good vigorous stirring (carefully so as to avoid sticky messes) to be sufficient.

Yeast comes powdered in packets, in liquid in vials, and in many other forms. As you become a more advanced wine maker, you might decide to use liquid yeasts. The liquid yeasts require amplification, but your initial use should be of powdered dry yeast in individual foil packets. These are very well-characterized and foolproof. Just open the packet and sprinkle on top of the must—and it works. Don't be fooled by the simplicity of use or the fact these yeasts are inexpensive. Dry wine yeasts are a very high quality product and I have used them successfully for years. If you skimp and use bread or beer yeast to make your wine, don't complain if your wine tastes like bread or is syrupy-sweet because the alcohol tolerance was too low.

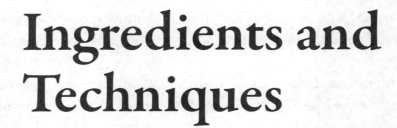

46

Ingredients and Techniques

Theoretically, you could make "wine" or at least a liquid containing alcohol, from just sugar, water, yeast and some nutrients. But the whole point of wine is to preserve the nutritional content of the starting fruits or vegetables, so we'll look at it from that point of view. Any fruit or vegetable can be used to make wine. Other than wine grapes, all fruits will require some amount of supplemental sugar. The juice of some fruits will require considerable dilution due to their high degree of acidity or astringency, and some will produce wines so tasty you'll wonder why you can't find them commercially. Others, like asparagus, will be downright unpalatable in some cases and suitable only for making marinades.

Fruits

Wine grapes are the perfect fruit for making wine. All you need to do is crush them and they make the perfect amount of juice with the perfect levels of acidity and sugar. Every other fruit is imperfect in some way. While fruits other than grapes are imperfect, they can be made perfect through proper adjuncts and technique.

With air transportation for produce so prevalent, there are more fruits available in our local markets than I could ever list, and quite a few I haven't tried because they are so expensive, such as starfruit and guava. In general, the higher the quality of the fruit, the higher the potential quality of your finished product. You will never make great wine from bad fruit—no amount of technique will improve its quality. But if you start with the highest quality fruit, there is at least the potential for creating great wine through solid technique.

You can use fruit in nearly any form to make wine: fresh fruits, dehydrated fruits, canned fruits, and frozen fruits. Fresh fruits and frozen fruits give the best results, and in many cases frozen fruits are superior to fresh because the process of freezing breaks down the cell walls to release more juice and flavor. Canned fruits often have a distinctly "cooked" taste that can detract from a wine, making it taste flat. They are best used for no more than half of the fruit in a wine. Wine-making shops sell specially canned fruits that come out better in wines than the canned fruit at the supermarket, but even these should constitute no more than half of the fruit by weight.

Dehydrated fruits retain their sugar, but have been subjected to oxidation and the loss of some of their more volatile flavor components. Usually, they are used in the form of raisins for purposes of adding some grape components to a wine so that it has a more vinous quality; dehydrated fruits in general, such as prunes and apples, are good for adding sherry-like taste qualities. Dehydrated banana is good for adding body to a wine such as watermelon wine that would otherwise be very thin. Very often, dehydrated fruits are sulfited to preserve their color. This is not a problem when they are added to a primary fermenter. In general, one cup of minced dried fruit will impart three ounces of sugar to the must, but this rule of thumb is no substitute for measuring with a hydrometer. Do keep in mind that making wine out of a dried fruit can concentrate the effects of that fruit, as I found to my chagrin with some prune wine I made.

Fruits, you will discover, are pretty expensive in the quantities you'd use for making wine. For example, you'll need twenty pounds of blueberries to make five gallons of blueberry wine. If you buy frozen organic blueberries at the supermarket for $3.69/lb, that means $73.80 just in fruit. Since you get twenty five bottles of wine from five gallons, that works out to just under $3/bottle, which is still a decent deal. Even so, it quickly becomes clear that your best bet is to either grow fruit yourself, go to a pick-it-yourself place or buy it in bulk from a farm stand. I

⊗ Always use unwaxed fruit. Waxed fruits will create a mess rather than wine.

pick the blueberries for my wine at Mrs. Smith's Blueberries nearby, and it's a lot more affordable. (You can also make wine in one-gallon batches so your initial outlay isn't so much. This is a good idea when experimenting!)

Fresh fruits for country wines are primarily processed using only one technique. In this technique, the fruit is placed in a clean nylon straining bag in the bottom of the primary fermenter, crushed with cleaned/sanitized hands, with the difference in volume being made up by adding water. The water helps to extract the dissolved sugars and flavor compounds, and as fermentation begins, the alcohol created helps to extract the color. This technique is best suited to softer fruits that are easily crushed by hand, though it is used for practically all fruits for the overwhelming preponderance of country wines.[1]

As an alternative, especially for harder fruits such as apples, I recommend using a high quality juice machine such as the Juiceman™ or Champion™. With these machines, the expressed juice goes into one container and the pulp goes into another. For darker fruits from which you want to extract color, such as cherries or blueberries, scoop the pulp from the pulp container into a nylon straining bag that you put in the bottom of the primary fermenter. (Note: Exclude the pits from stone fruits as they contain a cyanogenic glycoside that is poisonous.)

Juices

I have made very good wines from high-quality bottled juices. For example, two quarts of apple plus two quarts of black cherry with the sugar and acid levels adjusted and a hint of vanilla added will make a gallon of really great wine.

Bottled juice that hasn't been treated with an additive that suppresses fermentation (such as potassium sorbate) can also be used to make wine. Keep in mind that something like the generic apple juice you can buy cheaply by the gallon is hardly more than sugar water and doesn't make very good wine. But there is a big difference between brands, and sometimes you can make a really excellent wine out of a blended Juicy Juice™.

Bottled juices and juice blends from the natural food section of the grocery store are often 100% juice from the described fruit. These have

⊗ Organic fruit juices can make a valuable adjunct to homemade wine

---

[1] If you are using purchased fruits, please make sure they are unwaxed. The wax that purveyors use to make fruits look pretty will turn your intended wine into a useless mess.

been specifically formulated to retain the distinctive flavor of the fruit, and can be easily used as an addition to wines. You might want to be sparing in their use though, as they often cost as much as $10/quart.

Grape juice concentrates can help add "vinous" quality to a country wine, making its mouth-feel resemble that of traditional wines. These are special concentrates purchased from winemaking stores that have had the water removed under vacuum, and have been preserved with sulfites rather than through heat; therefore, they preserve a distinctive grape character. At roughly $16/quart (they make a gallon of must when water is added) they are expensive, but they make good additions as part of a must. They come in white and red varieties.

Vegetables

Vegetables are used for wine either by boiling them in water and including the water in the must, or by juicing the vegetables with a juice machine. Many vegetables, no matter how they are handled, will impart a haze to wines, but this effect is more pronounced when using boiled vegetables. This is because boiling tends to set the pectins while denaturing the natural enzymes in the vegetable that would otherwise break down the pectins over time. There's no reason why you couldn't try bottled vegetable juices so long as they haven't been treated with a fermentation inhibitor, but the results can be pretty iffy when using brands that include added salt. Salt is added to vegetable juice to balance natural sugars for a tasty beverage. But when you use salted vegetable juice in wine, the sugar is converted to alcohol during fermentation but the salt remains. The results can be good

for making marinade but decidedly not good for drinking. On the flip side, there's nothing wrong with having a variety of self-preserved marinades ready and waiting!

Speaking of marinades, both wines and vinegars are commonly used for this purpose, and both are self-preserving. You can make very good marinades by fermenting mixtures that include onions, herbs, celery, parsley, and similar ingredients. With their high alcohol content, they will keep for decades.

If you aren't making marinades but you are instead looking to make drinkable wines, both carrots and tomatoes can be excellent candidates for a wine. Carrots also blend quite well with apple. But don't let the fact that I've never made okra wine deter you if you want to give it a try.

Herbs and Spices

Though spices are not added to wines very much today, in past times spices were quite expensive so heavily spiced wines were an indicator of wealth and status. Unlike the traditional wine makers of France, as a home wine maker you don't have to contend with the traditional rules for making wine. One bonus is that you can add anything you'd like. You can add mulling spices to an apple wine, a hint of vanilla and cinnamon to a blueberry wine, and just a touch of rosemary to a carrot wine. The only rule is to make something that you and your friends will enjoy drinking, so if spices can enhance a wine to your tastes, then there's no reason not to use them. However, just as with food, it can be easy to over-do spice. Better too little than too much.

When adding spices, use whole rather than powdered ingredients. For one thing, powdered

Spice	Goes best with	Amount to use
Peppercorns	Used to add warmth to most wines	5–10 whole peppercorns per gallon
Cassia Buds	Apple, blueberry, cherry, and most fruit wines	10–30 buds per gallon
Cinnamon	Fruit wines	1 stick per gallon
Cloves	Fruit, vegetable, and grain wines	3–6 cloves per gallon
Allspice	Fruit, vegetable, and grain wines	4–10 berries per gallon
Nutmeg	Fruit and vegetable wines	No more than ½ meg per gallon
Ginger	Best in lightly flavored wines such as apple and carrot	2–8 ounces, grated
Star Anise	Fruit wines	1 star per gallon
Vanilla	Fruit wines	1 vanilla bean or less per gallon

spices tend to have lost some of their volatile flavor components and will give inferior results. For another, they often form a haze in wines that is harmless but unsightly.

The technique for use is straightforward. Put the chosen spices in a spice bag, and lightly boil the bag in a quart of sugar water for ten to fifteen minutes, then discard the bag. Allow the spiced sugar water to cool to room temperature before adding to the must.

Sources of Sugar

Because yeast contains enzymes that turn many forms of sugar into a sort more easily used, any common source of sugar will have the same result in terms of alcohol production. You can use granulated cane sugar, dextrose, glucose, fructose, honey, molasses, brown sugar, maple syrup, high-fructose corn syrup, dried fruits, concentrated fruit juices, and more.

Though the source doesn't matter in terms of creating alcohol, it can make a big difference in terms of taste—for example, many of the chemical compounds that make honey or brown sugar have a distinctive taste and aroma which will be preserved in wines that include them. For this reason, I would recommend against using brown sugar or molasses.

Glucose, dextrose, fructose, and sucrose (cane sugar) are all treated identically by yeast. If the sugar isn't in a form the yeast can use, the yeast employs an enzyme called invertase to change it into a usable form. Nothing is gained by using the more expensive fructose from a health food store over an inexpensive bag of granulated sugar from the grocery store. None of these contribute flavor to the wine, and simply serve as a source of sweetness or alcohol. They are a good choice for wines in which you want the tastes and aromas of the primary fruit to dominate their character.

Bottled juices and juice concentrates can also be used as a source of sugar, especially given that sugar is their primary solid constituent.

Containing a wide array of minerals, amino acids, and vitamins, honey is a tasty addition to many wines. A number of cultural traditions (including the honeymoon) have grown up around honey wines. Strictly speaking, a wine made from honey alone is called mead. Wine that combines honey with apples is called cyser, whereas wine made from honey and any other (non-grape) fruit is called melomel. Wine made from honey with added herbs is called metheglin, and wine made from honey and grapes is pyment.

When making mead variants, the source and quality of the honey you use makes a difference in the taste of the finished product. The generic blended honeys in the supermarket are fine when the honey is primarily used as a source of sugar. If you are making mead, however, blended honey is useless because it has been pasteurized and homogenized until it is nothing but sugar. If the tastes and aromas of the honey will be important to the end product, use a single-source honey from a bee keeper. The nectar that the bees collect positively affects the mineral content and flavor of mead. Clover, alfalfa, orange blossom, wildflower, and mesquite are just a few of the types of honey available; in general, darker honeys impart stronger flavors. You can get single-source and wild honeys from a local bee keeper, order them over the Internet or, if you are ambitious, start keeping bees yourself[2] and create your own honey.

Cleanliness and Sanitation

Before I get into the details of making wine, I want to delve a bit into cleanliness and sanitation,

---

[2] In my opinion, I don't have enough experience to write a book on beekeeping, however I have found Kim Flottum's *The Backyard Beekeeper* to be very good. If you are interested in keeping bees for honey, I highly recommend it.

as these are crucial for a successful outcome. You don't need a laboratory clean room or a level 3 hazmat facility to make wine. You can make wine in your kitchen or any room in your home. But you need to be attentive to detail. Everything that touches your must, wine, or wine-in-progress must be clean and sanitized.

"Clean" simply means "free of visible dirt or contamination." Dish soap and water are adequate cleansers. Wine bottles, fermentation vessels, wine thief, plastic tubing, and hydrometer along with all utensils that touch your wine need to be cleaned. Sometimes, all that is needed is to add some soapy water and shake. Other times, as with carboys, you may need to use a special brush. For subsequent sanitation procedures to work, the surfaces must first be clean. Once they have been cleaned, they should be thoroughly rinsed.

To sanitize the equipment, all surfaces that will touch the must or wine should be rinsed or wiped down with a sanitizing sulfite solution. Don't rinse afterwards. For bottles, vessels, and carboys you can add a portion of the sulfite solution and swish it around thoroughly so that it contacts all surfaces, and then pour it back into your container of solution. For other utensils, soak paper towels in sanitizing solution and use those towels to wipe them down immediately before use.

Your hand siphon and tubing might look to pose a problem at first, but there is an easy technique for keeping them clean. For this technique, you need two clean plastic gallon jugs that were previously used for water. Put one with soapy water on your counter and the empty one on the floor. Now, use your siphon to pump the soapy water all the way up into the tube and through the tubing into the empty container on the floor. Then, switch the containers and repeat

General Recipes for Making Wine from Common Fruits and Flowers

	Pounds	Fruit Preparation	Adjuncts	Pectic Enzyme	Tannin	Yeast Variety	Notes
Apple	10 lbs	Juice machine	½ lb raisins in straining bag	Double specified on container	¼ tsp	Red Star Pasteur Champagne	Use the juice but not the pulp
Blackberry	4 lbs	Crushed in straining bag	½ lb raisins in straining bag	As specified	None	Red Star Montrachet	
Blueberry	8 lbs	4 lbs juiced, 4 lbs crushed in straining bag	½ tsp vanilla and one stick cinnamon in bag	As specified	None	Lalvin ICV-D$_{254}$	
Cherry, Sweet	4 lbs	Juice machine, add pulp to straining bag	1 quart bottled cherry juice	As specified	None	Red Star Montrachet	Exclude the pits
Dandelion	5 cups flower heads	Put the flower petals (only!) in straining bag	1 lb raisins in straining bag	None	¼ tsp	Lalvin D$_{47}$	Ferment at under 70 degrees
Nectarine	3 lbs	Pitted and juiced in machine	½ lb raisins in straining bag	As specified	¼ tsp	Red Star Pasteur Champagne	
Peach	3 lbs	Pitted and juiced in machine	None	As specified	¼ tsp	Lalvin D$_{47}$	
Pear	10 lbs	Juice machine	½ lb raisins in straining bag	Double specified on container	¼ tsp	Red Star Pasteur Champagne	Add one stick cinnamon to straining bag
Plum	5 lbs	Pitted and crushed in straining bag	1 lb raisins in straining bag	As specified	None	Red Star Montrachet	
Raspberry	4 lbs	Crushed in straining bag	None	As specified	None	Red Star Montrachet	
Rhubarb	4 lbs	Crushed in straining bag	1 lb strawberry in straining bag	As specified	¼ tsp	Red Star Pasteur Champagne	
Strawberry	4 lbs	Crushed in straining bag	½ lb raisins in straining bag	Double specified on container	¼ tsp	Lalvin ICV-D$_{254}$	Comes out straw-colored rather than red
Watermelon	10 lbs	Juice machine	1 lb raisins in straining bag	As specified	¼ tsp	Lalvin D$_{47}$	Peel the outer skin off, and juice the rind and fruit

the process until the equipment is clean. Empty out the containers and rinse them thoroughly. Next, put the bottle of sanitizing solution on the counter, and siphon that into the empty container on the floor. Make sure to wipe down the outside of the equipment and tubing as well, as these may contact the wine.

Making the Wine Must

As noted previously, your wine must doesn't have to be made from a single source. You can use apples mixed with pears, carrots mixed with apples, juiced table grapes combined with bottled cherry juice, or whatever strikes your fancy. As long as you use good sanitation and technique, the results will be at least as good as most wines you can buy.

Some fruits are either highly acidic or highly tannic to such an extent that you wouldn't want to use their extracted juice exclusively to make wine because the results would be too sour or bitter. In those cases, only a portion of the must is made from that fruit, and the rest is made up from water or other juices.

What follows is a recipe table that indicates how many pounds of a given fruit to use in making a gallon of wine from that fruit, how much tannin to add to that wine per gallon, and any other adjuncts that I'd recommend. Any deficit in juice to make a gallon is made up with water.

The Primary Fermentation: Step-by-Step

1. **Start with fruit** juice obtained as described earlier in this chapter.

2. If needed, add enough water to the fruit juice to equal the amount of wine you wish to make. (It is helpful to add previously-measured amounts of water to your primary fermenter in advance and use a magic marker to mark gallons and quarts on the outside of the vessel for easy reference.) I use bottled water because my well water is sub-optimal, but if you have good water where you live, tap water is fine. Don't worry about whether or not your water is chlorinated, because the Campden tablets we'll be adding later serve to remove chlorine from the water.

3. Use your hydrometer to measure the specific gravity (SG) of the must. You are aiming for an SG of between 1.085 and 1.110, but in all likelihood your must measures much lower. Add the required amount of sugar or honey to your must. This will slightly increase the volume of your must, but that's fine.

4. Use your acid testing kit to test the acidity of your must. If needed, add acid. Try to use the specific acid (or acid blend) that will best enhance the character of the fruit. For example, malic acid will enhance apples and pears whereas citric acid will enhance watermelons and tartaric acid will enhance grapes. If you are in doubt, use an acid blend made up of equal parts of the three acids.

5. Add one teaspoon of yeast energizer for each gallon of must.

6. Add pectic enzyme as directed on the container, or double the amount if the recipe table specifies doing so.

7. Add tannin as appropriate for the fruit being used. (This is described in the accompanying recipe table.)

8. Crush and add one Campden tablet dissolved in a bit of juice per gallon of must. Vigorously stir the must.

9. Cover your primary fermenter, and plug the hole with a bit of cotton ball to keep foreign objects out. Wait 24 hours.

10. Vigorously stir the must to oxygenate. Once movement ceases, sprinkle yeast from the packet over the surface of the must. Do not stir.

11. Place the cover on the fermenter, and plug the hole loosely with a bit of cotton ball.

12. Allow to sit for a week. During this time, you should smell the fermentation. Also, it may foam heavily and come out through the hole in the lid. If it does, clean up on the outside and insert a new cotton ball. After the week, replace the cotton ball with an air lock filled with sanitizing solution.

13. Allow to sit for another week or two, until the air lock only "bloops" once every few seconds. This marks the end of the primary fermentation phase. Once the primary fermentation phase has ended, rack as soon as possible. If it sets for more than a couple of days, the dregs at the bottom (known as lees) will impart bad flavors to your wine.

Your First Racking: Step-by-Step

1. **A day before** you plan to rack, move your primary fermenter to a table or counter top. (By doing this a day in advance, you give any sludge stirred up by movement a chance to settle.) Put a wedge, book, block of wood, or something else from 1" to 2" high

⊗ Racking requires a bit of coordination but with practice it comes easily.

underneath the fermenter on the edge that is away from you. This will allow you to sacrifice the smallest amount of wine possible with the lees.

2. Clean and sanitize your racking tube, tubing, and your secondary fermenter and get your rubber stopper and fresh air lock ready. Put your secondary fermenter on the floor in front of the primary fermenter, and then carefully remove the lid from the primary fermenter, creating as little disturbance as possible. Put a bit of the wine in a sanitized glass, and dissolve one crushed Campden tablet per gallon, then add it back to the wine.

3. Put the plastic tubing from your racking setup in the secondary fermenter and the racking tube in the primary fermenter. Keeping the racking tube well above the sediment, pump it gently to get it started. It may take a couple of tries. Gently lower the racking tube as the liquid level diminishes. Watch the liquid in the tube very carefully. The second it starts sucking sediment, raise the racking tube up to break the suction.

4. Place the rubber stopper with an air lock filled with sanitizing solution in the secondary fermenter. Using a carboy handle if necessary, move the secondary fermenter to a location out of sunlight where even temperatures are maintained.

5. Immediately clean and sanitize your primary fermenter, racking tube, and tubing and stow them away. If you don't clean them immediately they will likely be ruined.

The Secondary Fermentation: Step-by-Step

1. **Wait. And wait.** Then wait some more. Patience, I have been told, is a virtue. After your first racking from the primary to secondary fermenter, the yeast will lag for a couple of days while it tries to catch up. Allow the secondary fermenter to sit unmolested until: the wine starts to become clear, you have more than a dusting of sediment at the bottom of the container, or the air lock only operates once every couple of minutes. This will likely take about a month.

⊗ The secondary fermentation in this vessel is almost complete.

Because the secondary fermenter sits for so long, don't forget to check the airlock periodically and top up the sanitizing solution in it so it doesn't evaporate and leave your wine vulnerable.

2. The day before racking, sit the secondary fermenter up on a table or counter, and tilt it using a book or other wedge, as before.

3. Boil some water in a pot on the stove and allow it to cool to room temperature while covered. Clean and sanitize another fermentation vessel as well as the racking tube and tubing. Place the sanitized vessel on the floor in front of the secondary fermenter, put the plastic tubing in the vessel,

and put the racking tube in the secondary fermenter. Operate the racking tube and transfer the wine from the old vessel to the new. Add one Campden tablet dissolved in wine for each gallon of wine.

4. Likely, there is an air space between the wine and the top of the new vessel. This will expose too much surface area of the wine to oxygen and potential infections. Pour in the sterilized water until the wine is just up to the neck.

5. Clean the rubber stopper and airlock, sanitize them, re-fill the airlock with sanitizing solution, and install them on the new secondary fermenter. Put the secondary fermenter in a location without sunlight and with even temperature.

6. Thoroughly clean and sanitize the empty secondary fermenter, the racking tube and the tubing.

7. Now it is a waiting game. Over weeks and months your wine will ultimately cease to ferment, and the haze within the wine will settle onto the bottom of the container. Keep an eye on the wine. Anytime a substantial sediment develops, rack the wine again and top up with sterilized water. Make sure the airlock doesn't go dry and permit foreign organisms to enter. Depending on ingredients, you may not have to rack again or you could have to rack one to three more times.

8. Once the wine has gone at least three months without requiring racking and is crystal clear, it is ready for bottling. You can allow it to age in the fermenter as long as you'd like—even several years.

Bottling Your Wine:

1. **Gather, clean, and sanitize** the wine bottles that will be accepting the wine. You will need five bottles per gallon of wine. Boil an equal number of corks for 15 minutes, and then allow them to sit in a covered pot. Clean and sanitize your corker.

2. Rack the wine, but do not add water to top off on this final racking. Add one Campden tablet per gallon by crushing the tablet and dissolving in a bit of wine and then adding that wine into the new vessel.

3. If you want to add potassium sorbate to prevent re-fermentation, dissolve that also in the wine and add back into the new vessel. Use ¼ tsp per gallon of wine.

4. Place the secondary fermenter holding the wine on a table or counter top, tilting as before.

5. Arrange the bottles on a towel on the floor in front of the fermenter and install the plastic hose clamp on the plastic tubing

⊗ Bottled blueberry wine. Magnificent!

so you can turn off the flow of wine when switching from bottle to bottle.

6. Put the plastic tubing in a bottle and the racking tube in the wine, pump the racking tube and start the flow of wine, pulling the tube higher in the bottle as the level of the wine increases. Stop the flow of wine when it is about half an inch into the bottom of the neck of the wine bottle. Put the tube in the next bottle and repeat the process until you run out of wine or there are no more bottles to fill.

7. One at a time, place the bottles on a solid floor, and use your corker to install one of the sterilized corks. Only work with one bottle at a time. As each bottle is corked, set it out of the way. Repeat until all of the bottles are corked.

8. Clean and sanitize your fermenting vessels, racking tube, and plastic tubing.

9. Now you can make and apply wine labels if you wish.

10. Enjoy at your leisure or give as a gift.

Creating Your Own Recipes

Most wine books are full of recipes. I'm sure they are useful, but I think it is more useful to understand how they are created so you can make your own recipes based upon what you have available. One of the reasons I went into so much detail in the chapter on the science of making wine is so you'd have all the tools you need to be self-sufficient.

When making a new wine for the first time, it is best to make it in a one-gallon batch. Overall, larger batches tend to come out better because they are less susceptible to temperature fluctuations, but I've made plenty of excellent wines in one-gallon batches, and the smaller amount may be less intimidating to a beginner.

In addition, even the cheapest wine ingredients are expensive at the scale of a five-gallon batch, so making a one-gallon batch is also best for experimental recipes. Reserve the larger five-gallon batches for tested recipes you know you'll be making for long-term storage or gifts. Some wine makers never make batches larger than a gallon, and they are quite happy with their results.

So let's look at the first critical decisions involved in making a wine recipe.

- Dominant and any secondary or tertiary fruits or flavors. This decision is purely aesthetic, and if you are someone with chronically bad taste you might consider consulting a friend or loved one for guidance. For example, I might want to make a wine with apple dominant, mulling spice secondary and honey tertiary. It would be rather daring as there would be little residual sweetness to balance the spice, so instead I'll make the apple dominant, honey secondary and mulling spice tertiary. Another example would be a wine with sweet cherry dominant and concord grape secondary.

- Check the tannin levels of each fruit. Any fruit that is high in tannin cannot be more than half of your must. If you want the fruit to be dominant anyway, you'll have to choose something unassertive such as generic white grape juice as a secondary. For example, if I want to make a wine with blueberry dominant, because blueberry is highly tannic, I am limited to four pounds of blueberries per gallon and will need to use adjuncts that won't overshadow the blueberry, such as white grape juice to make up the difference in volume.

- Check the acid levels of each fruit. Though the tables I've included are not a substitute for actual measurement, you can use them to get an idea that lemons are too acidic to constitute a major proportion of a wine must and that watermelon would need acid added. If the level of acid in the fruit is greater than 9g/L, then the quantity of that fruit should be limited to avoid excess acidity.

- Sugar level. Get a general idea of how much sugar will be in the major fruit ingredients, and how much will need to be added. Also, decide what form that sugar will take.

- Spicing. Look at the earlier tables when deciding how much spicing to add, if any.

- Pectic enzyme. Other than straight meads, all recipes will need pectic enzyme. Review the tables to see if the amount used is according to package directions or needs to be doubled.

- Yeast. Decide what type of yeast to use based upon its characteristics, and include yeast energizer in the amount recommended on the package.

One Gallon Example: Cherry Wine

Few can resist the idea of cherry wine, so it's a good start for a recipe. I've made cherry wine during the winter months and used a combination of bottled cherry juice, frozen cherries, and other adjuncts.

- I would like my dominant flavor to be cherry, my secondary flavor to be grape, and my tertiary flavor to be vanilla.

- Checking the tables, I see that cherries are high in tannin so they can't form more than half of my must, and they are high in acid too. So I will use one quart of bottled organic 100% black cherry juice, and one ten-ounce package of frozen sweet cherries, and make up the difference with organic white grape juice. Because less than half the recipe will have the higher tannins of cherry juice and the remainder of the recipe will come from white grape juice, tannin is likely to be a bit on the low side, so I'll add a quarter teaspoon of tannin.

- The two primary acids in cherries are malic and citric in that order, so if an acid test shows more acid is needed, I'll add a 2:1 mixture of malic and citric acids.

- Because I'm using bottled juices and frozen cherries with nutritional labels, I can add up how much sugar would be in the gallon: 200g from cherry juice, 42g from frozen cherries, and 480g from grape juice for a total of 722 grams. Converted to ounces that is 25.5 ounces. Looking at the hydrometer tables, I see that I need 31.6 ounces of sugar for a starting gravity of 1.090, so I figure I'll need about six ounces of sugar, though I will test with a hydrometer to be sure.

- Looking at the spicing table, and not wanting to overpower the cherry, I am including one vanilla bean in the primary fermenter.

- A lot of yeasts are available, but Montrachet looks like a really good match for what we're making.

So the final recipe looks like this:

Winter Cherry Wine

1 quart organic black cherry juice

1 ten-ounce package of frozen sweet cherries

3 quarts organic white grape juice

6-8 ounces of sugar, based on hydrometer test

1 vanilla bean

¼ tsp yeast energizer

¼ tsp tannin

2:1 blend of malic/citric acids as needed

1 packet Montrachet yeast

47

Advanced Techniques in Winemaking

Some of the techniques in this chapter truly are "advanced" in terms of difficulty or equipment, but most are merely extensions of what you already know that will help you produce wines with different characteristics.

Making Wine Without Sulfites

In the previous chapter I oriented procedures around the use of sulfites, because the use of sulfites makes it easier to produce a solid product. Even before modern times, sulfites were employed by burning sulfur to create sulfur dioxide gas to purify musts, and many yeasts generate their own sulfites during primary fermentation. There is no such thing as a sulfite-free wine. The best that can be managed is to make wine without adding them.

If you don't want sulfites added to your wine, here are some tips:

● Clean all equipment using scalding (140+ degree) water. Water this hot is, in fact, scalding. Use caution.

- Though it decreases the quality of the result somewhat, you can pasteurize your must by heating to 150 degrees and holding it there for ½ hour before putting it in your primary fermenter. Add bottled water to make up any difference in volume. Make sure the temperature has dropped below 80 before adding pectic enzyme or yeast. Musts that have been pasteurized often create very hazy wines, so don't do this with fruits that require a double dose of pectic enzyme.

- When using unpasteurized must, your yeast must out-compete all other yeasts and bacteria. So instead of sprinkling the yeast on top of the must, get your yeast ready two days in advance by sprinkling the yeast into a pint jar containing bottled apple juice mixed with a pinch of yeast energizer and then cap it with several layers of cheesecloth. Set it in a dark place at 60-70 degrees. When you add this yeast to your must, just pour it in smoothly and do not stir. Now your yeast has a head start so it can out-compete the wild yeasts and bacteria on the fruit.

Advanced Testing of Sulfite Levels

The sulfite test kits you can buy through wine hobby suppliers are fine for lightly colored wines but inaccurate when testing heavily colored wines because the phenolic coloring compounds in the wine take up some of the testing reagent. Errors can be as high as 20ppm. In an earlier chapter, I advised that you could "guesstimate" by subtracting 10ppm from the test results. If you aren't comfortable with guesstimates, you can do your own testing. The following procedures work on the principle of calculating total sulfite, calculating the error, and then subtracting the error from the total. You will be working with sulfuric acid in this procedure; safety goggles and a lab apron are required.

Equipment

50 ml beaker

3 ml syringe (no needle needed)

5 ml syringe (no needle needed)

10 ml graduated cylinder

250 ml volumetric flask (only needed if preparing your own iodine solution)

Scale (only needed if preparing your own iodine solution)

Chemicals

Distilled Water

.02N Iodine solution[3]

1% Starch solution

25% Sulfuric Acid solution

3% Hydrogen peroxide solution

Clean all equipment with distilled water. Put a 20ml sample of wine in the 50ml beaker. Add 5ml of starch solution, swirl to mix, then add 5ml of sulfuric acid solution to the sample and swirl

---

[3] This can be purchased from a lab supply company or made. To make it, mix .63g of iodine crystals and 1.3g of potassium iodide crystals together, place in a 250ml volumetric flask, and fill to 250ml with distilled water. Due to methamphetamine labs, iodine has been regulated since 2007 as a precursor. You can still buy elemental iodine, but your name goes on a list. Your name won't go on a list if you buy ready-made .02N iodine solution, but it is pretty expensive. If you aren't running a methamphetamine lab, don't worry about your name being on a list.

to mix again. Fill the 3ml syringe with iodine solution. Add iodine solution a little at a time, swirling after each addition, until a distinct color change (it will be dark blue) that remains for several seconds occurs. The measured amount of sulfite in ppm is:

(3ml−reading on syringe) x 32

Write this number down as we'll use it twice in the next part of the procedure. Now we need to measure the error. To do this, we'll need to remove the free sulfite from the solution. The 3% hydrogen peroxide solution is way too strong for a sample this small, so make some 0.012% solution by adding 1ml of hydrogen peroxide solution to 250ml volumetric flask and adding enough distilled water to meet the 250ml mark. Clean all equipment with distilled water. Put a 20ml sample of wine in the 50 ml beaker. Add an amount of your prepared hydrogen peroxide solution equal to 0.14 ml for every ppm detected in the earlier procedure. So if the first procedure gave a result of 57ppm, add 0.14 x 57 or 8 ml of hydrogen peroxide solution. Swirl to mix and wait a few minutes. Add 5ml of starch solution and 5ml of sulfuric acid solution to the sample. Fill the 3ml syringe with iodine solution. Add iodine solution a little at a time, swirling after each addition, until a distinct color change (it will be dark blue) that remains for several seconds occurs. The measured amount of error in ppm is:

(3ml−reading on syringe) x 32

The corrected amount of sulfite in the wine is: (measured sulfite)−(measured error) ppm.

Malolactic Fermentation

Most wine musts will contain some lactic bacteria. These are inhibited by sulfite levels greater than 20 mg/L, by alcohol concentrations of greater than 14%, low temperatures, and active yeast. If you have ever been quite certain that secondary fermentation has completed but later found your bottled wine to be slightly carbonated, it is likely that malolactic fermentation occurred spontaneously. Sometimes it even occurs simultaneously with alcoholic fermentation and you never notice.

Commercial wineries subject a large proportion of their red wines and a lesser proportion of their white wines to deliberate malolactic fermentation for a variety of reasons. The most obvious reason is that malolactic fermentation changes sharp malic acid to smooth lactic acid. It raises the pH and reduces the acidity slightly. The formation of lactic acid in the presence of ethanol also allows the creation of ethyl lactate, an ester that gives wines a fruity character. In addition, bacteria will produce diethyl succinate, another fruity ester along with diacetyl and other flavor compounds. Malolactic fermentation also serves to make wine more self-preserving by consuming pentoses and hexoses[4] not used by yeast, as well as malic acid that would otherwise serve as food for other bacteria. Malolactic bacteria secrete bacteriocins that inhibit the growth of other bacteria, which makes the wine more microbiologically stable. Finally, by deliberately conducting a malolactic fermentation, you can be certain that one won't occur spontaneously in the bottle.

---

[4] Pentoses and Hexoses are five-and six-carbon sugars, respectively.

There are a number of malolactic cultures available. Some are single species (usually *Oenococcus oenii*) and others contain a mix of species. Only *Oenococcus oenii* can work at pH values lower than 3.5, so all cultures contain at least that one bacteria.

Malolactic bacteria and wine yeast are often incompatible as one will inhibit the other. Therefore, malolactic culture is best introduced after the secondary alcoholic fermentation is complete unless the wine has a final alcohol level exceeding 14%. Though different products will require slightly different procedures and I based the following on the use of Lalvin's malolactic culture, it's a good guideline for malolactic fermentations generally.

- Wait until secondary fermentation has completed. It can be considered complete after the wine sits for three months without dropping any precipitate at the bottom of the fermenter and it is clear.
- About a week before adding the malolactic cultures, move the wine to an area with a temperature between 64 and 75 degrees. It must remain at this temperature throughout the fermentation.
- Rack the wine into a new, clean secondary fermenter. Do NOT add sulfite in this racking!
- If you have a sulfite test kit, you can test that the sulfite is under 20 ppm. If it is above 20 ppm, you can reduce it to that level via the addition of hydrogen peroxide as described in the chapter on wine chemistry.
- Add the packet of malolactic culture directly to the wine.
- Fit with an airlock. (The fermentation generates carbon dioxide.)

- Malolactic fermentations complete in one to three months, but because they proceed so slowly, it is hard to gauge. You could assess the progress using commercially available paper chromatography kits for malic acid detection, but these cost from $50 to $200 and their shelf life is only a few months. Unless you are making a LOT of wine, this doesn't make a lot of sense.
- After three months, rack the wine into a clean secondary fermenter, adding 50ppm sulfite to the must (one Campden tablet per gallon). This will inhibit any malolactic bacteria that remain. Allow to age for at least another month, then bottle.

Fortification

Fortification is the addition of distilled spirits to wine in order to increase its alcohol content. Wines are fortified for three reasons: to bring them to an alcohol level suitable for the development of what is known as a sherry flor; to arrest fermentation before all the sugar has been consumed so it retains sweetness; and to make a more biologically stable wine for purposes of long storage and shipping. Being distilled from wine, brandy is the most common spirit used for fortification.

Sherry wines are fermented to dryness, their alcohol content is assessed, and then they are mixed with brandy to reach an alcohol level of between 14.5% and 16%. This range is conducive to allowing the specific strain of yeast used in sherries to develop a cap known as a flor that protects the wine from further oxidation and promotes aldehyde production. If the wines were good but unexceptional, they are made into oloroso sherry by fortifying to a level exceeding 16% so that a flor isn't formed. If they were really bad, they are set aside to make vinegar or brandy.

Port wines are fortified to an amount of alcohol around 20% before the primary fermentation has completed. The high level of alcohol from fortification stops the fermentation very quickly so that high sugar levels remain.

Because distilled spirits are expensive (why would you use the cheap stuff?), the financially practical batch size for fortification will likely be limited to a gallon or so. Even though fortification will stop the yeast fermentation, the wine will continue to undergo small changes from aging for as long as forty years.

The first step in fortification is to assess the level of alcohol in the wine. For wines fermented to dryness, this is easy—you can just use the potential alcohol corresponding to the original hydrometer reading of the must. For wines that will retain sweetness, you will take a hydrometer reading every day or two during the primary fermentation and perform the fortification at a point corresponding to the degree of sweetness you want to retain. In general, you'll want to do this at a reading between 1.010 for slightly sweet to 1.040 for very sweet. The alcohol level can be determined by subtracting the potential alcohol at the point of fortification from the potential alcohol at the start of fermentation.

For example, if the original specific gravity of my must was 1.093 (12.8% potential alcohol) and I perform my fortification when the must reaches 1.027 (3.7% potential alcohol), the level of alcohol is 12.8% - 3.7% or 9.1%.

Once you know how much alcohol the wine already contains, you must decide how much alcohol you want it to contain after fortification. If you are wanting a sherry flor, you'll want 15%, but if you are making a sweet wine, you'll want 20%.

Then you need to calculate how much distilled spirit and how much wine to add to make a gallon at the desired strength. Though there are tables for this, algebra is the most flexible tool, and the equation is easy enough.

A = Percentage of Final Wine as Alcohol expressed as a decimal (e.g. 20% = .2)

B = Percentage Alcohol of Starting Wine expressed as a decimal

C = Percentage Wine of Distilled Spirit expressed as a decimal

D = Size of final batch in ounces

X = Ounces of Wine for the batch

$$X = D(A-C)/(B-C)$$

So, if I want a wine with 20% alcohol, my starting wine is 9.1% alcohol and I am fortifying with brandy that is 40% alcohol to make a batch of one gallon (128 ounces):

X = 128(.20 - .40)/(.091 - .40) = 82.8 rounded to 83 ounces.

So now I know I will use 83 ounces of wine and 128−83 or 45 ounces of brandy to make a gallon of my sweet fortified wine.

The procedure is straightforward. You put 45 ounces of brandy in a secondary fermenter, rack wine into the fermenter until you have a gallon, and then top it with an airlock. If you are making a sweet wine you'll need to rack it in another week or so, and then treat it like any other wine. If your starting wine was already completely fermented, you can wait a month before racking and then treat it like any other wine.

Oak Aging

Oak aging is traditional in wines, especially red wines. There's no question that the traditional aging of wines in oak barrels alters the flavor through the extraction of a variety of compounds from the oak. However, oak barrels are very expensive and require considerable care. Studies show that using a neutral container (such as glass) and adding toasted oak chips will impart the same compounds as aging in a barrel.[5]

Oak chips are available from both American and French oak, and in a variety of toasting levels. French oak imparts more tannin and spice notes, whereas American oak imparts more vanilla and sweet notes. Toasting oak cubes of either sort makes some of the compounds such as vanillin more available but also imparts a more charred character to the wine, especially at the highest levels of toasting.

Oak chips impart their character quickly at first, and then more slowly over time. Once they have been added, they can be removed and the compounds they add will remain and continue to work throughout the aging process. Though they can be retained in the fermenter for as long as nine months, little is gained by keeping them for longer than a month.

Before being added to the fermenter, the chips need to be sanitized so they don't infect your wine with something nasty. All you need to do is fill a quart canning jar with water, add a quarter

⊗ Oak chips are easier to work with than barrels and impart indistinguishable results.

teaspoon of potassium metabisulfite powder, put your oak chips in the water, and then put on the lid. After twenty four hours, the chips can be added to the wine by simply dumping them into the wine in the secondary fermenter. They won't fit through the racking tube, so they'll be removed at the next racking. Just rinse them out of the fermenter when you clean it.

Solera Aging

A solera is a grouping of containers (usually barrels) used to accomplish a unique blended aging technique in the production of certain vinegars, spirits, and wines. On a commercial scale, a solera is a substantial investment, but for an amateur with containers not exceeding five gallons, the larger concern is space. Though you can technically use this technique with as few as two containers and with no upper limit, I am going to describe it using three.

Label three containers as A, B, and C, filling them all with wine. After the wine has aged a year, withdraw and bottle half of the contents of

[5] A. Bautista-Ortín, A. Lencina, M. Cano-López, F. Pardo-Mínguez, J. López-Roca and E. Gómez-Plaza (2009), "The use of oak chips during the aging of a red wine in stainless steel tanks or used barrels: effect of the contact time and size of the oak chips on aroma compounds."

⊗ The technique of solera aging can be employed at home on a smaller scale using simple glass fermenters.

container C. Refill container C from container B, refill container B from container A and use new wine to refill container A. Do the same thing every year, and over time the average age of the wine bottled from container C will approach five years, even though you are bottling wine from it every year.

The average age increases with the number of containers and with bottling smaller portions according to the following formula:

Average Age = (Number of Containers– Fraction of Container Used)/Fraction of Container Used

So if you started with three five-gallon containers and only bottled one gallon (.2 of a five-gallon container) a year, the average age would approach (3 - .2)/.2 or 14 years. If you used four containers instead of three and drew off half of a container each year, the average age would converge upon seven years.

If you have a particular type or style of wine that you like and that requires substantial aging, setting up a solera of three containers can be an easy way of having your cake and eating it too, where over time you can consistently produce well-aged wine in small quantity every year.

Of course, this exact same approach is used with the higher quality balsamic vinegars, many of which have average ages exceeding a decade. Because vinegar is consumed in smaller quantities than wine, it is entirely practical to set up an inexpensive vinegar solera using five one-gallon containers. If you drew off and replenished a half gallon annually, the aging would converge upon nine years.

PART V
Greater Food Self-Sufficiency

48

Principles and Materials for Vinegar

There is vinegar, and then there is vinegar. Most often, we buy vinegar as a commodity product without giving much thought as to quality. The gallon jugs of distilled vinegar in the supermarket are indistinguishable. There is no point in making your own vinegar when you can buy it for $1/gallon in bulk; so this chapter is not about making that kind of commodity product.

Really good vinegar is a complex taste sensation to be savored and appreciated. It takes on the character of the malt, cider, or wine from which it is derived. It can also be improved by aging as the complex flavor and aroma compounds meld, recombine, and change. It is truly a gourmet product, and hand-crafted examples are usually more than $20/pint.

Vinegar in general is a healthy condiment. Vinegar increases satiety[1] thereby reducing caloric intake, it reduces the glycemic index of foods

---

[1] Östman, E; Granfeldt, Y; Persson, L; Björck, I (2005). "Vinegar supplementation lowers glucose and insulin responses and increases satiety after a bread meal in healthy subjects." *European Journal of Clinical Nutrition* 59 (9): 983–8

with which it is consumed,[2] and may reduce the risks of certain types of heart disease.[3] And just as wine preserves many of the vitamins and antioxidants in the original fruit, homemade vinegars made from those wines will likewise preserve vitamins and antioxidants; thereby making it even more healthy than the commodity vinegars used in the studies.

So this chapter is not about duplicating commodity products that are cheaper to buy than they are to make. Rather, it is about making a uniquely healthful product with gourmet qualities that will enhance your salads, greens, dressings, and anything else you make with vinegar.

If you make wine and beer, you will already have the raw materials at hand allowing you to make gourmet vinegar inexpensively. So I will focus on using wine and beer as the starting materials in this chapter, even though vinegar can also be made using similar techniques if you use hard cider, sake, or practically any other product containing alcohol.

Speaking of Wine and Beer

I really enjoy making wine and beer. I enjoy every aspect of the process, and I especially enjoy sharing my work with someone who will appreciate the results of my efforts. But sometimes my efforts result in a less-than-stellar product. The wine I made from bottled blueberry juice and brown sugar comes to mind as does the beer I made with far too much oatmeal. What on earth was I thinking? The good news is, I can use these to make vinegar. You will likely have some learning experiences of your own that will serve as excellent raw material.

Some commercial wines and beers are pretty poor. Even if wine or beer that you've purchased is pretty good, it may have sat in the refrigerator too long or be near its sell-by date. Rather than dump that effort or money down the drain, you might consider using it to make your own vinegar.

Wine that you use to make vinegar cannot have been preserved using potassium sorbate or sodium benzoate. Beer seldom has such preservatives. Any wine you use can be normally sulfited or it can be non-sulfited. The wine can be white or red, sweet or dry, and made from any conceivable edible fruit. The beer you use can be made from barley, wheat, or any other grain. And even though you will likely choose wines or beers for this process that were not optimal for drinking, it is very important that the starting material you choose be biologically sound.

Any sound wine or beer that you use, even if it isn't very good for drinking, will still yield a product far superior to the "wine vinegar" or "malt vinegar" you will find at the supermarket. The "wine" they use as a starting product was never intended for drinking in the first place, whereas yours was planned with drinking quality in mind and is hence a better material from which to make vinegar.

What is Vinegar?

Vinegar is a dilute form of acetic acid, ranging in strength from 4% to 8%. It is made by the

---

[2] Johnston, C. S.; Kim, C. M.; Buller, A. J. (2004). "Vinegar Improves Insulin Sensitivity to a High-Carbohydrate Meal in Subjects With Insulin Resistance or Type 2 Diabetes." *Diabetes Care* 27 (1): 281–2

[3] Johnston, Carol S.; Gaas, Cindy A. (2006). "Vinegar: medicinal uses and antiglycemic effect." *MedGenMed* 8 (2): 61

oxidation of ethyl alcohol into acetic acid through a fermentation process undertaken by acetic acid bacteria (AAB). Just as the yeast in wine derives its energy from sugar and produces ethyl alcohol as a waste product, AAB derive their energy from alcohol and produce acetic acid as a waste product. And just as the ethyl alcohol in wine acts as a preservative against organisms that cannot tolerate alcohol, acetic acid acts as a preservative against organisms that cannot tolerate the low pH created by acetic acid. This is how pickling foods in vinegar keeps them from spoiling.

Acetic Acid Bacteria

There are a great many specific strains of AAB. They are present on the surface of both healthy and damaged fruit as well as the nectar of flowers. They are also commonly transferred by the fruit flies that could have been attracted to your wine-making or brewing process.

Wine is produced in anaerobic conditions, meaning that oxygen is excluded. Vinegar, on the other hand, is produced under aerobic conditions as the AAB require oxygen to work. In the absence of oxygen, the bacteria go dormant.

Various strains of AAB[4] are present in wine must from the very beginning and remain in the wine even when it is bottled.[5] The primary factor that keeps it suppressed in wine is lack of oxygen and alcohol levels that are too high for the bacteria to process. So especially with newly-made wines, all that is theoretically necessary to turn wine into vinegar is to permit the entry of oxygen. In the presence of oxygen the bacteria would quickly proliferate as a film on the surface of the wine and turn the alcohol to acetic acid, especially if the alcohol level is under 10%.

Beer is even more susceptible to acetification because its lower alcohol content, lack of sulfites, and higher nutritional content make it an attractive target.

Acetic acid bacteria are not the only bacteria that can take hold in wine or beer, and leaving the results to chance can result in a product that is not only unusable, but thoroughly rotten. So for our purposes, just as a specific strain of yeast is used to make wine, a specific strain of bacteria is used to make vinegar. Acetic acid bacteria are commercially available in a form called vinegar mother. Vinegar mother, also known as *Mycoderma aceti*, is a gelatinous substance containing the AAB that forms on the surface of vinegar. Though vinegar could certainly be made from *Gluconobacter oxydans* or *Acetobacter pasteurianus* among many other possibilities, all of the commercially available vinegar mothers are *Acetobacter aceti*.

Acetobacter aceti needs to float on top of the wine or beer you use to make vinegar so that it has access to oxygen at all times. Without access to oxygen, it will go dormant. The vinegar mother you obtain may look like crude vinegar, or it may look like jelly. If it looks like jelly, it is very likely that when you put it in your vinegar crock, it will sink and thereby go dormant for lack of oxygen. To prevent this, a piece of thin wood about the size of a playing card is floated on top of the wine or beer, and the vinegar mother is placed on it. This piece of wood is usually made of oak and is called a vinegar raft.

---

[4] Acetobacter aceti, gluconobacter oxydans, and acetobacter pasteurianus predominate.

[5] A. Joyeux, S. Lafon-Lafourcade, and P. Ribéreau-Gayon (1984), "Evolution of Acetic Acid Bacteria During Fermentation and Storage of Wine," *Appl Environ Microbiol*. 1984 July; 48(1): 153–156

Vinegar mothers are available as white wine, red wine, beer/malt, and cider. All of them have the same acetic acid bacteria, and the only difference is the carrier. In small batches of vinegar—say less than a gallon—the carrier makes a difference in the flavor, but in larger batches of vinegar the carrier doesn't matter.

Some strains of acetic acid bacteria, such as *Gluconobacter oxydans*, will go dormant once all of the ethyl alcohol has been consumed. But the *Acetobacter aceti* that you'll be using does not go dormant once all of the ethyl alcohol is used. Instead, it starts consuming the acetic acid that it produced, with the end result being just carbon dioxide. So vinegar conversions using a commercial vinegar mother must be arrested once the conversion has completed or you'll end up with no vinegar at all.

The conversion process can be stopped in two ways. For purposes of aging the vinegar, it can be placed in a canning jar with a tight-fitting lid that excludes oxygen. This leaves the vinegar alive, but dormant. For purposes of long-term storage or use in an environment where oxygen might be admitted, the vinegar is pasteurized. Vinegar is pasteurized by heating it to 150 degrees for 30 minutes with the lid adjusted as for canning to prevent evaporation. Once it has been pasteurized, it can be stored in any clean container for a nearly indefinite period of time.

Ethanol to Acetic Acid Conversion

If you are using commercial beer or wine to make vinegar, the amount of alcohol (by volume) is listed on the label. If you are using your own, you should have a good idea how much alcohol is in your beer or wine from the hydrometer readings you recorded.

The chemical equation for the conversion of ethanol to vinegar is:

$$C_2H_5OH + O_2 \rightarrow CH_3COOH + H_2O$$

So ethanol plus oxygen gets converted to acetic acid plus water. Looking at the equation, each molecule of ethanol is converted into one molecule of acetic acid. The molecular weight of ethanol is 46.07 and its density is .789 g/cm³. The molecular weight of acetic acid is 60.5 and its density is 1.049 g/cm³.

This means that every gram of alcohol will result in 60.5/46.07 or 1.313 grams of vinegar. A gram of alcohol will occupy 1/.789 or 1.27 cm³. Alcohol percentages are done by volume, but vinegar percentages are done by weight. We can get a good idea of the conversion factor, that is, how much acetic acid a given amount of ethanol will create, by doing the math for a hypothetical 10% wine.

If I have a liter of 10% wine, that liter contains 100 ml of alcohol. 100 ml of alcohol has a mass of 100 cm³/1.27 cm³ or 78.7 grams. The mass of the vinegar produced will be 78.7 * 1.313 or 103 grams.

Therefore, a 10% alcohol by volume wine will create a 10.3% by weight vinegar. So in essence the percentages are identical. Knowing this fact will allow us to dilute the beer or wine we are adding to the vinegar mother to produce a vinegar of known strength. We'd still test it just to be sure, of course. But this allows us to make our vinegar very precisely.

How to Safely Use Homemade Vinegar in Canning

All canning books tell you to never use homemade vinegar in canning. That's because pickling recipes rely upon the vinegar having a certain strength of 5%, and if you use vinegar of a lesser strength you could wind up with botulism-tainted food that could kill you. So if you don't know for sure that the strength of your vinegar is 5% or greater, you can't use it safely. Of course, if the vinegar is substantially stronger than 5% you could wind up with pickled foods that are a lot more acidic than you'd like. You can always dilute it if it is too strong.

The solution to this problem is to figure out how much acidity is in the vinegar. You can do this easily by using the ingredients in a standard acid testing kit available from all wine-making suppliers, a pH meter, and a slight change in procedure. I specify using a pH meter rather than the phenolphthalein indicator because phenolphthalein turns pink when the endpoint is reached, and such a color change may be difficult to discern in vinegar of certain colors. A pH meter won't trick your eye.

Equipment

1 50 ml beaker
1 10 ml syringe (no needle needed)
0.2N Sodium Hydroxide solution
Distilled water
pH meter

Rinsing the syringe using distilled water after each use, put 2ml of the vinegar to be tested and 20ml of distilled water in the 50ml beaker. Fill the syringe with 0.2N sodium hydroxide solution to exactly the 10ml mark. Initially, add 1ml of sodium hydroxide to the beaker each time, swirl, then test with the pH meter. As the pH approaches its endpoint of 8.3, use lesser quantities. Repeat until the solution has a pH of 8.3.

The amount of acid in your vinegar is given by the following equation:

Percentage Acetic Acid = 0.6 x (10−reading of syringe at endpoint)

49

Vinegar Making Techniques

Making vinegar is easier than making wine or beer and requires minimal equipment or ingredients. Other than a vinegar crock and the wine or beer you'll be using, you can get everything else you need for under $30. Here are the items you'll need:

Vinegar Crock

Vinegar can theoretically be made in any sort of container. Traditionally, it is made in oak barrels called vinegar casks or in ceramic urns known as vinegar crocks.

There are three important features in a container used to make vinegar. The container should have a mouth wide enough that you can insert your vinegar raft and preferably your whole hand. It should have a tap, spout, or spigot near the bottom, but far enough from the bottom that it doesn't pick up sediment. Finally, it should be made of a material that will not react with the vinegar. Vinegar is a dilute acid, so it will react with most metals given time.

Given these features, you are not constrained to only use products officially sold as vinegar crocks. Anything officially sold as a vinegar crock will quite frankly be seriously over-priced. I looked on the Internet recently and found many of them priced at nearly $100!

I use two containers to make vinegar. One is a miniature ceramic water crock that holds a half gallon. It costs $24. The other is a one-gallon plastic beverage dispenser I picked up at a department store for $4. Both of these containers have the essential features, including the spigot. Normal ceramic water crocks hold 2½ gallons, an amount which may far exceed the amount of vinegar you plan to make. That's why I got a miniature ½ gallon crock.

You could go all out and get an oak vinegar cask, but that will set you back at least $80. If you want your vinegar to be oak-aged, just add oak cubes to the sealed pint or quart jar that you are using to age your vinegar.

Cheesecloth and Rubber Bands

These items are used over the mouth of your vinegar crock to allow oxygen to enter but keep fruit flies and other critters out. Not all cheesecloth is created equal. The material that is sold as

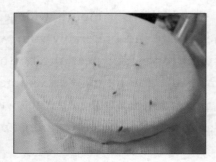

» Use a doubled piece of high-quality fine cheesecloth to cover your vinegar urn. Otherwise, fruit flies will get into your vinegar.

"cheesecloth" at the supermarket is not suitable for making cheese, and even doubled or tripled it won't keep fruit flies out of your vinegar.

Unless you have a good gourmet shop nearby that sells real cheesecloth, you may have to order it from a supplier of cheese-making supplies over the Internet. It is a bit expensive when you include shipping, so I recommend saving on shipping by ordering a couple of packages. They won't go to waste because you'll need the cheesecloth for making cheese in the next chapter.

The size of the needed rubber bands will be different depending upon the size of the mouth of your vinegar crock. The only caution worth mentioning is that light and vinegar fumes will degrade the rubber, so check the rubber bands weekly and replace them if you see signs of deterioration. Otherwise you'll look at your crock one day and find more flies in it than vinegar.

Miscellaneous Supplies

A vinegar raft is a small thin piece of oak that floats on top of your vinegar. Its purpose is to keep the vinegar mother from sinking because if the vinegar mother sinks, it will stop making vinegar. These are available in vinegar kits or individually from many Internet sites. Just type "vinegar raft" into a search engine.

Some people prefer the taste of vinegar that has been aged in oak, or the astringency contributed by the tannins leached from the oak. Oak barrels are expensive and time-intensive to maintain. An alternative is adding oak chips or oak cubes to the vinegar. Add a quarter cup per gallon, enclosed in a tied spice bag for easy removal later. The chips or cubes are added during the aging process and left in the vinegar for four to six weeks. For these purposes, you don't want to use oak from your building supply store. Instead, order it from a winemaking supplier. Winemaking suppliers can offer a range of oaks with different taste characteristics that you know aren't contaminated with anything nasty.

Canning jars are a good choice for aging and storing vinegars. They seal tightly, which will cause the vinegar mother to go dormant during aging, and they can be used repeatedly which makes them a good bargain.

One other thing you may find helpful is a funnel that you have attached to a piece of plastic hose such as the hose used for racking wine. As vinegar is being made, you need to add more beer or wine. The easy way to do this without risk of disturbing the vinegar mother is to insert the hose into the liquid in the vinegar crock, and add the liquid through the funnel.

A candy thermometer will be needed for pasteurizing vinegar, unless you plan to can it using a boiling water bath canner for long-term storage.

Consolidated Equipment and Ingredient List

- Vinegar crock
- Vinegar mother
- Cheesecloth

The materials for oak-aging vinegar are simple and inexpensive.

- Rubber bands
- Vinegar raft
- Canning jars
- Candy thermometer
- Oak chips or cubes (optional)

Making Your Vinegar

The first thing to do is pre-dilute your wine or beer if needed. At levels higher than 7% alcohol it might inhibit the AAB. You can always make it less concentrated, down to 3%, for purely culinary use or if your beer only has that much alcohol, and it isn't unusual for sherry vinegars to be as high as 7%. In general, I recommend diluting to 5.5% so the vinegar can be used with greater versatility. Always dilute with clean, non-chlorinated water. I use bottled water for this purpose.

So . . . how much water do you add to your beer or wine to get a certain percentage of alcohol? Start by dividing the current concentration in percent by the desired concentration in percent to get C. So if I have some 10% wine and I want 5.5%, I divide 10 by 5.5 to get 1.82. Next, multiply the volume of your wine (say 500 ml in a standard wine bottle) by C to get the total diluted volume: 500 ml × 1.82 = 910. Finally, subtract the volume of wine from the total volume to get the volume of water you need to add. 910 ml − 500 ml = 410 ml.

This also works with beer. Say I have some beer that is 6% alcohol and I want to dilute it to 5.5%. The standard beer bottle is 12 ounces. So C = 6%/5.5% = 1.09. Multiply 12 oz x 1.09 = 13. Finally, 13 − 12 = 1, so I would add one ounce of water.

The quantity of diluted wine or beer that you use is important because it takes a while for the vinegar mother to work, and in the meantime the underlying beer or wine is vulnerable to outside infection. You want to limit the amount you put in the crock to no more than triple the volume of the vinegar mother, which is eight ounces. So your initial ingredients of the vinegar crock will be 24 ounces of beer or wine diluted as needed and eight ounces of vinegar mother for a total of 32 ounces.

Making Vinegar, Step by Step

1. **Clean your vinegar** crock thoroughly and sanitize it using sulfite solution. (See the chapters on wine for how to make sulfite solution.)

2. Check the capacity of the container of vinegar mother you ordered. Usually it is eight ounces.

3. Add diluted wine or beer to the vinegar crock. The amount added should be twice the volume of the vinegar mother. So if you have eight ounces of vinegar mother, put 24 ounces of wine or beer in your crock. The alcohol percentage cannot exceed 7%.

4. Open your vinegar mother. If it is gelatinous, place your vinegar raft on top of the water/wine solution in the vinegar crock.

5. Add the vinegar mother. If it is all liquid, just gently pour it into the crock. If it is gelatinous, add it on top of the vinegar raft.

6. Cover the mouth of the container with cheesecloth and hold it in place with a rubber band.

7. Set the container in a dark place or at least someplace well out of the sun. The ideal temperature range is 80 to 90 degrees, but it will progress fine at 70 to 100.

8. Depending on temperature and other factors, the complete conversion of wine to vinegar can take anywhere from six weeks to three months. Check your vinegar weekly by sniffing it through the cheesecloth. It should smell like vinegar is forming.

9. To increase the volume of the vinegar being made, you can add more diluted wine or beer starting at the fourth week and every fourth week thereafter. Add by using a sanitized funnel and tubing.

10. Six weeks after the final addition of wine, start tasting small (less than ¼ tsp) samples of the vinegar to see if it is done. It's

done when all the alcohol flavor has been replaced with vinegar flavor. Your tongue and nose are amazingly sensitive and able to detect many substances in very low concentrations of parts-per-million. This is as accurate as any easily performed test in determining if the vinegar is done.

11. Once the vinegar is done, it is important to remove it from the vinegar crock because with all the alcohol gone, the vinegar mother will start consuming the acetic acid, and thereby destroy the vinegar. Take out as much vinegar as you can through the spigot and then start your next batch using the same vinegar mother in that container. As long as your vinegar doesn't become contaminated, you can use the same vinegar mother indefinitely.

Aging Vinegar

Just like wine, vinegar made from wine will mellow with age. Freshly-made vinegar is very sharp with a lot of pointed edges. When it is allowed to age, the compounds within the vinegar combine in various ways that make the vinegar more mellow and to bring out other flavor components.

Even though it is easy to visualize the vinegar mother as sitting on top of the wine, many of its bacteria are spread throughout the vinegar. When you draw off a sample, even if it looks clear, it is filled with acetic acid bacteria. (These bacteria, incidentally, are totally harmless to humans.) Freshly-made vinegar is teeming with life.

When vinegar is aged, it is aged with that life intact. The vinegar is drawn from the crock via the spigot and placed in a container sealed so as to exclude air. This renders the acetic acid

bacteria dormant. Vinegar can be kept in a sealed container for an indefinite period of time. In fact, genuine balsamic vinegar is aged for at least twelve years, and often for as long as 25 years. The minimum period of aging I would recommend is six weeks.

Vinegar can be aged in porcelain, glass, impervious plastic, or wooden barrels. A lot of the better traditionally-made vinegars feature oak aging. The oak aging serves to impart an astringent principle to the vinegar in the form of tannin. Tannin is not just one substance. The term "tannin" refers to literally dozens if not hundreds of related compounds formed around either a gallic acid or a flavone core. Tannins have in common not only their astringency, but also their ability to bind and precipitate proteins. This means that tannins introduced into vinegar will scavenge stray proteins left over from fermentation by combining with them to form an insoluble substance that will sink to the bottom of the container.

So over time, an initially high level of tannins is reduced and a number of protein- or amino acid-based substances are removed. This

⊗ The mother in this vinegar crock is doing nicely.

serves to alter the flavor in more ways than merely introducing astringency. In fact, the addition of tannin, through its ability to remove other substances, can paradoxically decrease the astringency of vinegar over a period of aging by removing other substances. Tannins also combine with metals in a process known as chelation. Chelation forms soluble compounds that include the metal but render it unavailable to combine with other substances. This likewise affects the flavor.

You can use oak in the aging of your vinegar by placing a quarter cup of the cubes or chips in a tied spice bag in your aging vinegar. Leave it in the container for six weeks, and then remove it using sterilized tongs and re-seal the container. The rest of the vinegar's aging will continue to be affected by the tannins imparted by the oak.

Keeping Vinegar

Eventually, the aging process ends and the vinegar is ready for storage. The next step is to filter and pasteurize. Perfectly adequate filtration is achieved by pouring the vinegar from the jar in which it is aging through a funnel lined with a coffee filter into a clean canning jar.

Fill the jar with vinegar to within a quarter inch of the top, and install the two-piece canning lid. Process for 10 minutes in a boiling water bath or steam canner and pasteurization is complete.

Making Herbal Vinegars

I'll confess that I have never purchased an herbal vinegar. Anytime I have seen herbal vinegar, it is usually in some sort of craft shop. The vinegar is in an ornate bottle with a sprig of some herb and has a fancy label. It also has an obscenely fancy price. The price seems crazy to me because I'm pretty certain that the vinegar they used was $1/gallon commodity vinegar and the sprig of herb cost about a penny, and the cost is $12 for six ounces. No thanks!

Herbal vinegars can be quite nice, though, and making your own is easy enough. You can make it using commodity vinegar from the supermarket or your own hand-crafted vinegar. I don't recommend using cider vinegars for herbs.

Chapter 31 reveals why growing your own herbs is easy. The hard part for beginners is choosing which herbs to use (and how much). To help you get started, I suggest the following single herbs: borage, thyme, rosemary, dill, basil, tarragon, and oregano.

I recommend making your herbal vinegars from fresh herbs when possible. Using fresh herbs, I recommend ½ ounce of fresh herb per cup (eight ounces) of vinegar as a starting proportion. Because the vinegar is a preservative, the herbs won't rot. When using dried herbs, use two tablespoons of dried herb per cup of vinegar.

The procedure is straightforward. Add the cleaned herbs to the container that will hold the herbal vinegar. Heat up the vinegar to a simmer (NOT a boil!), and then pour the vinegar into the container holding the herb. Seal the container. Allow the flavors to meld for three or four weeks to develop the full flavor before using.

If you want something really impressive for making an oil and vinegar dressing for salad, I would suggest making vinegar from pear wine, and then using the pear vinegar to make a borage herbal vinegar.

Oil and Vinegar Dressing

Ingredients:

11 ounces	Virgin olive oil
5 ounces	Hand-crafted wine vinegar
2 ounces	Water
1 Tbsp	Pulverized dehydrated sweet red pepper
1 Tbsp	Pulverized dehydrated onion
1 tsp	Sea salt
1 tsp	Garlic powder
1 tsp	Dried oregano
1 tsp	Dried basil
tsp	Xanthan gum OR ½ tsp dried powdered purslane or okra (optional)

Procedure

Add ¼ cup of water and ½ cup plus 2 Tbsp vinegar to your container. Add the remaining solid ingredients except for the xanthan gum/purslane. Shake and allow to sit for a few minutes. Add the xanthan gum/purslane and shake thoroughly. Add 1¼ cup plus 2 Tbsp of olive oil. Shake thoroughly.

The purpose of the xanthan gum or purslane in this recipe is to keep the mixture from separating too quickly for practical use because oil/vinegar and oil/water don't normally mix. The xanthan gum or purslane helps to keep it in suspension. If you use xanthan gum, don't use more than the recommended amount or you'll end up with a jelly-like substance rather than dressing.

50

Making Cheese at Home

Protein is an essential part of the human diet. Though vegetable sources can provide protein, in most cases the protein lacks crucial amino acids. The most readily available complete proteins are meats, eggs and dairy, of which the latter two are the least expensive. Continuing the theme of preserving nutritive content through fermentation, we arrive at cheese. Milk contains a lot of complete protein, but it is also highly perishable.

In the ages before refrigeration was reliably available, one of the few ways to make the nutritional value of milk last longer while also making it quite portable was turning it into cheese. Hard cheeses in particular, if waxed, can last for years.

Another advantage of cheese is that many hard cheeses lack lactose. Lactose is a sugar in milk that a substantial portion of the human population has not yet evolved the genetics to be able to digest. As a result, if they consume most milk products they will suffer severe gastrointestinal distress—sometimes for days. When the whey and curd are separated in the first phases of making cheese, 94 percent of the lactose stays in the whey. Most aged cheeses lack lactose and as a result provide lactose-intolerant people with a delicious way of obtaining the nutritional benefits of milk.

Cheese also has its own health benefits. It is rich in cancer-preventing conjugated linoleic acid and sphingolipids, fights tooth decay and helps maintain bone strength.

Like wine making, cheese making is both art and science. If anything, there is even more art to making cheese because it requires practice to master the various steps. So this chapter is enough to get you started, but you'll likely want to branch out once you've mastered the techniques covered here.

What Is Cheese?

Cheese is the coagulated fat and protein from the milk of domesticated dairy animals. The fats and proteins of milk are coagulated in various ways for the manufacture of different types of cheese. In some cases, a bacterial culture is added. The bacterial culture consumes lactose to make lactic acid, and this lactic acid causes the coagulation.

In other cases, rennet is added. Rennet is a complex mixture of enzymes that likewise coagulates milk. In yet other cases, an acid such as citric acid, tartaric acid or even vinegar is used to cause coagulation. Though the products of these various methods of coagulation are markedly different, they are all cheese because they have in common the coagulation of milk.

Milk: Where It All Begins

In the United States, cows are the usual source for milk, though goats are utilized to a lesser extent. In other countries, the milk of bison, buffalo, sheep, horses, yaks and other animals are also used. The nature of the milk of different species varies appreciably and this is reflected in the character of the cheese produced. Theoretically, you could make cheese using the milk of any mammal, though I wouldn't attempt this until you get good at making cheese from well-characterized herbivores such as cows and goats. Not only that, trying to milk a tiger or a bear is probably more dangerous than warranted.

Likewise, the components of the milk will vary between different breeds of dairy cattle and even the milk of a particular cow will vary with season and diet. Probably the most striking example of this was in the cream cheese my grandmother would make from cows that had been eating wild onions. The smell and taste of the wild onions was transferred to the milk and hence to the cheese. In the case of cream cheese, the results were delicious!

But for the purposes of this chapter we are going to work exclusively with pasteurized and homogenized cow's milk like you buy at the grocery store.

It is important to know that though pasteurized milk is fine, the *ultra*-pasteurized milk that you find in the store is unsuitable. This is too bad, because it is the organic brands that tend to be ultra-pasteurized. Ultra-pasteurization is used to extend the shelf life of expensive milk that wouldn't turn over very quickly. Unfortunately, that process damages the protein in milk so extensively that it is unsuitable for making cheese.

Milk from other animals can certainly be made into cheese, but doing so would require changes in timing, temperature, quantities of ingredients and so forth that are simply too extensive to be treated in a single chapter.

Most organic milk is ultra-pasteurized, making it unsuitable for cheese.

So we are going to use pasteurized, homogenized cow's milk from the grocery store as the learning medium for your first forays into cheese making. After you have mastered these skills, you can branch out from there. You can find specific types of milk suitable for your needs by finding a local dairy at www.smalldairy.com.

About Raw Milk

Cheese connoisseurs insist that the best cheeses are made from raw milk that has been neither pasteurized nor homogenized. The trouble is that raw milk is not readily available and quite often there are legal impediments to getting it directly from farmers. The basis for these legal impediments is widespread recognition of the likelihood of the presence of pathogens in raw milk.

Though in former times the largest risks were brucellosis and tuberculosis, today the risks are e. coli, salmonella and listeria. Testing of vats of milk in modern times shows that even from healthy cows, anywhere from 0.87 percent to 12.6 percent of raw milk harbors dangerous pathogens.[1] How do healthy cows give pathogen infested milk? They don't. Inadequate sanitation and cleaning of equipment introduces fecal bacteria into the milk. The reason pasteurization became a requirement in the first place was that farmers were actively falsifying their records so that tuberculosis-infected cows wouldn't have to be removed from milk production.[2]

The reason it continues to be required is because human nature hasn't changed, and that maintaining sanitation on an industrial scale of a biological product created by an animal that excretes feces requires extreme levels of conscientiousness that cannot be guaranteed. In essence, because the healthiness of cows and their milk can be tested to assure a safe product without pasteurization, it is possible to sell perfectly healthy raw milk. But pasteurization is required anyway to compensate for the existence of lazy or dishonest people that will prioritize the production of a single infected cow over the health and well-being of their customers. Most people I'm quite sure would do the right thing, but in an industrial system where the outputs of various farms are mixed together, it only requires one feces-contaminated vat to sicken thousands of people.

Obviously, raw milk that does not contain pathogens can be made. Humans have consumed raw milk for thousands of years before pasteurization was invented; it's just that such

---

[1] Position Statement on Raw Milk Sales and Consumption, Cornell University Food Science Department.

[2] "Not on My Farm!: Resistance to Bovine Tuberculosis Eradication in the United States, Alan L. Olmstead and Paul W. Rhode," January 2005, *The Journal of Economic History* (2007), 67 : 768-809 Cambridge University Press, Copyright © 2007 The Economic History Association, doi:10.1017/S0022050707000307.

milk was collected at home by the end users, so there was a direct correlation between shoddiness and adverse consequences that would result from collecting milk in a bucket that wasn't clean. The milk was used immediately rather than transported thousands of miles, and so any pathogens present had less opportunity to multiply to dangerous or infective levels. It is therefore possible to obtain raw milk that will not make you sick, provided it is supplied by an honest and conscientious farmer.

How to determine if someone is honest and conscientious, I can't say. If I could write a book describing a sure-fire technique of that sort, personnel managers across the world would rejoice. In the absence of that, I would instead look at the idea of mutual self-interest. If a farmer were to sell you raw milk that made you sick, your family could sue him into oblivion. So it is in his best interests, if he sells raw milk at all, to make sure it is pristine. Many such farmers use small-scale low temperature vat pasteurization just to be sure, and this process is less damaging to the milk proteins than standard pasteurization processes.

One other layer of protection is to only use raw milk to make hard cheeses that are aged for longer than two months. The process of cheese-making, when combined with the conditions of aging in cheese serve to eliminate potential pathogens and render the cheese safe. This only applies to aged hard cheeses! Soft cheeses and those eaten less than two months from manufacture should be considered as risky as raw milk, and I would personally avoid making them from raw milk, though that's an individual choice.

If you use raw milk in cheese making, there are only two procedural changes you'll need to adopt. The first is that you can avoid using calcium chloride (described later), and the other is that when heating the milk, especially for thermophilic cheeses, you will need to top stir the milk. Top stirring is just slowly dragging a utensil across the top quarter-inch of milk in order to keep the milk fats from separating out.

To find raw milk, I recommend the following Internet resources:

- A Campaign for Real Milk: www.realmilk.com
- The Weston A. Price Foundation: www.westonaprice.org
- Farm-to-Consumer Legal Defense Fund: www.farmtoconsumer.org

Categories of Cheese

Cheese can be categorized in various ways depending upon the substances from which it is made, its appearance or consistency, whether it is aged or eaten fresh and the procedures used to produce it. For our purposes, we will use fresh and aged cheeses as categories, as well as soft and hard cheeses, as these categories have the greatest differentiation.

Equipment

When it comes to the equipment needed to make cheese, quality matters. The good news is that most of this equipment is a once-in-a-lifetime purchase that can be passed along to kids or others. You will likely end up ordering most of these items over the Internet because you may have difficulty finding them locally.

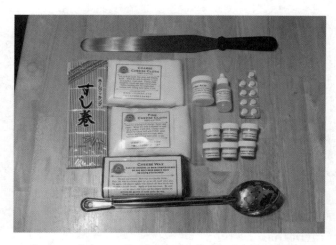
Quality ingredients and equipment will contribute to a quality product.

Measuring Cups and Spoons

You want both a large (2+ cup) and small (1 cup) Pyrex™ glass liquid measuring cups. You should be able to find these nearby if you don't already have them. You will also need measuring spoons, but not the ordinary cheap ones you get at the dollar store. You want high quality stainless steel measuring spoons that measure in 1/32, 1/16, 1/8 and 1/4 teaspoon increments, as well as the traditional sizes.

I have noted by comparing volumes to my laboratory standards that cheap measuring spoons are often undersized or over-sized. This is not a critical matter when making a cake, but when making cheese it can spell the difference between success and failure.

Large Double-Boiler

With batches of cheese starting with a gallon of milk or less and that use a mesophilic starter culture (more on starter cultures later), you can get by with a standard large pot that you set in a sink of hot water. But for batches of cheese

requiring more than a gallon of milk or using a thermophilic starter culture, you will need a double-boiler. In cheese making, this double-boiler is also called a "cheese pot." For very small batches of cheese starting with a quart of milk, you can improvise by setting a smaller pot into a larger one as long as the handles on the smaller pot will sit on the lip of the larger pot so the smaller one is surrounded by water.

Again, depending on the size of your largest intended batch of cheese, you may be able to use a double-boiler as small as eight quarts. But because it takes a large amount of milk to make enough curd to yield very much hard cheese after pressing, you wouldn't go wrong with one as large as twenty quarts. No matter what size you use, make sure it is stainless steel because acidified milk will leach aluminum or iron into your curd and impart metallic flavors.

If you don't already have a double-boiler, this is probably the most expensive item you'll need to get. Searching the Internet, I found prices ranging from $88 to $130 for a twenty-quart model. It won't come cheaply, but you'll be thankful that you got it. You can use it for batches of cheese starting with anywhere from one gallon to four gallons of milk, and its configuration will help to hold temperatures steady while preventing scorching. The results of your efforts will reflect the benefits of this device.

Colander

You'll need a large eight-quart colander that will fit into the cheese pot" with the handles resting on the edges of the pot. You'll use this to separate the curds from the whey, with the whey going back into the pot.

Special Utensils

You need a large stainless steel slotted spoon, a stainless steel skimming ladle and a stainless steel curd knife. This latter utensil is pretty specialized so you will probably have to get it via an Internet source.

Cheesecloth

You want high-quality coarse (twenty thread count) and fine (sixty thread count) cheesecloth. The fine cheesecloth is used for making soft cheese such as cream cheese whereas the coarse cheesecloth is used to hold harder cheeses during the pressing or curing process.

Cheesecloth is packaged in two-yard increments, so you get a piece that is three feet wide and six feet long. Cut off pieces as needed with good scissors. Before use, cheesecloth must be sterilized. Put it in a pan of water, boil for five minutes and then dump the cheesecloth and water into a colander in the sink. Cheesecloth can be reused. Rinse it under cool running water, and then work a few drops of dish liquid into it. Then rinse it thoroughly, and boil it for five minutes. After boiling, hang it up to dry then store the dried cheesecloth in an airtight bag. Don't forget to sterilize it before using it again.

Bamboo Sushi Mats

These allow good air circulation for cheese that is either draining or aging, and so are essential if hard cheeses will be made. Luckily, they are inexpensive at $4 each or less, because they can't be sanitized after use and hence should be discarded.

Cheese Wax or a Vacuum Sealer

Cheese wax is used to protect the cheese from air while it ages. This is a special kind of wax that melts at a low enough temperature that it won't hurt the cheese when you brush it on. Don't try to substitute canning wax for this! Another alternative is to use a vacuum sealer to seal the wax in an airtight bag from which all air has been evacuated. That's what I do because it is more convenient than waxing.

Cheese Press and Mold

A cheese press is used to knit the curds together into a solid mass while expelling excess whey. There are a variety of designs of varying expense and complexity. A search on the Internet will even reveal many free plans for making your own.

For the batches of cheese in this chapter, I am using a simple plastic press and mold that only cost $21. The downside is that you have to use external weights with it. Still, you can't beat it for the price and ease of use.

Instant-Read Digital Thermometer

Temperatures are critical when making cheese. Some types of cheese require gradually raising the temperature or holding at a certain temperature for a specified time. The best thermometer for such purposes is one that gives you an instant and accurate reading. A good digital thermometer is not expensive.

I have a Norpro electronic digital read thermometer/timer that only cost $16. It has programmed cooking temperatures for meat that make it a bit inconvenient, but you can set it for temperature-only so it doesn't beep. The reason I chose that model is because it has a stainless steel probe that makes it easy to clean and it was the only model I could find locally that suited my purpose. You could undoubtedly find other suitable digital thermometers at a nice cookware store.

Dedicated Small Refrigerator

Traditionally, many styles of cheese were quite literally aged in caves. Caves maintain a constant temperature and humidity throughout the year. Most of us don't have access to a suitable cave, and we don't have an area in the house that will reliably maintain a certain temperature for months on end.

If you decide to make cheeses requiring aging, you will find a dedicated refrigerator indispensable. A secondhand dormitory-sized refrigerator and an external thermometer set up to turn it on and off as needed will work perfectly for such an endeavor. A refrigerator dedicated to cheese making is called a "cheese cave."

Ingredients

Not all of these ingredients are needed for all cheeses, but you'll want them on hand. Some of these you likely already have from your excursions into wine and vinegar making.

Vinegar, Lemons, and Tartaric Acid

These common acids are used to make soft cheeses via the direct acidification method. In this method, the milk is heated to a certain temperature, a measured amount of acid is added and stirred into the milk, and then the milk clots after a period of time. This clotted milk is poured into a colander lined with cheesecloth, then the cheesecloth is tied into a bag. The bag is hung in a warm place for the whey to drain out of the soft curds. These are among the easiest cheeses to make, and they work especially well as dips and spreads.

Calcium Chloride, 30 Percent Solution

When milk is pasteurized, the calcium ion balance is upset in the milk, and this can impede proper curd formation. A small amount of calcium chloride solution diluted further in distilled water and mixed into the milk can correct this imbalance.

You can order food-grade calcium chloride and make the solution yourself (percentages are by weight!), or you can order the pre-mixed solution from various Internet stores specializing in cheese making supplies.

Calcium chloride, incidentally, is also an ingredient in some ice-melting pellets used on sidewalks and driveways. This is a very crude product that isn't suitable for human consumption, so make sure you get food-grade calcium chloride.

Flaked or Canning Salt

Salt is used as a flavor enhancer, a bacteriostatic preservative, a modulator for enzymatic action and to help expel water from cheese curds through osmotic pressure. Special "flaked" cheese salt is sold, and you can get that, but canning salt will do as well.

The important thing is to avoid the ordinary salts in the grocery store because not only do many of them contain iodine, they often contain anti-caking agents and other chemicals that could interfere with cheese making. So anything you use should be purely salt.

Starter Culture

Starter culture is an inoculant containing a mix of bacteria that eat the lactose in milk and excrete lactic acid. The first purpose of these bacteria is to lower the pH of the milk in order to encourage curd formation. The second purpose is the continuing development of flavor characteristics during the making and aging of the cheese. The nature of the starter culture strongly influences the flavor of the cheese.

Starter cultures are either mesophilic (meaning "medium heat loving") or thermophilic (meaning "high heat loving").

Mesophilic starter cultures work best at room temperature—around 72 degrees. They usually contain at least *Streptococcus lactis*, and many also contain *Streptococcus lactis var. cremoris* along with other lactic acid bacteria such as *L. delbrueckii* subsp. *Lactis, L. lactis* subsp. *lactis* biovar *diacetylactis and Leuconostoc mesenteroides* subsp. *cremoris* .

Streptococcus lactis is used to make buttermilk, so fresh buttermilk with active live cultures can be used to make a mesophilic starter culture for cheese making. Cheeses that begin with a mesophilic starter include farmhouse cheddar, edam, stilton and Monterey Jack, among others.

Thermophilic starter cultures work best at temperatures above 80 degrees and below 130 degrees. A specific recipe will dictate the best temperature within this range for the particular cheese being produced, but the culture works best at 110 degrees. Exceeding 130 degrees may kill a thermophilic culture. It may like heat, but it doesn't want to be scalded or boiled. Thermophilic starters are used to create Swiss and Parmesan cheeses among others. *Streptococcus thermophilus* is a common bacteria in thermophilic starter cultures, but *Lactobacillus delbrueckii* subsp. *bulgaricus, L. delbrueckii* subsp. *lactis, L. casei* and *L. plantarum* are all used.

Yogurt is made with thermophilic bacteria. One prominent brand of organic yogurt uses six live cultures that include *Streptococcus thermophilus, Lactobacillus delbrueckii subsp. Bulgaricus* and *L. casei*, so not only can plain yogurt be used to make more yogurt, it can also be used to make a thermophilic starter culture for cheese.

So you can buy starter culture in packets from a supplier, or you can make your own from buttermilk and yogurt.

If you opt to buy starter cultures from a cheese making supply store, there are only two important things you need to know: you want the sort of culture called a "direct vat" culture, and you should put it in the coldest part of your freezer the very second you get it. Keep it in the freezer until ready for use.

Rennet

Rennet is an enzyme that was originally derived from the stomachs of suckling animals. It is a proteolytic enzyme that breaks protein bonds in such a way as to turn liquid milk into solid curds. All infant mammals produce rennet. This turns milk into a solid form that stays in the digestive tract longer. That's why, when a baby spits up milk, it has mysteriously turned into a clumpy solid. Babies of all mammals have miniature internal cheese factories.

In practice, animal rennet is a byproduct of veal production. Animal rennet of this sort is extremely perishable and has to be kept refrigerated. It's also pretty expensive.

Rennet can also be made from certain fungi and plants. The sort made from plants has to be made fresh on the spot, which may not be feasible during winter or if you can't find the plants, so for our purposes I am recommending vegetable rennet, which is actually made from fungi. It is inexpensive and if you put it in the freezer it will stay good for at least a year. It comes in tablets that can be divided into halves and quarters, though this must be done carefully as it has a tendency to disintegrate.

Rennet is an extremely powerful enzyme. Tiny quantities will clot gallons of milk. When adding rennet, dissolve the required amount into a quarter cup of distilled water over a period of twenty minutes and then sprinkle it over the surface of the milk. Mix it into the milk using up-down and back-and-forth motions rather than swirling because swirling doesn't mix as efficiently. It's important that rennet be mixed efficiently because otherwise the curd it forms will be of uneven consistency.

Other Cultures and Enzymes

As your cheese making expertise increases, you'll want to try to make specific types of cheese. Toward that end, you will need different cultures and enzymes.

Lipase is an enzyme that splits milkfat into free fatty acids. It is used in manufacturing feta, blue, mozzarella and provolone cheeses, and develops a characteristic picante flavor in those cheeses. Like rennet, it is extremely powerful. Unless a recipe directs otherwise, use between 1/16 and 1/8 teaspoon of the powder per gallon of milk. Dissolve the powder in a half cup of cool water for thirty minutes prior to use. Lipase is added immediately before rennet by sprinkling it on top of the milk and mixing it in using an up-down and back-and-forth motion.

Propionic Shermanii culture is used to create the characteristic holes and flavor of Swiss cheeses. As it ferments, it creates carbon dioxide that expands to create the holes. This is added to thermophilic starter culture at the rate of 1/16 teaspoon per gallon of milk.

Not all mesophilic or thermophilic starter cultures are created equal. The specific varieties of bacteria make a difference in the ultimate flavor of your cheese. As you learn more about cheese, you will want to try other starter cultures.

How to Have a Lifetime Supply of Buttermilk and Mesophilic Cheese Starter

I have always loved buttermilk. Its thick consistency with sweet tartness is irresistibly delicious, and it makes wonderful pancakes as well! Buttermilk costs 70 percent more than regular milk, so if you like it, you can save money by making your own.

Start with buttermilk from the store that uses live cultures. You can make any amount of buttermilk you'd like from this by re-culturing. To re-culture, put the amount of milk you would like to turn into buttermilk into a stainless steel container. Using a double-boiler or putting the container of milk into a sink of hot water, raise the temperature to 86 degrees.

Hold at 86 degrees for ten minutes, then add 3/4 cup of buttermilk per quart of milk. (So that would be one and half cups of buttermilk for a half gallon and three cups of buttermilk for a gallon.) Remove the milk from the heat, cover with cheesecloth to keep out bugs but allow oxygen, and allow it to sit at room temperature undisturbed for twelve hours.

That's it. Really. Just refrigerate it after the twelve hours are up, and it will keep in the refrigerator for up to two weeks. Anytime you want more buttermilk, just repeat this procedure using a bit of the buttermilk you already made and you can have buttermilk forever unless your supply becomes contaminated.

Anytime a cheese recipe calls for "mesophilic starter" you can use your buttermilk at the rate of four ounces of buttermilk per one gallon of milk that you'll be turning into cheese. Though you can freeze this buttermilk for use later to make cheese, I don't recommend that as viability of the culture becomes spotty. I would only recommend using unfrozen buttermilk to make cheese.

How to Have a Lifetime Supply of Yogurt and Thermophilic Starter Culture

Yogurt is a bit more difficult to make than buttermilk because it requires the yogurt-in-progress to be held at a higher temperature for a long time. Though yogurt making machines are sold, this can also be accomplished by arranging to make yogurt on a weekend so you can keep an eye on it. Still, if you find that your family uses a lot of yogurt, you can find some pretty good machines out there for less than $100. Given that yogurt costs anywhere from 300 percent to 400 percent more than milk, if you eat a lot of yogurt you can save a lot of money by making your own.

You can make yogurt successfully from plain yogurt from the store, or you can buy a starter culture for the specific type of yogurt you wish to make. Viili culture produces a thick but mild yogurt similar to what you you mostly see in stores, whereas Piimä culture makes a thinner drinkable yogurt. There are many other cultures available, but no matter how you start your first batch, yogurt cultures are *serial cultures*, meaning that you can continue to propagate them indefinitely simply by using a quantity from the last batch to make the next.

If you decide to use plain yogurt from the store to make more yogurt, please read the ingredient label carefully to make sure you are buying a product made only from milk and cultures. There are some yogurt brands whose "plain" yogurt contains adulterants and other ingredients that won't be helpful. Pectin is often used as a thickener and this is okay.

First, heat your milk to 185 degrees in a double-boiler while stirring often. This is to kill off competing organisms. Then, remove the milk from the heat and allow it to cool to between 105 and 122 degrees. Once it is between these two temperatures, add either your starter culture or the live yogurt. Pour the mixture into cleaned and sterilized quart canning jars, and adjust the two-piece caps for a seal. Keep the temperature of these containers at 105 to 122 degrees for the next eight hours. Then, put your jars in the refrigerator where the yogurt will keep for two weeks.

Maintaining this temperature for so long will be difficult, but the bacteria have a better sense of humor than most regulatory agencies, and as long as you keep the temperature above 98 but below 130, your yogurt will still be fine. There are a lot of things that could work. A mattress heating pad or wrapping the jars in an electric blanket will likely work well; just be sure you keep an eye on things and check frequently so it doesn't overheat. Some ovens will maintain temperatures under 120. A slow-cooker with water on the lowest setting may work. You could set the jars in water in the slow-cooker and keep an eye on the temperature. You could also set them in a sink of water at 115 degrees and as the water cools add a bit of simmering water from a pan on the stove. The key is you'll need to improvise creatively.

The yogurt you create is plain yogurt. You can mix anything with it you'd like—fruit, nuts, granola, sweeteners, etc. If you decide to use it as a thermophilic cheese starter, use four ounces of your fresh plain yogurt per gallon of milk that you will be turning into cheese.

Okay, Let's Make Some Cheese!

Cheese is a pretty involved subject so there were a lot of preliminaries. And even with all of that, a single chapter in a single book can hardly scratch the surface. There are literally hundreds of types of cheese, all of which require differences in procedure, technique or ingredients. Rather than try to cover all of it, I am going to illustrate how to make three representative cheeses that are easily made at home using the ingredients and equipment described. Between these three cheeses, all of the basic techniques will be covered, and you will gain enough experience to experiment and branch out.

I am going to cover a direct acidification soft cheese. Using the same principle, you could make a soft cheese using a different acid. Then, I will demonstrate a soft cheese using a starter culture. Finally, I will demonstrate a minimally aged hard cheese using both starter culture and rennet.

Soft Cheese by Direct Acidification: Queso Blanco

Using a double-boiler, raise the temperature of 1 gallon of milk to 180 degrees while stirring so the milk doesn't precipitate protein. Add 1/4 cup of vinegar by slowly dribbling it into the milk while stirring. (You can use distilled vinegar or

Raising the temperature to 180 degrees before adding the vinegar. Notice the cheesecloth boiling on the right.

some of your homemade vinegar from the prior chapter. For a different taste, you can use the juice of three to five lemons.) Continue to stir for ten to fifteen minutes until the milk is completely clotted. If the milk doesn't clot, add up to four more tablespoons of vinegar while mixing for another ten to fifteen minutes.

The clotted milk draining in the colander.

Meanwhile, prepare the cheesecloth by boiling in a pan of clean water. After boiling, use the cheesecloth to line a colander. Pour the clotted milk into the cheesecloth lined colander, allowing the liquid to go down the sink. After the cheese has cooled, form the cheesecloth into a bag and hang it over a bowl until liquid no longer drains out of the bag. (This works best at standard room temperature. If the temperature is too cold, the cheese won't drain well. This process should complete within five to seven hours.)

Scrape the cheese out of the cheesecloth into a clean covered container. You can mix salt and dried herbs such as garlic powder, dill or basil into the cheese as desired. This is what is called a "fresh" cheese, and it should be refrigerated promptly after making and used within a week to avoid spoilage. Because of all the different things

I have a hidden hook under my cabinets for hanging cheese to drain.

you can mix with this, it is a very versatile cheese that can be used for bagels, dips and dressings.

Soft Cheese Using Yogurt Starter Culture: Farmer's Cheese

Add 1/2 teaspoon of 30 percent calcium chloride solution to 1/4 cup of water, and mix this

This easy cheese is great on bagels or mixed with herbs as a vegetable dip.

I'll add the yogurt once the milk reaches 105 degrees. You could also use commercial thermophilic starter culture for this step.

thoroughly with one gallon of milk in a double-boiler. Using the double-boiler, raise the temperature of the gallon of milk to 105 degrees. While the milk is heating, dissolve 1/4 of a rennet tablet in 1/4 cup of cool non-chlorinated water. Once the milk has reached 105 degrees, keep it there for five minutes and then add one cup of plain yogurt, stirring it in thoroughly. Keep the temperature at 105 degrees for ten minutes, then turn off the heat.

Here I am adding the dissolved rennet by pouring it slowly through a slotted spoon for better distribution.

Once the temperature has dropped to 95 degrees, add the rennet by sprinkling it over the milk and mixing using a gentle up-down and back-and-forth motion. Remove the pot and cover it with the lid. Allow the mixture to set for about an hour and then check for the development of the curd. Check the curd by inserting a clean and sterile blunt object (such as a glass candy thermometer). If it can be withdrawn cleanly without anything sticking to it and the hole it makes doesn't immediately fill with liquid, the curd is ready and you have what is called a *clean break*. If the curd isn't ready, allow the pot to set while covered for another thirty minutes and check again.

Now that you have a clean break, you need to cut the curd. The purpose of cutting the curd is to allow for uniform drainage of the milk liquid (known as whey) from the curd. (Yes, this is the famous "curds and whey"—a primitive predecessor to cottage cheese—likely eaten by Miss Muffet in the nursery rhyme.)

Your goal in cutting the curd is to cut uniform-sized curds for even drainage of whey. In general, the smaller you cut the curds initially, the harder the style of cheese you are making, though there are practical limits. In this case, you are cutting the curd into one-inch cubes. Do this by using your curd knife to first cut a grid at right-angles the entire depth of the curd so you end up with a one-inch checkerboard pattern. Then, you can make the horizontal cuts by positioning your curd knife at a 45-degree angle and cutting along one row of parallel lines in your grid. Though there are all sorts of other ways to do this and special gear you can buy, it is really that simple.

Once your curd is cut, cover the pot again and allow it to sit for another fifteen minutes so

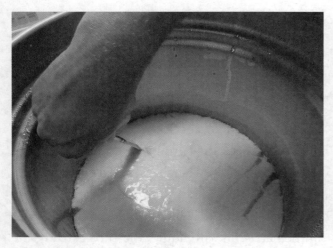

The horizontal cuts are being made by tracing the grid with the knife held at a 45-degree angle.

The curds will release whey and shrink. The metal device is the temperature probe.

some whey can gather at the bottom of the pot. Then, put your pot back into the double-boiler and slowly, over a period of thirty minutes or so, raise the temperature of curds to 110 degrees. As the curds are heating, gently—very gently so you don't break them—use your slotted spoon to stir the curds in such a way as to exchange those on the top with those on the bottom in order to promote even heating. Once the curds have reached 110 degrees, keep at that temperature for thirty minutes while gently mixing every five minutes or so. You will notice the curds getting smaller and the amount of whey increasing. While this process is ongoing, prepare a large piece of cheesecloth by boiling.

Line your colander with a double layer of cheesecloth, and gently pour the curds and whey into the colander. You can save the whey for baking later, add it to your compost pile or just let it go down the sink. (If the whey is greenish, do not be alarmed—this

is normal!) Let the curds drain in the colander for an hour or so, and then put the curds into a bowl and salt to taste, turning the curds evenly for uniform distribution. I prefer sea salt for this, but you can also use cheese salt or canning salt. Do NOT use regular table salt (iodized or not)

The cheese is being mixed with flaked cheese salt.

or you will be sorry because your cheese will be bitter.

Prepare some more coarse cheesecloth by boiling, and then use a double layer to line your clean cheese mold. Add the curds to the mold, fold the cheesecloth over top of the curds, and put the top of your mold on top of the cheesecloth. Put your mold in a shallow pan (a disposable pie plate would be ideal) to catch whey that is expelled, put two pounds of weight on top of the mold, and place the whole works in the refrigerator.

Once the cheese and press have been allowed to work in the refrigerator for four or five hours,

I used a 2.5 pound weight on the cheese press, and it worked fine.

The completed cheese before wrapping it in plastic and storing in the refrigerator.

turn the cheese out of the mold, unwrap it, and place in a closed container in the refrigerator. Use within a week.

Hard Aged Cheese Using Mesophilic Starter: New Ipswich Jack

Mix one teaspoon of 30 percent calcium chloride solution into a quarter cup of water, and mix this with two gallons of milk in a double-boiler. Bring the temperature of the milk up to 85-90 degrees, and add either 1/2 tsp of powdered mesophilic starter or one cup of fresh buttermilk, mixing thoroughly. Cover the mixture and allow it to ripen for thirty to forty minutes while maintaining the temperature between 85 and 90 degrees.

While the mixture is ripening, prepare your rennet solution by mixing 1/2 tablet of rennet with 1/4 cup of cool non-chlorinated water. Once the mixture has ripened, add the rennet solution by dripping it around the milk and mixing it gently but thoroughly using up-down and back-and-forth motions. Continue to maintain a temperature of 85 to 90 degrees while allowing the mixture to sit covered for an hour. At this point, the curds should give you a clean break.

Use your curd cutting knife to cut the cubes into 1/4-inch cubes. Continue holding the temperature at 85 to 90 degrees for another forty minutes while gently stirring the curds every five minutes or so. Keep the curds covered while not stirring or checking the temperature. You'll notice the curds shrinking and the volume of whey increasing.

Slowly increase the temperature to 100 degrees over a thirty-minute period while stirring every five minutes or so. This amounts to about two degrees every five minutes. Hold the temperature at 100 degrees for another thirty minutes while stirring every five minutes.

Now, very gently so as not to damage or lose curds, pour off as much of the whey are you can. This may be easier to do with a helper holding back the curds using the slotted spoon while someone else tips the pot over the sink.

Put the pot back into the double-boiler and continue to stir for another thirty minutes while maintaining the temperature at 100 degrees. Meanwhile, prepare a double layer of coarse cheesecloth by boiling, and use it to line a colander. Pour the curds into the cheesecloth-lined colander. Add two tablespoons of cheese salt and mix the curds gently.

Line your cheese mold with cheesecloth, and then pack the mold closely with the curds. Fold your cheesecloth over top of the curds, install the top of your mold, and put your mold in a shallow pan to catch the whey that will be expelled.

Put a ten pound weight on top of the mold to press the cheese for fifteen minutes. Then, remove the cheese from the mold, take it out of the cheesecloth, flip it over in the cheesecloth, and put it back in the mold.

This time, press the cheese for thirty minutes with a thirty-pound weight. (I recommend just stacking three ten-pound dumbbell weights as ten-pound weights are easier to handle.) Then, take the cheese out of the press, take it out of the cheesecloth, flip it again in the cheesecloth, re-cover it, and put it back in the mold. Press it this time with forty pounds for twelve hours.

After this, take it out of the mold and cheesecloth, and lay it on a bamboo sushi rolling mat. Flip it on the mat once a day so that it dries evenly. After three to five days, it should be dry to the touch. Once it is dry to the touch, it is ready for aging.

This cheese should be aged at temperatures of from 50 to 60 degrees for anywhere from one to three months. Maintaining such temperatures is a tall order in most homes, but any temperature range from 45 to 68 will do. Luckily (at least in this respect) my house is old and drafty, so I can age cheese in a kitchen cabinet anytime from November to April without need of maintaining a special environment.

If, however, you happen to either live in a warmer climate or have a more energy-efficient home, you will likely need to create a cheese cave from a dorm refrigerator as described earlier in this chapter.

Larger cheeses will form a natural rind that will protect them from invasion, but smaller cheeses (like the size that we have made in this example) will need to be protected by either wax or plastic.

If using plastic, first wash the cheese using vinegar on a clean paper towel to reduce bacterial counts, then seal it in plastic using a vacuum sealer.

If you are using cheese wax, melt it by putting a small stainless steel bowl in a pot of boiling water and adding wax to the bowl. (This bowl will be almost impossible to clean after, so you might want to get a cheap bowl at a department store for this purpose.) After you have washed the cheese with vinegar, use a natural bristle brush to dip in the melted wax and then paint it onto the cheese. Once the wax has hardened on one side of the cheese, turn the cheese over and coat the other side. Check the cheese over thoroughly to make sure you haven't missed any spots and that

Despite a couple of imperfections in uniformity of coating, this waxed cheese is aging nicely.

the cheese is coated uniformly, and then set the cheese aside to age.

After this cheese has aged for a month, it is safe for people who are lactose-intolerant; and after it has aged for two months, it is safe even if made from raw milk.

Experiment and Keep a Log

A lot of times people want to make cheeses like those they buy. If you want to do that, there are a host of sites on the Internet that give specific recipes. But what I would like you to do, instead, is experiment and keep a log. I have covered all the fundamental principles you need to know in order to make your own unique cheeses so long as a few basics are understood. Fresh cheeses have to be refrigerated to be safe and should be used in less than a week. Cheeses made from raw milk have to be aged for at least two months to be safe. Hard cheeses need to be pressed with increasing amounts of weight. But now, from just the three cheeses I have given in this chapter, I'd like you to think about the variations.

The Queso Blanco recipe was a direct acidification cheese made with vinegar. What would happen if, instead of adding vinegar, you added a mesophilic starter and held it at 88 degrees for an hour before pouring into the cheesecloth? It would certainly taste different!

The soft Farmer's Cheese described earlier used a yogurt (thermophilic) starter culture. What if you used the same technique, but instead used a buttermilk (mesophilic) starter and varied the temperature accordingly?

The Jack cheese recipe is pretty interesting. Don't you wonder what would happen if you used a thermophilic starter and some lipase instead of a mesophilic starter? How would it come out? What would it taste like? What would happen if you added a pint of heavy cream and a tablespoon of wine vinegar to one of the recipes?

So rather than copying other recipes, what I am encouraging you to do is follow the general principles I have described here to make your own and keep notes. I think you will be very pleasantly surprised at how easy it is to make astonishingly good cheese that is uniquely your own and can't be bought anywhere at any price, and that is ultimately what will make cheese making a worthwhile thing for a mini-farmer.

51

Ten Further Secrets of Food Self-Sufficiency

Because I'm interested in helping people take charge of the food portion of their budgets, it's only natural that I'd pay close attention to studies and statistics pertaining to family food budgets. One thing I learned is that over 40 percent of the average household food budget for Americans is spent on eating out.[3]

It stands to reason that if 40 percent of a family's food dollars are spent on food prepared by others, even the most comprehensive approach to producing food at home will have a limited effect. Maximizing the positive economic role of mini-farming requires that a dent be made in the budget spent eating out.

Why do people eat out? Obviously, there are those special celebratory occasions or dates. But most often Americans eat out because they lack the time or energy to prepare food at home. It's a simple mathematical equation. If you get out of work at half-past five, pick up your son at daycare at half-past six and get home at half-past seven with junior's bedtime only a scant ninety minutes away, you simply do not have time to make a meal and clean up after.

---

[3] Duquesne, B., Matendo, S. Lebailley, Ph. (2011), "Profiling Food Consumption: Comparison between USA and EU," Gembloux Agricultural University.

A lot of times this is a chicken-and-egg problem. You go to the grocery store in good faith and buy food you plan to prepare, but you end up working late or there is a last-minute project one of your kids forgot to mention, and you literally end up throwing food away. Why waste money? So eventually you stop buying it because you don't want to take the risk of waste. So not only do you not have the time to cook, but if you did have the time, you wouldn't have the ingredients.

Mini farming takes you a step closer to having the ingredients because of the vast quantities of food you will be putting in the freezer or cans. Almost all of it can be prepared in the microwave in five minutes.

And there is another insidious aspect to the amount of money we spend at the grocery store. Most of that money is spent on pre-made foods and meals, rather than on raw ingredients. Breakfast cereals that you can just pour into a bowl and top with milk have an entire aisle dedicated to them. The same applies to cookies and crackers. There is a pretty large selection of pre-made soups, stews, pastas and more. And then, in the freezer section, the amount of freezer space dedicated to what used to be called "TV dinners" is several times larger than the space devoted to frozen vegetables.

So even the portion of the food budget that isn't spent on eating out is largely dedicated to pre-made foods. Again, the primary reason for this is speed and convenience. Frying up some bacon and eggs in the morning takes more time than pouring some cereal in a bowl, and every minute seems to matter.

I am not a nutritionist or dietitian, but I can certainly see the obvious correlation between what we eat and how healthy (or unhealthy) we

are. All of these convenience foods are not helping our waistlines or health. Though I disagree with the official guidelines of what constitutes "overweight" or "obese," I think most of us realize that as Americans have moved from home-cooked meals to eating out and eating pre-made meals, we have become heavier. I was just reading the label on a canned lasagna marketed by a famous national brand. The ingredients include glyceryl monostearate, modified food starch and high fructose corn syrup. None of these is a deadly poison, but I think it is safe to say that they contribute nothing to the nutritional value of food and you are unlikely to add them to your own cooking.

This seems like an inescapable cycle, but it isn't. There are ways to take charge of this aspect of your food budget so you can become more economically self-sufficient while reserving trips to a restaurant for those truly special occasions. Here are the closely guarded secrets of the thirty-second degree of the inner-sanctum of food self-sufficiency.

Secret #1: Preparing Two Meals Takes the Same Amount of Time as Preparing One

To be 100 percent honest, it doesn't take exactly the same amount of time, but the difference in required time is only marginal. I've done this a lot, and I have concluded that with only a 10 percent increase in the amount of time, you can double the amount of food you prepare when you make a meal.

The reason for this is because most of the time involved in making a meal is spent in getting all the ingredients together, waiting for the stove and cleaning up the mess. The actual time spent chopping and mixing is quite small.

If you are already cooking, the marginal increase in time to cook other items simultaneously is inconsequential.

When I make London Broil steaks in the oven, I don't put in just enough for the current meal. Instead, I put in enough for two or three meals. It takes the same amount of time. I just put the extra steaks in containers and pop them first in the refrigerator, and then the freezer. Now, in addition to having made the main course for the current meal, I have also made the main course for two other meals. Even better, those main courses only require being zapped in the microwave for five minutes on an evening when I am too time-pressed to cook.

I do the same thing when I make salad. If I make salad for dinner, I get out some containers and just go ahead and put salads in those too and put them in the refrigerator for the next day.

Over time, this builds up. If I do this four days a week—say, Saturday, Sunday, Tuesday and Thursday—I will start building a reserve

stash of ready-made main courses. Let me trace this through the week.

On Saturday I make three meals of London Broil steak. I eat one of them and put two in the freezer. On Sunday I make three meals of baked chicken thighs and drumsticks. I eat one of them and put two in the freezer. On Tuesday I make three meals of swordfish steak. I eat one and put two in the freezer. On Thursday I make three meals of pork chops. I eat one and put two in the freezer.

Let's say that on Monday I eat London Broil from the freezer, on Wednesday I eat chicken and on Friday I eat swordfish. At the end of the week, I still have one London Broil, one chicken, one swordfish and two pork chop main courses in the freezer.

This same holds true for practically anything. Mashed turnips, squash, beef bourguignon, stir-fried broccoli and even spaghetti with sauce all freeze fine. They can all be cooked in just five minutes in the microwave.

Secret #2: Freeze Main Courses and Side Dishes Separately

Except for one-dish meals, freezing side dishes separately from main courses will make it easier to maintain dietary variety. If roast beef is served with broccoli one night, it can be served with squash on another night and carrots the next time.

When you do this, you can even customize meals. Would you like salmon or turkey this evening? Would you prefer parsnips, Swiss chard or braised squash as your side?

Secret #3: Use the Weekend to Get a Head Start

You don't have to work and slave all weekend. All you need to do is spend a couple of hours on a weekend day doing something else while a big beef roast or a couple of broiler chickens cook in the oven. While those are cooling, steam a large batch of carrots and fry up some summer squash.

These are the sorts of dishes you simply won't have time to make during the week, but you can often put away more than eight servings of each food cooked, and these will serve as a sort of "go-to" base in your freezer for times where you may be tied up and home too late to cook for an entire week.

The weekend gives a head start in prepared meals.

Secret #4: Aluminum Baking Pans

I know that using anything disposable is politically incorrect, and with good reason. But at the same time, one major hurdle to cooking is the time required for cleanup, and scrubbing baked-on grease splatters from the edges of a baking pan is pretty time-consuming. And anyone who has ever tried to use a dishwasher to clean baking pans knows it is a futile endeavor.

Recycling aluminum saves 95 percent of the energy of making new aluminum, and every pound of aluminum recycled prevents the mining of four pounds of bauxite. So even though I am encouraging you to use a disposable product, I encourage you to give the pans a quick rinse with soapy water and take them to your local recycling center. This way, most of the harm resulting from using a disposable product is averted.

Using disposable baking pans makes a tremendous difference in terms of efficiency because it eliminates the most time consuming cleanup chore associated with baking. This has a worthwhile psychological effect on your willingness to bake things in the first place. Furthermore, you can often fit several of these in the oven at once, and this serves to get the most out of your baking time.

Secret #5: Use the Cooking Methods Requiring the Least Active Intervention

You've likely noticed that I have mentioned baking a lot. The reason is because baking and broiling are the sorts of cooking methods that allow me to get the food ready, put it in the oven, and then go about other important tasks. The stove has a timer, so it will get my attention when it is needed, but otherwise I am free.

Unless I am making an artisan bread as a special treat, when I make bread, I use a bread machine. My bread machine has a custom cycle that I have programmed, and all I have to do is pour in my ingredients and press two buttons. When the beeper goes off, the bread is ready. To make this even easier, whenever I make bread, I leverage my time by packaging all the solid ingredients (except the yeast) together in a vacuum-sealed bag.

I make three or four bags like this, because the time consuming part is just gathering the ingredients. Now, to bake bread, all I have to do is put water in the bread pan, dump in my mix, put a tablespoon of yeast in the center, and add a tablespoon of butter cut into chunks. Then I push two buttons. Making bread literally takes me less than five minutes. Anytime I have made bread this way, nobody in the family has ever complained of the lack of mono- and di-glycerides either.

Cooking methods such as pan frying and boiling require your active presence, whereas baking and steaming do not. That is not to say you should never pan fry or boil your food. Some food simply tastes better when prepared using those methods. Rather, I am saying you should consider broiling a London Broil steak instead of frying it in a pan, because you can broil a lot of steaks at once while you are busy doing something else.

Secret #6: Disposable Plastic Containers

One of my personal hurdles is that I tend to be forgetful about food containers. Maybe I'll eat my peas and leave the container in the back seat for a couple of days because I forgot to bring it in. At that point, it is unusable for food again. The durable name-brand plastic food containers are

expensive, sometimes costing more than $4 each. At that price, being forgetful about three containers can make bringing my own food as expensive as eating out.

The solution is reusable but disposable plastic containers. These cost in the neighborhood of 50 to 70 cents each, so even forgetting three of them is less expensive than buying a burger. If I am not forgetful, they can be reused several times. Likewise, if used for something like fish or spaghetti sauce that often ruins containers, I am still way ahead financially.

The fact a container can't be reused because I allowed food to rot in it or it was used for baked tuna doesn't mean that it has to be thrown away. Disposable plastic containers are made of polypropylene, with recycling resin identification code "5." Recycling these containers will save both energy and fossil fuels while saving space in landfills.

So whenever I've cooked extra, that additional food goes into a container and is placed in either the refrigerator or the freezer. It is simple, fast, inexpensive and most importantly makes it *easy*.

Secret #7: Use Insulated Bags and Cold Packs to Pack Meals

There are three major impediments to packing lunch. The first is that the commute is so long that the food could go bad on the way. The second is the lack of a refrigerator at work. The third is the lack of time to pack the lunch.

The third impediment has already been addressed. Just grab some containers out of the freezer. Packing lunch takes thirty seconds. It could take a bit longer if you also take some time to throw in an apple and a banana; but even so, that's less time than the drive-thru window, so you are going to be saving time too.

The first and second impediments are answered with insulated bags and cold packs. Insulated bags are the new "lunch box" and they work far better than their ancestors. The re-usable cold packs available in stores for as little as $1 apiece, when enclosed in your insulated bag, will keep your food cold and fresh for a long time.

Secret #8: Adopt Time-Saving Cooking Methods

Other than baking, I should also mention pressure cooking, crock pots, outdoor grilling and thermos cookery.

Very often, people forget their outdoor grills except for the occasional burger or family event, but grills offer the advantage of reducing cleanup of bakeware. Most meats and vegetables can be grilled; if not directly then wrapped in aluminum foil. Cleanup time is reduced.

A good stainless steel pressure cooker is not cheap, but it is a wise long-term investment because it can dramatically compress cooking times for roasts, stews, beans and other foods that can often require hours to cook. I have a Fagor™ pressure cooker, and using the included recipe book I've cooked dried bean and meat stew dishes in less than an hour that would otherwise take practically all day. You can cook a two pound beef roast, including prep time, in thirty-five minutes.

Crock pots have been around for a long time, but seem to have fallen off the radar for most people. If you get a crock pot with an insert (something I highly recommend), you can get the food ready the night before and leave the insert in the refrigerator. In the morning, just put the insert in the device and turn it on. You'll come home to the aroma of a delightful slow-cooked meal. Crock pots come with recipe books and there are a good many recipes on the Internet. I use mine for thickening homemade ketchup and spaghetti sauce as well.

Very few people have heard of thermos cookery, and that's too bad. Cooking with a thermos is one of the most time and energy saving methods of cooking imaginable—especially for whole grains such as wheat, dried beans and other foods that would require overnight soaking and long periods of cooking on the stove. If filled with food heated to boiling, a good thermos will still maintain a temperature exceeding 160 degrees (the internal temperature to which meats need to be cooked in order to be safe) twelve hours later, and a temperature exceeding 140 degrees (hot enough to kill pathogens) twenty-four hours later.

You can't use just any old thermos. You want one that is lined with stainless steel rather than glass or plastic, and with a wide mouth. I use a Stanley Aladdin, but have also used a good Thermos brand stainless steel bottle for many years. You can find hundreds of recipes on the Internet and once you get the hang of the underlying principles, you'll soon be adapting. I mainly used mine to get my whole wheatberry and oatmeal with strawberry and banana ready. A hot, delicious breakfast was ready for me the moment I was ready!

Secret #9: Make Your Own Drinks

It adds up over time. Coffee with breakfast ($2.50), a soda with lunch ($1.74) and some bottled water on the way home ($1.29). It adds up to $110/month. You can make a large dent in that by getting an iced tea maker, a coffee maker, some coffee and tea or herbal teas and a couple of stainless steel beverage bottles.

Like a coffee maker, an iced tea maker offers the advantage of making the iced tea in one step. Mine only cost $22, so it paid for itself in short order.

Stainless steel beverage bottles are durable, easily cleaned, and are unlikely to accumulate crud that would make drinks stored in them unpalatable. Their chemical makeup renders them impervious to acidic drinks, so that the

This iced tea maker has paid for itself many times over by reducing the purchase of bottled products.

metal isn't leached into the beverage. I got mine for $1 each at an end-of-season sale.

Secret #10: Meals in a Jar

My local supermarkets have large sections dedicated to what could be called "meals in a jar." These include canned soups, pastas, stews and similar items. But when you look at the ingredients and nutritional content, most of these are little more than caloric energy—mostly from sugar or carbohydrate.

All editions of the *Ball Blue Book of Preserving* that were printed in the past couple of decades include sections on canning your own stocks, soups, stews and even baby foods. Likewise, in *Mini Farming: Self Sufficiency on 1/4 Acre*, I give guidelines that will allow you to can practically any prepared food made of mixed ingredients. This way, you need not rely on a particular recipe in a cookbook. If your family is used to meals in a jar, you can easily make your own. And those that you make yourself will be far superior to anything you purchase in terms of the quality of ingredients.

Of course, making and canning food can be time-consuming, which sort of defeats the purpose. I use two methods for dealing with this. The first is that I keep a stash of cleaned jars handy. If I make a good stew, I can dump it in the jars, heat up the canner, and can a few jars right away. I have both a large and a small pressure canner, and the smaller one is no larger than the pot in which I cook pasta.

The second is that I freeze rather than can. If I just made a delicious bowl of glop but don't have the time to even heat up the canner, I dump my glop into a disposable plastic container destined for the freezer.

Canned foods can be eaten right out of the can or require only sixty seconds to heat up in the microwave, whereas frozen foods take five minutes or more to be properly heated in a microwave. So in aggregate, you will tend to save time overall by canning instead of freezing, but you have to grab your time where you can and no matter the means used, anything made at home contributes to your food self-sufficiency.

The Secret That Is Not a Secret

Before I finish this book and drop you into a seemingly endless alphabetical index, I want to share one other thing I consider to be important. As an engineer, you could say that my daily task is to accomplish things that others would consider impossible. Because of this, I'm likely to have an almost naively positive attitude about what is or isn't possible. Even so, I believe that too often people invent their own limitations from their own untested assumptions about things they "can't" or "could never" do.

One of my goals in writing about mini-farming and self-sufficiency topics is to show people just how easy it really is for you to achieve levels of self-sufficiency that most people would deem "impossible." And I hope that within these pages I've also imparted some ideas that will help make things easy.

The last secret I wish to divulge in this book isn't a secret at all: you *can*. You *can* grow a substantial portion of your own food, you *can* make your own wine or cheese, you *can* reduce your dependence on eating out and quite frankly if you are willing to work at it, you *can* achieve nearly anything you believe is within your capacity.

From Markham Farm to your home: best wishes to you and yours!

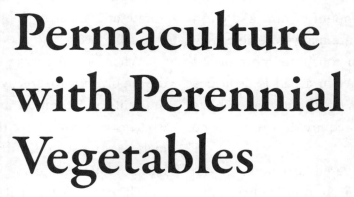

52

Permaculture with Perennial Vegetables

As described in Chapter 14, plantings of berry canes, fruit or nut trees, and grapevines are all a form of permaculture. Though such plantings require some degree of maintenance, overall they require very little time, effort, and money for the amount of food derived. Unfortunately, most vegetables planted in the garden need to be replanted every year. This entails a great deal of time and effort.

A little-known fact is that most of the vegetables that we plant as annuals for purposes of efficiency and high yield are derived from wild ancestors that are perennial. These wild ancestors are far less susceptible to pests and diseases than their domesticated progeny and therefore don't require the degree of crop rotation that would otherwise be needed to maintain a healthy crop. It wouldn't be practical to grow perennial vegetables exclusively, but it is entirely practical to dedicate three, four, or more beds to selected perennials because of the savings in time and effort.

For example, rather than growing kale (which is grown as an annual), you could grow sea kale. Sea kale is perennial and will return year after year. Sea kale is not only perfectly edible, it was featured in Thomas Jefferson's garden and contains all of the familiar nutrition of cabbage family plants. In addition, as long as the pH is adjusted to higher than 6 to avoid clubroot, sea kale will never experience a serious pest or disease problem.

Sea kale is just one example of how you can grow perennial vegetables that were an important part of our diet until very modern times, while saving a tremendous amount of time and effort in the long run. There are many vegetables that if handled correctly can constitute more or less permanent plantings. When a bed is dedicated to this sort of crop, it is taken out of availability for other vegetables but requires far less time and effort to maintain.

I have already covered asparagus in an earlier chapter. If properly prepared initially, asparagus beds can remain productive for decades. If you keep the bed weeded and harvest prudently, you'll have plenty of asparagus every year without ever having to put shovel to soil. The same applies to the herbs discussed in the chapter on herbs—many of them will return every year either due to their perennial nature or from self-reseeding. Examples include mints, balms, sage, and thyme, among others. My mini farm has two 4 ft. x 8 ft. beds dedicated strictly to culinary and medicinal herbs and another 4 ft. x 8 ft. bed that produces impressive quantities of asparagus. Though I rotate where I plant annual herbs year to year, my herb beds require less maintenance than any of the others.

You aren't limited to sea kale, asparagus, and herbs, however. There are a number of other vegetables that make an excellent choice for permanent plantings in raised beds.

Soil Preparation and Care

In general, the beds for perennials need to be prepared just as you would prepare for any other crop by correcting for nutrient deficiencies, adding micronutrients, correcting the pH, and incorporating plenty of organic matter. Because perennial vegetables by definition remain in that bed a long time, you should make sure you incorporate at least eight cubic feet of compost per 4 ft. x 8 ft. bed.

When planting more typical crops, you have the opportunity to directly incorporate additional nutrients and compost annually via admixture, whereas you don't have this luxury with perennials because such disturbance of the soil could harm or kill the plants.

The good news is that most perennial vegetables put nowhere near the strain on soil as their annual and biennial cousins, so they require less fertilizer. In fact, a properly prepared bed may, in some cases, require no amendments at all for several years thereafter. This is another good reason why establishing a few beds of perennial vegetables makes sense.

At least every year, compost should be added to the beds. You can't turn it in, so just spread it as evenly as you can on top. I prefer that it be added twice annually: once in the fall and then again in the spring. After a while, you'll be able to judge how much compost is needed just by digging up a bit of soil and looking, but a good guideline is you'll need three cubic feet annually per 4 ft. x 8 ft. bed. The winter weather helps to break down the compost added in fall, and the famous April showers will help incorporate both that and the compost added in early spring.

The compost should be well finished so that it won't leach nutrients. If you find that your compost particles are too big to spread effectively, you can use a piece of half-inch hardware cloth to strain your compost. Put the pieces that don't fit through the holes back into the pile and use the smaller pieces for spreading.

You should use a soil test kit to test your beds for nitrogen, phosphorus, and potassium annually. If a perennial bed requires the addition of one or more of these, you should thoroughly mix the needed amount with the compost you will be adding. You should make sure to also add micronutrients to the compost that you spread on the beds. This could take the form of kelp solids, sea solids, some Celtic Sea Salt (no more than six ounces per 4 ft. x 8 ft. bed annually), or some wood ash, among other sources. These will get leached into the bed via rain and weather, as well as by the action of earthworms and other soil organisms.

Weeds are the greatest enemy of perennial vegetables because, unlike your annual beds that you can aggressively hoe or flame or from which every living green thing can be removed before planting cover crops, perennial plants can't be disturbed like that and survive.

An ounce of prevention will get your beds off to a good start. As most perennial vegetables are planted in early summer, you have ample opportunity to presprout and remove as many weeds as possible. Just let the weeds sprout in the bed, and then hoe them. You can do this several times in the spring before time to plant. Then, just before planting, flame the bed thoroughly to kill any seeds in the top one-quarter inch of soil.

Once you have planted, you will have to hand-weed the beds in most cases, though there may be some instances when you can use a stirrup hoe. A stirrup hoe only disturbs the top quarter to half inch of soil and so will do the least damage to the root systems of desired plants. In the fall, when plants die back, you can also mulch to create a barrier that will keep new seeds from falling into the beds and prevent many that are already in the bed from sprouting. You can use shredded leaves or shredded straw as a mulch, but you should make sure to remove it in the spring so it doesn't inhibit the emergence of desired crops.

Onions

The standard bulbing onion discussed in an earlier chapter is planted annually, but if you are willing to deal with smaller bulbs, there are several varieties of onion that divide into clusters of onions underground and regrow every year. These include Welsh onion, garlic chives, potato onions, walking onions, and shallots.

I maintain a bed of potato onions. Late every summer when they die back, I pull the clusters

⬢ The onions on the right are perennial potato onions. They are smaller, but delicious.

of onions and replant about 15 percent of them equally spaced around that bed to grow back the next year. This way I have an infinite supply of small onions that go great in stews, and the amount of work I have to invest is minimal.

These onions are smallish but have vastly superior flavor to the standard bulbing onions. Once you have used these in a stew, you'll see why so many pioneers carried these with them for their homesteads out West.

Garlic as a Perennial

Garlic is most often grown as an annual, but once you have established a bed of garlic, it can be grown as a perennial. Before you plant the bulbs in fall, make sure you till in a good quantity of finished compost—at least four cubic feet per 4 ft. x 8 ft. bed. Then make sure to add micronutrients. After that, use the techniques covered in the chapter on onions, such as presprouting to reduce weed problems, as much as possible. Then, plant your bulbs at a six-inch spacing in all directions.

In early summer, many of the plants will form blossoms. Pinch off the shoots once they are a couple of feet tall so the plants will form bulbs. (You can collect them earlier and fry them up as garlic scapes.) Harvest the bulbs from the large plants in the late summer, and let the smaller plants die back. The next year, those smaller plants will sprout.

The biggest problem you will have in such a planting is weeds. I recommend mulching in the fall with dead leaves you rake off the yard. These leaves will compost over time and enrich the soil, and they will prevent many weeds as well. Come spring, if they haven't rotted down enough to let the garlic sprout, gently remove them. You can control weeds the rest of the season with a carefully used stirrup hoe.

Jerusalem Artichokes

A friend in Connecticut introduced me to Jerusalem artichokes several years ago, and I have maintained a bed of them ever since. Jerusalem artichokes are an indigenous root vegetable that is high in an indigestible starch called inulin. You'll find special pastas for diabetics made using inulin in some stores.

Jerusalem artichokes are propagated by ordering some tubers and planting them in a bed in the spring. In the fall, you will harvest about twenty times as many tubers as you originally planted. This will continue year after year ad infinitum. In fact, if you aren't vigilant, they will invade and take over your entire yard!

Jerusalem artichokes are usually thoroughly scrubbed, boiled, and then either sliced or mashed and served with butter. In this form, they are delicious. If you have never eaten them before, just eat a little bit the first few times because your large intestine likely lacks sufficient numbers of the bacteria needed to process inulin. This lack of bacteria will cause diarrhea. If you eat a little at a time and build up to it, you'll soon find that you can pack away a whole plate of these delicious roots without any trouble at all.

Groundnut (*Apios americana*)

I have included the scientific name of this plant because there are several plants called "groundnut" that might be confused. This groundnut is

⊗ These Jerusalem artichokes are tasty, but start off eating only a small quantity.

a member of the same family as fava beans. It is a perennial vine native to the United States. During the regular growing season, it grows a bean vine that bears numerous bean pods. These pods can be harvested young as green beans or allowed to ripen into dried beans. Over the course of the season the vines store up energy in the tubers, from which the groundnut will resprout for the next season indefinitely. The tubers are likewise edible and unusually rich in protein for a root vegetable.

Scorzonera or Black Salsify

Common salsify or oyster plant (*Tragopogon porrifolius*) is a biennial root crop (which is well worth growing, incidentally), but the closely related scorzonera (*Scorzonera hispanica*) is perennial. Common salsify roots should be harvested in their first year because, once the plant flowers in its second year, the roots become unappetizing and the plant dies. Scorzonera, however, can be grown year after year. The roots of scorzonera are typically thin but can grow as long as three feet, making harvest difficult. Growing it as a perennial, you can get thicker roots that have more food plus are less likely to break by waiting

until the second year to harvest. Meanwhile, simply allow it to make flowers and seeds as it wishes, and the bed will be liberally reseeded to replenish those plants that you harvest.

The black skin of the roots is inedible and needs to be removed. When you remove it, though, the white flesh almost immediately turns black. To prevent this, have a bowl of water with salt or lemon juice mixed in and throw the roots in there as soon as they are peeled. Scorzonera is usually boiled and served with other vegetables. I prefer to blanch it (and salsify), dehydrate, and serve in winter stews.

Good King Henry

Good King Henry is a perennial relative of amaranth that is native to Europe. It is planted from seed the first year. Thereafter, each spring the new shoots are blanched and eaten like asparagus, and a few leaves are harvested throughout the summer and prepared like spinach.

Perennial Broccoli

Perennial broccoli is a form of broccoli that, instead of forming a head, sends up slender stalks with just a few flowers on each. The entire slender stalk is cut and eaten. Perennial broccoli is transplanted in late summer. In northern areas such

⊗ This mulched scorzonera produces abundantly with little effort.

as New Hampshire, it will need to be overwintered in a high tunnel or similar environment, but no such care is required south of Maryland. Once overwintered, it starts sending up stalks in the spring. These stalks can be harvested until the next winter when the plant is overwintered again. Three high-yielding varieties of perennial broccoli are Nine Star, Red Arrow, and Bordeaux.

Rhubarb

Rhubarb was once so valuable in Europe that its cost was four times that of saffron and almost three times that of opium.[6] Luckily, you can grow it for yourself at trivial cost. In warmer parts of the country, rhubarb will grow year-round, but in colder zones it will die back during the winter and re-emerge in spring. The leaves are poisonous both due to a high concentration of oxalic acid and the likely presence of an anthraquinone glycoside. (This is a drastic purgative, for which purpose rhubarb was used in medicine.) The

⊗ An embarrassment of riches, this rhubarb is destined for a strawberry-rhubarb dessert.

[6] Lloyd, J. (1921) *Origin and History of all the Pharmacopeial Vegetable Drugs, Chemicals and Preparations with Bibliography*, p. 270

concentration of oxalic acid in rhubarb stalks, however, is so low as to be harmless.

Rhubarb stalks taste highly acidic, but almost all of this is from malic acid—the same acid that gives green apples their tartness. Rhubarb should be started indoors from seeds in the spring, transplanted in early summer, and then allowed to overwinter. You can harvest up to half the stalks each year. Just gently pull them from the plant and strip the green matter of the leaves from them.

Sea Kale

I mentioned sea kale in the introduction to this chapter because it is such an excellent example of a perennial vegetable. It is tasty, nutritious, and can grow anywhere in the continental United States. It should be started indoors and then transplanted in early summer. Germination can take as long as five weeks but can be accelerated a bit if you make several shallow nicks in the seed coating with a sharp knife and soak in water overnight before sowing.

It should be transplanted into deeply worked, very rich soil that is high in organic matter. Because its origin is near the sea, it will particularly benefit from the use of trace minerals in the form of unrefined sea salt. Add about six ounces of unrefined sea salt (for example, Celtic Sea Salt) annually to the bed. Its first shoots can be harvested and treated like asparagus, but its leaves and stalks can be eaten year-round.

Watercress

Closely related to annual garden cress, watercress is a reliable perennial that is one of the oldest leaf vegetables known to have been eaten by humans. It is rich in numerous essential vitamins and is a proven cancer fighter.

Because it is semiaquatic and will whither and die in still water, it can be difficult to maintain suitable conditions for its culture in most gardens. However, it is in sufficient demand that it might be worthwhile to set up a dedicated area.

Watercress can be easily grown using the inexpensive white two-gallon buckets, a kiddie pool, and a small pond aerator. Drill several holes in the bottom of each bucket and fill the bottom half with gravel. Marble chips would be ideal as watercress prefers its water to be slightly alkaline, and marble is simply a supercompressed form of lime that dissolves very slowly. Then fill the container the rest of the way with rich garden soil. Set the containers in the kiddie pool, fill the pool with six inches of water, and make sure to run the pond aerator for at least four hours a day. Change the water completely once a week.

Once freezing weather arrives, empty the kiddie pool, and store your containers of cress in an unheated outside area until spring.

Wood Nettle (*Laportea canadensis*)

I've listed the scientific name so there's no misunderstanding the plant I'm describing. Don't confuse wood nettle with horse nettle. Horse nettle is an unrelated plant, all the parts of which are poisonous. Wood nettle is a perennial plant usually found in moist woodlands in dappled shade. Wood nettle is a monoecious herb that has separate male and female flowers on the same plant. Not only will wood nettles reseed themselves from the fruits they develop from the upper female flowers, but they will also spread through their root system.

If you have an area of your lawn that only gets a couple of hours of sun daily but is shaded the rest of the time, wood nettle can be an ideal solution for making that area productive. If you can't find wood nettle seeds, stinging nettle (*Urtica dioica*) will work just as well in these conditions and is just as tasty.

Start the seeds by storing in the freezer for six weeks and then planting them in well-watered peat pots three months before last frost. Transplant at a spacing of one foot into your bed. Water the bed about twice as often as you water your other beds.

Eating a plant that wants to sting you as self-defense is a bit tricky. Wood nettle is covered with hairs, and some of those hairs·are hypodermic syringes that inject a mixture of formic acid, histamine, and acetylcholine, among other compounds. Formic acid and histamine in particular will make it sting. The juice of jewelweed will cure the rash, but it is best avoided altogether by handling the fresh plant with heavy gloves. Once collected, strip the leaves from the stem, and sauté or steam them. The cooking process softens the needles so they can't sting and inactivates the chemicals. You'll be surprised at how delicious they are, as well as rich in vitamins and minerals.

⊗ Wood nettles can be grown in beds and are also found in the wild.

Index

hybrid plants, 19, 91, 117–118, 267, 327–328, 363

hybrid vigor, 19

hydrogen peroxide solution, 426, 427

hydrometers, 414–415, 437, 441, 449

I

iced tea maker, 495, *495*

illustrated double-dig, *34–35*

imidacloprid, 340

immunity boosters, 93

inbreeding depression, 119, 246, 261, 271, 343, 370–371

"The Incredible Egg Washer," 157

indeterminate tomatoes, 358, 359, 361–362

infectious bronchitis (IB), 149

inoculant, 239, 320

insect repellents, natural, 94–95, 98, 303

insecticides, 96–97, 98, 142, 303, 340, 350, 352

insulated bags, 493–494

Intensive Agriculture. *see also* Raised Beds

  Average Crop Yields Planted Intensively, *86–87*

  Biodynamic method, 13–14

  drip irrigation, 79–80

  French Intensive method, 13, 14, 41

  Garden Watchdog, 132

  Grow Biointensive method, 10, 11, 13, 22, 29, 62–63, 78, 107

  learning and observation, 14–15

  and "living mulch," 10, 20, 51

  mini farm method, differences to other methods, 13–14

  plant-spacing and thinning distance, 10, 12, 14–15, 116

  space requirements, 20

  Square Foot method, 10, 11–12, 13, 29, 31, 42, 78

  vertical gardening, 12

Intensive Culture of Vegetables (Aquatias), 13

Internet resources

  American chestnut, 143

  baby chicks, 148

  botanical potato seeds, 343

  chicken housing, 153, 161

  Cooperative Extension Service, and other support organizations, 105, 212–213

  garden supplies, 109

  gardening companies, 132

  for hoop houses, 126

  The Humanure Handbook (Jenkins), 58

  for raw milk, 474

  sealer bags, 196

  weather and climate, 105, 117

  websites of interest

    accf-online.org, 143

    alaskagiant.com, 94

    ars-grin.gov/npgs/orders.html, 343

    bountifulgardens.org, 138

    davesgarden.com, 132

    fairviewhatchery.com, 148

    farmtoconsumer.org, 473

    hoophouse.com, 126

    mcmurrayhatchery.com, 148, 153

    newworldcrops.com, 343

    pvcplans.com, 126

    realmilk.com, 473

    simplici-tea.com, 94

    smalldairy.com, 473

    strombergschickens.com, 148

    vacuum-sealer-bags.com, 196

    Weather.com, 105, 117

    westonaprice.org, 473

    westsidegardenerr.com, 126

interplanting, 72–73, 292–293

intervenal chlorosis, 223

inulin, 502

iron, 67, 418

irrigation. *see* Watering and Irrigation

IRS (Internal Revenue Service), 209

isolation methods, 120, *122*, 261, 332

isothiocyanates, 368

Italian plum tomatoes, 358

J

Japanese beetles, 239–240, 268

Jarden Corporation, 185

Jeavons, John, 13, 22

Jeffers Livestock, 149

Jefferson, Thomas, 500

jellies, 189–191, *202*

jelly bags, 190

Jenkins, Joseph, 58

jerky, 199

Jerusalem artichokes, 502, *503*

Journal of Agricultural Food Chemistry, 418

journal-keeping, *14*, 15, 23, 53, 93, 118, 487

the Juiceman™, 430

juicing fruit, 190, 430, 431–432

Juicy Juice™, 431

K

kale, *87*, *104*, *122*, 127, *202*, 254, 284, 499–500. *see also* Greens

Keep It Simple, Inc., 94

kelp, 65, 193, 227, 501

Kenosha County Commuter Study, 2001, 23

kielselsol, 419

killing cone, *162*

Kimball, Herrick, 164

Wyeast 4632 Dry Mead Yeast, 410–411

winnowing, 121, 240

winter squash, 73–74, 352–353. *see also* Squash

winter wheat, *51*

wintercress, 127

wireworms, 33, 74, 95, 220, 259–260, *260*, 338, 339–341

wood ashes, 46, 47, 221–222, 225, 258, 260, 313

wood chipper conversion to thresher, 179–180, *180*

wood nettle (*Laportea canadensis*), 505, *505*

World Health Organization, 309

Wyandotte chicken, 148

Wyeast 4632 Dry Mead Yeast, 410–411

X

xanthan gum, 469

Y

yarrow, 91, *92*

yeast, 426–427, *435*, 441, 445, 446, 448

yeast energizer, 409, 424–425, 436, 441

yogurt, 478, 480–481, 482–483

Z

zinc, 68

Notes